These Hallowed Grounds

VOLUME 2

A Record of the Memorials in Christ Church Cathedral and Friends' Burying Grounds, Lisburn with some biographical notes and other interesting information on associated Families

Published by

LISBURN BRANCH OF THE NORTH OF IRELAND FAMILY HISTORY SOCIETY

ISBN 0-954-00151-6

Printed by NORTHERN WHIG LTD., BELFAST

CONTENTS

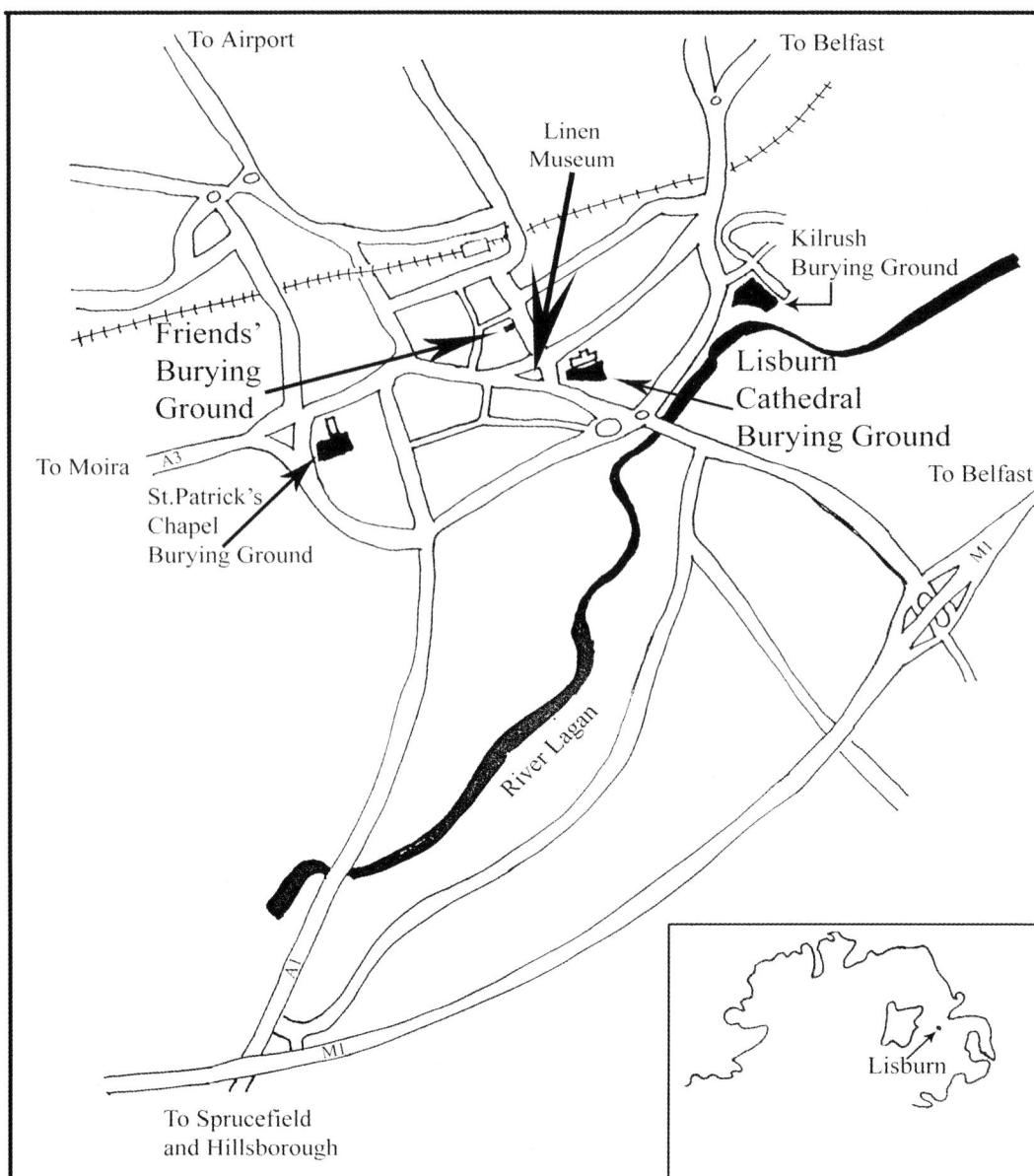

ACKNOWLEDGEMENTS

In compiling this book we acknowledge the help received from the staff of the Irish Linen Centre & Lisburn Museum, especially Brenda Collins, Elaine Flanigan and Trevor Hall. We also acknowledge the valuable help and information received from Robert Apsley, Rev. William Bell, Sam Bracegirdle, Muriel Cameron, Dr. Alan Dempsie, Trevor Fulton, Jim McAdam, Trevor Neill, William Parker, Victor Sefton, William Swain, Dolores Whittaker and all Lisburn Branch Members of the North of Ireland Family History Society - past and present.

To the Deputy Keeper of the Public Record Office of Northern Ireland, the Irish Linen Centre & Lisburn Museum and Queen's University Belfast Art Collection our grateful thanks for permission to use archival material, photographs and portraits, as individually acknowledged.

Project Team   Pat Allen, Harry Curry, Dr. Richard Gray, Eleanor McFadzean, Sean Minshull, Evelyn Patterson, Ted and Margaret Rolston, Ann Robinson, and Yvonne Simpson.

Photographs   Dr. Richard Gray, Ann Robinson and George Scott.

The printing of this book was funded by "Awards for All", Lisburn Historic Quarter and Lisburn City Council

INTRODUCTION

The four oldest burying grounds in Lisburn are those at Christ Church Cathedral, Kilrush, Millbrook Road, The Society of Friends, Railway Street and St. Patrick's, Chapel Hill. Volume 1 of "These Hallowed Grounds" (thereafter referred to as THG Vol. 1) contained the surviving inscriptions of headstones in Kilrush and St. Patrick's, as well as other relevant material and information on some of the associated families. This book, Volume 2, contains the surviving inscriptions for Lisburn Cathedral and Friends' Burying Ground, Lisburn Cathedral memorials, maps, photographs, other relevant material and biographical notes on some of the associated families.

Over the years several attempts have been made to record inscriptions of headstones and memorials in Lisburn Cathedral. The journals of "The Association for the Preservation of the Memorials of the Dead in Ireland", which then became "The Journal of the Irish Memorials Association", published several of the Lisburn gravestone inscriptions between the years 1902 and 1931. We have indicated where these are and have used the abbreviation "M.D.". It is fortunate that these were recorded, as now some of them are illegible, or missing altogether. Rev. William Carmody in his book "Lisburn Cathedral and its Past Rectors," published in 1926, recorded most of the memorials in the Cathedral.

In the summer of 1958 John and Doris Harper, William and Ann Stewart, John, Joseph and Patrick Holden and Agnes McComish, members of the Church of the Latter Day Saints, recorded dates and relationships from the Lisburn Cathedral gravestone inscriptions, but not the actual wording of the inscriptions. In the 1970's Trevor Neill, Sharon Adams, William Parker, Ivan Cameron, Sam Dixon and Valerie Harkness of Lisburn Historical Society recorded the Lisburn Cathedral gravestone inscriptions. Part of this record has gone missing and only the details from the north part of the graveyard now survive. In 1992 Evelyn Patterson (a member of the Lisburn Branch of the North of Ireland Family History Society) recorded details from the surviving stones. Apart from "M.D." and Rev. Carmody's book, none of this information was ever published in a written form. This we are rectifying now, before time and vandalism mean that the information is lost forever. We have attempted to record the exact inscriptions, and are grateful for the work done previously. Again, due to age and weathering, it has not been possible to decipher everything. Full names, dates etc. may be missing. We have tried, where possible, to check and verify information, but, although there are good burial records surviving, they are not continuous. In one case there is a gap of forty years.

In 2002 William Swain, of the Society of Friends, extracted all the relevant burial details for the Railway Street Burying Ground from the burial records of The Society of Friends. We have included these, together with the gravestone inscriptions from Railway Street Burying Ground.

In the mid. 19th century the Lisburn burying grounds were becoming full, so, in 1878, the New Cemetery on the Hillsborough Road, Lisburn, was opened and there was a special section for burials of members of the Society of Friends. This meant there were fewer burials in the older grounds. Since the publication of Volume 1 the exact date of the closure of the Cathedral and Kilrush Burying Grounds has been discovered. The Lisburn Standard of Saturday May 6th 1911 had a notice inserted by Lisburn Urban District Council stating that burials in the two Burial Grounds were to be discontinued from 1st May 1911, except for several named people who continued to hold rights of burial. (There were thirty-six people for the Cathedral and twenty-three for Kilrush. It is unlikely that all these people were eventually buried in the two grounds.)

In 1752 the use of the Julian calendar was abandoned in favour of the Gregorian calendar. Under the Julian calendar the year began on 25th March and continued until the 24th March the following year, so dates from 1st January to 24th March could have had double dating. We have recorded these dates as thus:- 1695/6

LISBURN URBAN DISTRICT COUNCIL

Cathedral and Kilrush Burial Grounds

IMPORTANT NOTICE

NOTICE IS HEREBY GIVEN THAT THE LOCAL GOVERNMENT BOARD FOR IRELAND have made Orders under their Seal dated 22nd April, 1911, to the effect that Burials shall be discontinued in the CATHEDRAL and KILRUSH BURIAL GROUNDS on, from and after the 1st day of May, 1911, subject to the right of sepulture or interment being reserved to the persons named or described in the schedules annexed to the Orders, of which the undernoted is a copy

The Orders may be inspected at my office.

Dated this 4th day of May, 1911.

T. M. WILSON, Town Clerk.

Town Hall, Lisburn.

CATHEDRAL BURIAL GROUND

SCHEDULE OF EXCEPTIONS

NAME	Description	Address	Age in Years
Robert M'Henry	Married	Windsor Gardens, Malone Road, Belfast	61
Sarah M'Henry	Married	Windsor Gardens, Malone Road Belfast	60
Henry Musgrave	Bachelor	Drumglass House, Belfast	76
Edgar Musgrave	Bachelor	Drumglass House, Belfast	73
William Fairley	...	60 Dee Street, Belfast	70
Catherine Johnston	Spinster	Workhouse Hospital, Lisburn	83
Sarah Jane Pelan	Widow	Lisburn	
Lucy Pattison	Spinster	42 Willowbank St., Antrim Road, Belfast	63
Sarah Flurel	Widow	Wallace Avenue, Lisburn	70
Mary Gelston	Spinster	Fortwilliam Terrace, Belfast	70
David C. Tinsley	Bachelor	11 Ulsterville Avenue, Belfast	35
Matthew Tinsley	Bachelor	11 Ulsterville Avenue, Belfast	42
Eliza Tinsley	Spinster	11 Ulsterville Avenue, Belfast	43
Minnie Tinsley	Spinster	11 Ulsterville Avenue, Belfast	41
Joseph Hill	Bachelor	1 Smithfield, Lisburn	40
James Hill	...	17 Smithfield, Lisburn	60
Stewart Lavery	Married	18 Linenhall Street, Lisburn	75
William Johnston	Widower	22 Millbrook Road, Lisburn	58
Magdalene Johnston	Spinster	22 Millbrook Road, Lisburn	26
Eleanor Johnston	Widow	Seymour Street, Lisburn	60
John Johnston	...	Seymour Street, Lisburn	31
John M'Bride	Married	40 Bow Street, Lisburn	62
Margaret M'Bride	Married	40 Bow Street, Lisburn	50
Isabella Wilson	Spinster	9 Smithfield, Lisburn	46
Wm. Alex. Wilson	...	9 Smithfield, Lisburn	42
Agnes Crockard	Married	Low Road, Lisburn	58
John Crockard	Married	Low Road, Lisburn	60
Mary Allen	Widow	Wallace Drive, Lisburn	76
Emily Margt. M'Kee	Spinster	24 Market Square, Lisburn	62
Agnes M'Kee	Spinster	24 Market Square, Lisburn	60
Margt. J. M'Donald	Widow	Hill Street, Lisburn	75
Jane Hull	Spinster	25 Smithfield, Lisburn	75
Sarah Doyle	Spinster	157 Albertbridge Road, Belfast	74
Jane Maria Purdon	Widow	56 Eglantine Avenue, Belfast	88
Alex. M'Camley	Married	29 Brookmount Street, Belfast	75
Frances M'Camley	Married	29 Brookmount Street, Belfast	75

KILRUSH BURIAL GROUND

SCHEDULE OF EXCEPTIONS

NAME	Description	Address	Age in Years.
Sarah Burns	Widow	7 Antrim Street, Lisburn	71
Margaret Cahoon	Widow	4 Blythe Street, Belfast	72
Robert Corbett	Widower	Old Warren, Lisburn	70
Letitia Corry	Widow	29 Antrim Street, Lisburn	64
James Dickey	...	Bridge Street, Lisburn	75
Susannah Dougan	Widow	90 Hill Street, Lisburn	94
Catherine Gardiner	Widow	14 Old Barracks, Lisburn	73
Jane Graham	Widow	6 Market Lane, Lisburn	50
Mary Innes	Widow	25 Millbrook Road, Lisburn	70
Mary Lennigan	Widow	52 Antrim Street, Lisburn	69
Eliza Lappin	Widow	118 Longstone Street, Lisburn	68
Lucy M'Connell	Widow	Palmer Street, Belfast	75
Wm. Jas. M'Coubrey	Widower	44 Seymour Street, Lisburn	70
Mina M'Creedy	Spinster	Hillhall, Lisburn	66
John M'Dowell	Widower	Fitzroy Avenue, Belfast	63
Thomas Robinson	...	52 Chapel Hill, Lisburn	68
Matilda Spratt	Widow	94 Gainsborough Drive, Belfast	53
Mary Strange	Widow	1 Shandon Street, Belfast	53
Sarah Stewart	Widow	Hill Street, Lisburn	60
Isabella Wiggins	Widow	31 Rosebank Street, Belfast	64
J. R. T. Mulholland, J.P.	...	30 Derryvolgie Avenue, Belfast	80
Anna Mulholland	Spinster	30 Derryvolgie Avenue, Belfast	83
Jane Towe	Widow	54 Richardson Street, Belfast	...

HISTORY OF CHRIST CHURCH CATHEDRAL, LISBURN

In 1611 Sir Fulke Conway, a substantial Warwickshire landowner, with Welsh roots, was given, by James I, a grant of the manor of Killultagh in south-west County Antrim, bounded on one side by the River Lagan, and so acquired the area previously controlled by the O'Neills of Clandeboye.

Sir Fulke Conway built his manor house on an easily defended site overlooking the river and in 1623 built a church as a chapel-of-ease which was originally for the use of the manor house. This church was known as the Church of St. Thomas. Sir Fulke died in March 1624, as the result of a fire which was said to be caused by smoking his pipe in bed, in one of his residences, and was succeeded by his elder brother, Sir Edward Conway, who in 1626 became 1st Viscount Conway of England and Killultagh in Ireland. He died on 3rd January 1630/31 aged 67 and his son, also Edward, succeeded him. This Edward became the 2nd Viscount Conway and died in 1655. In 1631 he appointed George Rawdon, from Rawdon Hall, near Leeds in Yorkshire, as his land agent in Ireland. Rawdon developed the town of Lisnagarvey, and the estate of Killultagh. It was around this manor house that a new settlement with inhabitants from Conway's family estates in the midlands of England and Wales was established. The 2nd Viscount was succeeded by his son, also Edward, who became the 3rd Viscount, and was then created Earl of Conway on the 3rd December 1679. He died in August 1683 and as he had no direct heirs his Irish and English estates passed by will to his nephew Popham Seymour. In 1699 Popham was killed in a duel in London at the age of 24 and the estates then passed to his brother Colonel Francis. Both of these Seymours took the surname Conway. The next to succeed was Francis, the son of Colonel Francis, and he became the 1st Marquis of Hertford in 1793. The estates then passed in turn to Francis, the 2nd Marquis, Francis Charles, the 3rd Marquis, Richard, the 4th Marquis and then by will to Sir Richard Wallace. Sir Richard Wallace, who was an illegitimate son of the 4th Marquis, died on the 25th January 1884.

The first surviving register for the church of St. Thomas starts 12th September 1639, but has an entry of 30th December 1637, up to 22nd August 1641, with a gap, and then continues from 2nd March 1643 until 23rd December 1646. The gap is probably due to disruption caused by the fact that the 1641 rebellion had broken out on the 23rd October of that year. The rebels, who were led by Sir Phelim O'Neill, Sir Con Magennis and General Plunkett, were defeated at Lisburn by the King's force under the command of Sir George Rawdon.

The first church, along with the manor house and the town, was destroyed at this time. The first register of baptisms, marriages and burials survived. It is believed that this first church was 80 feet long and 25 feet wide, with a porch on the south side. The map of Lisnagarvey, of about 1632, shows a plan of the church.

The church, the manor house, and the town were rebuilt in the 1660's, and on 27th October 1662, when Jeremy Taylor was Bishop of Down and Connor, the church of Lisburn was granted a charter by Charles II, making it the Cathedral of the United Diocese of Down and Connor, and allowing it to elect two members to the Irish Parliament. Blaris and Lisnagarvey Parishes now became Blaris Parish, otherwise Lisburn Parish, and the church became known as Christ Church Cathedral.

In 1674 a tower was constructed to provide access to the gallery, which was also erected in the same year. In 1697 the vestry decided to "raise £60 for the repair of the church and churchyard of Lisburn, and also for enlarging said church."

Disaster struck again when in April 1707 an accidental fire destroyed the Cathedral, manor house and most of the town. Fortunately the main structure of the church tower survived, but the church had to be rebuilt for a third time. The foundation of the new Cathedral was laid in 1708, but the construction took several years to complete. This is the Cathedral building that exists today. Fortunately the records also survived this fire, probably due to the Rev. Joseph Wilkins, who was the rector at this time.

The vestry was added to the cathedral in 1727. The inscription on the wall is as follows:-

This
Vestry was built
in the year
1728.
The Reverend
Anthony Rogers
Rector
Thomas Crawford Esq.
William Seeds
Church Wards

Nearly a century later, in 1805, the spire, which today is still a very fine and easily recognisable landmark in Lisburn, was added. David McBlain of Limavady had the contract for this work. It replaced an earlier wooden spire.

In 1824, in order to provide additional seats, a gallery, supported on cast iron pillars, was added to the present building. 1834 saw the organ, which had been a gift from the Marquis of Hertford in 1790, being re-located to the gallery.

In the Ordnance Survey Memoirs for 1835 a very comprehensive description is given of the Cathedral. This said that it was built of stone and lime, and was about 91 feet by 40 feet, with walls about 3 feet thick. It was 1 storey high and slated, with a large door on the west and a second door from the Vestry room on the north. The windows were Gothic in design, with 4 on the south and 3 on the north and 1 in the east gable. Inside, there were 2 metal stoves for heating and a chandelier suspended from the ceiling. It was estimated the Cathedral could hold almost 900 people.

The entrance to the Cathedral was by 2 wrought iron gates, one on the west from Market Square and the other on the north side of the cathedral.

The steeple and spire were also built of lime with 5 Gothic windows and a clock. In the steeple were a large bell, 2 chime bells and a fire bell, which was also used on market days at 10 o'clock a.m. The large bell has the following inscription on the outside: "This bell recast by the Honorable Francis, Earl of Hertford, anno 1751, Thomas Lester of London, fecit." The fire and market bell has the following inscription on the outside: "The gift of Lord Conway, 1721, recast 1746, Roger Hodgkinson Esquire, seneschal." The clock and 2 chime bells have the following inscriptions on them. On the clock: "The gift the most noble Marquis of Hertford, 1796, John Briant, Hertford, England, fecit." This is a four-quarter clock. On the bells: "John Briant, 1796." These bells proclaim the hour by 8 strokes and the quarter hour by 2 strokes. The large bell was recast in Dublin in 1861.

When a new fire station was opened in Railway Street the part-time men could not hear the fire bell and so from October 1884 until after the First World War the Select Vestry allowed the large Cathedral bell to be rung as well. This bell was also used as a curfew bell and each evening, at 9 p.m., there were one hundred strokes. This went on until 1923.

In 1940 the Cathedral clock chimes stopped working and in 1996 the clock stopped working. In 2004 a modern clock mechanism was installed by Canavan Clockmakers, Lurgan, to electronically control the clock and bells.

THE GROUND PLOTTE OF LISNEGARVEY

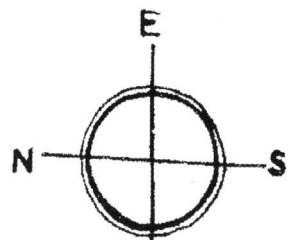

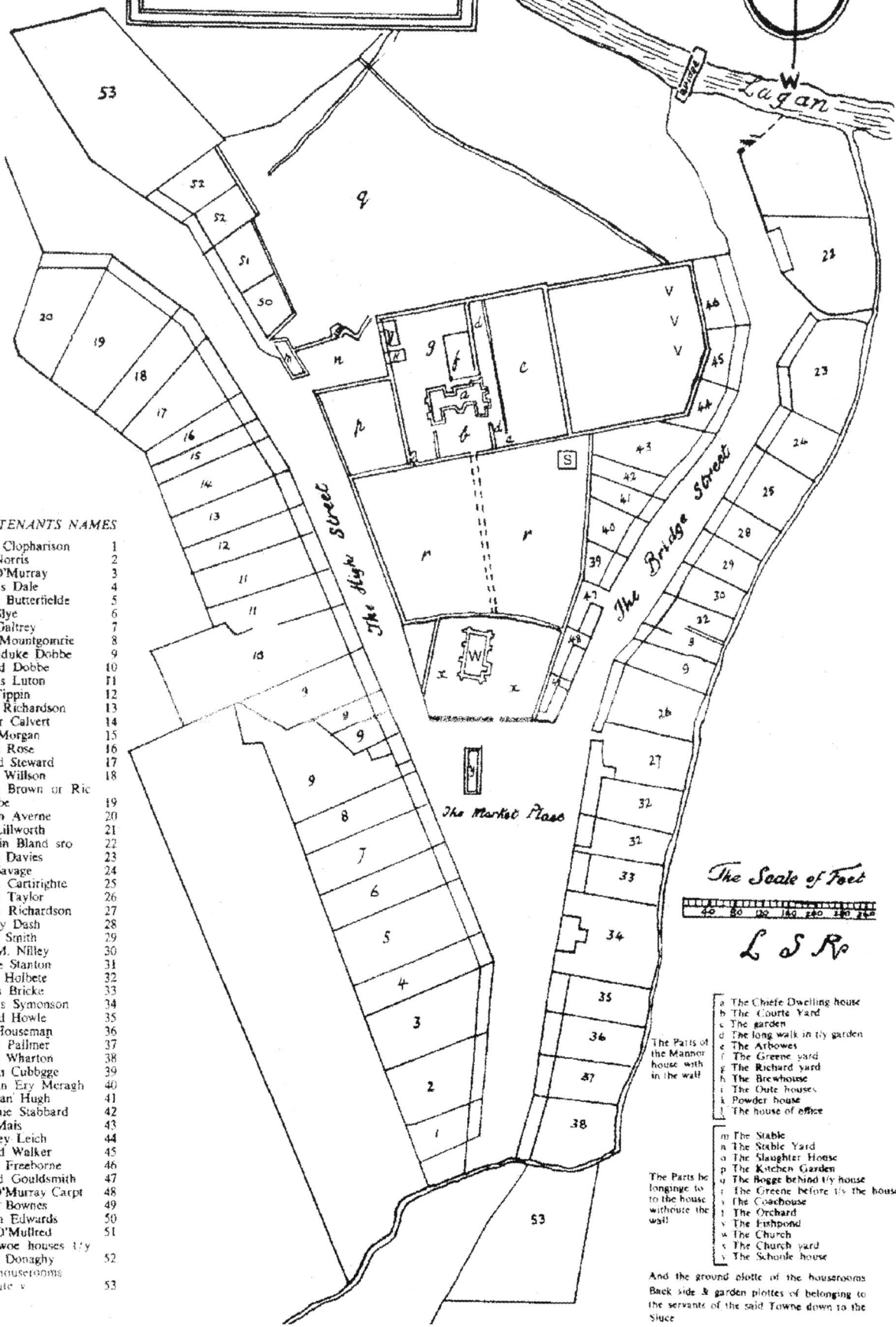

E
N — W — S

Lagan

Bridge

The High Street

The Bridge Street

The Market Place

53 52 51 50 49 48 47 46 45 44 43 42 41 40 39 20 19 18 17 16 15 14 13 12 11 10 9 8 7 6 5 4 3 2 1

q v c d f g h b a i k l m n o p r s w x y z

21 22 23 24 25 28 29 30 32 26 27 32 32 33 34 35 36 37 38 53

THE TENANTS NAMES

Name	No.
Henry Clopharison	1
John Norris	2
John O'Murray	3
Thomas Dale	4
Symon Butterfielde	5
John Slye	6
John Galtrey	7
Hugh Mountgomrie	8
Marmaduke Dobbe	9
Richard Dobbe	10
Thomas Luton	11
John Tippin	12
Heven Richardson	13
Chrofer Calvert	14
Anne Morgan	15
George Rose	16
Edward Steward	17
Henrie Willson	18
Robert Brown or Ric Dobbe	19
William Averne	20
John Lillworth	21
Katherin Bland sto	22
George Davies	23
John Savage	24
Joumie Cartirighte	25
Robert Taylor	26
Tymon Richardson	27
Humfrey Dash	28
Willim Smith	29
John M. Nilley	30
Ashuffe Stanton	31
Henrie Holbete	32
Francis Bricke	33
Thomas Symonson	34
Richard Howle	35
John Houseman	36
Patrick Pallmer	37
Robert Wharton	38
William Cubbgge	39
John an Ery Meragh	40
Owen an' Hugh	41
Anthonie Stabbard	42
John Mais	43
Humfrey Leich	44
Richard Walker	45
Hernie Freeborne	46
Edward Gouldsmith	47
John O'Murray Carpt	48
Robert Bownes	49
William Edwards	50
Peter O'Mullred	51
The Twoe houses t/y were Donaghy	52
Small houserooms W'oute v	53

The Scale of Feet

40 80 120 160 200 240 280 320

L S R

The Parts of the Mannor house with in the wall

a The Chiefe Dwelling house
b The Courte Yard
c The garden
d The long walk in t/y garden
e The Arbowes
f The Greene yard
g The Richard yard
h The Brewhouse
i The Oute houses
k Powder house
l The house of office

The Parts he longinge to to the house withoute the wall

m The Stable
n The Stable Yard
o The Slaughter House
p The Kitchen Garden
q The Bogge behind t/y house
r The Greene before t/s the house
s The Coachouse
t The Orchard
v The Fishpond
w The Church
x The Church yard
y The Schoole house

And the ground plotte of the houserooms Back side & garden plottes of belonging to the servants of the said Towne down to the Sluce

Due to the increasing growth and prosperity of the congregation over the next fifty years the Cathedral was now ready to be extended in a major way. These major changes to the building were in the years 1884 - 1917 when Canon Pounden was rector. In 1889 the present chancel was added, and the east wall was replaced by a Gothic arch. Buttresses of dressed stone were put in to reinforce the external wall of the nave. When this work was being carried out a vault was discovered with two burials. They were of Theophilus Mimmings, of Lambeg, who was buried 22nd May 1668 and Abigail, wife of Thomas Ricaby, Lambeg, who was buried 17th August 1680. It is possible that when the new chancel was added to the Cathedral it was extended over part of the graveyard to the east of the building. The Parish Hall was built in 1884, and was used as a Sunday School. In 1890 four pictorial stained glass windows in the Cathedral were dedicated, two windows in memory of Sir Richard Wallace and two windows in memory of former Bishops and Lisburn Rectors.

In the early hours of August 1st 1914 damage was caused to the chancel window in the east end of the Cathedral. Dynamite was used to cause an explosion, but, because it had not been buried deeply enough into the ground, it was only the window that suffered damage with twenty-nine panes being either cracked or broken. Several suffragette handbills were found in the grounds and later that day four suffragettes, Mrs. Metge, Miss Dorothy Evans, Miss Maud Wickham and Miss Carson, were arrested by the police at Mrs. Metge's house in Seymour Street.

After two appearances in Lisburn Courthouse they were released from prison on 11th September, as the Home Secretary remitted the sentences of all persons who were undergoing imprisonment for crimes connected with the Suffrage agitation.

In 1950 the East window was presented by John Milne Barbour in memory of his wife, Eliza Barbour, and his son, John Milne Barbour, who had died in an air crash in Scotland. This depicts Christ in Glory. [For Barbours see THG Vol. 1 page 147.]

For some years First World War regimental colours carried at the Battle of the Somme were displayed in the Cathedral. These were the colours of the 11th Battalion Royal Irish Rifles and the Fourth Antrim Battalion of the Ulster Volunteer Force.

1924 saw the widening of the entrance to the grounds from Market Square, when an adjacent building was demolished and double gates were erected. These gates were repaired in 2003.

The most recent internal major change was in 1990 when the chancel area was altered by moving the choir seating to a raised area below the pulpit. The communion rail was extended, new chancel steps in white marble were installed and the stone pulpit was replaced.

In 1609 the Chapter of the Church of Connor was remodelled, by a charter of King James I, as the Chapter of St. Saviour, Connor. This Chapter sits in the Cathedral of Christ Church, Lisburn. Nowadays the titles of Chapter members are honorary and the members all serve in the Diocese of Connor in other full time capacities.

RECTORS

ST. THOMAS, LISNAGARVEY

1634/5	Rev. William Chambers
1637	Rev. Martin Tinley
c1641	Rev. Thomas Ives
1641–1646	No details known
1661	Rev. Jeremiah Piddock
1661	Rev. James Mace

BLARIS

1622	Rev. Patrick Hamilton
1636/7	Rev. Alexander Forbes/Forbisson
1637/8	Rev. James Hamilton
1664	Rev. George Rust

1668 UNION OF BLARIS AND LISNAGARVEY
NOW KNOWN AS LISBURN

1668	Rev. James Mace	1876	Rev. Hartley Hodson
1671	Rev. Joseph Wilkins	1884	Rev. William Dawson Pounden
1716	Rev. George Wilkins	1917	Rev. William Patrick Carmody
1727	Rev. Anthony Rogers	1924	Rev. John Sinclair Taylor
1741	Rev. John Welsh	1950	Rev. Stephen Parnell Kerr
1743	Rev. Richard Dobbs	1960	Rev. Richard Adams
1775	Rev. Thomas Higginson	1976	Rev. Gilbert Wilson
1781	Rev. William Traill	1982	Rev. John McCammon
1796	Rev. Snowden Cupples	1999	Rev. Samuel Wright
1836	Rev. James Stannus		

CURATES OF LISBURN CATHEDRAL

1651	Rev. Andrew Wyke	1877	Rev. George Gardiner Parkinson
1658	Rev. Philip Tandy	1880	Rev. John Paterson Smyth
1661	Rev. Michael Matthews	1884	Rev. George Patton Mitchell
1661	Rev. Thomas Haslam	1889	Rev. George Robert Bell
1716	Rev. Thomas Finlay	1909	Rev. Edward Parkinson Riddall (honorary)
1731	Rev. Thomas Johnston	1916	Rev. John Balfour Bradshaw
1743	Rev. John Arthur	1925	Rev. William Hall
1743	Rev. Roger Vere	1932	Rev. Frederick William Robert Knowles
1763	Rev. Richard Dobbs (jun)	1934	Rev. Thomas Maxwell Orr
1769	Rev. Edward Fletcher	1937	Rev. Leslie Aidan Elliott
1771	Rev. Philip Johnson	1940	Rev. Thomas Herbert Frizelle
1775	Rev. Patrick Parker	1944	Rev. James Andrew O'Brien Rogers
1785	Rev. Philip Fletcher	1947	Rev. James Nelson McCullough
1792	Rev. Samuel Smythe	1953	Rev. William Henry Lendrum
1792	Rev. Roger Moore Dillon	1961	Rev. Charles Robert Jordeson Rudd
c1806	Rev. Hill Coulson	1962	Rev. James Clyde Irvine
1817	Rev. Thomas Edward Higginson	1964	Rev. Clive West
1824	Rev. Thomas Cupples	1966	Rev. John Wadsworth Ellis
1829	Rev. Thomas Thompson	1968	Rev. Harold George Whitty
1832	Rev. Ralph Bridge	1970	Rev. William John Bridcut
1835	Rev. Cecil Smyly	1973	Rev. William Albert Murphy
1838	Rev. William Reeves	1977	Rev. Thomas Raymond McKnight
1840	Rev. Edward Loftus Fitzgerald	1979	Rev. William Warren Russell
1842	Rev. Edward James Cordner	1980	Rev. William Matthew Adair
1842	Rev. John Nash Griffin	1984	Rev. Christopher Lind Peters
1845	Rev. J. Hudson	1988	Rev. James Roland Heaney
1846	Rev. Hartley Hodson	1991	Rev. William Alan Capper
1843	Rev. Andrew Craig Neely	1994	Rev. Jan Hales
1856	Rev. James John Hall	1999	Rev. Roger Thompson
1860	Rev. Robert Lindsay	2003	Rev. Ken McGrath
1870	Rev. Thomas Agmondisham Vesey		

CATHEDRAL RECTORS AND CURATES

REV. HARTLEY HODSON
Rector 1876 – 1884

REV. EDWARD PARKINSON RIDDALL
Hon. Curate 1909 – 1919

REV. JOHN SINCLAIR TAYLOR
Rector 1924 – 1950

REV. THOMAS HERBERT FRIZELLE
Curate 1940 – 1943

REV. STEPHEN PARNELL KERR
Rector 1950 – 1959

REV. WILLIAM HENRY LENDRUM
Curate 1953 - 1961

CHURCHWARDENS OF LISBURN CATHEDRAL

1667	Henry Godyer	1736	John Fletcher and Wm. Shaw
1668	William Stephens and Mr. Ferne	1737	Arthur Johnson and John Abbot
1669	Bryne Magee and Wm. Conway	1738	Edward Smyth and Lieut. Frederick Porter
1670	Richard Smyth and Thomas Taylor	1739/40	Edward Smyth and Sam Delacherois
1671	Ezekiel Clough and Henry Hoole	1741	Thomas Howell and Thomas Seeds
1672	John Peers and Matthew Wolfe	1742	William Connor and John Gordon
1673	Francis Garnet and John Darling	1743	Joseph Masklin and John McClure
1674	John Templeton	1744	Henry Bell and Richard Barnsley
1675	John Kennell and Anthony Le Roy	1745	William Close and Richard Roberts
1676	John Templeton and Robt. Ransom	1746/47	Thomas Dixon and William Brison
1677	George Rogers and Thomas Blair	1748	John Carlton and William Nickle
1678	James Bodkin and Richard Clough	1749	Roger Hodgkinson and Abraham Crommelin
1679	Thomas Danby and John Hamilton	1750	Marmaduke Dempster and James Fulton
1680	Will Crow and Thomas Granger	1751/52	Thomas Johnson and Alexander McAuley
1681	Joseph Burgess and Thomas Abbot	1753	Thomas Carlton and Henry Betty
1682	William Mastin and James Taffe	1754	Thomas Bingham and Robert Fulton
1683	John Clarke and John Waring	1755	Cornelius Carlton and James Wightman
1684	John Tate and Will Beane	1756	Thomas Mussen and Francis Burden
1685	Richard Robison and Will Close	1757	William Dillon and David Betty
1686	Richard Pitts and Richard Swinerton	1758	William Johnson and Andrew Shanks
1687	Edward Peers and William McKetrick	1759	Reney Bullmer and James Kennedy
1688	William Smyth and William Barwick	1760	Arthur Johnson and John Whitla
1689	Richard Fitzachery and Thomas Lassels	1761	Samuel Betty and John Ward
1690	Robert Nixon and Richard Fitzachery	1762	William Wheeler and John Fulton
1691	Antony Kinning and Thomas Dixon	1763	James McBurney and John Patten
1692	John Blackhall and Robert Harrison	1764	Edward Ross and Thomas Betty
1693	James Martin and James Burney	1765	John Kinley and Robert Bell
1694	Thomas Welch and Henry Conway	1766	Saml. Townsend and John Stirling
1695	Arthur Brooks and Capt. Cornelius Carlton	1767	Lewis Hastings and David Willson
1696	Thomas Cornwall and Daniel Mildway	1768	Roger Johnson and Henry Welsh
1697	Thomas Rogers and Matthew Pailing	1769	James Higginson and Robert Masklin
1698	Edward Ellis and George Hodgeskinson	1770	George Tandy and Robert Murray
1699	Michael Jackson and Francis Irwin	1771	Robert Duncan and Edward Peers
1700	John Peers and John Cooke (also Michael Jackson and Arthur Bradley)	1772	Cornelius Carlton and Robert Brady
1701	John Cooke and William Ellis	1773	Edward Marsh and John Smyth
1702	Edward Obery and John Hamilton, jun.	1774	John Hunter and Mr. De Lacherois Crommelin
1703	Edward Obery and Thos. Parkinson	1775	John Hastings and William McCracken
1704	Richard Hawkins and Christopher Barker	1776	William Boyle and Henry Morrison
1705/6/7	Anthony Kennen and Thos. Dixon	1777	William Masklin and William Darby
1708	Walter Brerton and Christopher Whiting	1778	William Dillon (jun) and Arthur Johnson
1709	Walter Abbot and Joseph Hignet	1779	John Bolton and Thomas Ward
1710	Eaver Magee and Edward Peers	1780	Henry Marmion and Archibald Mussen
1711	Edward Peers and Ethelred Wogan	1781/82	William Rogers and Jas. Stewart
1712	Edward Peers and Eaver Magee	1783	Poyntz Stewart and John Elsey
1713	Francis Obre and Philip Robinson	1784	Thomas Carlton and Wm. Patten
1714/15/16	William Seed and John Busby	1785	Sam De la Cherois and Joseph Chapman
1717	Thomas Benson and Chas. Frankelin	1786	William Hogg and John Johnson
1718	Thomas Welsh and Lewis Rushet	1787	John Crossley and Richard Greer
1719	Peter Cullenan and Elisha Bodkin	1788	Joseph Garner and Thos. Hunter
1720/21/22	Thomas Rose and John Tone	1789/90	George Morewood and Robert Mussen
1723	No record for this year	1791	William Hogg and William Johnston
1724	Henry Close and William Wogan	1792	Richard Barnsley and James Townley
1725	Ambrose Towle and Ed. Masline	1793	John McDowell and William Dillon, jun
1726/27	John Reed and Anthony Carter	1794	George Dixon and John Bulmer
1728/29	Thomas Crawford and Wm. Seeds	1795	Thomas Carlton and Richard Brison
1730/31	Edward Masklin and James Crouch	1796	Thomas Townley and Robt. Sterling
1732/33	Henry Close and Joseph Ellis	1797	Henry Mussen and Samuel Warring
1734	George Walsh and Jaques Marquis	1798	James Pelan and Edward Phillips
1735	Jeremiah Falloon and William Shaw	1799	Samuel Tucker and Wm. Wheeler
		1800	James Mussen and James Mussen

1801	George Boomer and Richard Cohoon	1865	H.J. Manley and Jacob Bannister
1802	William Coulson and Henry Marmion	1866	Lucas Waring and W. Taylor
1803	Robert Coulson and Wm. Williams	1867	John Morton and John Pennington
1804	Francis Smyth, Esq., and Capt. James Cordner	1868	William Johnston and Samuel Young
1805	John Garret and Benjamin Neely	1869	H.J. Manley and W.T. Stannus
1806	Walter Coulson and Richard Greer	1870/71	James Mack and Ralph Robson
1807	John Marshall and James Williams	1872	Capt. Whitla and William Johnston
1808	Arthur Davis and James Hodgens	1873	W. T. Stannus and Samuel A. Johnston
1809	Matthew Mussen and Richard Pelan	1874/75	Claude L. Capron and T.R. Stannus
1810	James Richardson and Matthew Jordan	1876	Claude L. Capron and J.A. Mack
1811	William Phillips and John Woods	1877/78	Claude L. Capron and T.R. Stannus
1812	William Caldbeck and William Graham	1879/80	R.H. Bland and T.R. Stannus
1813	James Stewart and William Johnson	1881	R.H. Bland and Mr. Garrett
1814	Thomas Higginson and Henry Fisher	1882-88	R.H. Bland and T.R. Stannus
1815	Thomas Johnson Smyth and Thomas Wilson	1889	R.H. Bland and Dr. George St. George
1816	Charles Lutton and John Smith	1890	Robert Henry Bland J.P. and Thomas J. English
1817	Rowley F. Hall and Charles Lutton	1891	R.H. Bland and John Trousdell
1818	?	1892	R.H. Bland and Hugh Smith
1819	Joseph Beatty and Sam. Johnson	1893	R.H. Bland and George B. Wilkins
1820	William Higginson and George Pelan	1894	Robert H. Bland J.P. and John M. Barbour
1821	Robert Stewart and Henry Magee	1895	R.H. Bland and Robert Bannister
1822	Robert McCall and Henry Magee	1896	Robert H. Bland and Robert Rice
1823	Hugh Seeds and John Major	1897	Thomas J. English and Richard Young
1824	James Smyth and John Clarke	1898	Dr. George St. George and W.J. Greene
1825	Henry Higginson and Charles Casement	1899	John Trousdell and W.H. Hancock
1826	George Boomer and John Moore	1900	Hugh Smith and George B. Wilkins
1827	James Thompson and Parker Major	1901	Charles McGowan and George Mearns
1828	William Moore and David Beatty	1902	Alexander Gardiner and Robert McCreight
1829	Capt. Samuel Delacherois Smyth and Robert McClure	1903	Joseph Lockhart and W.J. Wilson
1830	David Mack and John Singleton	1904	Robert McCarrison and Saml. Greene
1831	Thomas Weatherhead and George Emerson	1905	T.J. English and Dr. St. George
1832	John Woods and James Ward	1906	Charles McGowan and Robert Bannister
1833	William Collins and John Reid	1907	W.H. Hancock and George Mearns
1834	Samuel Gamble and George Major	1908	T.J. English and Robert McCreight
1835	Thomas Beckett and John Chapman	1909	Joseph Lockhart and W.J. Wilson
1836	Robert Mussen and Thomas Johnston	1910	Robert McCreight and Robert Bannister
1837	Henry Mussen and George Duncan	1911	Joseph Lockhart and T.J. English
1838	William Whitla and Richard Jefferson	1912	Robert Bannister and Samuel Greenfield
1839	William Stewart and John Millar	1913	H.V. Pegg and Samuel Greene
1840	Richard Robinson and Robert Alderdice	1914	Joseph McKibben and W.J. Greene
1841	John Shaw Smyth and Francis Weldon	1915	Joseph Lockhart and T.J. English
1842	William Bullick and Henry Seeds	1916	J.A. Woods and W.J. Wilson
1843	James Coulson and John Jefferson	1917	Dr. St. George and T.J. English
1844	John Heron and John Campbell	1918	T.J. English and Robert Bannister
1845	John Vernon and Robert Hall	1919	Robert Bannister and Samuel Greenfield
1846	Robert Stewart and Craig Ward	1920	Samuel Greenfield and James Shanks
1847	Henry J. Manley and Arthur McCartney	1921	James Shanks and T.J. English
1848	James Bolton and Thomas McCreight	1922	Joseph Lockhart and Robert McCreight
1849	Henry John Garrett and Richard Murray	1923	W.J. Greene and Frank Hewitt
1850	James Mussen and Michael Woods	1924	James Shanks and Samuel Greenfield
1851	Thomas Sharp and Edward Lemon	1925	Samuel Greenfield and Joseph McNeice
1852	Thomas Sharp and Henry Seeds	1926	Samuel Greenfield and J.C. McNeice
1853	Henry John Garrett and George Pelan	1927	R.C. Bannister and R.K. Megran
1854	Robert Stewart and Michael Linn	1928	R.K. Megran and A. Refausse
1855	James Ward and Alexander Titterington	1929	A. Refaussé and T. Creggan
1856	W. Mussen and R.G. Hill	1930	T. Creggan and D. McKibben
1857	Lucas Waring and W. Whitla	1931	D. McKibben and J. Doran
1858	Walter T. Stannus and Samuel Young	1932	J. Doran and J. Clarke
1859	Mr. Manley and W. Graham	1933	A. Refausse and J.C. McNeice
1860	Mr. Stephenson and T.R. Stannus	1934	T. Leckey and S.J. Keery
1861	James Ward and William Thompson	1935	S.J. Keery and T.A. Long
1862	Robt. Barbour and James Cairns	1936	T.A. Long and S.J. Keery
1863	David Beatty and Redmond Jefferson	1937	J.H. Creen and W.F. Keery
1864	J.K. Green and George Thompson	1938	J.H. Creen and W.F. Aughey
		1939	A. Refaussé and J. Forsythe

Year	Names	Year	Names
1940	J. Forsythe and J. Doran	1973	W.A. Galashan and F. Bailie
1941	J. Doran and W.J. Parks	1974	A.S. Orr and D.H. Robinson
1942	W.J. Parks and J. Morrison	1975	T. Cherry and J.S.M. McKibben
1943	J.B. Iago and J.C. McNeice	1976	T. Cherry and J.S.M. McKibben
1944	H.J. Buchanan and R.K. Megran	1977	R.J.M. McConnell and D. McCormick
1945	J. Forsythe and J.H. Creen	1978	G.A.E. Gillespie and S. McCabe
1946	J. Forsythe and J.H. Creen	1979	D. Wright and J.A.G. Gibson
1947	F.R. McClure and E. Shaw	1980	Dr. J. Geddis and M.J. Heaney
1948	F.R. McClure and E. Shaw	1981	R.A.M. McKinnon and J. Sommerville
1949	T.A. Long and M. Stevenson	1982	J. Sommerville and W. Milne
1950	J. Malcolm Smith and W. Corkin	1983	Dr. K. Fullerton and W. Milne
1951	Ernest Creery and W. Beattie	1984	Dr. G. McCartney and J. Quigley
1952	J. Barbour and W. Gibson	1985	R. Norris and J. Quigley
1953	Ernest Keery and W. Beattie	1986	R. Norris and R. Robinson
1954	F.A. Cox and S. Allen	1987	T. Hull and R. Robinson
1955	T.A. Long and W. Scott	1988	T. Hull and A. Clarke
1956	F. McClure and J. Lord	1989	D. Reilly and A. Clarke
1957	J.A. Gilmore and T. Malcolm	1990	D. Reilly and D. Culbert
1958	W.C. Rollins and D.H. Roberts	1991	Mrs. K. McCullough and D. Culbert
1959	W. Gibson and W.J. Allister	1992	Mrs. K. McCullough and Mrs. I. Nichol
1960	W. Gibson and W.J. Allister	1993	Mrs. I. Nichol and Mrs. E. Stevenson
1961	D.H. Robinson and L.P.A. Stewart	1994	Mrs. E. Stevenson and J. Breadon
1962	H.W. Gillespie and B. Patterson	1995	J. Breadon and Miss B. Hilland
1963	Roy Irvine and John Hull	1996	Miss B. Hilland and A. Johnston
1964	E. Shaw and F.R. McClure	1997	Miss D. Mahood and A. Johnston
1965	R.J. Fitzimmons and R.J. Heaney	1998	Miss D. Mahood and T. Bruce
1966	E.H. Christie and J.S. McKibben	1999	B. Bell and T. Bruce
1967	W.C. Rollins and J.S. McKibben	2000	B. Bell and Mrs. E. Robinson
1968	R.A.M. McKinnon and T. Jordan	2001	J. Price and Mrs. E. Robinson
1969	T. Murdock and D. White	2002	J. Price and Mrs. A. Hall
1970	R.J.M. McConnell and E. Gillespie	2003	B. Welsh and Mrs. A. Hall
1971	W. Gibson and C. McCormick	2004	Mrs. M. Kennedy and B. Welsh
1972	Dr. J. Geddis and J. Briggs	2005	Mrs. M. Kennedy and P. Duggan

LISBURN CATHEDRAL c1920

Courtesy of the Irish Linen Centre & Lisburn Museum

THE HUGUENOTS

The Huguenots were French Protestants, or Calvinists. From 1598, when the edict of Nantes was proclaimed in France, until 22nd October 1685, when the edict of Nantes was revoked, the Huguenots were relatively free to worship as they wished, although some of them fled France during this time. After this date, as well as now suffering horrendous religious persecution, hundreds of buildings owned by the Huguenots were either burned or levelled to the ground, and they had to flee for safety to other Protestant countries. These countries included the Netherlands, Germany, Denmark, Switzerland, England and Ireland.

In Ireland a great number of Huguenots came to Waterford, others settled in Dublin, where they brought their skills of silk weaving, others went to Portarlington, but a large group moved north and settled in Lisburn, Belfast and Lurgan. It is thought there could have been Huguenots in Lambeg in the late 1640's, or earlier. In 1658 Louis Gaston is mentioned in Lisburn Cathedral records and Huguenots had also come over in Cromwell's army in the 1660's.

Among the army of William of Orange were a considerable number of Huguenots. Fredrich, Duke of Schomberg, was Commander-in-chief of the Williamite army in Ireland, and colonel of the Huguenot cavalry. Lisburn was his headquarters in the winter of 1689/90 and during his stay in Lisburn he lived in Castle Street. The burial records of Lisburn Cathedral record the deaths of some members of Schomberg's army, including some Huguenots.

Louis Crommelin had first come to Ireland about 1697 to survey the country for the representatives of the Earl of Galway, and then in 1698 King William invited Louis Crommelin to Lisburn where he was employed as "Overseer of the Royal Linen Manufacture in Ireland." Louis advanced money for this enterprise and also brought family members with him. Daniel De la Cherois had been a lieutenant in Lord Lifford's Regiment and also had experience in trading and linen. He married Marie Angélique, a cousin of Louis Crommelin. Nicholas De la Cherois was also in Lisburn and c1699 joined his brother in the linen industry. As well as members of his own family Louis invited other Huguenots to join him. The colony consisted of about 27 families, including those who worked for him, possibly about 120 in number.

The Lisburn Huguenot colony was the only one in the north of Ireland and it had its own Church and Pastor. The French Church was built in Castle Street. The first Pastor, Rev. Charles De la Valade, was a Minister who had conformed to the Anglican Church, and was appointed about 1704. The government paid £60 per year for the salary of the pastor. The services in the French Church were conducted in French. It is said of Charles De la Valade that if any members of the congregation did not attend services on the Sunday he would visit them next day. A list of the principal members of his congregation from about Queen Anne's reign is as follows:- Richard Bouchier, James De Berniers (sic), Israel Brethet, René Bulmer, Louis Crommelin, Louis Crommelin, jun., John Chartrex (sic), Wm. Colbert, D. Delap, Wm. Dillon, Thomas Drewett, Nicholas De la Cherois, Daniel De la Cherois, Henrie Du Pré, Peter Goyer, R. Gimblette, James De Ermaine, J. Frizzle, Matthew Jellett, John Martine, J. Maslin, William Noblette, James Obré, Mark Pettigrew, Thomas Lascelles, Matthew Roche, Mark Perrin, Jean Truefit, Francis Tournier and Louis Valentin. Charles De la Valade died in 1755 and his wife about 1759. The first clerk of the church was Peter Goyer, who was buried in Kilrush Burying Ground (see THG Vol. 1). La Valade was succeeded briefly by his brother, and in 1756 Rev. Saumarez Dubourdieu, son of Rev. Jean Armand Dubourdieu and great nephew of the Rev. Charles De la Valade, was appointed pastor. For 56 years Saumarez was also principal of the Lisburn Classical Academy, situated in Bow Street.

After the descendants of the original Huguenots had become intermarried with the local population there was no longer any need for a French Church with services held in their native tongue. In 1768 Saumarez had been appointed Curate In Perpetuity of Lambeg, and in 1780 he was appointed Vicar of

Glenavy. Saumarez died 14th December 1812, aged 96 years and 3 months, and is buried in Lambeg churchyard. The monument to him that is in Lisburn Cathedral was erected by his former pupils.

With the death of Saumarez Dubordieu and the decline in the number of Huguenot worshippers the French Church closed in 1818 and the building became the courthouse. Later, c1850, the old Lisburn Town Hall was erected on the site. This building now has a blue "Ulster History Circle" sign on it to commemorate the original site of the French Church. After the church closed the worshippers used Lisburn Cathedral.

The Bible and prayer book of the French Church are now preserved in PRONI in CR/1/35K. The records of Lisburn Cathedral also include the record of 23 children baptised by Charles De la Valade from 1709 to 1736. [see MIC/1/3/1]

UNVEILING OF CROMMELIN PLAQUE – 3rd AUGUST 1964   *(Courtesy of PRONI CR1/35J/2)*
(L – R) Rt. Hon. John Andrews, D.L., MP, Sir Graham Larmor, Capt. R.M. Crommelin

LISBURN CATHEDRAL BURYING GROUND

According to the first surviving Register of St. Thomas burials were made from 1639, with the earliest recorded burial being of "Stephn Mardsdene, Clarcke of the parish" on the 19th September.

In June 1700 there is a mention of the churchyard in the vestry books :

"It was agreed & ordered that a wall of stone & lime, eight foot high, without any doors, or windows, should be built on the north side of the churchyard of Lisburn, and that about four yards of ground should be lent & allow'd for the convenience of the tenemts near said wall, which ground so lent & allowed doth still of right belong to the sd church-yard."

The earliest legible date now found on a surviving tombstone is 1670, which is on the Atkinson stone, No. 110. Perhaps this stone and several others survived the fire of 1707. Thomas Molyneaux in "Journey to the North" said:

"When I stood in the churchyard I thought I had never seen so dreadful a sight before, all around us. The church burned to the ground, the tombstones cracked with fire, vast trees that stood around the graveyard burned to trunks. Lord Conway, to whom this town belongs, had his house, though at a distance from the rest of the town, burned to ashes and all his gardens in the same condition as the trees in the churchyard. 'Tis scarcely conceivable that such dismal effects should arise from so small a cause and in so short a time as they relate. Only some turf ashes thrown on a dunghill with a fresh wind blowing towards the town, raise and threw on the shingles of the next house, which, they being like spunk (timber) by a long drought of weather which then happened, took fire, and the wind continuing what it had begun, the whole town in half an hour was irrevocably in flames."

The following is a description of the churchyard from the Ordnance Survey Memoirs of 1835, with a record of some of the names of people buried in the graveyard:

The yard is tolerably large, enclosed partly by buildings and partly by a stone and lime wall, and contains a large number of handsome tombs and headstones and a beautiful square monument topped with a handsome marble urn representing a blazing light, and on its side, engraven tablets. This [was] erected by the seneschal over the remains of his late wife, Mrs. Gregg. The graveyard is also sheltered on the north and east by lofty forest trees which, together with the cathedral and its elegant and lofty spire on their elevated site, form a great ornament to the town and neighbourhood in which they are situated.

Names and Surnames in Cathedral Burial Ground.

The following are the principal names and surnames of families who bury in the cathedral graveyard at Lisburn. [First names] male: Edward, Joseph, William, Richard, Hugh, Francis, George, James, Thomas, Patrick, Alexander, Samuel, Roger, Henery, John, Nicholas, Ralph, Robert, Isaac, Poyntz, David. Female: Dorothea, Elizabeth, Emily, Margaret, Anngelica, Charlotte, Isebella, Jane, Martha, Maria, Sarah, Cathrine, Mary Ann, Mary, Ann, Elenor. Surnames: deLacherois, Crommelin, Caldbeck, Cupples, Clarke, Coulson, Crossley, Crofton, Corrant, Carleton, Barnsley, Bells, Blackburn, Boyd, Bowes, Bensons, Brigs, Bannister, Brereton, Bracegirdel, Buttle, Fletchers, Forrast, Fulton, Foster, Fergusson, Gibson, Gregg, Gamble, Gurk, McGurk, Gillott, Galston, Hudson, Hill, Hurst, Heron, Hawkshaw, Irving, Jefferson, Marsh, Macartney, McCallister, McCaul, McAnally, McBlane, Murray, Maginnes, Dobbs, Davis, Dukes, Johnson, Johnston, Logan, Pennington, Pelan, Parkinson, Ross, Williams, Whitla, Weldon, Ward, Wilson, Wood, Watson, Stewart, Sefton, Simon, Smyth, Shannon, Spratt, Thompson, Truffett, Turner, Kernes, Kibbins, McKibbins, Dillon, Boomer.

The Ordnance Survey Memoirs also said that in 1835 the oldest stone legible was one on the south side of the cathedral erected 1682 to Elizabeth Sarah and John Baxter. Their ages were not given, but the word "children" followed the names.

In 1996 some headstones were relocated from the north side to the south side to give more room for vehicular access.

The Garden of Remembrance, for the interment of ashes of parishioners after cremation, was created in the southeast corner of the churchyard. This peaceful area was provided by Dr. Garry McCartney in 1988, in memory of his wife, Marilyn, who died in 1986. Dr. McCartney's ashes were interred in 1992.

From the burial records it is evident that several people were buried inside the Cathedral building. We include a list of these.

Bearing in mind all the "mishaps" to the Cathedral there is a very good record of burials in the graveyard, but unfortunately there are gaps in this record. The surviving burial records are as follows:-

Book 1 Burials 1639 – 1646
Book 2 Burials 1661 – 1720
Book 3 Burials 1720 – 1749
Book 4 Burials 1763 – 1779 & 1781
Book 6 Burials 1820 – 1848
Book 7 Burials 1849 – 1853, 1856 – 1869
Book 8 Burials 1870 – 76, 1882, 1884, 1885 – 1917, 1920, 1929

These records can be found in P.R.O.N.I. under MIC/1/3/1, MIC/583/9-10 and CR/1/35C/3.

The first register was published by the Representative Church Body in 1996 as "The Register of St. Thomas, Lisnagarvey, Co. Antrim 1637 – 1646" and was edited by Raymond Refaussé.

The last burial recorded in the burial book for the Cathedral Burying Ground is for Isabella Wilson in February 1929.

CATHEDRAL 74   **DETAIL OF RAILING**

LISBURN CATHEDRAL BURYING GROUND

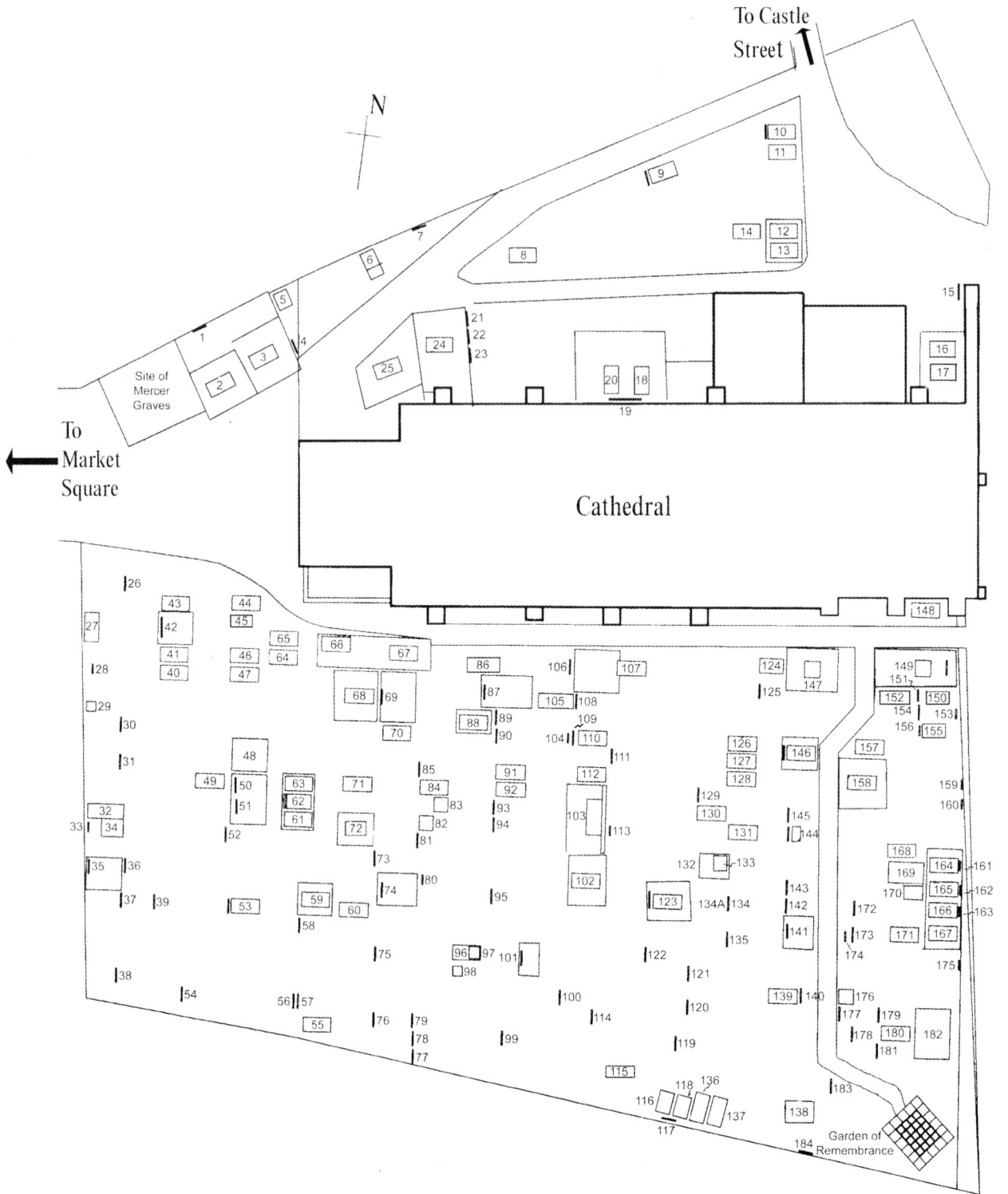

To Castle Street

N

10
11

9

7

6

14 12
      13

8

5

21
22
23

15

24

25

16
17

Site of Mercer Graves

1

4

3

20 18

2

19

To Market Square

Cathedral

26

43 44
42 45

148

27

41 65 66 67
40 64

46
47

86

106

107

124

149
151
152 150
154 153
156 155

28

68 69

87

105 108

125

147

29

88 89

109

126

157

30

70

90

104 110

127
128

146

158

31

85

91
92

111

112

159
160

48

84

49 50

63 71

83

93

103

129
130

145

168
169 164 161

51

62

82

94

113

131

144

170 165 162

32
34

52

61

72

81

73

102

132 133

143
142

166 163

171 167

33

35 36

59

74

80

95

123

134A 134

135

172

173
174

175

37 39

53

60

123

141

139 140

176
177 179

38

54

56 57

55

75

76 79

78

77

96 97
98 101

100

99

114

122

121

120

119

115

118 136

116

117

137

138

183

178 180 182
181

184

Garden of Remembrance

18

LISBURN CATHEDRAL BURYING GROUND

1. CALDBECK
2. STANNUS
3. CUPPLES
4. WHITEFORD
5. UNKNOWN
6. CLARKE
7. WETHERED
8. REILLY
9. FLYNN
10. WILSON
11. UNKNOWN
12. HOGG/BOLTON
13. HOGG/NICHOLSON
14. SIMON
15. McCLURE
16. PURDON/DE LA CHEROIS-CROMMELIN
17. DOBBS/DE LA CHEROIS-CROMMELIN
18. JOHNSON SMYTH
19. STEWART
20. STEWART
21. CAMPBELL
22. UNKNOWN
23. UNKNOWN
24. WRAY
25. MUSSEN
26. FERGUSON
27. HOWARD
28. YOUNG
29. REID
30. SIMPSON
31. CROCKARD
32. FULTON
33. UNKNOWN
34. McMULLEN
35. JEFFERSON
36. JEFFERSON
37. UNKNOWN
38. FLEMING
39. MACARTNEY
40. HULL
41. CROSSLEY
42. THOMPSON
43. MARTIN
44. CARLETON
45. BRERTON
46. UNKNOWN
47. CARLETON
48. WHITLA
49. BLACKBURN
50. McHENRY
51. McHENRY
52. DAVIS
53. ALLEN
54. DOYLE
55. POWELL
56. COCHRAN
57. McCANN
58. LACKEY
59. WIGHTMAN
60. TURNER
61. ROGERS
62. GILBERT
63. McKEE
64. BARNSLEY
65. UNKNOWN
66. NEELY
67. JOHNSON SMYTH
68. DILLON
69. O'FLAHERTY
70. CLOSE
71. FULTON
72. COULSON
73. UNKNOWN
74. KELLY
75. JOHNSON
76. JOHNSTON
77. UNKNOWN
78. BANNISTER
79. BANNISTER
80. STEWART
81. WILSON
82. BLACKBURN
83. BRIGS
84. BLACKBURN
85. BLACKBURN
86. MOREWOOD
87. WOODHOUSE
88. MARMION
89. TRAINOR
90. FORREST
91. JACKSON
92. GARNET
93. REID
94. BRADY
95. RUSSELL
96. STORY
97. RICHMOND
98. THOMPSON
99. NEWBURN
100. CUMMINS

101. WATSON
102. UNKNOWN
103. MUSGRAVE
104. ATKINSON
105. UNKNOWN
106. MURRAY
107. STEWART
108. NEWBURN
109. FULTON
110. ATKINSON
111. TOWNSON
112. FULTON
113. GIBSON
114. McCALL
115. FAIRLEY
116. McGURK
117. MURRAY
118. WELDON
119. FULTON
120. HAMMOND
121. UNKNOWN
122. BOYD
123. CROCKARD
124. CHARTERS
125. HERON
126. KIDD
127. FFAREWELL
128. IRVING
129. HURST
130. VERNON
131. PELAN
132. BUSBY
133. MOMENTO MORI/UNKNOWN
134. BROOKE
134A. WHEELER
135. RICHARDSON
136. SMITH
137. FULTON
138. McKEE
139. MATEER
140. HALLIDAY
141. BULLICK
142. HUGHES
143. UNKNOWN
144. GORDON
145. TINSLEY
146. TINSLEY
147. GREGG
148. OBRE
149. HAWKSHAW
150. DAVIS

151. HART
152. DRAKE
153. GELSTON
154. GELSTON
155. HASLAM
156. STALKER
157. DRAKE
158. SHANNON
159. NEELY
160. BURDEN
161. CROMMELIN/GILLOTT
162. CROMMELIN
163. DE LA CHEROIS
164. SMYTH
165. SMITH
166. CROMMELIN
167. DE LA CHEROIS
168. HULL
169. McMILLAN
170. MARTIN
171. ROCHET
172. UNKNOWN
173. SORBY
174. THOMPSON
175. TRUEFET
176. PENNINGTON
177. PENNINGTON
178. BRACEGIRDEL
179. UNKNOWN
180. CROSSLEY
181. CROSSLEY
182. UNKNOWN
183. HERALD
184. UNKNOWN

ADDINGTON	See **SIMON**	14
ALLAN	See **WHITLA**	48
ALLEN	[*ornate, upright marble, with scroll design, iron railings*]	53

In loving memory
of
James Allen,
born 12th August 1831,
died at Bow Street, Lisburn, 19th Octr 1873.
Also his daughter Mary Elizabeth,
who died in infancy.
Also his daughter Margaret,
born 26th Feby 1866, died 13th January 1870.
Also his Mother-in-law Mary Elizabeth Short,
born 23rd Decr 1815, died 19th Septr 1871.
Also his son Andrew,
born 23rd Decr 1858, died 8th Nov^b 1887.
Mary Allen,
wife of the above named James Allen,
born 23rd Decr 1835, died 26th Feby 1912.
---ooo---
"I am the resurrection and the life."

ALLEN

{*Recorded in M.D. Vol. XII-XIII 1926-31.*}

ATKINSON	[*upright, red sandstone, crumbling, rope design, faint outline of hour glass carving. Inscription also around the border*]	104

HERE LYETH THE
BODY OF MARY
ATKINSON OF LI
SBURN DESEACED (sic)
THE FIRST DAY
OF SEPTEMBER
1689.

HE S[AVED M]Y SOUL WHEN MY MORTAL DAYS WERE
DONE.

{*Inscription around border.*}

HERE LYETH ROBERT ATKINSON, THE
FATHER, WHO DIED THE 6 OF DEC
EMBER 1670, AND HIS DAUGHTERS.
DOROTHIE, WHO DIED THE 5 OF JUNE
1672. MARY, WHO DIED THE FIRST
OF SEPTEMBER 1670. AND SARAH, WHO
DIED THE 23 OF JULY 1697.

HERE LYETH THE BODY OF MARY
WADE WHO DEPARTED THIS
LIFE THE 9 OF OCTOBER
1723, AGED 80 YEARS.
UNDER THIS MARBLE LYETH
THE BODY OF THOMAS WADE.

BANNISTER   [*upright sandstone*]   79

Sacred
to the memory of
Robert Bannister who died 30th
January 1836, aged 78 years. Also
his son Robert who died 20th august (sic)
1822, aged 15 years.
Also Ezekiel Thomas Bannister,
son of the late Jacob Bannister,
who died 3rd May 1853, aged 3 years
and 5 months.

{*Recorded in M.D. Vol. XII-XIII 1926-31.*}

BANNISTER   [*upright sandstone, almost illegible*]   78

Erected
by
James Bannister
of Lisburn in memory of his
mother Catharine who departed
this life ** June 1869,
aged 77 years.
Also his daughter Mary who
departed this life 1st January
1851, aged 4 years.
Also his father James Bannister
who departed this life 8th February
1875, aged 84 years.

BARNSLEY *[sandstone ledger, with cement sides]* 64

Interred beneath this stone is the
body of Richard Barnsley
who departed this life 23rd June,
Anno 1792, AE 75.
Also the body of Richard Barnsley,
son of above, who departed this
life the 21st April Anno 1827, aged 57.
Also his son Richard Barnsley
who departed this life the 20th May 1847,
in the 31st year of his age.
Also here rests the body of Sarah,
wife of the second Richard Barnsley,
who departed this life April 1st 1867,
aged 89 years.

{1824 – Richard Barnsley was a merchant of Bridge Street.}

BELL
Site
not
found
2004

In memory of
James Bell, late Sergeant of
His Majesty's 67th who died 23 Jan 18**
Age 70 years

{Recorded in 1958.}

BERNIERE/
BERNIER
See **CROMMELIN**
162

BLACKBURN *[iron railings with metal plaque]* 49

The
Burying Ground of
Robert Blackburn
of
Belfast
1845

[front]

Erected
by
Alexander Blackburn
………………………..
…………………………..

{Rest illegible.}

[side]

And of
Alexander Blackburn
who died 19th Sep[t] 1891.
And
John Blackburn
who died 26th June 1909.

BLACKBURN   *[flat, red sandstone]*   84

Erected
by
Catherine Blackburn,
of Laurel Hill,
in memory of her beloved husband,
Alexander Blackburn,
who departed this life the 7th June 1840,
aged 53 years.
Also sacred to the memory of the above
named Catherine Blackburn, who departed
this life the 20th May 1841, aged 35 years.
Also their daughter Isabella, who departed
this life the 6th June 1843, aged 8 years.
Also their eldest son William John who died in
Barbados the 27th June 1855, aged 24 years.

Sacred to the memory
of
Mary,
the beloved wife of Adam Blackburn, *Lissue,*
who departed this life 18th March 1863,
aged 54 years.
Also three of their children
and one grandchild who died young.
Also the above named
Adam Blackburn
who died the 21st May 1879, aged 78 years.
His daughter Ann, wife of the late James Blackburn,
who died 28th February 1882, aged 42 years.
His grand-daughter Charlotte MooreAlso his son William Blackburn
died 8th May 1900, aged 69 years.

BLACKBURN

Site
not
found
2004

Erected
to the memory of
Joseph Backburn, Ballymacash,
died 3rd May 1853, aged 75 years.
Ann Blackburn, his wife, died
22nd April 1851, aged 72 years.
William Blackburn died
17th July 1824, aged 14 years.
Thomas Blackburn died
2nd April 1843, aged 29 years.
Alexander Blackburn died
11 July 1876, aged 57 years.

*{Burial record gives Ann Blackburn's burial as August 1851, the
newspaper death notice gives her name as Agnes.}*

{Recorded in M.D. Vol. XII-XIII 1926-31.}

BOLTON See **HOGG/BOLTON** 12

BOLTON See **FULTON** 71

Erected
by
Hugh Boyd
of Lisburn
in memory of his wife Elizabeth
Boyd, who departed this life the 1st
of March 1806, aged 34 years.
Also his son Hugh Boyd who depa
rted this life the 27th January 1813,
aged 7 months.
---ooo---
Hugh Boyd Sen. died January 1837,
aged 59 years.
Agnes McNally, his daughter, wife
of the late Richard McNally, died
May the 21st 1863, aged 61 years.

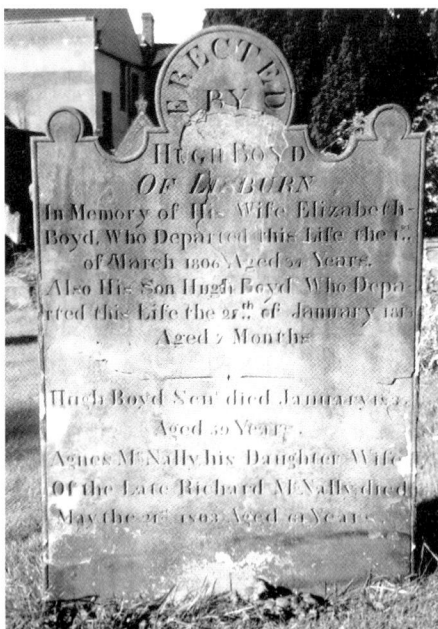

CATHEDRAL 122
BOYD

BOYES See **SIMPSON** 30

BRACEGIRDEL *[upright sandstone, parts flaking off, almost illegible]* 178

Here lieth the body of Sarah
Bracegirdel daughter to Samuel
............e Bracegirdel of Lisburn
who departed this life the
...... 1801 aged 2 years.

my parents

{Rest of inscription illegible.}

BRADY

Sacred
to
the memory of
Thomas Brady who died May 1805,
aged 30 years.
Also Robert Brady who died
Sept. 1807, aged 70 years.
Also Ann, wife of Thomas Brady,
who died May 20th 1843,
aged 68 years.
Also Oliver Brady,
son of Thomas & Ann Brady,
who died June 24th 1843,
aged 42 years.
And Matthew Brady their last sur
viving son who died 15th July 1847, aged
4[9]. Much regretted universally res
pected by all who knew his worth.

BREATHWAITE See **McKEE** 63

BRERETON [*sandstone ledger*] 45

Here lyeth the body of William
Brereton who departed this life
the 17th day of October 1793
7* years.

BRIGS [*small, flat, slate stone with carving*] 83

HERE   LYETH
THE   BODY OF
ROBERT BRIGS WHO
DIED THE 22 OF DECEM^{BR}
[17]54, AGED 80 YEARS.
ALSO HIS WIFE MARGARE^T
STEED WHO DIED THE
7 OF SEPTEMBER
1748, AGED 68 YEARS.
AND ALSO HIS DAUGHTER
ALACE BRIGS WHO DEPARTED
THIS LIFE NOVEMBER THE 27TH
1781, AGED 82 YEARS.

BROOKE [small upright sandstone, on the reverse of **WHEELER** No. 134A] 134

H♦THE♦BODY
Y♦WIFE♦TO
OKE♦CHYRUP
URN♦WHO
THIS♦LIFE

*{Rest underground. Inscription is not complete as the side edges appear rough, and the stone would appear to have been reused for **WHEELER** No 134A. It would also appear to be for the wife of "Brook Chirurgeon" who was mentioned in Rev. Carmody's book.}*

CATHEDRAL 134 **BROOKE**

BULLICK *[marble headstone, iron railings, double grave.]* 141

Erected
by
Moses Bullick,
Lisburn,
in memory of his brother
William,
died 15th May 1865, aged 23 years.
Also his sister Mary,
died 7th June 1904, aged 55 years.

{Moses Bullick was a painter and glazier of Railway Street.}

BURDEN *[upright sandstone, weathered.]* 160

HERE LIETH THE BODY OF
MARY BURDEN, WIFE TO
JOHN BURDEN OF LISBURN,
WHO DEPARTED THIS LIFE
THE 21 DAY OF AUGUST
1749, AGED ** YEARS.
HERE LYETH THE BODY
OF JANE BURDEN, DAUGHTER
TO JOHN BURDEN OF
LISBURN, WHO DEPARTED
THIS LIFE APRIL 12TH AN
DOM 1740, AGED 11 YEARS.

BUSBY *[flat red sandstone]* 132

HERE LIES THE BODY OF
MR JOHN BUSBY WRITING MAST[ER]
IN LISBURN WHO DEPARTED
THIS LIFE THE 19 DAY OF JANUR^Y
1737, AGED 63 YEARS.
---ooo---
HERE LIES THE BODY OF
KATHERINE, WIFE OF JOHN
BUSBY, WHO DIED NOVEMBER
ANNO 1707. ALSO 8 CHILDREN.

CATHEDRAL 132
BUSBY

CALDBECK *[sandstone tablet, with carved top, attached to the wall, originally had railings]* 1

THE BURYING GROUND OF W. CALDBECK

CALVERT See **PURDON/DE LA CHEROIS-CROMMELIN** 16

Erected
to
the memory of
William Campbell
who died July 20th 1847, *aged 27 years.*
And of his brother,
John Campbell. M.D.,
who died Sept[r] 6th 1867.
And of Sarah,
the wife of John Campbell,
who died Jan. 16th 1914.

{*Although named on this stone both John and Sarah Campbell are
buried in Blaris Burial Ground, where they are named on a second
stone.*}

CARLETON [*raised slate ledger stone, with cement sides*] 44

Here lie the remains of
Sarah Carleton, wife of Edward Carleton
of Blaris, who departed this life 20th
December 1761, *aged 21 years.*
also of Cornelius Carleton of Blaris
who died the 5th April 1781, *aged 64 years.*
and his brother, the above named
Edward Carleton of Blaris, who departed
this life the 24th June 1781, *aged 54 years.*
Mary Carleton, widow of
the above named Cornelius Carleton,
died on the 22nd of June 1811,
aged 88 years.

CARLETON [*flat sandstone, almost illegible*] 47

Here in lie the remains of
Cornelius Carleton, late of Lisburn,
who departed this life 29 of March 1819 (sic),
aged 69 years.
Also the remains of Elizabeth,
wife of Cornelius Carleton, who died
9 Sept 1824, aged 72 years.
Also the remains of Mary Sproull
who died 16 May 1860, aged 57 years.
And of her mother Eleanor Sproull,
who was a daughter of the above named
Cornelius Carleton of Lisburn.
Also of her daughter Eliza Sproull
died 9th June 1868, aged 55 years.

{*Cornelius Carleton died in 1818.
Eleanor Sproull died 17th May 1863 aged 88 years.*}

CARLETON	See **GILBERT**	62
CARY	See **DILLON**	68
CHARTERS	[*flat, red sandstone, crumbling and almost illegible*]	124

HERE LYETH THE BODY OF
JOHN CHARTERS MERCHANT
IN LISBURN WHO DIED AUGUST
THE 31 17[19 AGED 75] YEARS.

HERE [LYETH THE BODY] OF
FRANCES [MARSHALL] THE WIFE
TO JOHN [CHARTERS] MERCHANT
WHO ……………….. THE 12
[DECEMBER] 1691 [AGED 40 YEARS.]

HERE ……………………………. OF
BET…………………………………..
CHARTERS ……………………… JULY 6
1712 …………………………………..

HERE …………………………… OF
ELIZA………………………………….TO
……………………………………… DIED
JUNE? …………………………… YEARS.

CLARKE	[*flat sandstone*]	6

SACRED TO THE MEMORY
OF MARY, WIFE OF LIEU[T] CLARKE, ROYAL
ARTILLERY, WHO DEPARTED THIS LIFE 11TH DEC[R]
1836, AGED 58 YEARS. AND THEIR SIX CHILDREN.
JOHN AGED 21 YEARS
JAMES 1*?
THOMAS 10
MARY ANN 11
MARGARET 5
ELIZABETH 2

CLARKE	See **STEWART**	107

[HERE] LYETH THE BODY OF
WILLIAM CLOSE OF
LISBURN WHO DEPARTED
THIS LIFE THE 13th DAY OF
[JUNE] ANN DOM 1698,
AETATIS SUAE 61.
HERE ALSO LYETH
THE BODY OF REBEKKA
CLOSE, WIFE TO THE
ABOVE NAMED WILLIAM
CLOSE, WHO DEPARTED
THIS LIFE THE 11TH DAY
OF MARCH 1690 AND
.... YEAR OF
HER AGE.

---ooo---

HERE LYETH THE BODY
OF EDMUND ELLIS WHO
DIED THE 19 OF APRIL
1714 AGED ** YEARS.
HERE LYETH THE BODY
OF M^{RS}. SARAH ELLIS WHO DE
PARTED THIS LIFE 22 DAY
OF JANUARY 1710, AGED 57.
HERE LYETH THE BODY OF M^R.
HENRY CLOSE, OF PLANTAT
ION, WHO DEPARTED THIS
LIFE ** DAY OF AUGUST
1741, AGED ** YEARS.
ALSO THE BODY OF WILLIAM CLOSE,
SON TO THE ABOVE HENRY CLOSE,
WHO DEPARTED THIS LIFE JANUARY
THE 19TH 1781, AGED 59 YEARS.

CLOSE   See **DILLON**   68

COCHRAN   [*loose, broken sandstone, very weathered, only part remaining*]   56

Erected
by
James Cochran,
of Lisburn,
to the memory of his son James
Cochran, who departed this life
4th January 1841, aged 3 years.
Also his daughter Ellen, who
departed this life on 2nd July 1845.

{*Recorded in M.D. Vol. XII-XIII 1926-31.*}

COCHRAN	See **WOODHOUSE**	87
COLSON	See **STORY**	96
COULSON	[*box tomb, with slate top, surrounded by tall iron railings*]	72

[*top*]

Here lieth the remains of
Ann Coulson
who departed this life 3rd June 1790, aged 42 years.
also of
William Coulson
who died 6th Jany 1801, aged 62 years.
Also of
Mary Hannigan
who died 9th March 1803, aged 94 years.
And also
Reverend Hill Coulson
who departed this life 15th August 1815, aged 38 years.
Ann J. Coulson
died 14th Jany 1830, aged 4 years & 8 months.
Ann Coulson
died 27th June 1834, aged [47] years.
Walter Coulson,
son of aforesaid Wm. Coulson,
died 14th Feby 1836, aged 53 years.
Jane Coulson,
Grand daughter of above Wm. Coulson,
died 9th July 1840, aged 6 years.
William Coulson died 18th August 1851,
aged 77 years.
James Coulson died 26th day of March
1854, aged 76 years.

[*side*]

In memory of
The Rev. Hill Coulson.
Mild were thy virtues to suspicion slow,
Men's arts thou knews't not or refused to know
Thy faith a bounteous spring in stillness ran
Reflecting heaven and doing good to man.

[*side*]

In memory of
Ann J. Coulson
Meekness like thine sweet child and holy love,
The arms of saving mercy from above,
Stooped to embrace, and lifting them to view,
He thence the pattern of our virtues drew.

COULSON	See **LACKEY**	58

COULSON	See **RUSSELL**	95

CROCKARD [*upright sandstone*] 31

Erected
in
memory of Robert Crockard,
who departed this life Feby 8th 1836,
aged 55 years.
Mary Crockard, died 26th April 1867,
aged 67 years.
Adam Crockard died 23^{th (sic)} May 1869,
aged 36 years.
Also Mary Crockard, *of Hillhall,*
died 15th April 1870, aged 38 years.
Mary, the wife of William Crockard,
died 2nd May 1873, aged 31 years.
Archibald Crockard
died 27th Decr 1876,
aged 86 years.
Robert Crockard, Grandson
of above, died 12th Feby 1883,
aged 18 years.

CROCKARD [*upright granite stone with granite surround, older sandstone stone* 123
lying flat in the grave]

In
memory
of
John and Agnes Jane Crockard.
Also their children
William and Charlotte.

[*flat sandstone, almost illegible*]

Erected by
Henry Curry in memory of
George Jacke A..... died 10th of July
1821 also of Ag...... Grand-
daughter of said .... who
....

CROCKARD	See **LACKEY**	58

SIX FOOT OPPOSITE LYES
THE BODY OF LOUIS CROMM
ELIN BORN AT ST. QUENTIN
FRANCE. ONLY SON TO LOUIS
CROMMELIN AND ANN CROMM
ELIN, DIRECTOR OF THE LINEN
MANUFACTORY, WHO DIED BEL
OVED OF ALL, AGED 28 YEARS,
THE 1 OF JULY 1711.

SISTE VIATOR ET ILLE DUM
VITA MANEBAT ET RESPICE
FINEM
ALSO THE BODY OF MARY
MADEL[N] BERNIERE, WIFE OF
CAPTAIN BERNIERE, ONLY DAUGH
TER OF LEWIS CROMMELIN,
DECEASED THE 8 OF JULY 1715,
AGED 24 YEARS.
HERE ALSO LYETH THE REMAINS OF
LOUIS CROMMELIN SEN[R] WHO DIED
7 JULY 1727, AGED 75 YEARS.
ALSO THE BODY OF ANNE,
WIFE OF LOUIS CROMMELIN,
DECEASED THE 15 AUGUST 1755,
AGED 97 YEARS.

[*small slate stone below No. 162, very faint, almost illegible*]

[Catherine] wife of John Smith, daughter of John De Bernier
grand daughter of Lewis Crommelin dec.
Also
John Smith, Ballenaskea, County Westmeath, dec.
December 11 1799, aged 54.
Judith, wife of John Smith, daughter Sam. De la Cherois
dec. August 22 1821,
[aged 74 years.]

[Here lyeth the body of]
Elizabeth [Crommelin who departed this life the] 2[nd][day]
[of January] 1777, aged 30 years.
Also the remains of her husband,
De La Cherois [Crommelin] Esq., who departed this life
31st December 1804, aged 80 years.
Here also is laid the body of their son in law, the Rev. Francis
Hutcheson D.D., Archdeacon of Down and Connor, who died 24th
February 1814, aged 57 years.

[Also the remains of
Mary Angelica, daughter of Delacherois Crommelin,
and wife of Doctor William Stewart of Lisburn,
who died 24th August 1833 (sic), aged 65 years.]

*{Mary Angelica Stewart died 26th May 1832
and was buried 5th June 1832.}*

*{Last inscription given in article on Huguenots in Northern Whig,
Thursday October 22 1885, and not found 2004.}*

CROMMELIN   COPY OF INSCRIPTION ON CROMMELIN GRAVE
[*Copy made onto 3 brass plaques in 1964, and is attached to the front
of the iron railings*]

Here are interred the body of
ABRAHAM GILLOTT who died the
8th of July 1711. Aged 55 years.
ANN, wife of SAMUEL LEWIS
CROMMELIN, who died the 30th
of August 1718. Aged 30 years.
GILLOTT their son who died 2nd
December 1715. Aged 2 years.
JANE their daughter who died
the 31st of January 1718. Aged 5
months. HENRIETTE, second
wife of SAMUEL LEWIS CROMM-
ELIN, who died the 19th of May
1739 (sic). Aged 57 (sic) years. EASTHER
wife of JAMES CROMMELIN
died the 2nd of September 1739.
Aged 41 years. SAMUEL LEWIS
CROMMELIN who died the 2nd
of September 1713 (sic). Aged 57 years.
His daughter ANN died 21st of
June 1751. Aged 27 years.
HENRIETTE 28th of March 1752.
Aged 23 years. MAGDALEN 18th
April 1753. Aged 25 years.

Six foot opposite lyes the
body of LOUIS CROMMELIN
born at St. Quentin France,
Only son to LOUIS CROMM-
ELIN and ANN CROMMELIN
director of the Linen Manufactory who died beloved
of all, aged 28 years, the 1st of
July 1711.
Siste Viator et ut ille dum vita
mannebat suspice coelum des-
pice mundum et respice finem.
Also the body of MARY MAD-
ELIENE BERNIERE, wife of
Captain Berniere, only daugh
ter of LEWIS CROMMELIN,
deceased the 8th of July 1715.
Aged 21 (sic) years
Here also lieth the remains of
LOUIS CROMMELIN SEN[R]. who
died the 7th July 1727. Aged 75 years.
Also the body of ANNE, wife
of LOUIS CROMMELIN, deceased the 15th August 1755. Aged
97 years.

Here lyeth the body of
NICOLAS De La CHEROIS, Major
in the Lord Lifford's Regiment
of Foot, deceased June 13th 1702.
Aged 53 years. Also the body of
NICOLAS De La CHEROIS his son
who deceased October the 22nd
1708. Aged 12 years. Also the
body of MARY De La CHEROIS,
wife of said Major De La Cherois,
who deceased December 22nd
1724. Aged 66 years.

HERE ARE INTERRED THE BODY
OF ABRAHAM GILLOTT WHO DIED THE
8TH OF JULY 1711, AGED 55 YEARS.
ANN, WIFE OF SAMUEL LEWIS CROMMELIN,
WHO DIED THE 30TH AUGUST 1718,
AGED 30 YEARS.
GILLOTT, THEIR SON, WHO DIED THE 2ND
OF DECEMBER 1715, AGED 2 YEARS.
JANE, THEIR DAUGHTER, WHO DIED THE
31ST OF JANUARY 1718, AGED 5 MONTHS.
HENRIETTE, SECOND WIFE OF SAMUEL
LEWIS CROMMELIN, WHO DIED THE 19TH
OF MAY 1732, AGED 37 YEARS.
EASTHER, WIFE OF JAMES CROMMELIN,
DIED THE 2^{D} OF SEPT^{R} 1739, AGED 41 YEARS.
SAMUEL LEWIS CROMMELIN WHO DIED
2ND OF SEPT^{R} 1743, AGED 57 YEARS.
HIS DAUGHTERS. ANN DIED 21 OF JUNE
1751, AGED 27 YEARS. HENRIETTE 28TH
OF MARCH 1752, AGED 23 YEARS.
MAGDALEN 18 APRIL 1753, AGED 25 YEARS.

VIEW OF SOME OF THE HUGUENOT GRAVES

To the memory
of
John Crossley Jun[r]
of Lisburn,
who, in the year 1810
Established the first Free School
on the System of Bell and Lancaster
in this Province,
and
although struggling with a feeble constitution
continued until his last illness
to exert himself
with great zeal and judgment
in communicating the blessings
of Religious and Moral Knowledge
to many Poor Children.
---oOo---
A pious and practical Christian,
humble in himself, charitable to others,
affectionate to his friends
and devout towards his God.
He did much good with limited means
and was called to his Everlasting Reward
on the 10th March, 1816
aged 31 years.
---oOo---
Here also are interred
the remains of His Excellent father
John Crossley Sen.
who departed this life on the 11th March
1830, aged 84 years.

CATHEDRAL 41
CROSSLEY

CROSSLEY *[flat sandstone]* 180

This tomb
is erected by Sarah Crossley to the
memory of her beloved husband, John
Crossley, who departed this life in the
year of our Lord 1838 on the 20th day
of April, aged 30 years.
Invidious grave how dost thou rend in sunder
Whom love has knit and sympathy made one.
---ooo---
Beneath this stone a husband lies
How gentle is his sleep?
Does he not hear his loved one cry?
Does he not see her weep?
Ah no! Her grief he may not hear,
Nor wipe away the falling tear.
The eye which on the captive heart
Its beams of brightness flung.
The form of envied loveliness
Lies mouldering here beneath the soil
Discernable by none but God.

CROSSLEY *[upright sandstone]* 181

This stone
is erected
by Mary Ann Crossley in memory
of her husband Thomas Crossley,
who departed this life feb[y (sic)] 13th A.D.
1819, aged 42 years.

{*Recorded in M.D. Vol. XII-XIII 1926-31.*}

CUMMINS *[upright sandstone, crumbling, buried in ground]* 100

Erected
by
John Green of Belfast
to the memory of his motherinlaw
Mary Cummins
who departed this life 16th February
1856, aged 56 years.

{*Recorded in M.D. Vol. XII-XIII 1926-31.*}

[*top*]

Here lie the remains
of the Revd Snowden Cupples D.D.,
Vicar General of Down & Connor
and 39 yrs Rector of Lisburn, *alias* Blaris,
who died 22nd of October 1835,
in the 82nd year of his age.
Also
of his son Rev. Edward Cupples L.L.B.,
Vicar General of the Diocese of Down and Connor
and Vicar of Glenavy, who died on the 22nd
day of November 1857, aged 72 years.
Also of
Frances Cupples, daughter of the
Revd Snowdon Cupples, who died
28th Sep^t 1869, aged 65 years.

[*side*]

In memory of
William Cupples Esqr., who died on 26th
of November 1833, in the 49th year of his age.

"Deus me Resurgat!"

DAVIS   [*upright sandstone, pieces flaking off*]   52

Here lieth
the
remains of
Arthur Davis,
who departed this life on 13th of April,
1847, in the 79 year of his age.
Also Mary Davis his wife, who died
on March the 11th 1860, aged 96 years.

DAVIS   *[flat sandstone, in pieces, almost illegible, surface flaking off]*   150

HERE LYETH THE ....
................AM..............
...DEPART..........
...... THE ....
.......P**AR AND

---ooo---

.... body of Edward
Thomas Davis who
.... this life July the
.... years.

---ooo---

.... the body of Thomas Davis
of Lisburn who departed this life
[19th September 1813?] aged 8? years.

DE LA CHEROIS   *[red sandstone, attached to the wall]*   163

HERE LYETH THE BODY OF
NICOLAS DE LA CHEROIS, MAJOR
IN THE LORD LIFFORD'S REGI
MENT OF FOOT, DECEASED JUNE
THE 13 1702, AGED 53 YEARS.
ALSO THE BODY OF NICOLAS
DE LA CHEROIS, HIS SON, WHO
DECEASED OCTOBER THE 22
1708, AGED 12 YEARS.
ALSO THE BODY OF MARY
DE LA CHEROIS, WIFE OF
SAID MAJOR DE LA CHEROIS,
WHO DECEASED DECEMBER
THE 22 1724, AGED
66 YEARS.

DE LA CHEROIS   *[flat sandstone set in cement]*   167

Underneath this stone
are deposited the mortal remains of
Nicholas De La Cherois Esquire,
who departed this life
on the 23d day of Jany 1829,
in the 92nd year of his age.
And also of Charlotte, his wife,
who departed this life
on the 2nd day of Feb 1828,
aged 65 years.

DILLON   [*sandstone ledger, on four low pillars, tall iron railings*]   68

Here lyeth the body of
William Dillon, of Lisburn,
who departed this life 11th
Sept 1784, aged 68 years.
Here also lyeth the body of
Elizabeth Dillon, wife of the
above William Dillon, who de
parted this life May the 29th 1786,
aged 69 years.
Here lieth the body of
Jane Dillon, daughter of
Arthur Cary Esq. of Bangor,
wife to William Dillon Junr
of Lisburn, who departed this life the
6th June 1795, aged 20 years.
Here lyeth the body of
William Dillon Senr, Merchant,
of Lisburn, who departed this life the
7th March 1796, aged 41 years.
Susanna Dillon, departed this life the 22nd
June 1805, aged 52 years.
Isabella Tennent Dillon died the 25th day of
November 1831, aged 9 years.
Jane Dillon, only daughter of William Close
Esq. of the Forge, Magheralin, County Down, and wife of
William Dillon, of Lisburn, departed this life on
the 22nd November 1834, aged 56 years.
William Dillon died 24th November 1837, aged
65 years.

{*1811 William Dillon – Conveyancer.*
1824 William Dillon - Proctor of Down & Connor, Castle Street.}

DOBBS/DE LA CHEROIS- CROMMELIN

[flat sandstone, set in cement]

Here lie the remains of the Rev[d] Rich[d]
Dobbs D.D. 32 years Rector of the Parish
of Lisburn and formerly Fellow of T.C.D. He
was a man of extensive learning, great
piety, and strict honesty. He lived respected
and esteemed and died lamented, in charity
with all men on the 28th of May 1775, in the 80th
year of his age.

---oOo---

Here also lie the remains of the Rev[d] John
Dobbs, the [4th] son of the above named Richard
Dobbs who, during the short period of his
Ministry, displayed such talents and such
attention to the Pastoral Office that it may
be truly said he was an ornament to his
holy profession. He died on the 28th Oct[r]
1773, in the 23[d] year of his age.

---oOo---

Here rests the remains of Mrs Hariet Dobbs,
wife of the Rev[d] Rich[d] Dobbs, Dean of Connor,
in whom the affectionate wife, the tender
mother and the pious christian where (sic)
eminently united She died the 25th March 1784,
in the 45th year of her age.

---oOo---

Here lieth the remains of Mary, wife of
the late Rev[d] Richard Dobbs D.D., who departed
this life April 1796, aged 82 years.

---oOo---

Here lieth the remains of Maria Dobbs, wife of
Samuel De la Cherois-Crommelin, Esq., who
departed this life December 12th 1815,
aged 57 years.

{Continued on *PURDON/DE LA CHEROIS-CROMMELIN*
No. 16.}

DOYLE

[red sandstone, weathered]

Erected by
James Doyle in memory of his
son Henry who died January 10th 1841,
aged 14 years.
Also his daughter Elica died 18th
December 1852, aged 24 years.

{Recorded in M.D. Vol. XII-XIII 1926-31.}

DRAKE   *[broken, small flat, red sandstone]*   152

IN MEMORY OF
FRANCIS DRAKE WHO DIED
FEBRARY(sic) 24 1810,
AGED 81 YEARS.

DRAKE   *[upright sandstone, iron railings]*   157

Departed
this life the 12th of July 1830,
Elizabeth Drake, aged 52 years.
Also her husband, William Drake,
who departed this life 17th of July
1835, aged 69 years.
---ooo---
This stone was erected by their
beloved son, William Drake, of
New York, North America.

Also his niece Eliza Mateer, who died
20th January 1855, aged 19 years.
---ooo---
Renovated 1899
by their Grand-son
Stewart Lavery, of Lisburn,
in loving remembrance of his
Grand-father and Grand-mother
William and Eliza Drake.

ELLIS   See **CLOSE**   70

FAIRLEY   *[flat, broken sandstone, top part missing since c1926]*   115

…….. departed
………… aged
…………………
died young.
Also his wife Hannah Fairley,
who died on the 12th October
1840, aged 79 years.
Also two of his grand-
children, William, who died
18th June 1846, aged 8 years.
James, who died 15th Jany 1847,
aged 1 year 11 months. Also
their mother Margaret Fairley,
who died 18th December 1847, aged
38 years, and an infant who died young.

{Recorded in M.D. Vol. XII-XIII 1926-31.}

FERGUSON   [*small, upright sandstone, pieces flaking off*]   26

This stone was erected
by James Ferguson to the
memory of his wife, Jane
Ferguson, who departed
this life the 4th of May 1813,
aged 56 years. She lived
a pious religious life
and died the same.

FERGUSON   See **McKEE**   63

FFAREWELL   [*flat, red sandstone*]   127

HERE♦LYETH♦THE♦BODY
OF♦THOMAS♦FFAREWELL
DEPARTED♦THE♦FIRST♦DAY♦OF
MARCH♦1704.
---ooo---
HERE♦LYETH♦THE♦BODY♦OF
MARY, ♦THE♦DAUGHTER♦OF
THOMAS♦FFAREWELL, ♦GENT,
WHO♦DEPARTED♦THIS♦LIFE
THE♦8♦DAY♦OF♦SEPTEMBER
ANNO♦DOM♦1690,   AE♦19.

FLEMING   [*upright sandstone, becoming illegible*]   38

Erected
by John Fleming,
in memory of his daughter, Jane
Fleming, died 1st February 1828, aged
7 years. Also his son, James
Fleming, died 1st March 1829, aged 9
years.
And his wife, Mary Fleming, died Oct.
18th 1847, aged 48.
Also the above John Fleming died March
30th 1851 aged 54.

{*Recorded in M.D. Vol. XII-XIII 1926-31.*}

FLYNN   *[upright sandstone, iron railings]*   9

Erected
by
John Flynn to the memory of his
father, Charles Flynn, who died
26th July 1826, aged 77 years.
Also his Mother, Sarah, who died
23d Sep. 1843, aged 63 years.
Also his wife, Elizabeth Cecelia,
who died 11th Nov 1866, aged 46 years.
Also the above named John Flynn
who died 13th April 1895, aged 76 years.

FORREST   *[upright sandstone]*   90

Erected
by
David Forrest in memory
of his daughter Nina who died
14th April 1876, aged 7 years.

FULTON   *[flat stone, broken and part of the stone missing]*   71

This stone is erected
as a tribute of affection by Colonel Fulton
to the memory of his beloved parents, brothers
and sisters whose names are inscribed underneath.
Ann Fulton, daughter of Richard Fulton,
February 17th 1799, *aged 22 years.*
Sarah Fulton died February 1st 1802, *aged 16 years.*
Elizabeth Fulton, wife of Richard Fulton, died
July 21st 1812, *aged 60 years.*
Margaret Wightman March 30th 1819, *aged 44 years.*
Andrew Fulton died June 5th 1822, *aged 43 years.*
also Andrew and Richard Fulton, sons of Andrew Fulton,
the former died *aged 4*, the latter *aged 8 years.*
Richard Fulton, husband of Elizabeth Fulton, died
April 9th 1823, *aged 70 years.*
Richard Fulton, Captain of Her Majesty's 12th
Lancers died February 24th 1827, *aged 38 years.*
Robert Fulton died May 6th 1830, *aged 56 years.*
Isabella Fulton, wife of Andrew Fulton, died
17th March 1850, *aged 70 years.*
Sophia Matilda Bolton, the wife of William Fulton
of Lisburn, who died 26th June 1879,
aged 78 years.
Mary Jane Fulton, wife of Robert Watson, died
8th August 1880, *aged 30.*
William Fulton died 5th September 1881.

*{The wife and children of Robert Fulton, who died May 1830, are
buried in **FULTON** No. 119.}*

FULTON *[broken sandstone, some parts now missing]* 112

Here lyeth the remains of Joseph Fulton
the son of John Fulton of Calcutta who de[parted]
this life the 19th of September 1814.
Also
Ann Fulton daughter of John Fulton ………..
…….. who departed this life the 10th Oct [1814?]

['Tis past, the fleeting] dream of life [is o'er,
And she] has reached that happy [peaceful shore,]
where kindred angels [Hallelujahs sing
And …………. the ……. spring
Her …………. of a liberal mind,
A heart correct, unsullied and refined,
A Christian steady, and a friend sincere,
A daughter duteous, and a sister dear,
Such] were the virtues [claimed their native heaven,
Then] can we weep the [dispensation given?]

{Only a few words of this inscription now exist.}

FULTON *[sandstone]* 119

Sacred
to the
memory of Jane Fulton,
wife of Robert Fulton
of Lisburn,
who departed this life
August 11th 1831, aged 63 years.
Also two of her children.
James and Eliza Ann Fulton.
Also Joseph Fulton, her son,
who departed this life
Decemb^r 7th 1831, aged 36 years.

*{Robert Fulton, husband of Jane, is buried in **FULTON** No. 71.}*

{Recorded in M.D. Vol. XII-XIII 1926-31.}

FULTON *[upright sandstone]* 109

Joseph Fulton *Esq.* 6th April 1823.
Ann Fulton, *his wife,* 12th Feby 1833.

FULTON *[flat sandstone]* 32

Sacred
to the memory of
Ellen Fulton
widow of Lieu^t Fulton, Enniskillen Dragoons,
who died 28th June 1846, aged 75 years.

James Bell Fulton
Died 21st June 1817, aged [25] years

James Fulton
Died July 1817 aged 62? Years

John Fulton
[Died 17th] March 1829, aged 44 years.

Eliza Reid
Died 27th April 1829 aged 35? years

Ann Fulton
Died 5th January 1834, aged 75 years

Jane Sproull
daughter of Robert Bell Fulton
died 2nd Sep. 1845, aged 25 years.

Also Alicia Charlotte Fulton his
daughter who died on the [24th]
of June [1852], aged 30 years

*{This stone was moved from the north side and was originally
surrounded by railings.}*

GAMBLE   See **MACARTNEY**   39

GARDNER   See **McKEE**   63

GARNET   [*flat sandstone*]   92

HERE LYETH THE BODY OF
FRANCIS GARNET MERCHANT
IN LISBURN WHO DEPARTED
THIS LIFE THE 17 OF JUNE
1693, AGED 71 YEARS.
HERE LYETH THE BODY OF
RUTH GARNET, WIFE TO FRA
NCIS GARNET, WHO DEPARTED
THIS LIFE THE 26 SEPTEMBER
1701.

GELSTON   *[upright, polished granite stone]*   153

In loving memory
of
Mary Gelston
who died 12th February 1915,
aged 80 years.
Also of her Father & Mother.
Samuel Gelston
who died 24th September 1864,
aged 80 years.
And Alice Gelston,
daughter of
Arthur Johnson, *Lisburn,*
who died 21st January 1853,
aged 59 years.
---ooo---
"They rest in peace."

R. Hanna

GELSTON   *[upright sandstone, crumbling]*   154

Sacred to the memory
of
Sarah Gelston,
who was born in Lisburn
27 Decr 1752, and departed this life
in Belfast 15th Decr 1820.

{Recorded in M.D. Vol. XI 1921.}

GIBSON   *[upright, red sandstone, with skull and crossbones carving in high*   113
relief]

HERE LYETH THE
BODYS OF JANE &
MARY DAUGHTERS
TO JOHN GIBSON.
JANE DIED OCTOB^R
THE 12TH 1709.
MARY DIED APRIL
THE 24TH 1711◆

Erected

in

memory of John Gilbert of Blaris
who died 10th April 1810, aged 63 years.
also his wife, Allice Gilbert,
who died 16th April 1838, aged 83 years.
Their children *viz*
Thomas Gilbert died 15th Sep 1826, aged
40 years.
Sarah Gilbert died 7th December 1836,
aged 48 years.
Mary Tollerton died 9th April
1855, aged 63 years.
Cornelius Carlton Gilbert died
11th April 1867, aged 82 years.
John Gilbert died 6th April 1875,
aged 74 years.
Robert Gilbert died 5th Sep.
1877, aged 85 years.
Also his wife, Sarah Gilbert,
died 9th April 1884, aged 74 years.
Their grandchildren.
Elizabeth Tollerton died
17th May 1848, aged 21 years.
Sarah Tollerton died 28th Feb
1849, aged 15 years.

{*John Gilbert and Alice Carleton married 19th December 1782.*}

{*Recorded in M.D. Vol. XII-XIII 1926-31.*}

[flat stone]

In memory
of
John Gilbert of Blaris who died 10 April
1810, aged 63 years.
And Alice relict of the above died 16th
Apl. 1838, aged 82.
Their children.
Thomas died 15th Sep 1826, aged 40 years.
Sarah died 7th Dec 1836, aged 48.
Mary Tolerton died 9th Apl. 1855, aged 63.

Also their grandchildren Tolerton.
Elizabeth died 17th May 1848, aged 22 years.
Sarah died 28th Feb. 1849, aged 19 years.

[upright marble stone, with carving of dove, and an older flat,
sandstone slab lying in front]

Sacred to the memory of
John Gordon, of Belfast,
who departed this life 13th January 1866,
aged 47 years.
Also of his mother,
Jane Gordon,
born May 12th 1790, died August 24th 1864.
Also of his father Nicholas Gordon,
born October 1792, died July 1876.
Norris Gordon,
died 20th December 1889, aged 62 years.
---ooo---
Until the Morning of the Resurrection

[flat sandstone slab]

Sacred to the memory
of
John Gordon, of Belfast,
who departed this life
13th January 1866,
aged 47.
Also his mother, Jane Gordon,
born May 12th 1790,
died August 24th 1864.
Also his father Nich..........

{*Rest broken.*}

CATHEDRAL 144
GORDON

GREEN	See **CUMMINS**	100

GREGG   *[large, tall, pillar with very large Greek urn on top, set into a raised* 147
cement plinth, with a sandstone surround]

Sacred
to the memory of
Anne,
the dearly beloved wife of
William Gregg,
of Lisburn,
who departed this life
the 3ᵈ of April 1834,
in the 24ᵗʰ year of her age.
And also of
her husband
William Gregg,
who departed this life
the 2ⁿᵈ of Febʸ 1870,
in the 73ʳᵈ year of his age.
---ooo---
It is finished
and.we have no right to doubt
His word "Thanks be to God
who giveth us the victory thro'
our Lord Jesus Christ."

HALLIDAY   *[upright sandstone]*   140

Erected
by
James Halliday, of Lisburn, in
memory of his daughter Ann,
who died 24ᵗʰ Sept. 1841,
aged 18 years.

HAMILTON   See **HOWARD**   27

HAMMOND   *[broken sandstone, sunk in ground]*   120

In memory of
Hannah,
the beloved wife of David Hammond
(Officer of Excise), who departed this life
January 18ᵗʰ 1841, aged 33 years.
Also to
Mary Anna, William, William Henry
and Albert children of the above who
died in infancy.

{*Recorded in M.D. Vol. XII-XIII 1926-31.*}

HART   [*sandstone, broken and in pieces*]   151

…………………………………
………..♦MARGRAT
[AND ANN] ♦DAUGHTERS♦
OF♦JOHN♦HART, ♦WHO
DEPARTED♦THIS♦LIFE
THE♦21 & 24♦OF♦JUNE
1680. ♦ALSO♦ELNOR,
HIS♦WIFE, ♦WHO♦DEP
ARTED♦THIS♦LIFE
THE♦1♦OF♦JANUARY
1680.

{*Only the base with "1680" is in its original place in the ground.
This stone was destroyed by vandals in 2005.*}

CATHEDRAL 151   **HART**

HASLAM   [*worn, flat slate, lying in front of **STALKER** No. 156*]   155

HERE LYETH THE BODY OF M^R
SILVANUS HASLAM OF LISBURN,
WHO DEPARTED THIS LIFE
17 SEPTEMBER 1711.

Erected

by

Eleanora Frances Hawkshaw

in

memory

of

her beloved Father,

John Stewart Hawkshaw Lieut. Col.,

of Divernagh, Co. Armagh,

died 10th February 1848, aged 71 years.

Also her beloved mother,

Sophia Hawkshaw, daughter of

Thomas Dawson Lawrence Esq.,

of Lawrencetown, Co. Down,

died 10th December 1859.

Also of her brother,

William Hawkshaw, who died in infancy.

Also her beloved sister,

Emilie Hawkshaw, who died 12th July 1841.

---ooo---

The Lord gave and the Lord will take

away. Blessed be the name of the Lord.

[small flat stone]

Erected

to

William Hawkshaw,

of Divernagh, Co. Armagh,

father of

John Stewart Hawkshaw Lieut Col.,

who died 1826, *aged 82 years.*

Also Eleanor Hawkshaw, his wife,

who died 1826, *aged 84 years.*

Also to

Jane Hawkshaw, their daughter,

who died 1855, *aged 82 years.*

HAYNES   See **WHITLA**   48

Erected
by
Thomas Herald,
of Lisburn, to the memory of his
father John Herald, who died on the
23rd of July 1849, aged 55 years.
Also his son Thomas, who
died on the 24th April 1860,
aged 9 months.

{*Recorded in M.D. Vol. XII-XIII 1926-31.*}

HERON   *[tall, upright sandstone]*   125

Sacred
to the memory of
Samuel Wallis Heron,
son of Lieut^{t} Saml Heron R.N.,
who departed this life
on the 25th day of June in the
year of our Lord 1839, aged
13 years and ten months.
Asleep in Jesus.
Sacred to the memory of
Lieut^{t} Samuel Heron R.N.
who departed this life 18th of May 1840.
Also Charlotte Smyth, widow of the
late James Smyth, Ballylintough House.
Also Anne Heron, widow of Lieutenant
Edward Heron R.N., aged 91 years.
Also of Eliza, widow of the above Lieutenant
Samuel Heron R.N., who departed this life
October 22nd 1885, aged 92 years.

{*Charlotte Smyth died 20th December 1870, aged 47 years.*
Anne Heron died 24th February 1879.}

HICKS   See **JOHNSTON**   76

HIGGINSON   See **MARMION**   88

HOGAN   See **NEELY**   159

HOGG/BOLTON   *[raised sandstone ledger on four pillars, within a granite surround*   12
with No. 13]

Sacred
to the memory of Rose Hogg, who died
30th of June 1813, aged 102.
Also her grand Son, Edward Hogg Bolton,
who died Nov 1st 1836, aged 49 years.
Dorothea Bolton died 17th March
1846, *aged 56 years.*
Abigail Bolton, mother of the
above, departed this life 28th October
1846, *aged 89 years.*
James Bolton Esq.,
Commander Royal Navy,
son of the above Abigail Bolton,
died April 3rd 1867,
aged 72 years.

HOGG/NICHOLSON   *[sandstone box tomb, within a granite surround with No. 12]*   13

[top]

Here lieth the body of
Clara Nicholson,
widow of Alexander Jaffray
Nicholson M.D., of Dublin,
and eldest daughter of
William & Mary Hogg,
whose remains are also
interred under this stone.
Died February (sic) 17th 1874,
aged 85 years.
---ooo---
Blessed are the dead which die in the Lord
from henceforth. Yea, saith the spirit
that they may rest from their labours
and their worths do follow them.
Rev. 14 v 13

[side panel]

Sacred
to the memory of
William Hogg Esq.,
who departed this life 25th July 1824,
aged 70 years.
And of Mary, his wife,
who departed this life 28th Feb[y] 1856,
aged 92.

{Belfast News Letter says William Hogg died 12th August 1824.
Burial record says he was buried 15th August 1824.}

[HERE LYETH THE BODY OF
MRS. MARY HOWARD, MOTHER
OF] THE [RIG]HT HO[NBLE. LTT.
GENERAL FREDERICK]
HAMILTON,[WHO DIED IN]
THE YEAR OF OUR LORD,
1705. AGED [91 YEARS.]
HERE [LYETH THE BODY OF
CAPTAIN JOHN PORTER, WHO
DEPARTED THIS LIFE THE **
OF DECEMBER, 1719,
AGED 77 YEARS.
HERE LYETH THE BODY OF
MARY PORTER, WIFE
OF FREDERICK PORTER,
WHO DEPARTED THIS LIFE
2 *** 1745.
AGED ** *****]

{Only a few words are now visible.}

{In "Lisburn Cathedral & its Past Rectors" the Very Rev. Carmody records that an old gravestone was found in 1920 when the central aisle of the Cathedral was being tiled. Number 27 would appear to be this stone. Carmody notes that they must have been of some note in their day otherwise they would not have been buried in the Cathedral building. The Cathedral records have the following burials:-

- *Mrs. Mary Howard of Lisburn December ye 28th 1706 aged 91 years. [Aged 91 years is written in the margin.]*
- *Captn. John Porter Dec 25th 1719*
- *Mary, w. of Captain Frederick Porter, Lisburn buried March 22 1745/46.}*

HUGHES   *[upright sandstone]*   142

Erected
by the
Rev James Hughes, Wesleyan
Minister, to the memory of Hariet,
his excellent and beloved wife, who
died 14th April 1858, aged 62 years.

{Rev. James Hughes was a Methodist Minister on the Lisburn Circuit 1856-1857. The Methodist church was in Market Street until the present Methodist church was opened for public worship in Seymour Street on Sunday 21st November 1875.}

HULL

HERE LYETH THE BODY OF
WILLIAM HULL SON TO ARTHUR
HULL WHO DECEASED THE [2?]
DAY OF JANUARY ANNO
DOM 1689 AETAT
24.
HERE LYETH Y^E BODY ....
DELAP WHO DEPARTED THIS
LIFE Y^E 14 OF JAN 1716
.... 47 YEARS.

HULL   [*flat, broken sandstone*]   168

Sacred to the memory
of Joseph Hull
who died 26th Dec 1869, aged 69 years.
And of his sons.
Hugh 2nd Sep 1842, aged 12 years.
Joseph 19th Sep 18[54?], aged 18 years.
Also
four children who died in infancy.
And of his ....
Ellen 18th Oct [1882], aged 36 years.
Also his wife,
Eliza 5th March 1886, aged 86 years.
And of his daughter,
Jane Hull,
who died 22nd January 1913,
aged 82 years.
---ooo---
I am the resurrection and the life; he that
believeth in me, though he were dead,
yet shall he live. John 11. 25

HURST   [*upright sandstone*]   129

Here
lyeth the body of Captain
Hurst of the Donegall Reg^t
who died the 25th of may (sic)
1801, aged 43 years.

HUTCHESON   See **CROMMELIN**   166

HUTCHINSON   See **SMYTH**   164

IRVING   *[flat sandstone]*   128

TO THE MEMORY OF
THOMAS IRVING M.D.

JACKSON   *[flat, red sandstone]*   91

HERE LYETH THE BODY OF
ROGER JACKSON WHO DEPARTED
THIS LIFE THE 26TH OF FEBRUARY
1694, AETAT IS SUAE 74.
HERE LYETH THE BODY OF MR MICHAEL
JACKSON SURGEON AND APOTHECARY
WHO DEPARTED THIS LIFE THE 1ST
DAY OF MAY 1727, AGED 31.
---ooo---
HERE LYETH THE BODY OF
JOHN JACKSON WHO DEPARTED
THIS LIFE THE 1 OF JUNE
ANNO DOMMINI 1738, AE 36.

JEFFERSON   *[upright sandstone, with Greek urn, iron railings]*   35

Erected
by
Redmond Jefferson,
of Lisburn, in memory of his son, John,
who departed this life 24th September 1850,
aged 2 years and 6 months.
Also of four children who died in infancy.
Also of his wife, Eliza Jefferson,
who departed this life 4th April 1879,
aged 61 years.
Redmond Jefferson,
died 31st January 1891,
aged 77 years.

{Redmond Jefferson died 31st January 1892.}

JEFFERSON   [*tall, upright, sandstone*]   36

Sacred
to the memory of
John Jefferson,
of Derriaghy,
who departed this life 24th of
May 1856, in the 89th year of his age.

"When Christ who is our life, shall appear,
then shall ye also appear with him in glory"
Colossians 111 Chapt. 4th verse.

Also his wife, Ann Jane Jefferson,
who departed this life June 2nd 1864,
aged 86 years.
Also their son Robert Jefferson,
who departed this life 9th April 1888,
aged 84 years.

{*Recorded in M.D. Vol. XII-XIII 1926-31.*}

JEFFERSON   See **NEELY**   66

JOHNSON   [*upright sandstone, sunk into ground*]   75

....
... [ANN] ....JOHNSON,
DAUGHTER TO ARTHUR JOH
NSON, WHO DIED 22ND JULY 1726,
AGED 4 YEARS.
ALSO JAMES JOHNSON
DIED SEPTEMBER 12, AGED
2* YEARS 1774.
ALSO THE BODY OF
WILLIAM JOHNSON WHO
[DIED 7 JAN 1735
AGED 65]

....
....

JOHNSON   See **GELSTON**   153

JOHNSON   See **JOHNSTON**   76

JOHNSON SMYTH

[*top*]

Sacred
To the memory of Roger Johnson Smyth [Esq.]
of Lisburn who departed this life the 28th
of March 1816, aged 71 years.
Also his grandson,
Roger Johnson Smyth, Member for this Borough,
eldest son of Thomas Johnson Smyth J.P. D.L.,
who departed this life
on the 26th August 1853,
aged 39 years.
And also of
Thomas Johnson Smyth, J.P. D.L.
who died 22nd April 1860, aged 75 years.
Also his son,
Matthew Johnson Smyth Esq., who died
23rd September 1865, aged 47 years.
also of Madeline,
daughter of Thomas Johnson Smyth J.P.,
Goremount, and Great Granddaughter of the
above Thomas Johnson Smyth J.P. D.L.,
who died 8th August 1870, aged 10 months.
Also of
Charlotte Johnson Smyth, relict
of the above Thomas Johnson Smyth J.P.D.L.,
who died 25th April 1875, aged 83 years.
Also of
Thomas Johnson Smyth Esq.
elder son of the Revd. E. Johnson Smyth,
and grandson of the above named
Thomas Johnson Smyth J.P. D.L.,
who died 8th April 1879.

[*side*]

Also
Thomas Roger Johnson Smyth
Major Durham L.I.
Killed in action at Vaal Krantz S. Africa
Feb[y] 5th 1900,
Aged 42 years.
Elder son of the above
Matthew Johnson Smyth
He is buried ……
Where he……..

[side]

Rose daughter of [Thomas] Johnson Smyth
………. Caen in Normandy
…………….… 1825 aged 12 years
……………….. lamented by her parents

{*Rose was baptised 26th November 1812.*}

[side]

Also
Matthew Bruce Johnson Smyth,
second son of the above
Matthew Johnson Smyth,
died August 8th 1901,
aged 41 years.

[side]

Sacred
To the memory of Harriet daughter of Thomas Johnson Smyth Esq.
who departed this life on the 7th January 1838 aged 17 years. She
lived
beloved and died universally regretted that she was
may be hoped ………… departing words to her

{*Rest of inscription illegible.*}

JOHNSON SMYTH	*[flat sandstone, set in cement]*	18

Sacred
to the memory
of
Aemelia, the beloved wife
of the
Revd Edward Johnson Smyth,
Vicar of Glenavy,
who fell asleep in Jesus
the 1st of April 1876,
aged 67 years.
---ooo---
Them also who sleep in Jesus will
God bring with Him.

1 Thessalonians
IV 14

JOHNSON SMYTH	See **STEWART**	19

JOHNSTON   *[upright sandstone, now almost completely illegible]*   76

HERE
lieth the body of
William Johnston who departed
this life the 19th November
1816, aged 65 years.
Also his daughter Mary Ann
who departed this life 15th December
1824, aged 21 years. Also his wife
Mary Johnson who departed this
life April 2nd 1829, aged 70 years.
Also his son Robert who departed
this life 29th July 1829, aged 27 years.
Also John Hicks who died on
22nd July 1800, aged 42.
Also Catherine Hicks,
wife of the late …….. Hicks,
who entered into her rest
7th April 1878(?), aged 69 years.

{*Recorded in M.D. Vol. XII-XIII 1926-31.*}

JOHNSTON   See **PURDON/DE LA CHEROIS-CROMMELIN**   16

JONES   See **WRAY**   24

KELLY   *[upright sandstone with slate insert, enclosed by tall railings]*   74

1857

By
John Kelly
to the ever
lamented memory
of the best of mothers
who departed this life
17th September 1854.
"Trusting solely to the merits
of her Redeemer"
---ooo---
William *died 2nd May 1847,*
aged 17 years.
Hugh died 27th August 1869,
aged 32 years.
Also the above named
John Kelly who died 17th August
1872, aged 41 years.
---ooo---
Erected by John Kelly
1857

{*John Kelly was a carpenter of Railway Street. William Kelly died
after an epileptic fit caused him to fall into the dam which supplied
Lisburn with water. W.H. Pennington tried in vain to rescue him.*}

Erected
by
James Kidd,
of Lisburn, in memory of his wife Ann,
who died 24th March 1849,
aged 33 years.
Also Thomas, his son, who died March 17th 1855,
aged 18 months.
Also William, his son, who died August 10th
1856, aged 3½ years.
Also his son, Edmund Henry, died May 19th
1861, aged 15 months.
Also his daughter, Caroline, who died
19th May 1865, aged 6 years 8 months.
Also the above named James Kidd, who
died 19th February 1866, aged 43 years.
Also his daughter Anne, who died
2nd March 1878, aged 20 years.

LACKEY *[upright sandstone]* 58

Erected
by
William Coulson & Sons Esqs.
and the workmen of their (sic) Factory
as a mark of respect to the memory
of William Lackey who died 10th of
March 1849, aged 46 years.
---ooo---
Also his father William Lackey
died 3rd Sep[r] 1833, aged 63 years.
Also John Lackey who died 6th
September 1848, aged 39 years.
Also James Crockard
who died Sept. 6th 1854,
aged 21.

{Recorded in M.D. Vol. XII-XIII 1926-31.}

LAVERY See **DRAKE** 157

LAWRENCE See **HAWKSHAW** 149

Erected
by Arthur Macartney,
of Lisburn, in memory of Agnes,
his wife, who departed this life
May 29th 1866, aged 73 years.
Their children-
William, who died April 12th 1837,
aged 16 months.
Richard, who died April 10th 1839,
aged 7 years.
Margaret, who died August 6th 1840,
aged 2 ½ years.
Hugh, who died Dec. 20th 1840,
aged 7 years.
Arthur & Agnes M. Gamble, their grand children,
who died in infancy.
Surgeon John Macartney, their eldest son,
who died in Barbadoes, Jan. 30th 1864,
aged 35 years.
The above-named Arthur Macartney,
died 28th May 1874,
aged 70 years.
Also Arthur Macartney, son of the above,
who died at Dublin on the 24th April 1877,
aged 45 years.

Blessed are the dead who die in the Lord.

{Arthur Macartney was a baker in Bow Street, Lisburn.}

{Recorded in M.D. Vol. XII-XIII 1926-31.}

CATHEDRAL 39
MACARTNEY

MARMION	[*sandstone box tomb with stone surround*]	88

In this vault
lieth the mortal remains of the late
Henry Marmion Esq., also his wife Eliza
Marmion and five of their children. Margaret,
who died an infant, Henry, their eldest son,
Richard Waring, their third son, and
Margaret and Eliza, their daughters.
Here also
is buried the remains of the late Lieut
Charles Talbot Higginson R.N., youngest
son of the late Capt. Phillip Talbot
Higginson of Dublin, who died in Lisburn
July 1818, aged 31. Also Marg^t. Higginson, 4th
daughter of the late Capt. Phillip Talbot
Higginson, who died 18th Feb 1852.

These all died in sure and certain hope.
Job 19th ver 25   26

{*Charles Higginson died 8th June 1817.*}

MARSHALL	See **CHARTERS**	124

MARTIN	[*flat, red sandstone*]	43

HERE LYETH THE BODY OF
MR. ROB^T MARTIN WHO DEPARTED
THIS LIFE Y^E 4TH OF APRIL 1731
AGED 40 YEARS. ALSO ELANOR Y^E
WIFE OF ROB^T MARTIN.

ALSO TWO SONS AGED ABOUT 3 YEARS,
EDWARD & CHARLES MARTIN.
ALSO ……………………... GRANDOUGHTER
WHO DEPARTED THIS LIFE THE 3 OF
JANUARY ****

MARTIN	[*flat stone broken, almost illegible*]	170

Erected
by
[Robe]rt Martin in memory
of his beloved children
….thea who died 26 ………..
……………. aged 1 yea…………….
…………. died 8th Nov………..
…………... aged 7 years …………….
……………..ve………………..

MASLIN

Site
not
found
2004

HERE LYE THE REMAINS
OF WILLIAM MASLIN,
WHO DEPARTED THIS LIFE
THE 20TH DAY OF MARCH, 1707,
AGED 55 YEARS.

*{Inscription given in article on Huguenots in Northern Whig,
Thursday October 22 1885.}*

MATEER

[flat, red sandstone] 139

Erected
by
Joseph Mateer,
in memory of his wife, Isabella,
who departed this life 12th of May 1849,
aged 64 years.
Also the above named Joseph Mateer,
who departed this life 31st of October 1870,
aged 79 years.

MATEER

See **DRAKE** 157

McALESTER

See **WIGHTMAN** 59

McCALL

[upright sandstone, bottom half almost illegible] 114

David McCall, of Lambeg,
died 8th November 1762, aged 99 years.
William McCall, his son, died
5th April 1799, aged 66 years.
David McCall, son to William,
died 8th May 1806, aged 28 years.
Edward McCall died 14th May 1810,
aged 25 years.
Judith McCall died 4th March 1821,
aged 75 years.
William McCall died [6th?] November .....
Aged [67?] years.
Richard McCall died ....
aged 55? years.

{Recorded in M.D. Vol. XII-XIII 1926-31.}

Erected
by
Alexander McCann
of Lisburn, in memory of his beloved
Mother, who departed this life the 19th
day of February 1852, in the 75th
year of her age.

Such were her dying words.
"O Lord grant that when I am gone to
Heaven my son may receive the reward of
what he has done for me while on earth."

{Recorded in M.D. Vol. XII-XIII 1926-31.}

McCLURE [*slate stone attached to wall*] 15

William Thomas McClure
died 14th May 1835, aged 6 weeks.
Agnes McClure died 13th May
1866, aged 19 years.
Leonard McClure died
14th June 1868, aged 33 years.
Buried in Lone Mountain
Cemetery, San-Francisco.
Adam McClure, father of the
above, died 28th March 1874,
aged 76 years.
Joseph McClure died
21st February 1881, aged 47 years.
Martha McClure died
16th February 1887, aged 57 years.
Margaret, relict of
Adam McClure, died
14th December 1889, aged 86 years.

{Agnes McClure died in 1865.}

McDOWALL See **WHITLA** 48

McGURK   *[flat sandstone]*

Erected
by
Arthur McGurk
to the memory of his wife Frances who
died on the 24th Dec 18**(23?) aged 36 years.
Also
three of his children who died young.
And John who died on the 9th Dec 1835,
aged 26 years.

{*This stone was moved from the north side.*}

McHARRY

Erected
by
Margaret Reid,
of Belfast, to the memory of Margaret
McHarry, who died 17th June 1852,
aged 28 years.
Also of M. Ann McHarry, who died
28th Nov. 1852, aged 21 years.
Also the above named Margaret
Reid, who departed this life 24th day
of September 1860, aged 65 years.
No condemnation to them who are in
Christ Jesus.
Death separates the strongest
ties of Friendship.

Site
not
found
2004

{*In the burial records a Margaret McHarry was buried 19th May
1852, and a Mary Anne McHarry was buried 16th Feb 1853.*}

{*Recorded in M.D. Vol. XII-XIII 1926-31.*}

McHENRY   *[upright black, polished, granite stone, enclosed in railings*   50
with No. 51]

In
loving memory
of
Robert McHenry,
of Belfast,
born 13th April 1849,
died 6th January 1914.
Also his wife,
Sarah McMaster McHenry,
died 26th December 1921.
---ooo---
He giveth His beloved sleep.

{*Sarah McHenry died 26th December 1920.*}

Erected
by
Robert McHenry
to the memory of his beloved daughter
Jane, who departed this life
21st August 1867, aged 15 years.
Also her Grandfather, who died
18th September 1852, aged 76 years.
Also the above named
Robert McHenry,
who died 14th May 1881, aged 68 years.
and Jane, his wife,
who died 24th October 1890, aged 76 years.

"Blessed are the dead who die in the Lord."

CATHEDRAL 51   **McHENRY**

Erected
by his wife
in memory of her husband,
John McKee, who died 3rd
February 1837, aged 53 years.
Also her daughter, Phebe
Gardner, who died 11th April
1860, aged 17 years.
Also her Grand-daughter,
Phebe Breathwaite, who died
24th Aug 1866, aged 4 years and
9 months.
Also the said Phebe Gardner
who died 1st Dec 1869,
aged 71 years.
Also her daughter, Ellen
Ferguson, who died 11th Feb
1871, aged 50 years.
Also her Grand-son,
William David Breathwaite,
who died 4th January 1877,
aged 7 months.

McKEE *[sandstone with marble insert, fallen and in piece, decorative carving* 138
on three sides, no inscription now remaining]

Erected
by G.W. McKee

In memory of
George McKee
who died 6th Oct. 1861,
aged 52 years.
And of three of his children
who died in infancy.
Also his son, George, who died
31st October 1867, aged 23 years.
And of Eliza McKee
who died 25th February 1891.
Hannah McKee
who died 25th December 1896.
And Jane McKee
who died 13th March 1900.
Also Emily Margaret McKee
who died 18th Nov 1911.

"The righteous shall be in
Everlasting remembrance."

{Recorded in M.D. Vol. XII-XIII 1926-31.}

| McMILLAN | [*metal plaque, tall iron railings*] | 169 |

The
Burying Place
of
Thomas McMillan
1872.

| McMULLEN | [*flat sandstone*] | 34 |

Erected
by
Mary McMullen
in memory of her husband,
James McMullen, who
died at Knockmore on the 17th day of March
1878, aged 61 years.

| McNALLY | See **BOYD** | 122 |

MERCER

{*The site of the Mercer vault is now a flower bed near the main gate of the Cathedral. There are three memorials to this family inside the Cathedral.*}

**MOMENTO MORI/
UNKNOWN**

[*flat sandstone, with skull, crossbones and hour glass symbols in high relief*]   133

NTO
MEME   MORI

REMEMBER◆MAN◆AS
THOU◆GOES◆BY
ON◆DEATH◆JUDGMENT
AND◆ETERNETY

{*The Latin inscription of "Memento Mori" on this stone means "Remember you must die". The three symbols of crossbones, a skull and an hour-glass represent these words visually. These words and symbols were common on memorials of Scottish settlers in the late 17th and early 18th centuries.*}

| **MOORE** | See **BLACKBURN** | 85 |

| **MOREWOOD** | [*flat, red sandstone*] | 86 |

JANE MOREWOOD 1820

GEORGE MOREWOOD
1828

MURRAY [upright sandstone, surface flaking]

Sacred
to the memory of
William Murray
who departed this life May the 5th
1827, aged 24 years.
Also of his sister Frances Charlotte,
dearly beloved wife of
Isaac Sefton of Lisburn,
who departed this life
in the 27th year of her age.
Jane, the dearly beloved wife of
Richard Murray, and mother of
the above children named William and
Frances Charlotte, died June 29th 1856.

MURRAY *[metal plaque on wall]* 117

The Family
Burying Ground
of
James Murray
Lisburn
1806.

*{This stone was moved from the north side and was originally
surrounded by railings.}*

MUSGRAVE *[large, impressive, grey vault, carved decoration, enclosed with tall
iron railings]* 103

Family Burying Place of Doctor Samuel Musgrave.
---ooo---
I know that my redeemer liveth
Job xix 23

CATHEDRAL 103
MUSGRAVE

Erected by
James Mussen, *Lisburn,*
in the memory of his daughter Sarah,
died the 30th of Oct. 1803, aged 11 days.
Also his son James,
died the 21st Dec 1816, aged 19 months.
And his daughter Eliza,
died 2nd June 1819, aged 15 years.
Likewise his daughter Margaret,
died 8th June 1822, aged 18 months.
And his daughter Anna,
died 18th March 1843, aged 26 yrs.
The above named James Mussen
died 13th July 1851, in the 82nd year of his age.
His son Edward Cupples Mussen,
died 8th Nov 1852, in the 39th year of his age.
Also Mary Richardson Mussen,
daughter of James Mussen,
died 15th March 1854, in the 52 year of her age.
Also Deborah, wife of the above James Mussen,
died 21st March 1856.

{1824 James Mussen – tallow chandler.
1852 James Mussen – woollen draper, Market Square.}

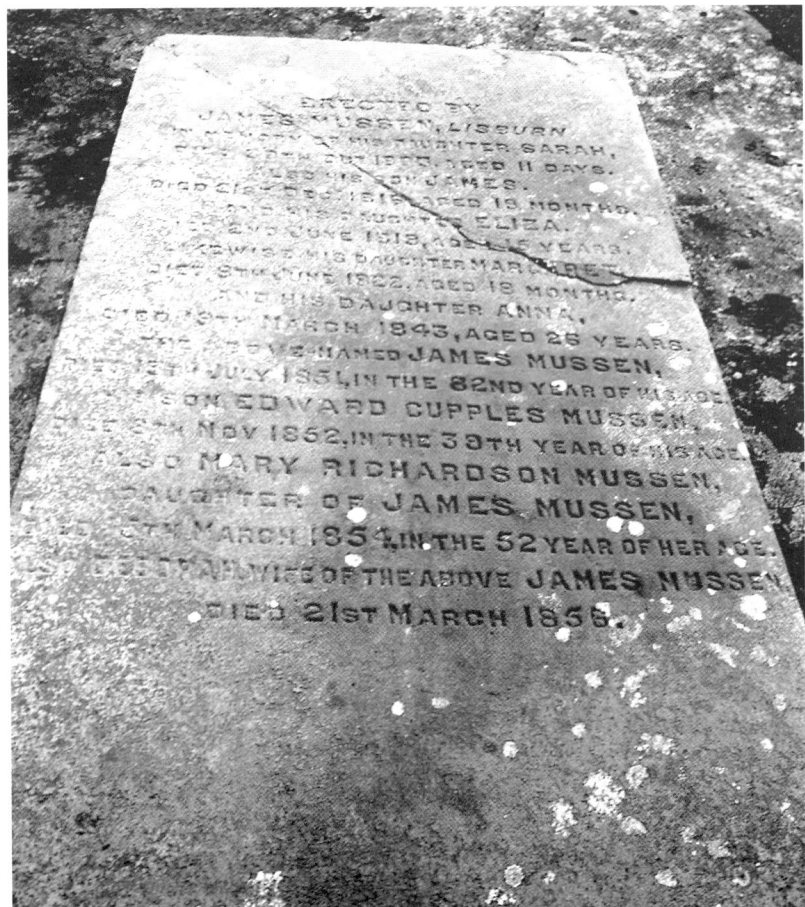

CATHEDRAL 25
MUSSEN

[*top*]

Sacred
to the memory
of John Boyes Neely,
the beloved son of Erskine Neely,
of Lisburn,
who departed this life March 29th 1841,
aged 23 years.
Sarah Neely departed this
life the 8th of Feb. 1856,
aged 79 years.
Erskine Neely departed this
life on the 17th December 1861,
aged 77 years.

John Jefferson departed this
life 29th of Sept[r]. 1855,
aged 46 years.
Anne Jane Jefferson departed this life the
30th Nov. 1860, aged 47 years.
Thomas Rutherford Pelan
departed this life 3rd April 1875,
aged 41 years.
Also
Sarah Jane Pelan, his wife,
died 21st April 1923,
aged 94 years.

[*side*]

On the ** day of August 1849
John Neely Jefferson aged three years and three months.

{*Side inscription almost illegible.*}

{*1852 John Jefferson – woollen draper, Bow Street.*}

[John Neely Jan. 1823, aged 68.
His wife Mary who died Nov. 1829, aged 67.
Also their son Benjamin, Principal of
Lisburn Academy, who died Oct. 1838, aged 60.
Also his wife Mary who died 1841 aged 58.
of the] family of Benjamin and Mary Neely.
Mary an infant who died Dec. 1803.
Jane an infant who died Dec 1816.
Snowden Cupples an infant who died Sep 1820.
Benjamin aged 23 and Violet aged 18 who
died on same day June 11th 1831.
Eleanor Cupples who died Mar 18th 1836.
Their 5th son
William Mills Neely died at Melbourne
on the 26th January 1864 in the 46th year of
his age.
Mary Neely who died at Lisburn
Oct 5th 1863, aged 57.
Margaret Craig Hogan who died in U.S.A
in 1871, aged 58 years.
Rev^{d}. John Neely who died at Augusta
U.S.A. 5th March 1873, aged 68.
Alexander Neely who died at Baltimore
U.S.A. 27th July 1879, aged 55 years.

{*Mary Neely died 5th October 1864.*}

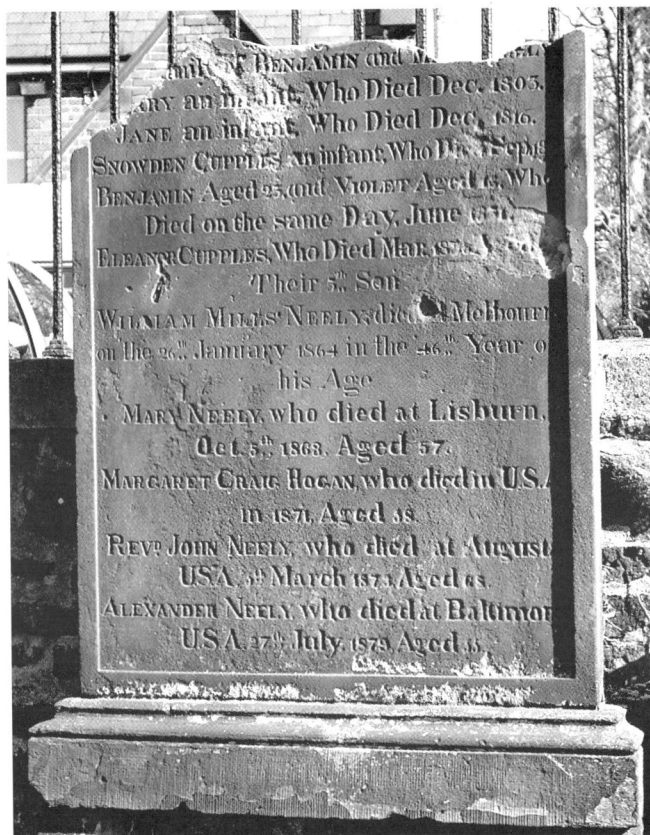

CATHEDRAL 159
NEELY

Erected
by Thomas Newburn
in memory of his beloved children viz
Thomas Newburn who died July 15th 1842,
aged 5 years.
Abigail Newburn died August 7th 1845,
aged 4 years.
Thomas Newburn died April 15th 1849,
aged 1 year and 6 months.
Thomas Newburn died April 8th 1854,
aged 2 years and 6 months.
William Newburn died Feb[y] 15th 1855,
aged 1 years and 7 months.
Robert Newburn died Feb. 23rd 1855,
aged 5 years.
Elizabeth Newburn died March 28th 1855
aged 10 years
And the above named
Thomas Newburn died Sept. 4th 1855,
aged 46 years.
And also his beloved wife Eleanor
21st Sept 1856,
aged 36 years.
Jane Newburn died 25th Nov 1858, aged 18 years.

{Recorded in M.D. Vol. XII-XIII 1926-31.}

Erected
by
William Newburn
in memory of his wife
Mary Newburn
who died 13th October 1884,
aged 47 years.
Also the above named
William Newburn
who died 23rd February 1890,
aged 56 years.

NICHOLSON   See **HOGG**   13

O'FLAHERTY   *[upright sandstone, white marble insert, shaped top]*

Erected
to
the memory of
Francis Hale O'Flaherty
of Lisburn
who died 18th October 1859,
aged 58 years.
And
Eleanor O'Flaherty, his wife,
died 30th May 1875, aged 62 years.
Also of their children.
John Greaves
died 27th March 1841, aged 9 months.
John Hale
died 17th July 1849, aged 7 years.
Thomas Alexander O'Flaherty M.D.
Staff Surgeon R.N.
died 26th October 1888, aged 51 years.
Francis Hale Hill O'Flaherty
died 5th May 1901, aged 53 years.
Douglas Hill O'Flaherty,
Captain 15th Royal Irish Rifles,
killed Thiepval, 1st July 1916,
aged 36 years.

OBRE   *[raised, slate ledger stone, on four pillars, close to the wall of the*   148
Cathedral. The only legible inscription starts half way down the
stone.]

HERE LYETH THE BODY OF
FRANCIS OBRE
[CLANTILEW] THE COUNTY OF ARMAGH
WHO DEPARTED THIS
LIFE THE 19 MARCH 1709
AGED 6[5] YEARS.
[ALSO EDWARD SMITH O'BRE,
WHO DIED 12 MAY 1824,
AGED 75 YEARS.]

{*Last part of inscription given in article on Huguenots in Northern*
Whig, Thursday October 22 1885.}

PARKINSON

Robert Parkinson died 11th July 1859 aged 17 (son of Thomas)
Susanna Parkinson died 16th May 1868 aged 21 (daughter of Thomas)
Alice Parkinson died 29th December 1892 aged 74 (wife of Thomas)
Thomas Parkinson died 30th April 1877 aged 61 years.

Site
not
found
2004

{*Information recorded in 1958.*}

PATTERSON	See **WOODHOUSE**	87

PELAN	*[flat sandstone]*	131

Erected
by Samuel Pelan, of Lisburn,
to the memory of his wife,
Eliza Jane Pelan, who died
11th July 1834, aged 28 years.
Thomas Pelan Jun. who died
3^d Novr 1829, aged 34 years.
Thomas Pelan Sen. who died
4th Octr 1830, aged 80 years.
John Richard Pelan
died 11th May 1836, aged 4½ years.
Also the above named Samuel
Pelan died July 2 1862, aged 69 years

PELAN	See **NEELY**	66

PENNINGTON	*[tall, upright sandstone, pieces flaking off]*	176

Sacred
to
the memory of John Pennington
who departed this life 3rd March
1874, aged 83 years.
And to the beloved memory of
his wife Isabella, who departed
this life 6th Nov 1878, aged 87 years.
Also his son John
who departed this life 11th Nov.
1877, aged 59 years.
and William Henry who was
drowned at Sandhurst
Victoria Australia 18**
aged 44 years.

{*Stone damaged in February 2003. Pieces now cemented and lying
flat on the ground.*}

PENNINGTON	*[upright slate]*	177

Here lieth the remains
of
Thomas Pennington
who departed this life
the 16th of February 1813,
aged 47 years.

PORTER	See **HOWARD**	27
POWELL	*[flat sandstone]*	55

.... [LYE]TH THE BODY OF
.... POWELL IN LISBURN
.... DEPARTED THIS LIFE THE
.... DECEMBAR[SIC] ANNO DOM
.... AE TATIS   34

HERE LYETH THE.......................
ROBERT MAR...........................
CHILDREN................................
OF LISBURN..............................

PURDON/ **DE LA CHEROIS-** **CROMMELIN**	*[flat sandstone, set in cement, continuation of No. 17]*	16

Also the remains of
Samuel De la Cherois-Crommelin Esqr.
her husband, who departed this life
September 7th 1816, aged 71 years.
Also the remains of their Grand Child,
Samuel De la Cherois, son of Doctor Henry
Purdon, who departed this life August 12th 1814,
aged 5 years.
Henry Purdon M.D., died 11th September 1843,
aged 73 Years.
Ann De la Cherois, his wife, died
February 27 1853, aged 73 years.
Amelia Stott, wife of their son Thomas Henry,
died January 8 1861, aged 44.
Kate Frances Purdon, her daughter,
died October 14^{th (sic)} 1871, aged 29.
Also Andrew John Johnston, husband of
Kate Frances Purdon, who departed this life
3rd of November 1871, in his 28th year.
Charles De la Cherois Purdon A.M., M.B.,
T.C.D., F.R.C.S.I.,
died 8th January 1882, aged 63 years.
Thomas Henry Purdon. M.A., M.B.,
T.C.D., F.R.C.S.I.,
born 1806, died 6th August 1886.
Jane Maria Calvert,
wife of Charles De la Cherois Purdon. M.B.,
born 12th August 1822, died 6th February 1916.

READE	See **WOODHOUSE**	87
REED	See **STORY**	96

REID   [*sandstone pillar, white marble insert*]   29

Erected
by
William Reid, Lisburn,
in memory of his father,
Samuel Reid, who died
5th Dec 1868.

REID   [*upright sandstone, flaking*]   93

Erected
by
Robert Reid in memory of his son,
John, who died 2nd November 1834,
aged 7 months.
Also his wife, Mary Ann, who died
9th August 1865, aged 59 years.
Also his daughter, Matilda, who
died 17th March 1867, aged 26 years.

REID   See **FULTON**   137

REID   See **McHARRY**

REILLY   [*flat, broken sandstone stone*]   8

Memorial of affection
by a
Widow and Mother
Sorrowing not, as without hope,
after a beloved Husband and dutiful Child.
"not lost but gone before."
John Lazarus Reilly,
of Reilly's Town, Carrickfergus,
who departed this life 18th Decr 1811?,
aged 73 years.
And Harriet Reilly
who departed this life the 31st day of October 1811
aged 28 years.
James Reilly departed this
life 3rd November 1854, aged 54 years.
Harriet Gilmore, alias Reilly,
died 13th March 1856, aged 26 years.
And her only child, George Gwynne, died
1st January 1856, aged 4 months.
Bridget, widow of J.L. Reilly, died
16th July 1859, aged 83 years.

RICHARDSON   [*upright sandstone*]   135

Erected
by
Margaret Richardson, to the memory
of her husband, John Richardson,
who departed this life 24th November
1825, aged 37 years.

RICHMOND   [*broken sandstone and in pieces, lying loose on gravestone No. 96*   97
                    STORY]

In memory
of
Maria Watts Richmond,
daughter of
Quartermaster John Richmond
of the Royal Scots Greys,
who died 21st November
aged 7 years.

{*Recorded in M.D. Vol. XII-XIII 1926-31.*}

ROCHET   [*raised, flat, red sandstone, with cement sides*]   171

HERE LYETH THE BODY OF MR LEWIS
ROCHET OF LISBURN MERCHANT WHO
DEPARTED THIS LIFE THE 1 OF OCTOBER
IN THE YEAR OF OUR LORD GOD 1726
AND IN HIS 51 YEAR OF HIS AGE

ROGERS   [*broken, flat sandstone, very worn*]   61

HERE LYETH THE BODY OF
DORETY, WIFE OF CORNET
GEORGE ROGERS IN LISBURN,
WHO DEPARTED
THIS LIFE THE 11 DAY OF
MARCH 1682.

{*In the burial records there is also a Dorothy, dau. of George Rogers
buried "May ye 8 1689".*}

RUSSELL [*sandstone, only part remaining, very weathered*] 95

Sacred
to the memory
of Ew^d Russell ………………
Aged
……………………………..
……………………………..
……………………………..
……………………………..
aged 1* years *
Cathrina Russell
died July 21st 18**………..
W. Coulson ……..
died July 12 18**……..

RUSSELL See **TINSLEY** 146

SEFTON See **MURRAY** 106

SHANNON [*sandstone box tomb, raised cement surround*] 158

Mary Shannon,
died 5th February 1834,
aged 83 years.
John Babtist Shannon,
her son,
died 23rd May 1856,
aged 82 years.
Mary Shannon,
wife of John Babtist Shannon,
died 22nd February 1838.
Their children.
Rachel Shannon
died 4th October 1806,
aged 6 months.
Mary Shannon
died 27th April 1814,
aged 11 years.
John Shannon
died 26th August 1827,
aged 21 years.
James Shannon
died 3rd November 1837,
aged 28 years.

SHORT See **ALLEN** 53

SIMON   *[flat sandstone]*   14

Sacred
to the memory of
Julia Simon
who departed this life the 4th of April 1824,
aged 73 years.
Also
her husband John Simon
who departed this life the 15th of April 1827,
aged 82 years.

*{Julia Simon had formerly been **ADDINGTON**.*
1824 Directory - Capt. John Simon, gent, Market Square.}

SIMPSON   *[upright, granite stone]*   30

Erected
by
James Simpson
to the memory of his beloved wife,
Elizabeth, (daughter of
the late James Boyes,
of Stoneyford)
who died 4th September 1859,
aged 82 years.

SMITH   *[flat sandstone]*   136

Here lieth
the body of
Abraham Smith who died
20th October 1802, aged 2 years.
Also John Smith who died
10th April 1832, aged 9 months.
Also Mary Smith who died the
26th January 1837, aged 63 yrs.
Also William Smith who died
the 16th March 1843, *aged 68 yrs.*
Also Mary Smith departed
this life 6th April 1847, aged
37 years.

{This stone was moved from the north side.}

SMITH	*[flat sandstone, set in cement]*	165

Interred beneath this stone is the body
of Captain Samuel Delacherois Smith,
of Lisburn,
late of the Regiment of Foot, who
died 17th June 1829, aged 55, son to the
late John & Judith Smith.

{*Burial records say he was buried 21st May 1829.*}

SMITH	See **CROMMELIN**	162

SMYTH	*[flat sandstone, set in cement]*	164

Here lies intered (sic) the remains of
Mrs. Martha Smyth,
relict of the late Thomas Smyth
of Drumcree, County of Westmeath. Esq.,
and daughter of the
Revd Francis Hutchinson
Archdeacon of Down & Connor,
Ob^t 5th Jan^{ry} 1818, AE 81 years.

SMYTH	See **HERON**	125

SMYTH	See **STEWART**	19

SORBY	*[tall, upright sandstone]*	173

Erected
by
John Sorby.
In memory of
his mother,
Abigail Sorby,
who departed this life the 24th of June 1837,
aged 61 years.
---ooo---
Plucked from my children in their youthful days
When most their mother's tender care they need.
Oh, let a faithful friend direct their ways
To that bright path which will to Heaven lead.

SPRATT

Site
not
found
2004

Erected
To the memory of Isabella Spratt
Daughter to Joseph Spratt of G**ttets
Ga** who departed this life May 15
1821(?) Aged 1(?)years

{This stone cannot now be found. It is thought to have been where the Remembrance Garden now is.}

From the burial records:-
- *Joseph Spratt, Innkeeper, Lissue buried 19th February 1825.*
- *Isabella, widow of the late Joseph Spratt, Lissue, buried 7th January 1826.*
   {They may be from Gawley's Gate.}

{Recorded in M.D. Vol. XII-XIII 1926-31.}

SPROULL	See **CARLETON**	47
SPROULL	See **FULTON**	137
STALKER	*[small, upright, worn sandstone]*	156

HERE◆LIETH
THE◆BODY◆OF◆DAN
IEL◆STALKER◆WHO
DIED◆JULY◆THE◆17
1717, ◆AGED◆19◆YEARS.
ALSO◆MARY◆&◆ANN,
CHILDREN◆TO◆JOHN
STALKER, ◆WHO
DIED◆NOVEMBER◆YE
19◆1724.

CATHEDRAL 156
STALKER

[*side*]

The
Very Reverend
James Stannus A.M.
Dean of Ross
and
Rector of Lisburn.
Born 1788.
Died 1876.
---ooo---
Erected
by
their children
in
affectionate memory of
dearly
beloved parents
---ooo---
Elizabeth Stannus
his wife.
Born 1793.
Died 1873.
---ooo---
"Them also which sleep
in Jesus will God bring
with him." 1 Thess iv 14

[*side*]

Also
Harriet Jane Stannus
dearly beloved.
Died February 16 1893.

STEED   See **BRIGS**   83

STERLING

Erected
in memory of
William Sterling, of
Old-Warren, who died 4th June 1866,
aged 84 years.
Also his beloved wife
Mary Jane Sterling, who
died 22nd April 1879,
aged 54 years.
Also their grandchild who died in infancy.

{*Recorded in M.D. Vol. XII-XIII 1926-31.*}

Site
not
found
2004

STEWART *[large slate monument fixed to the north wall of the Cathedral,* 19
becoming worn]

Within the railings affixed to this monument are deposited the
remains of Mrs Rose Stewart (relict of the late Capt[n]
Charles Stewart) who died in the Month of February
1779, aged 92 years. Of Poyntz Stewart, third son of
Poyntz Stewart Esq., of Lisburn, who died on the 5th
day of November 1773, aged 9 years. Of Hannah Smyth,
fourth daughter of M[rs.] Charlotte Smyth, of Lisburn, who
died on the 3rd day of august (sic) 1792, aged 24 years. Of M[rs.]
Ann Stewart, second wife of Poyntz Stewart Esq.,
of Lisburn, who died on the 21st day of July 1793, aged 67
years. Of Ann Stewart, daughter of the above mentioned
Charles & Rose Stewart, who died on the 26th of July
1804, aged 78 years.
Here also are interred the bodies of Margaret
Stewart, the 6th daughter of Doctor William
Stewart, of Lisburn, who died on the 13th day of
May 1816, AET 3 months and of Margaret Stewart,
his wife, who departed this life on the 15th day of May
1816, AET 39.
Also the body of Charlotte, relict of the late Wm.
Smyth Esq, *of Ballintoy,* who died July 26th 1822,
aged 94 years. Also the body of Poyntz
Stewart Esq., of Lisburn, who died April 9th
1823, aged 87 years. Also the body of the Rev[d]
James Smyth, Vicar of Dysert and in Diocese
of Lismore, who died November 29th 1823, aged 61 years.
Also of Mary Ann, 4th daughter
of Dr. William Stewart and of the above named
Margaret, who died 24th August 1833, aged 23 years.
Also of Arabella, the wife of Major
William Stewart, son of Dr. Stewart, who
died on the 21st of February 1840, aged 45
years.
Also of Dr. William Stewart, who died on the
22nd of October 1844, in the 76th year of his age.
Also of Magdalene Stewart, who died at Glenavy,
the 5th December 1871, aged 66 years.
Also of Aemelia, the beloved wife of the
Rev[d] E. Johnson Smyth, who died on
the 1st of April 1876, aged 67 years.

*{Mrs. Rose Stewart's death is recorded in the Belfast News Letter
February 1782.}*

{Recorded in M.D. Vol. XII-XIII 1926-31.}

Sacred
to
the memory
of
Magdelene Stewart
who died in the Lord
the 5th of December 1871,
aged 66 years.
---ooo---
Blessed are the dead who
die in the Lord.
Revelations
XIV 13

STEWART *[upright slate stone]* 80

Erected
by
William Stewart
in memory of his daughter Elizabeth,
who departed this life on 11th April
1840, aged 2 years.
Also his son Robert who died
15 June 1859, AE 14.
Blessed are the dead who die in the
Lord.
Also his son Henry who died 21st June
1861, aged 19 years.

{*Recorded in M.D. Vol. XII-XIII 1926-31.*}

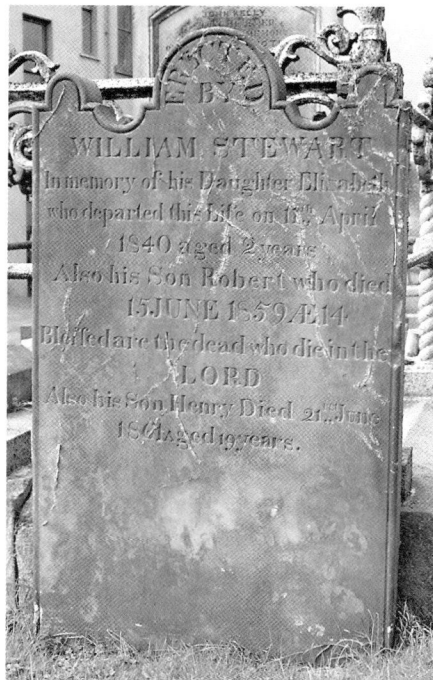

CATHEDRAL 80
STEWART

Here lieth the body of
Robert Stewart, *of Lisburn,*
who departed this life on the 6th of
May 1837, aged 83 years.
Also his wife Ann Stewart, who
departed this life on the 29th of Dec[r]
1835, aged 94 years.
Also their son James Stewart,
who departed this life on the 26th Dec[r] 1847,
aged 66 years.
Also Lucinda Stewart, wife of
Robert Stewart (son of Robert Stewart and Ann Stewart)
who departed this life on the 11th Sept[r] 1853,
aged 60 years.
Also Robert Stewart
who departed this life on the 4th of June 1858,
aged 75 years.
These all died in faith
Also Elizabeth, eldest daughter of
Robert Stewart, who departed this life
25th March 1887, aged 66 years.
Also Marianne, third daughter of
Robert Stewart, and dearly loved wife of
Rev. Samuel Clarke, who departed this life
30th September 1888, aged 61 years.

STEWART See **CROMMELIN** 166

STORY *[sandstone box tomb]* 96

Here lieth the body
of
Anthony Makepeace Story
Lieu. In His Majesty's 22nd Reg. of Light Dragoons
who departed this life
on the 20th May 1797,
aged 20 years.
---ooo---
This tomb having become dilapidated
was restored A.D. 1850
by the surviving brothers and sisters
of the deceased viz.
Henry Story Esq. of Worton, Stockton on Tees,
Mary Ann Reed, Widow,
and
Julia Colson,
wife of the Rev. John Morton Colson Clk.

{Recorded in M.D. Vol. XII-XIII 1926-31.}

THOMPSON   *[grey, polished, upright, granite stone with two curved, polished*   42
granite tombs, iron railings. Lettering is on the upright stone]

In
memory of
William Thompson
born 5th Jan. 1763, died 7th Oct. 1843.
Dora Thompson, his wife,
born 1749, died 11th April 1823.
Their children:-
James Thompson born 1784, died in infancy.
William John Thompson, born 1791, died in infancy.
Jane Thompson, born 8th Nov. 1787, died 1805.
Francis Thompson,
born 3rd Aug. 1783, died March 1865.
Interred at Hill Hall, Co. Down.
Jane Thompson,
wife of the above named Francis Thompson,
born 30th April 1782, died 9th July 1840.
Interred at Hill Hall, Co. Down.
Their children
Richard Thompson,
born 25th Aug. 1810, died 5th Sept. 1856.
Interred at Hill Hall, Co. Down.
James Thompson,
born 9th June 1821, died 12th Oct. 1854.
Interred at Coimbatore, India.
William Thompson M.D., F.R.C.S.I.,
born 7th March, 1806, died 22nd Sep. 1882.
His children:-
William Thompson,
Colonel 3rd Madras Cavalry,
born 1st Sep. 1834, died 7th July 1882.
Stewart Thompson,
born 6th Dec. 1835, died 26th Dec. 1862.
and his widow,
Rosina Thompson,
born February 1803, died 8th December 1884.
---oOo---
Erected by Rosina Thompson, widow of
William Thompson M.D., F.R.C.S.I.
1883.

Erected
by
James Thompson
in memory of his beloved wife,
Eliza,
who died 17th February 1890, aged 58 years.
Also their son
Samuel,
who died 20th May 1874, aged 1 year & 5 months.
Also their daughter
Esther,
who died 28th August 1878, aged 16 years.
also his son Samuel, who died
5th July 1894, aged 18 years.
The above named James Thompson
who died 29th July 1898, aged 68 years.
---ooo---
"For so He giveth His beloved sleep."

Robinson
Belfast

THOMPSON *[small, upright sandstone]* 174

HERE LIETH
THE BODIES OF
MARY ANNE DYED
AP[R] Y[E] 27, AGED
ONE YEAR, 1726.
THOMAS THOMP
SON DYED AUGUST
Y[E] FIRS[T] 1726, AGED
TWO YEARS.
CHILDRN TO W[M]
THOMPSON.

CATHEDRAL 174
THOMPSON

Erected
to the memory of
Thomas Tinsley, *of Lisburn,*
who dep. this life on the 1st July 1865,
AE 67 years.
His beloved wife Mary, who dep.
this life on Oct 27th 1847, AE 39 years.
His 3 daughters Martha, Sarah
And Eleanor, who died in infancy.
Lettitia, who dep. this life on May
11th 1861, AE 22 years.
---ooo---
His Grandson John Tinsley, who
dep. this life on Dec 31st 1864, AE 15 *months.*
Also his son John Tinsley,
who died 26th Jan 1886, AE 42 years.
Also Agnes, the beloved wife of
John Tinsley,
who died 10th Jan 1908, AE 63 years.

TINSLEY *[upright black polished marble, with black polished marble surround,* 146
also a flat black polished stone]

[upright stone]

TINSLEY

[flat stone]

In affectionate remembrance
of
Arthur Tinsley,
who died 6th October 1875.
His wife Mary,
who died 1st December 1910.
Their son John,
who died in infancy.
Their son David Charles,
who died 9th September 1921.
Their son Arthur Stanley,
who died 8th March 1934,
and was interred in City Cemetery Belfast.
Their daughter Eliza Jane Russell,
who died 15th March 1944.
Also Matthew Tinsley,
who died 17th February 1949.
Also his sister
Marianne (Minnie),
who died 16th July 1951.

TOLLERTON	See **GILBERT**	61
TOLLERTON	See **GILBERT**	62
TOWNSON	*[upright, worn, red sandstone]*	111

HERE♦LYETH♦THE
BODY♦OF♦ROBERT
TOWNSON♦WHO
DEPARTED♦THIS♦LIFE
THE♦30♦OCTOBER
1691.

TRAINOR	*[broken, upright sandstone, formerly on a plinth, resting against* ***MARMION*** *No. 88]*	89

Erected
by
John Trainor
in memory
of his family.

TRUEFET	*[red sandstone, attached to the wall]*	175

HERE LIETH THE BODY OF
M^R. JAMES TRUEFET WHO
DEPARTED THIS LIFE THE 6 OF
JANUARY 1722.
AND ALSO M^RS. JAINE HIS
WIFE WHO DEPARTED THIS
LIFE FEBRUARY THE 27
1725.
6

CATHEDRAL 175
TRUEFET

TURNER   [*sandstone, lower part illegible*]   60

Erected
by Francis Turner of Lisburn to the memory
of his mother, Mary Turner, who departed
this life 4th day of April 1836, aged 71 years.
Also his daughter, Ann Turner, who
departed this life 12th November
1832, aged 2 years.
Also his son Archibald Turner who
died 14th November 1844, aged 16 years.
Also two of his children, Jemima
and Stewart, who died in infancy.
His sister, Ann, aged 63 years.
His son, James, died 18th August 1869,
aged 47 years.
Also the above Francis Turner
died 8th Dec 1873, aged 77 years.
His wife, Ann Turner, died
26th June 1874, aged 69 years.
His daughter, Margaret Ann, died
26th Jan 1875, aged 41 years.

{*Recorded in M.D. Vol. XII-XIII 1926-31.*}

UNKNOWN   [*loose sandstone headstone, illegible*]   5

UNKNOWN   [*low box tomb with granite top, illegible*]   11

UNKNOWN   [*upright, red sandstone, very weathered and illegible*]   22

UNKNOWN   [*loose sandstone headstone, illegible*]   23

UNKNOWN   [*upright sandstone, very weathered*]   33

Erected
.... on

{*Only legible letters.*}

UNKNOWN   [*upright sandstone, very weathered,*   37
carved dove of peace]

Erected

{*Only legible word.*}

UNKNOWN   [*flat granite, illegible*]   46

UNKNOWN   [*low box tomb, with granite top, illegible*]   65

UNKNOWN	[*upright sandstone, flaking and illegible*]	73
UNKNOWN	[*stump*]	77
UNKNOWN	[*fallen stone, illegible, carved hour glass and wings. Ornamental iron railings*]	102

Time is short

{*only visible words*}

UNKNOWN	[*flat, red sandstone*]	105
UNKNOWN	[*flat stone, crumbling and illegible*]	121
UNKNOWN	[*upright sandstone, flaking and illegible*]	143
UNKNOWN	[*upright sandstone, flaking and illegible*]	172
UNKNOWN	[*upright sandstone, illegible*]	179

This stone erected

{*only visible words*}

UNKNOWN	[*Now a flower bed.*]	182
UNKNOWN	[*large sandstone tablet with carved surround and curved top, attached to the wall*]	184

{*No inscription legible.*}

VERNON	[*flat sandstone*]	130

Erected
by James Vernon in memory of his
Family. Margaret, died 6th July 1838,
aged 2 years.
Hugh died in infancy.
John died 16th July 1840, aged 10 years.
Catherine, his Mother, died 17th July 1842,
aged 65 years.
Alis died 29th Dec 1831, aged 9 years.
Prudence died 11th April 1857, aged 14 years.
Alis his beloved wife died 3d August
1867, aged 59 years.
The above named James Vernon died
28th April 1886, aged 83 years.

WADE	See **ATKINSON**	110

WATSON	[*upright, black polished granite, with leaf carving and granite surround*]	101

In
loving memory
of
Henry Watson,
of Lisburn,
who departed this life January
21st 1880, aged 58 years.
Also of his beloved wife,
Mary Anne,
who died at Bangor, May
3rd 1903, in her 80th year.
Also four of their children
who died in infancy.
---ooo---
"Until the day break and
The shadows flee away."
---ooo---

**1904
WATSON**

WATSON	See **FULTON**	71

WELDON	[*flat sandstone, only a piece remains, parts are illegible*]	118

Erected
by
Christopher Weldon in memory of
his beloved wife Anne Weldon
died much lamented on the ....
1833 aged * years
also Catherine ....
the ....

{*This stone was moved from the north side.*}

WETHERED	[*sandstone, cemented into wall*]	7

Erected
by
Thomas Wethered M.D.,
of Lisburn, in memory of his wife,
Mary, who died 3rd February 1839.
Thomas Wethered M.D
died 7th September 1842.

WHEELER   *[small upright sandstone]*   134A

HERE LIETH YE
BODY OF FRAN
CIS WHEELER
DIED JUNE 10
1769 AG^D 3 MONTHS.

{On the reverse of **BROOKE** *No. 134. This stone would appear to have been re-used as the side edges are not smooth and the inscription on No.134 appears to be incomplete.}*

WHITEFORD   *[upright sandstone]*   4

Hugh Boyd Whiteford M.D.
Died 13th Dec 1830,
aged 56 years.

WHITLA   *[sandstone box tomb]*   48

[side]

Sacred
to the memory of John Whitla. Esq. Late of H. M. 14th Light
Dragoons
who departed this life 21st March 1821, in the 25th year of his age.
This tomb was erected as a small tribute to his worth
by his affectionate widow.

[side]

Sacred
to the memory of George Whitla Esq. of Lisburn
who departed this life May the 12th 1831, aged 66 years.
Also his wife Margaret Allan who died Dec 25th 1842, aged 74 years.

"We look for the Saviour the Lord Jesus Christ." Phil. 3rd 20.

[top]

To the memory
also of Eleanor Haynes,
widow of Lieut. John Whitla
and of
Dr. McDowall.
She died July 1890, aged 93 years.

Here are
interred the bodies
of
James Wightman,
died Octr 1767.
John Wightman,
of Lisburn, Merchant,
died Decr 1801.
Margaret, his wife,
died Novr 1780.
His Mother, and his sons
John and Robert.
Mary, relict of John Wightman,
died Mar 1819.
Eliza McAlester,
his daughter,
relict of Charles McAlester
of Belfast, Merchant,
died July 1855.

WIGHTMAN See **FULTON** 71

WILSON *[upright sandstone, very worn]* 10

Erected
in
memory of
Adam Wilson,
who departed this life 11th June 1833,
aged 48 years.
Susanna, his wife, died 29th March 1837,
aged 33 years.
William, their son, died 15th July 1845,
aged 18 years.
Sarah, their daughter, died 5th June
1868, aged 45 years.
Robert, their son, died 17th Nov 1877.
Susanna, their daughter, died 22nd Feb 1884.

Erected

by
William Wilson
of Ballymacash
in memory of his son James who
departed this life ** May ****
aged * years
Also …………………….. who
departed this life ………….. er
186* aged ** years
Blessed are the dead who die in the Lord.

WOODHOUSE   *[tall, upright sandstone, white shield insert, urn on top, tall iron   87
railings]*

In memory
of
Margaret, the beloved wife of George Woodhouse,
daughter of the late John Cochran Esq. Londonderry.
Her disposition was most amiable
and her trust in the Lord Jesus Christ most confident
and so trusting. She died at Lisburn 2 March 1849.
And of his dear wife Mary Cairns,
daughter of the late R.P. Reade Lieut. 22 Dragoons,
who, in the certain hope of everlasting life,
died at Fintona 5 Nov[r] 1877.
And of his dear wife Catherine Jane,
daughter of the late W. Patterson Esq. J.P. Fivemiletown,
who, also in the faith of the Gospel,
died in Dublin, 27 Nov[r] 1890.
And of George Woodhouse
who died at Bray, Co. Wicklow
on 8th March 1898, aged 84 years.

"Blessed are the dead who die in the Lord."

Sacred
to the memory of
Lieutenant Colonel Henry Wray, late of the Honourable East India
Company's Service, departed this life on the 22nd day of August
1809,
aged 66 years.
Also his widow Charlotte Wray died on
the first day of June 1849, aged eighty-nine.
Also of Mary Jones, of Lisburn, spinster,
who died 20th day of February 1838, aged 82 years.
Mullis ille habilis

John Young
aged 5 years & 8 months.
Assasinated (sic) 23rd August 1822.

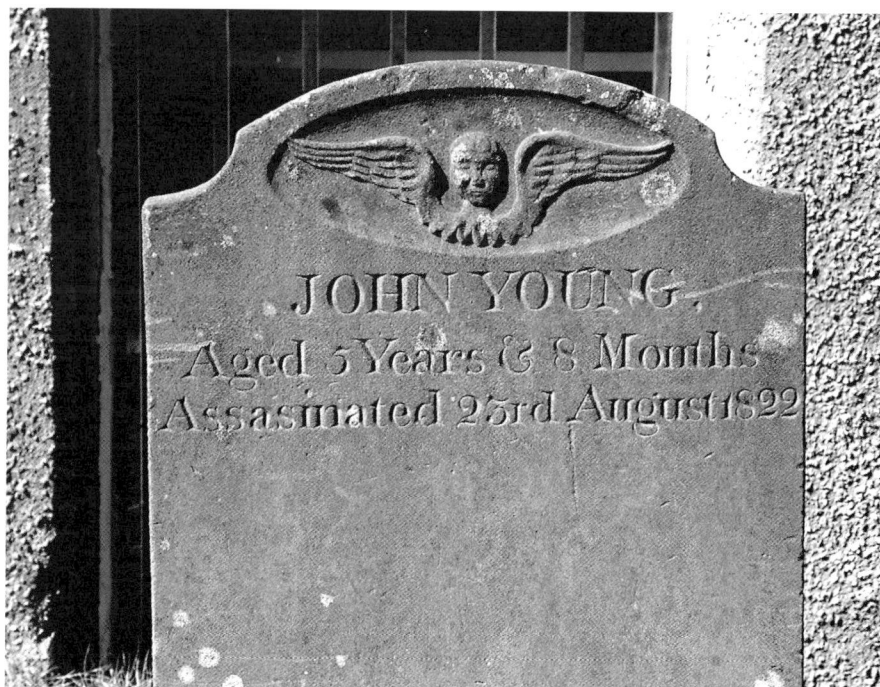

CATHEDRAL 28   **YOUNG**

GARDEN OF REMEMBRANCE

[pink polished marble, on wall]

This garden of rest
is dedicated
to the glory of God
and
in loving memory
of
Frances Elizabeth Marilyn McCartney

4th August 1930 – 8th November 1986

"The Lord is my Shepherd."

[pink polished marble, below stone on left]

This pathway was laid
in loving memory
of
Doreen Reilly

14th June 1937 – 6th March 1988

Be still and know that I am God
Psalm 46 v. 10

[upright pink polished marble stone set into the ground]

The one you love is not here.
The one you love is risen!

[small flat pink polished marble stones set into the ground]

Marilyn McCartney 1930 – 1986 Garry McCartney 1928 – 1992	Doreen Reilly 1937 – 1988	Robert J. Taggart 1913 – 1989 Elizabeth Taggart 1918 – 1997	Wilhelmina Topping 1917 – 1990 Charles Topping 1915 – 1992
Anna B. Smyth 1901 – 1988 Dr. George B.P. Smyth 1900 – 1989 M.I. Weir 1895 – 1992	John Doak 1908 – 1991	Walter Glass 1923 – 1994 Elizabeth C. Glass 1925 – 2004	Isabel McVittie 1911 – 1994 Stewart McVittie 1911 – 2000
Eileen Rix 1956 – 1994	Elizabeth Green 1923 – 1997	John Geddes 1939 – 1998	William Robert Nelson 1925 – 2004

LISBURN CATHEDRAL MEMORIALS

NAVE - NORTH

[brass plaque, mounted on ebony wood]

{R.I.C. crest}

In proud and ever loving
memory of
Oswald Ross Swanzy, D.I.,
Royal Irish Constabulary,
who gave his life in Lisburn,
Sunday, 22nd August, 1920.
And of all his gallant comrades who
like him have been killed in the
unfaltering discharge of their duty
and in the service of their country.
"Be thou faithful unto death and I will give thee a crown of life."
Erected by his mother and Irene his sister.

[white marble, mounted on marble, with regimental motto]

Pro Patria
To commemorate the self sacrifice
of
Garratt Primrose Jenkins,
Second-Lieutenant, R.F.A.,
who gave up his young life in his
Country's defence in the Great War.
This tablet is erected as a mark of sympathy with his Father,
Major A. P. Jenkins,
11th Battalion Royal Irish Rifles,
who suffered wounds and imprisonment in the same cause.
by his colleagues of the Lisburn Urban District Council.
---ooo---
1917.

{Garratt Primrose Jenkins died 7th September 1917 and is buried in Canada Farm Cemetery, Belgium.}

[*brass plaque*]

In loving memory of
William Graham of Lisburn,
who died on 23rd Aug. 1850,
aged 66 years.

{*N'oubliez*}

His wife,
Elizabeth Graham,
who died on the 19th Feb. 1865, aged 77 years,
and their children, **William Graham**, who
died on the 27th July 1889, aged 62 years,
and **Anne Graham**, who died on the
19th Oct. 1892, aged 72 years.
---oOo---
"Until the day break and the shadows flee away."
---oOo---
Erected by Colonel James Graham, 1894

[*brass plaque*]

To the Glory of God,
and In Memory of
Colonel James Graham,

{*N'oubliez*}

son of
William and Elizabeth Graham,
of Lisburn,
who died at Wimbledon, Surrey,
on April 26th 1905,
Late H.E.I.C., 14th N.I. Regiment,
and Bengal Staff Corps, 1849-1879.
Served in the Indian Mutiny Campaign including
the Siege and Capture of Lucknow, 1857-1858.
---oOo---
Erected by His Widow and Children,
1905.

NAVE – NORTH

[brass plaque]

Sacred
To the Memory of

George Whitla	Died 1831 aged 66
Margaret, his Wife	Died 1842 aged 74
William, their Son	Died 1861 aged 69
Elizabeth, his Wife	Died 1886 aged 75

Their Children

John	Died 1842 aged 7
Sydney Herbert	Died 1853 aged 10
Seymour Conway	Died 1853 aged 8
Elizabeth Clarke, wife of T.P. Carr, R.I.C.	Died 1871 aged 34
Eleanor Margaret, wife of Col. L.M. Buchanan, C.B.	Died 1877 aged 39
Emma Hardcastle Haldane, wife of Major H. Lucas	Died 1899 aged 58
James Buchanan, Capt. Late Connaught R^{grs}	Died 1911 aged 76
William, Col. Late Lincolnshire Regt.	Died 1917 aged 77
George, Surgeon-General late A.M.S.	Died 1919 aged 86
Ada, wife of Col. T. Higginson C.B.	Died 1919 aged 73
Jane Alicia, wife of C.C. Bridges	Died 1929 aged 84
Valentine Herbert	Died 1933 aged 80

---oOo---

"If we believe that Jesus died and rose again, even so them
also that are fallen asleep in Jesus, will God bring with Him."

I. Thess. Iv. 14

---oOo---
VIVE UT VIVAS.

[marble, with decorative carved surround]

To the
Glory of God,
and
in brotherly and loving memory
of one whose name in this parish will be
held in lasting remembrance,
REVD. HARTLEY HODSON, D.D.
Canon of Cairncastle,
and for seven years Rector of Lisburn,
who died February 3 1884, aged 66 years.

This Tablet
is erected by the Orangemen of the District of
Lisburn, in testimony of the regard felt by
them towards one who for many years was
identified with their institution, and who in
the most critical times of their history, when
ministering in Christ Church, Lisburn, held the
office of District Master.
---oOo---
"The memory of the just is blessed."

NAVE – NORTH

[white marble, with carved urn]

Memoriae Sacrum
Rev^{di} viri **GUY ATKINSON**, D.D.
Per multos annos Parochiae Ahoghill
Rectoris
Obiit vicessime quarto die Octobris 1804
nonaginta et Septem annos natus
Nec non
Uxoris ejus observantissmae
JANE ATKINSON
Quae obiit tricessimo die Decembris 1798
anno aetatis suae sexagessimo secundo
Et
Mariae filiae earum unicae
uxoris Revdi Georgii Golding
quae hanc vitam reliquit
Novembris vicessimo sexto die 1793
novendecim annos nata
Reliquae earum mortals
in Cemeterio vicino conquiescent.

{Recorded in M.D. Vol. V 1902}

Translation

Dedicated to the memory of
the Rev. GUY ATKINSON, D.D.
for many years the Rector of Ahoghill Parish.
He died on the 24th day of October 1804
aged 97 years.
And also
to his most attentive wife,
JANE ATKINSON,
who died on the 30th day of December 1798
in the 62nd year of her life.
And
to their only daughter, Mary,
wife of the Rev. George Golding,
who left this life
on the 26th day of November 1793
aged 19 years.
Their mortal remains
rest in the neighbouring cemetery.

{Rev. Atkinson's first wife was Jane, daughter of Charles Maule, his second wife was Jane, daughter of Jackson Wray, Donegal. He also had two sons Rev. Charles Atkinson and Jackson Wray Atkinson.}

[marble, with urn and decorative carved surround]

In memory of
One who lived a life of faith in the Son of God,
blessed herself in blessing others, it was her
high privilege to spend and be spent in the service
of Him "Who loved her and gave Himself for her."
To
JANE DEBORAH
Eldest daughter of the late Hugh Moore of Eglantine
and Mount Panther, in the County of Down, Esquire,
formerly Captain in the 5th Dragoon Guards,
and of Priscilla Cecilia his wife.
This tablet
is erected by those who knew her worth and mourn her loss.
She died "looking unto Jesus"
December 6, 1863, at Warren Cottage, Lisburn.

"Be thou Faithful unto Death."

[marble, with carved urn]

This tablet is erected
to the memory of
Major Charles Johnson Nicholson,
of the Bengal Staff Corps,
and brother of Brigadier-General Nicholson,
at Doomree,
On his way to join his station he died,
on 18th December 1862,
from the effects of a wound received at Delhi.
---ooo---
Also to the memory
of his wife, **Lizzie Nicholson,**
who died of decline, at Cheltenham,
on the 17th May 1863,
surviving her husband only five months
---ooo---
"They were lovely and pleasant in their lives,
and in their death they were not divided."
2. Samuel 1.23

R. Montgomery
Belfast

[marble, with ornate carving]

Sacred
to the memory of
William Hogg, Esq.
who departed this life 25th July 1824
Aged 70 years,
and of **Mary**, his wife
who departed this life 28th Feb[y] 1856
aged 92 years.
Their remains are interred near this spot.
This tablet was erected by their son
Sir James Weir Hogg Bar[t.] M.P.

[marble, with carved sarcophagus]

Sacred to the memory of
Jane Hawkshaw,
(daughter of William Hawkshaw Esq.
of Lisburn.)
OB. 25 Feb. 1855. Aetat 81.
---ooo---
During a long life of usefulness
she adorned the doctrine of God her Saviour
by deeds of piety and benevolence
imparting the means of spiritual instruction
as well as temporal relief, but without ostentation;
not resting her hope on personal merit
she ascribed her whole title to salvation
to the favour and mercy of the Father, son & spirit,
in and through the great redeemer.
To her this tablet is affectionately inscribed
by her sorrowing friends.

"Blessed are the dead which die in the Lord."

[marble, with very ornate surround]

In
Loving memory
of
Marianne,
the dearly beloved and devoted wife
of the
Rev. Samuel Clarke.
She departed to be with Christ
on 30th September, 1888,
aged 61 years.
---ooo---
"For ever with the Lord."

DOBBS

This memorial was the work of Edward Smyth (1749 – 1812) and was erected in 1780. At the top is a Bas Relief of Lieut. William Dobbs with below it a representation of the sea engagement in Belfast Lough. The inscription on the memorial was composed by Councillor Dunn.

NICHOLSON

This memorial by John Henry Foley R.A. (1818 – 1874), shows in relief the circumstances of Brigadier-General John Nicholson's death in Delhi. The three soldiers in the foreground are two fusilier guards and a member of the 75th Regiment. The dead include a Brahmin, a Hindoo, a Mussulman and a British Officer. To the left is a wounded private of the 75th who has struck down a Sepoy. Victory is represented by the British flag planted in the wall. The church in the background is the English church of St. Paul.

[marble, with angel, carved portrait and naval scene]

This Marble is sacred to the Memory
Of **Lieutenant William Dobbs**,
A Naval Officer
Who terminated his Career of Virtue,
By an illustrious Display of Valour
On board one of His Majestie's Sloops of War;
Where endeavouring to snatch Victory from Fortune,
In Opposition to superior Force,
He fell a self-devoted Victim to his Country.
His Body rests in that Element,
On which Great Britain has long rode triumphant,
By the Exertions of Men like Him.
His afflicted Townsmen,
By strewing Laurels over this empty Monument,
Derive Honour to themselves:
They can add nothing to his Fame.
---ooo---
He was born at Lisburn on the 22nd day of September, 1746, and died
of his Wounds on board the Drake the 26th of
April, 1778.

[white marble, with engraved scene of the Siege of Delhi. Sculptor J.H . Foley R.A. London 1862]

The Grave of **Brigadier-General John Nicholson, C.B.**, is beneath the fortress which he died to take.
This monument is erected by his Mother, to keep alive his memory and example among his countrymen.

Comrades who loved and mourn him add the story of his life.
He entered the army of the H.E.I.C. in 1839, and served in four great wars – Afghanistan, 1841-42;
Sutlej, 1845-46; Punjab, 1848-49; India, 1857.
In the first he was an Ensign; in the last a Brigadier-general and Companion of the Bath. In all, a Hero.
Rare gifts had marked him for great things in peace and war. He had an iron mind and frame, a terrible
courage, an indomitable will.
His form seemed made for an army to behold, his heart, to meet the crisis of an empire. Yet was he gentle
exceedingly; most loving; most kind.
In all he thought and did, unselfish, earnest, plain, and true. Indeed, a most noble man!
In public affairs he was the pupil of the great and good Sir Henry Lawrence; and worthy of his master.
Few took a greater share in either the conquest or government of the Punjab. Perhaps none so great in both.
Soldier and civilian, he was a tower of strength; the type of the conquering race.
Most fitly, in the great siege of Delhi, he led the first column of attack and carried the main breach;
Dealing the death-blow to the greatest danger that ever threatened British India.
Most mournfully, most glorious, in the moment of victory, he fell mortally wounded on the 14th and died on the
23rd of September, 1857, aged only 34.

{Recorded in M.D. Vol. XII-XIII 1926-31.}

[marble, with carved crest]

Malo Mori Quam Foedari

In ever loving memory
of
Colonel Theophilus Higginson,
Companion of the Bath,
Fourth son of H.T. Higginson, M.A., J.P.,
of Lisburn, Co. Antrim, and Carnalea House,
Co. Down, who died at Farnham, Surrey,
30th August 1903,
aged 64.
The gift of God is Eternal life through
Jesus Christ our Lord.

[marble, with carved crest]

Et vi et virtvte

Sacred
to
the Memory of
Thomas Robert Stannus, B.A., J.P.,
of Maghraleave, Lisburn,
Eldest son of The Late Very Reverend James Stannus,
Dean of Ross and Rector of Lisburn.
Born 21st September 1818,
Died 8th November 1907.
---ooo---
"The Memory of the Just is Blessed."

[brass diamond plaque, with crest, now on the wall, but originally on the floor of the old chancel]

Lisi Dominus Frustra

Beneath this place is buried
Sir George Rawdon, Bart., 1684,
who defeated the Rebels at Lisburn
in the Great Rebellion, 1641.
Also buried here is his son,
Sir Arthur Rawdon.
1695.

CHANCEL – NORTH

[marble, with ornate carved sarophagus]

Non magnus   sep vivimus

Not to perpetuate the memory of one
Whose works will be his most enduring memorial,
But that there may not be wanting
A publick testimony to his memory in the diocese
Which derives honour from his superintendence,
This tablet is inscribed with the name
of **JEREMY TAYLOR,, D.D.**,
Who on the restoration in MDCLX
Of the British Church and Monarchy
In the fall of which he had partaken,
Having been promoted to the Bishoprick
of DOWN & CONNOR.
And having presided for seven years in that see,
As also over the adjoining diocese of DROMORE,
Which was soon after intrusted to his care,
"On account of his virtue, wisdom, and industry;"
Died at LISBURN, Aug (XIIIth). 13 MDCLXVI.,
In the 55th (LVth) year of his age:
Leaving behind him a renown,
Second to that of none of the illustrious sons
Whom the Anglican church
Rich in worthies, hath brought forth;
As a Bishop, distinguished
For munificence & vigilance truly Episcopal;
As a theologian, for piety the most ardent,
Learning the most extensive & eloquence inimitable:
In his writings, a persuasive guide,
To earnestness of devotion, uprightness of practice,
And Christian forbearance & toleration:
A powerful assertor of episcopal government,
And liturgical worship,
And an able exposer of the errors of the Romish Church;
In his manners, a pattern of his own rules
Of holy living & holy dying,
And a follower of the GREAT EXEMPLAR of sanctity,
As portrayed by him in the person
Of our LORD and SAVIOUR JESUS CHRIST.
---ooo---
Reader, though it fall not to thy lot
To attain the intellectual excellence
Of this Master in Israel,
Thou mayest rival him in that,
Which was the highest scope even of his ambition.
An honest conscience & a Christian life.
---ooo---
This tablet
was inscribed by the Bishop & Clergy
of Down & Connor in the year of our Lord 1827

{Erected by Bishop Richard Mant.}

CHANCEL - NORTH

[bronze tablet]

Thomas Ross, O.B. 1756, Aet 74.
Wife; three sons; three daughters.
Edward Ross, O.B. 1768, Aet 46.
Mary Ross, O.B. 1765, Aet. 36.
Elinor, wife of Snowden Cupples,
D.D., Rector Lisburn, Vicar General
Down and Connor, O.B. 1828, Aet. 67.
Elinor Cupples, O.B. 1803, Aet. 3.
Charles Cupples, M.D.R.A., O.B. 1848, Aet. 57.
Rest beneath this Chancel.
1889

[brass plaque]

In memory
of
John Sinclair Taylor
Rector of this Parish 1924 – 1950
Treasurer of Connor

[brass plaque]

In memory
of
Stephen Parnell Kerr
Rector of this Parish 1950 – 1959
Precentor of Connor

[brass plaque]

To the Glory of God, and to Commemorate
the 60 years faithful Ministry in the diocese, of
THE REV[D.] WILLIAM DAWSON POUNDEN, B.A.,
Rector of Lisburn, and Treasurer of Connor.
This brass has been placed here by
The Primate of All Ireland, and The Bishop of the Diocese
and His Brother Clergy,
in whole-hearted Affection and Admiration,
for a brother greatly beloved in the Lord,
September 1915.
---ooo---
Lord I have loved the habitation of Thy House.

CHANCEL - NORTH

[*brass plaque*]

To the Glory of God
and in ever loving memory of
Rev. Edward P. Riddall, M.A.,
For 10 years
Honorary Curate Assistant of this Parish.
He died 30th June 1922.
Erected by the Parishioners
as a mark of their affection and esteem.
"A servant of Jesus Christ."
Rom. 1., 1

REREDOS

[*small, brass plaque*]

To the Glory of God
and in loving memory of
Walter Charter Boomer, M.C.,
Captain 12th Batt. R.I.R.,
Ulster Division,
who died of wounds
on the 2nd October, 1918.
Aged 27 years.
Buried in
Molenhoek Military Cemetery,
Becelaere, Belgium.
---ooo---
[*separate brass plaque*]

Re-Interred Dadizeele,
New British Cemetery,
August, 1920.

CHANCEL - SOUTH

[brass plaque]

Pro Patria

Lisburn   Cathedral

ROLL OF HONOUR
To the Glory of God and in Grateful
Memory of the Men from this Parish who
gave their Lives in the World War, 1939 – 45.
These Chapter Stalls were erected by
the congregation.

Rank	Name	Unit
Pte.	David Smith	R.A.S.C.
Flt. Lieut.	Harry Connolly	R.A.F.
Sgt.	William H. Waring	R.A.F.
Sgt./Major	William J. Mulholland	R. Inn. F.
2nd Lieut.	Arthur B. Bradshaw	R.Sig.
Pte.	Samuel Topping	R.U.R
Sgt.	James McGeown	R. Inn. F.
Sgt.	Robert Willis	R.A.F.
W/O	Ian R.H. Iago	R.A.F.
Pte.	John Troy	K.O.S.B.
Sgt.	John J. Caves	R.A.F.
L/Cpl.	R. Henry Haire	R.A.F.
Cpl.	Norman Jefferson	R.U.R.
Cpl.	William Jefferson	R.U.R.
Steward	Moses Hall	M.N.
C. Steward	Robert Elkin	M.N.
Gnr.	James Roy	R.A.

Faithful unto Death

MEMORIAL
HODSON

CHANCEL - SOUTH

[marble, with carved surround, formerly with sarcophagus and bust of Dubourdieu]

Lector
Cenotaphium spectas **Reverendi viri Saumarez Dubourdieu A.M.** Ecclesiae
Gallicae Reformatae in hoc municipis positae ministry eccleslae Glenevensis
Vicarii et scholae Lisburnensis per sex et quinquacinta annos praefecti
Vir comis simplex pius candidus integer.
Qui gallica stirpe ortus sed exul patriae
sibi nomen et locum et novam patriam
apud exteros
virtutibus meruit
nullis mundi illecebris distractus
juventutem bonis litteris
gregem puros fidei praeceptis
omnes exemplo vitae bene actae
instruxit et ornavit
E charissima conjuge quatuor liberos natos
tali patre dignos
Reliquit
obiit XIX calend Januarii (sic)
Anno Salutis MDCCCXII
Ex actis jam annis XCVI mensibus III
Discipuli bene merentis haud immemores
Hocce P.P.

Jn° Smyth D.

[translation by Rev. Carmody]

Reader,
This monument is erected to the memory of the
Rev. Saumarez Dubourdieu, A.M. Minister of
The French Protestant Church in this town,
Vicar of the Parish of Glenavy, and fifty-six
years master of the Classical School of Lisburn.
In manners he was courteous, and unaffected.
In conduct pious, candid, and of strict integrity.
Descended from French parentage
who had been forced from the land of their nativity
by religious persecution,
he merited and obtained for himself
a name, a habitation, and a country among strangers
unwarped by worldly allurements,
he instructed the youth committed to his care,
in learning, useful and ornamental;
in the pure principals of the Christian Faith;
and all who were witness of his conduct,
by the bright example of a life well spent.
By a wife deservedly dear to him,
he left four children,
worthy of such a parent.
Departed this life the 14th December (sic) 1812
aged ninety-six years and three months.
His scholars
in grateful remembrance of his virtues,
have caused this marble
to be erected.

NAVE – SOUTH

[marble]

In loving memory of
Charles Curtis Craig
Born 1869 Died 1960
Privy Councillor for Ireland
Deputy Lieutenant for C° Down
Member of Parliament at Westminister
South Antrim 1903 – 1922
Antrim 1922 – 1929
and his beloved wife
Lilian Bowring Craig
Born 1875 Died 1954.

[marble]

In loving memory of
Lieutenant Commander
Lisburn Curtis Craig R.N.,
Elder son of
Captain the R^t Hon. Charles Curtis Craig
Formerly M.P. for C° Antrim
who with 35 of his comrades gave his life
for his country when H.M.S. Venetia
of which he was in command was sunk by
a mine in the Thames Estuary on
19th October 1940.

[white marble, with carved regimental symbols]

Pro Rece et Patria

In Loving Memory of
Major Thomas Roger Johnson Smyth,
of the 68th Regt. Durham Light Infantry, age 42.
Who was killed while gallantly leading
his men at the action of Vaal Kranz,
Natal, South Africa, on the 5th Feb. 1900.
"They that sleep in Jesus will God bring with Him."

[white marble]

Erected by Margaret A. Ozelton
To the sacred memory of her devoted friend
Everina Eliz. Adams Johnson Smyth
Died 20th April 1970
And her brother
Roger Henry Ellis Johnson Smyth
Died 7th February 1969
Son and daughter of the above.
{i.e. of Major Thomas Roger Johnson Smyth.}

NAVE - SOUTH

[brass plaque, in wooden surround]

HUGH McCALL
1805-1897

One who was given to Philanthropy,
Justice and Truth.
A Journalist without fear.
An Accurate Historian,
A Painstaking Chronicler.
---ooo---
This Tablet
Is Placed Where He Worshipped
To His Remembrance By His Friends.
---ooo---
This, above all, to thine own self be true,
And it must follow, as the night the day,
thou canst not then be false to any man.

*{Buried in Kilrush Burying Ground. For more information on the **McCall** family see "These Hallowed Grounds" Volume 1, Kilrush No. 77 and page 159.}*

[marble, with carved crest]

Malo Mori Quam Foedari
Erected
in memory of **Henry T. Higginson, Esq.,**
A.M., T.C.D., and J.P. for Counties of Antrim
and Down, formerly of this Parish, and for
50 years Registrar of the Diocese of Down
and Connor, who died at Carnalea House,
County Down, 20th June 1869, aged 71 years.
And
of His Wife, **Charlotte,** who died at Carnalea
House, 15th June 1875, aged 75 years.
And
of their children, **Thomas E. Higginson**, Lieut.
39th Regiment Bengal Infantry, who died in
India, 20th January 1850, aged 22 years.
Charles H. Higginson C.E., who died
at Trenton, U.S. America, 7th April 1869,
Aged 39 years.

J. Thompson,
sculptor,
Lisburn.

[marble, with carving]

Erected by Personal Friends, to the Memory of
Thomas Johnson Smyth, R.N.,
Lieutenant of Her Majesty's Frigate Juno, who
lost his life, in an heroic attempt to save
the lives of a boat's crew, upset in the surf
off the coast of California, 16th May, 1846,
aged 29 years.
He was an honour to the service, esteemed by
his Captain and beloved by his
shipmates & friends.

Johnston, Belfast

[marble]

To the Glory of God
and in ever affectionate remembrance of
Elizabeth Ann Johnson Smyth.
Born 9th March 1833. Died 27th February 1923,
youngest daughter of
the Rev[d] John Corken, of Ingram,
and Vicar of Aghalee in the County Antrim.
Widow of Matthew Johnson Smyth, of Lisburn
who died 23rd September 1865

Holy, Holy, Holy, Lord God Almighty

MEMORIAL
JOHNSON SMYTH

VESTIBULE

[*marble*]

Sacred
to the memory of
Edward Smyth Mercer,
Lieutenant 94th Regiment,
who died at Umballa, East Indies,
on the 25th April 1867,
aged 23 years.
---ooo---
Erected by his brother officers,
in token of their esteem

[*marble*]

Sacred to the Memory
of
Annie, born August 6th 1851, died April 26th 1852
John William Lake, born July 25th 1854, died August 10th 1854.
The infant children of John Henry Mercer, Esq., Captain Royal Marines, and Annie his wife.
The daughter of William Lake, Esq., of "Woodstreet House," near Sittingbourne, Kent.

S.M. also of **Elizabeth Frances**, the infant daughter of Capt. Arthur Hill Hasted Mercer
and **Elizabeth Ann**, his wife, daughter of Major R. H. Ord, K. H., Deputy-Lieutenant for the County of Essex,
who died June 5th 1849.
S.M. also of **Captain Henry Mercer**, second son of Colonel Edward Smyth Mercer, R.M., late Commandant
of the Plymouth division, who died July 22nd 1855, leaving a wife and daughter to lament his loss.

Sacred to the memory also of **Captain Henry Mercer**, Royal Artillery,
youngest son of Colonel Edward Smyth Mercer
who fell in action
at Rangiriri, New Zealand,
on the 20th Nov. 1863, while leading in forlorn hope his escort of Artillerymen
to retrieve the losses of that disastrous day.
Aged 38 years
---ooo---
"I deeply deplore, in common with all under my command, the loss the service has sustained in the
death of Captain Mercer, Commanding Royal Artillery in this colony, who died from the effects
of the wound he received whilst gallantly leading his men to the assault on the Redoubt. I regard
it as a serious misfortune that the force should be deprived at such a moment of the services
of so able and energetic an officer."
Extract from Despatch dated camp Rangiriri Nov. 26th 1863, of Major General Sir Duncan Cameron
K.C.B.
To the Right Honourable the Secretary of State for War.

VESTIBULE

[marble, with engraved surround]

DIED IN THE FIRST WORLD WAR
Pro Patri
To the Glory of God
And in grateful memory of the men
From this parish who fell in the
Great War 1914 - 1918

W. Atkinson	A. & S.H.	B. Lyness	R.I.RFL[S]
W.C. Boomer, M.C.	R.I.R.	A. McBride	R.I.RFL[S]
D. Boyd	R.I.R.	R. McBride	R.I.RFL[S]
G.R. Bell	I.G.	R. McBride	R.I.RFL[S]
A. Cairns	C.E.F.	F. McKibben	R.I.RFL[S]
C.J. Caldwell	I.G.	J. McDowell	R.I.RFL[S]
R.J. Clarke	C.E.F.	J.E. Martin	R.I.RFL[S]
A. Clarke	R.I.R.	A. Moore	R.I.RFL[S]
H. Corkin	R.I.R.	J. Mulligan	R.I.RFL[S]
J. Corkin	R.I.R.	J. Murphy	R.I.RFL[S]
R.J. Corken	M.G.C.	S. Patterson	R.I.RFL[S]
J. Corry	R.I.R.	R. Porter	R.I.RFL[S]
A. Cowan	R.I.R.	R. Sally	R.I.RFL[S]
J. Fenton	R.I.R.	G. Smith	R.I.RFL[S]
G.E. Flynn	R.I.R.	J. Tate	R.I.RFL[S]
A. Griffen	R.I.R.	G. Tate	R.I.RFL[S]
R. Heron	R.I.R.	W. Thompson	R.I.RFL[S]
W.H. Hughes	R.I.R.	S. Topping	R.I.RFL[S]
G.H. Hull	R.I.R.	G.F. Walker	R.I.RFL[S]
H. Harvey	R.I.R.	W. Walsh	R.I.RFL[S]
F.C. King	M.G.C.	T. Walsh	RI.RFL[S]
G. Laird	R.I.R.	D. Walsh	R.I.RFL[S]
W. Leathem	R.I.R.	A. Welch	R.I.RFL[S]
H. Lovie	E. Lanc[s].	J. Wilson	R.F.Art[y].
D. O'Hara	R.I.F.		

MEMORIAL   **JENKINS**

121

VESTIBULE

[wooden plaque]

Pro Patria

The following
in addition to those who fell
Volunteered for service 1914 – 18

W. Allen	R.I.R.		S. Dalzell	R.I.R.
S. Allen	R.I.R.		A. Dowling	R.I.R.
G. Allen	R.I.R.		R. Dowling	R.I.R.
F.E. Ashe	R.I.R.		A. Dowling	R.I.R.
M. Atkinson	R.I.R.		F. Dowling	C.R.
T.J. Atkinson	R.I.R.		J. Downey	K.L.
D. Allen	I.G.		W. Dodds	L.C.
T.J. Allen	R.N.		J.S. English	R.A.M.C.
J. Allen	Inn. D.		W. Elliott	R.I.F.
S. Alister	T. C.		H. Elkin	R.I.R.
A. Alderdice	N.I.H.		A. Fryer	K.R.
T. Andrews	R.I.F.		J. Frazer	R.N.R.
G.W. Bannister	R.N.A.S.		J. Fulton	R.I.R.
R.G. Beattie	R.I.R.		J. Gallaher	R.I.R.
R. Beattie	R.I.R.		J.R.A. Gell	R.I.R.
R. Bell	R.I.R.		J. Gilliland	R.I.R.
W.J. Bingham	R.I.R.		T. Gilmour M.M.	R.I.R.
I. Brown	R.I.R.		R. Graham	R.I.R.
S. Brown	R.I.R.		J. Gilmour	R.Inn.F.
W. Bratty	R.I.R.		S. Graham	R.E.
W. Bell	R.I.F.		W. Griffin	R.E.
F. Boyle	R.A.F.		H. Greenfield	R.G.A.
J. Burke	R.Inn.F.		J. Gilmour	C.E.
R. Booth	R.E.		J. Gilmour	C.A.
W. Calvert	R.I.R.		J. Hamilton	R.C.A.
G. Clarke	R.I.R.		W. Harvey	R.A.S.C.
J. Clarke M.M.	R.I.R.		H. Hawthorn	R.I.R.
C. Clarke	R.I.R.		W.J. Heron	R.I.R.
W. Corkin	R.I.R.		W. Higginson	R.I.R.
R. Crone	R.I.R.		D. Hasley	S.L.
J. Crone	R.I.R.		T. Higginson	R.E.
R. Cairns SR	L.C.		J. Higginson	R.E.
R. Cairns JN	R.I.F.		V. Hunter	R.E.
J.A. Cooke	R.I.F.		W.T. Hughes	R.N.R.
W.J. Clarke	L.S.		W. Hall	S.L.I.
S. Coulter	R.Inn.F.		J.P. Henderson	C.E.F.
A. Crone	S.F.		W. Jefferson	R.I.R.
J. Coard	I.G.		W.D. Johnston	R.I.R.
R. Cargo	R.E.		W. Jones	N.I.H.
J.K. Crawford	N.Z.E.F.		J. Johnston	C.E.F
W.J. Dalzell	R.I.R.		W. Keery	R.I.R.

J. Kidd	R.I.R.	R. Nash	A.S.C.
R. Kidd	R.I.R.	J.D. Neill	R.A.S.C.
S. Kidd	R.I.F.	G. Patterson	R.I.R.
W. Kidd	R.Inn.F.	W.E. Peel	R.I.R.
J.. Kerr	R.F.A.	W. Reid	R.I.R.
I. Kerr	R.A.F.	J.E. Reid	R.I.R.
G. King	T.C.	T. Roy	R.I.R.
A. Kidd	L.C.	W.H. Rainey	R.A.F.
J. Leckey	R.I.R.	F. Rice	R.F.
Jas. Lovie	R.I.R.	N. Russell M.C.	R.I.F.
John Lovie	R.I.R.	J. Shields	R.I.R.
G. Lyness, SR	R.I.R.	W. Shields	R.I.R.
G. Lyness, JN	R.I.R.	J. Stevenson	R.I.R.
J. Lyness	R.I.R.	D. Stewart	R.I.F.
T. Lyness	R.I.R.	R. Stevenson	R.E.
J. Lannigan	C.E.F.	H. Smyth	M.C.C.
J. Matier	R.I.R.	W. Sloan	E.L.
R. Matier	R.I.R.	J. Shields	C.E.F.
T. Megran	R.I.R.	R. Tacy	R.I.R.
J. Mearns M.C.	R.I.R.	J. Thompson	R.I.R.
J. Megran	D.C.L.I.	H.J. Thompson	R.I.R.
T. Mulligan	A.S.C.	R. Thompson	R.I.R.
T. Megarry	R.E.	S. Walsh	R.I.R.
J. McNeice	R.I.R.	A. Watson	R.I.R.
T. McKinley	R.I.R.	T. Wilson	R.I.R.
W. McCartney	M.R.	W. Wilson	R.A.S.C.
J. McCormack	R.Inn.F.	W. Welch	R.A.S.C.
E. McKibben	R.M.	A.E. Welch	R.A.M.C.
W. Nash	R.N.	P. Wilson	M.G.C.
T. Nash	R.I.R.	W.F. Wilson M.C.	M.G.C.
J. Norwood	R.I.R.	G. Wilson	R.E.
F. Norwood	R.I.R.	J.A. Woods	R.A.F.
J. Norwood	R.A.F.	R.H. Haire	R.A.F.
S. Poots	R.I.R.		

SACRED
TO THE MEMORY OF
WILLIAM HOGG, ESQ.,
WHO DEPARTED THIS LIFE 25TH JULY 1824,
AGED 70 YEARS.
AND OF MARY, HIS WIFE
WHO DEPARTED THIS LIFE 28TH FEBY 1856,
AGED 92 YEARS.
THEIR REMAINS ARE INTERRED NEAR THIS SPOT
THIS TABLET WAS ERECTED BY THEIR SON
SIR JAMES WEIR HOGG, BART M.P.

MEMORIAL   **HOGG**

[marble, carved surround]

Sacred
to the
Memory
of
Major Robert Bell Fulton,
of the Bengal Artillery,
who died at Futteyghur, in Hindoostan, on the 11th
May, 1836, aged 47 years.
As a soldier, keenly alive to the honour of his profession,
he filled several high and responsible staff appointments
with acknowledged zeal, talent and integrity. As a friend
he was generous, affectionate, and constant; as a
Christian, humble, devout, and sincere.
To record, in his native town, the high character he
established in that distant land.
THIS CENOTAPH
Is inscribed by his
Brother Officers and Friends
who have also erected a suitable monument
over his grave in the
FORT OF FUTTEYGHUR

Hugh Ferguson

[engraved marble, depicting the Good Samaritan]

Go thou and do likewise.

Erected
to the memory of
Rowley F. Hall, Esq[r].,
Attorney at Law.
By personal friends in Lisburn,
in testimony of their affection and of his worth
in the discharge of the laborious duties
of his profession,
he was more studious to prevent litigation,
than to derive emolument.
He exemplified the conduct of the Good Samaritan,
in visiting and relieving the sick and afflicted,
in seasons of epidemic and infectious disease.
He was indefatigable in promoting
the education of the poor,
and the charitable institutions of this parish.
Of the practice of religion and virtue,
the uniform tenor of his life
afforded a bright example.
Died September 22nd, 1826,
in the 39th year of his age.

{*Rowley Hall was law agent to the Marquis of Hertford. In 1822 he presented the bell for the cupola*
of the Lisburn Male Free School.}

[marble, originally in the vestibule, but now lying against the wall]

S.M. **John Mercer, Esq**., from Scotland		
	died about	A.D., 1636
S.M. **Captain John**, son of the above, died		A.D., 1650
S.M. **John**, of Castle Robin, Derryaghy,		
	son of the above, died	A.D., 1726
S.M. **John Mercer, Esqr**., of Hillhall Court,		
	son of the above, died	A.D., 1731
S.M. **John**, son of the above, also of		
	Hillhall Court, died	A.D., 1814
S.M. **Samuel,** eldest son of the above, died		A.D., 1839
S.M. **John**, 3rd son of the above, died		A.D., 1843
S.M. **Waring**, 5th son of the above, died		A.D., 1810

also

Edward Smyth Mercer, Esq., youngest son of the above, Died Decr., 24th, 1847. He entered the Royal Marines 1797, and for upwards of half-a-century, and during the wars of that period, served his King and country with zeal, gallantry and honour. He died while Colonel Commandant of the Plymouth Division. His parting advice to his four sons, also engaged in the service of their country, was to live honourable, as soldiers, united as brothers, and sincere as Christians. His last days were those of the Christian soldier, and his best epitaph is engraved on the sorrowing hearts of his widow and his Children.

Arthur Hill, 2nd son of the above, died A.D., 1848, aged 86.

Henry Beauchamp, fourth son of the above, who died May 26th, 1852.

S.M., also of **Nelly**, the lovely, amiable and affectionate wife of Edward Smyth Mercer, Esquire, Captain H.M. 34th Regiment, and daughter of **Thomas Turner**, Esquire, of Arcot and Palmanair, in the East Indies, who died June the 1st, 1852, aged 26 years.

Also three of her children,

Edward Smyth, Arthur Hill Hastedd, Henry Beauchamp,

Who died in infancy.

GO THOU AND DO LIKEWISE

MEMORIAL   **HALL**

GALLERY – SOUTH

[marble, with carved surround]

Sacred
to the memory of the
Rev. Ralph Bridge, A.B.,
Curate of Lisburn.
Ob 15 Jan. 1838, AE 31
From Typhus Fever
contracted in the performance
of his duties.

"The Friend, the son, the Christian, the Divine;"
"Let those who knew him, those who loved him, speak."

Thus speaks the Rector
and certain of the parishioners
"Who knew him and loved him."
And
who have caused this tablet
To be erected.
1838.

[marble, with ornate carving, three cherubs carved at the bottom]

Well done thou good & faithful servant
Enter thou into the Ioy of thy Lord

Near this stone is deposited the body
of **Mrs. Alice Smyth**,
Daughter of Cap^n. Brent Smyth, of Dublin,
Who died in the 45th year of her age.
To the world a loss, to herself an infinite Gain;
A superior understanding,
And a most sweet & generous Temper.
Always imployed in the Practise of Religion
Both to God & Man,
And improved by the purest influences of it,
Made her such an amiable pattern of Virtue
As we never knew to be excelled.
Such was her whole Life
And her Death was equall (sic) to it.
Go Reader & do thou likewise
That thy Soul may be happy with her's,
When like her's thy Body shall moulder in the Grave
And this World be nothing to thee.
Her only Sister & her Husband,
In return for numberless Favours
And that so much Virtue may not be forgotten,
Have with the deepest sorrow for her Death
Erected this Monument to her Memory,
Well knowing the mean while that it is more criminal
To Write & Publish then (sic) to speak a Lie.
She was born February the 13th, 1706 Died May 31 1751.

GALLERY - SOUTH

[marble, with carved surround]

Sacred to the memory of the **Rev. A. Rogers**,
many years rector of this Parish, who died on 15th Jan^{ry}. 1741.
His remains are deposited in a Vault which his Parishioners caused to be
made under the Chancel from respect to the Memory of so excellent a Pastor.
Also to the memory of **Anne Rogers**, otherwise Redmond, his Wife,
who died 28th Septr. 1751.
Also to that of their children. **Conway Rogers**, who died 26th Novr. 1737.
Henrietta Anne Rogers.
Margaret Alice Rogers.
William Rogers, who died 21st Septr. 1817.
Sacred also to the memory of **Anne Stewart**, otherwise Rogers, the
beloved Wife of Major William Stewart, of His Majesty's 30th Reg^t of Foot.
She was the eldest daughter of William Rogers, Esqr. of Lisburn,
and Granddaughter of the Revd. A. Rogers above named.
She departed this Life on the 8th Augt. 1824, in giving birth to her fifth child.
To those who knew her no Memorial is necessary to perpetuate the
Memory of her many and exalted Virtues.
Such was the gentleness of her Nature, the humility and benignity of her Mind,
that it may be truly said: "of such is the Kingdom of Heaven."
Her afflicted Husband and a beloved and only Sister
unite in erecting this Monument to her Memory.
Also to the Memory of **William Anthony Rogers Stewart**.
the only son of Major William Stewart and Anne his wife,
who died in Dublin on the 10th Sept^{t.} 1826, aged 3 years and 7 months.
"I will ransom them from the power of the Grave.
I will redeem them from Death."
Hosea 13 chap.1 4 v

[Not found in 2004, but recorded in Rev. Carmody's book.]

Perseverence
To the Glory of God,
Sacred to the memory of
Eleanor Frances Hawkshaw,
Daughter of the late Lieut-Col. John Stewart Hawkshaw,
31st (Huntingdonshire) Regt. And 91st (Argyllshire)
Highlanders,
Of Divernagh, Co. Armagh, and Blaris Lodge,
Co. Antrim.
She died in Dublin, Feb. 7 1907, in her 93rd year.
"Jesus Christ the same yesterday, to-day and for ever."

WINDOWS

NAVE - NORTH

Alexander Forbisson AM		1628
James Mace		1650
Joseph Wilkins	DD	1670
George Wilkins		1718
Anthony Rogers		1727
Richard Dobbs	DD	1740
Thomas Higginson		1775
William Traill	DD	1781
Snowden Cupples	DD	1796
James Stannus Dean of Ross		1835
Hartley Hodson	DD	1876

Erected to the Glory of God and in Memory of
The Rectors of the Parish from AD 1628
Whose names are written above.

NAVE - SOUTH

To the Glory of God and also to
Record the names of **Jeremy Taylor** 1660.
& his successors Bishops of Down
& Connor and who ministered in this Cathedral.

1667	**Roger Boyle**	1752	**Robt Downes**
1672	**Thomas Hacket**	1753	**Arthur Smyth**
1694	**Samuel Foley**	1765	**James Traill**
1695	**Edward Walkington**	1783	**William Dickson**
1699	**Edward Smith**	1804	**Nathan^l Alexander**
1720	**Francis Hutchinson**	1823	**Richard Mant**
1739	**Carew Reynell**	1849	**Robert Knox**
1743	**John Ryder**	1886	**William Reeves**
1752	**John Whitcombe**	1892	**Thos J. Welland**

CHANCEL - SOUTH

[*Wallace windows*]

Go and do thou Likewise

Erected to the Glory of God and in loving memory
of **Sir Richard Wallace** Bart KCB by his widow

(Mayer & Co Munich and London)

[*smaller window*]

RW
I was hungry and ye gave me meat
I was thirsty and ye gave me drink

CHANCEL - EAST

[*Barbour window*]

Heaven and Earth are full
Of the Majesty of thy Glory

To the adornment of this house of almighty God
And in grateful and fondest memory of the beloved wife **Eliza Barbour** born 8th March 1873 died 24th April
1910 and of the dear and only son **John Milne Barbour** born 20th August 1906 died 3rd July 1937
This window has been erected by the Right Hon. Sir John Milne Barbour Bart., D.L. of Hilden, Lisburn and Conway, Dunmurry.

CHANCEL

[*round the bottom of the wooden panelling in the Chancel*]

In memory of **Samuel Dornan** – Given by his wife.
In memory of **James and Ellen J. McNeice**, Given by their family.
In memory of **Richard John Hall**, and his sons Richard William John and Moses.
Given by his wife and family.

[*small wooden table (behind Communion table)*]

In memory of **Samuel H. Taggart**.

[*Communion table*]

In memory of those who lost their
Lives in the World War 1939 – 1945.
Given by the choir.

[*wooden prayer desk*]

To the Glory of God
In memory of the men
Of the parish who fell in
The Great War 1914 – 18
"They loved not their lives unto death".
Rev XII. XI

[*two prayer desks*]

In memory of **John Rush**.
Given by his wife.

[*reading stand*]

Given in loving memory of
Cecil R. Whitcroft
By his wife & family.
17 June 1990.

CHANCEL

[marble steps beneath the Communion table}

In memory of **Mrs. Charters**

NAVE

PEWS

In memory of **Louisa Malcomson Kelsey** by whose benefaction these pews were given. Dedicated by the Bishop of Connor. February 18th 1973.

GLASS CASE ON STAND

[brass plaque]

The case for the "Blow" Bible
was presented by Tom Murdock
and dedicated to the Glory of God
In loving memory of
his dear wife **Nancy**
who departed this life on 5th October 1974.

[handwritten on the fly leaf of the Bible]

This book – a copy of the
first Bible published in Belfast
was given to the Rev. Canon Taylor,
Rector of Lisburn, to be preserved
with the other local records, by
Thomas Sinclair, a Lisburn Citizen
July 15th 1927

{Bible printed by James Blow.
Bible has Jan[y] 1st 1808 written on it.}

IN EVER LOVING MEMORY
OF
COLONEL THEOPHILUS HIGGINSON,
COMPANION OF THE BATH,
FOURTH SON OF H. T. HIGGINSON, M.A. J.P.
OF LISBURN CO. ANTRIM, AND CARNALEA HOUSE
CO. DOWN, WHO DIED AT FARNHAM, SURREY,
30TH AUGUST 1903,
AGED 64.
The gift of God is Eternal life through
Jesus Christ our Lord.

MEMORIAL
HIGGINSON

GALLERY

ORGAN

[small brass plaque]

This organ was restored
By the gifts of parishioners
And an anonymous gift
In memory of
Isabel King M.B.E. J.P.
February 1973

[originally on the organ were the following two inscriptions]

Presented by the **Marquis of Hertford** through the very Revd. Dean Stannus.

Snowden Cupples, D.D., Rector
Thos. Thompson, Curate
Surgeon Thomas Wethered
George Emerson
C. Wardens 1832.

CASTLE STREET GATE

[plaque in the archway]

These gates were given
in memory of
Clara Cregan
and dedicated by
The Bishop of Connor
Easter Day 1963

THIS
VESTRY WAS BUILT
IN THE YEAR
1728
THE REVEREND
ANTHONY ROGERS
RECTOR
THOMAS CRAWFORD ESQ
WILLIAM SEED
CHURCH WARDS

VESTRY

BURIALS RECORDED AS BEING INSIDE LISBURN CATHEDRAL BUILDING

1684

- The R^t Honble Sr George Rawdon knight & Bar^{net} died ye 18th of Aug. 1684, between nine & ten in ye evening, & was interred the 28th day following, honourably & decently by his son, Sir Arthur Rawdon, in the chancell at Lisburn.

1695

- The body of the Right Rev^d. Father in God, Samuel, Lord Bishop of Down & Connor, was interred in the Quire of the Church of Lisburn, at the South end of the Communion table. May 23 1695. [*Bishop Samuel Foley*]
- Mr. Thomas Ward, late Dean of Connor buried at the entrance into the Chancel. July the 10th 1695.

1696

- Edward, son of ye Reverend Lord Bishop Walkington of Down & Connor in the quire on the north side – August y^e 22nd 1696.
- Henrietta da^u. of Captn. John Chichest^{er} deceas^d. Augst. 31 96 in ye quire.

1697

- Dr. Thom$^{s.}$ Hacket, late Bishop of Down & Connor, Augst 31st. Interr'd in the chancel part, the part of the grave under M^r. Conway's seat, next to the wall.
- Mrs Dorothy Dawson of Lisburn, November y^e 10th in the new ile below the uppermost pillars.

1698

- Ann da of Henry Kenly of Lisburn March y^e 27th in the new ile over against Mr **** ****.
- Lieutenant Thomas Conway lays at ye head of M^r. Francis Brooke stone in ye body of ye church. April ye 5th 1698. [*A kinsman of Lord Conway. His wife was a sister to Edward Harrison.*]
- M^{rs}. Dorothy Lovel buryed before M^r. Tandy's pew in the old Ile – Septemb^r. 24 1698.
- Mrs. Jane Edwards buried in the new ile against M^r. Lathom's seat – Octb^r 10 1698.
- Mrs. Mary Lindon buried at the south end of the Comunion (sic) table three foot and a half from the south wall of the Church Octob^r 12 1698.
- Elizabeth wife of Rev^d. M^r. Edwd. Goldsmyth buried in the new Ile below the middle pillar Novemb^r 6 1698.
- The Right Rev^d. Fath^r. In God Edwd. L^d B^p. of Down & Connor was interr'd on the north side of the Quire close by the wall. Jan. 10 1698. [*1698/9*] [*Bishop Edward Walkington*]

1699

- M^s. Jane Hilas buried near the pulpit staires Augst 1st 1699.
- Joseph son of M^r. Thomas Mildmay lies in y^e ally against the church dore on the south side. Aug. the 9$^{th?}$ 1699.

1700

- Edward Harrison Esqr. of Maghreleve, buryed in Lisburn Church, under the reading desk Octob^r. 13 1700. [*Jeremy Taylor's son-in-law. He left £10 to be distributed to the poor of Lisburn.*]
- Mary wife of Cristopher Barker lieth at James Martin's pew dore in the New Ile. January the 17th 1700. [*1700/1*]

1703

- Mrs. Mercy Tandy buried in the church of Lisburn close before the Castle seat Decemb^r. the 10th 1703.

1706

- Mr. George Lovel Rector of Lade buried July 4th 1706, under his wife's grave stone in the church of Lisburn. [*Aged 77 written in the margin.*]

1721

- Oct. 25 Arabella, d. of the Right Honble Francis Lord Conway buried under the Communion table.

1725

- Sept. 28th Captn Anthony Welsh buried under his seat near the ally going to ye pulpit.

SELECTED ENTRIES FROM THE BURIAL BOOKS 1661 – 1724

These entries have been chosen because of their relationship to other people mentioned in this book, or because of their age on death.

1661

- Edward ye son of Jeremy Lord B^{p}. of Downe, Conor & Dromore March 10th.

1663

- Moses ye son of Lieut. Coll. Moses Hill of ye parish of Drumboe July ye 22nd.

1675/6

- The hon^{bl} Lady Dority Rawden (sic) of Lisburn Feb. ye 25th.

1681

- Mrs. Mary ye wife of Mr. Joseph Wilkins of Lisb. Rector Nov. ye 30th.

1684

- Mr. Francis Brooks Chirurgion of Lisburn Novem^{b} y^{e} **.

1683

- Mr Michael Harrison of Dirr Sept ye 6th. [*Early Belfast trader and tanner.*]

1695

- Grace Holland widow of ye late Lord Bishops Thomas? November ye 11th.
- Francis son of Mr. Arthur Brooks of Lisburn July ye 31st 1695.
- Thomas Loe of English Town being as he himself said 132 years of age buried ye 16th of August. 1695.
- William Simson of Lisburn aged about 103 years Oct ye 8 1695.
- Mr Thom^{s} Haslam reader in the Church of Lisburn aged eighty-two years. Feb 12 1695. [*1695/6*]

1696

- Edward son of Mychal Read & grandson to Edward Obre Sept. 1696.

1698

- Jane Hart of Lisburn aged 106 – July the 16th 98.

1716

- The Rev Joseph Wilkins D.D. Dean of Clougher & Rector of this Parish buried May 22 1716.

1720

- Jane Cole buried Ap 11 1720. [*Aged 107 written in the margin.*]
- Eliz. Watson bury'd June 15 1720. [*Aged 102 written in the margin.*]

1724

- Dec. 9 The Honble. George Augustus Charles son of the Right Hon. The Lord Conway.

LISBURN CATHEDRAL DEATH NOTICES

Tuesday October 21 1873
ALLEN Oct. 19, at his residence, Bow Street, Lisburn, after a lingering illness, Mr. James Allen, aged 42 years.

Tuesday February 27 1912
ALLEN February 26th, at her residence, Wallace Avenue, Lisburn, Mary, widow of the late James Allen. Funeral to family burying-ground, Cathedral Churchyard, Lisburn, to-morrow (Wednesday) morning 28th inst. at eleven o'clock.

Friday June 22 – Tuesday June 26 1792
BARNSLEY Died at Lisburn on Saturday last, Mr. Barnsley, at the advanced age of 78 years; a gentleman who through life, supported a most unblemished character.

Tuesday April 24 1827
BARNSLEY On the 21st instant, at his house in Lisburn, Richard Barnsley, Esq.

Tuesday May 25 1847
BARNSLEY On the 20th inst. at his residence, 11 College-square, Belfast, Richard Barnsley, Esq., M.D. aged 30 years.

Wednesday April 3 1867
BARNSLEY April 1, at Shamrock Vale, near Lisburn, Sarah, relict of the late Richard Barnsley, Esq., of Lisburn.

Tuesday March 18 1834
BLACKBURN On the 13th instant, at her residence, near Ballyskeigh (sic), Mrs. Eleanor Blackburn, relict of the late John Blackburn. In her was exemplified every quality which adorns a pious christian, a tender parent, and a sincere friend; her decease will be long and deeply lamented by a large family of children, and a numerous circle of friends.

Friday June 19 1840
BLACKBURN On the 7th inst. at his residence, Laurel Hill, near Lisburn, Mr. Alexander Blackburn, aged 53 years, much and deservedly regretted by a numerous circle of friends.

Friday May 28 1841
BLACKBURN On the 20th inst. of consumption, in the 35th year of her age, at her father's residence, in this town, Catherine Blackburn, relict of the late Mr. Alex. Blackburn, of Laurel-hill, near Lisburn, much lamented by all who knew her.

Tuesday April 11 1843
BLACKBURN On the 2d inst. at his father's house, Ballymacash, near Lisburn, of a lingering consumption, Thomas, youngest son of Mr. Joseph Blackburn, aged 28 years.

Friday August 29 1851
BLACKBURN August 22, aged 72 years, Agnes, relict of Mr. Joseph Blackburn, of Ballymacash, near Lisburn.

Friday May 6 1853
BLACKBURN   At his residence, Ballymacash, near Lisburn, Mr. Joseph Blackburn, aged 75 years.

Saturday April 13 1872
BLACKBURN   April 12, at his residence, No. 27, Mill Street, Belfast, James Blackburn, aged 44 years. His remains will be removed for interment in Lisburn churchyard, on to-morrow (Sunday) afternoon, at three o'clock.

Thursday July 6 1876
BLACKBURN   July 4, Mr. Alexander Blackburn, Ballymacash, aged 57 years. His remains will be removed for interment in Lisburn Churchyard, this (Thursday) afternoon at three o'clock. Friends will please accept this intimation.

Friday May 23 1879
BLACKBURN   May 21, at Lissue, Lisburn, Adam Blackburn, aged 78 years. His remains will be removed for interment in Lisburn Churchyard, to-morrow (Saturday) morning, at ten o'clock. Friends will please accept this intimation.

Monday November 3 1879
BLACKBURN   November 2, at 55 Percy Street, Belfast, Robert Percy, infant son of R.T.I. Blackburn. His remains will be removed for interment in Lisburn Cathedral, to-morrow (Tuesday) morning, at ten o'clock.

Wednesday March 1 1882
BLACKBURN   February 28, at the residence of her brother, William Blackburn, Lissue, Ann, widow of the late James Blackburn, Belfast. Her remains will be removed for interment in the Cathedral Churchyard, Lisburn, to-morrow (Thursday) morning at eleven o'clock. Friends will please accept this intimation.

Monday September 21 1891
BLACKBURN   September 19, at his residence, Hillview Street, Belfast, Alexander Blackburn, formerly of Lisburn. The remains of my beloved husband will be removed from the above address, for interment in the family burying-ground Aghagallon, this (Monday) morning, at ten o'clock passing through Lisburn about half past eleven o'clock. Friends will please accept this intimation. Jane Anna Blackburn.

Tuesday January 5 1892
BLACKBURN   January 2, at his residence, Knockmore, Lisburn, Robert Blackburn, aged 87 years.

Tuesday January 31 1893
BLACKBURN   January 29, at 4, Twickenham Street, Isabella, youngest and dearly loved daughter of Robert Blackburn. Her remains will be removed for interment in Lisburn Cathedral Churchyard, to-morrow (Wednesday) morning at ten o'clock. Friends will please accept this (the only) intimation.

Monday November 15 1897
BLACKBURN   November 14, at his residence, No. 4 Twickenham Street, Belfast, Robert Blackburn, in his 76th year. His remains will be removed for interment in Lisburn Cathedral Churchyard, on Wednesday morning, 17th instant, at ten o'clock. Friends will please accept this intimation.

Wednesday May 9 1900
BLACKBURN   May 8th, at the residence of his brother-in-law (Mr Henry Monroe) Lissue, Lisburn. William Blackburn, aged 69 years. His remains will be removed from the above address for interment in the family burying-ground, Cathedral Churchyard, Lisburn, to-morrow (Thursday) morning at eleven o'clock.

Henry Monroe.

Monday June 28 1909
BLACKBURN   June 26th, at his residence, Ballymacoss, Lisburn, John, the dearly loved husband of Rebecca Blackburn. His remains will be removed from above address for interment in Lisburn Cathedral Churchyard, this (Monday) afternoon, at two o'clock. Friends will please accept this intimation.

Rebecca Blackburn.

Friday March 20 1863
BLACKBURNE (SIC)   March 19, at Lissue, near Lisburn, Mary, wife of Adam Blackburne (sic) aged 54 years.

Tuesday January 31 1837
BOYD   In Lisburn, on Thursday se'nnight, Mr. Hugh Boyd, tailor, in the 59th year of his age.

Friday November 11 1836
BOLTON   On the 2d inst. at Lisburn, E.H. Bolton, Esq. a gentleman, greatly esteemed and regretted.

Friday October 30 1846
BOLTON   On Thursday morning last, at the residence of her brother James Hogg, Esq., Castle-street, Lisburn, Abigail Bolton, aged 89, widow of the late John Bolton, formerly of Island, county Wexford. Her remains will be removed for interment on Saturday, October 31st, at half-past 3 o'clock, p.m.

Thursday April 5 1867
BOLTON   April 3, at Lisburn, James Bolton, Esq., Commander Royal Navy, aged 73 years. His remains will be removed for interment in the Cathedral Graveyard, Lisburn, on to-morrow (Saturday) afternoon at five o'clock.

Thursday October 10 1918
BOOMER   Oct. 1 killed in action, Captain Walter Charter Boomer, M.C. Royal Irish Rifles, only son of Mr. Richard W. Boomer, Knockmore House, Lisburn.

Friday July 7 1843
BRADY   On the 24th ult. at his residence, Lisburn, Mr. Oliver Brady, aged 42 years.

Friday January 5 1877
BREATHWAITE   January 4, at Longstone Street, Lisburn, William David, infant son of Mr. Thomas Breathwaite, aged 7 months. His remains will be removed for interment in the Cathedral Churchyard to-morrow afternoon, at three o'clock. Friends will please accept this intimation.

Friday January 19 1838
BRIDGE   On the 15th inst. at Lisburn, of typhus fever, caught in the discharge of his ministerial duties, the Rev. Ralph Bridge, Senior Curate of Lisburn, in the 32d year of his age – most sincerely and deeply regretted by all who had the pleasure of his acquaintance.

Friday September 28 1877

BRIGGS   September 26, at his residence, Knockmore, Lisburn, Mr. Ralph Briggs, aged 62 years. His remains will be removed for interment in the Cathedral Churchyard, Lisburn, this (Friday) afternoon, at half-past two o'clock. Friends will please accept this intimation.

Tuesday April 3 1877

BUCHANAN   April 2, of inflammation of the lungs, at Edenfel, Omagh, Eleanor Margaret, the beloved wife of Major L.M. Buchanan, and eldest surviving daughter of the late William Whitla, Esq., of Lisburn, deeply regretted. Funeral on Thursday morning, the 5th instant, at ten o'clock.

Tuesday April 24 1827

CALDBECK   At Lisburn, on the 21st inst., in the 14th year of her age, Dora, second daughter of William Caldbeck, Esq.

Tuesday April 14 1835

CALDBECK   At Lisburn, on Tuesday last, of scarletina, Elizabeth, youngest daughter of William Caldbeck, Esq. in the 9th year of her age.

Tuesday August 25 1840

CALDBECK   At Lisburn, on Saturday, the 1st of August inst., in the 21st year of his age, Joseph Caldbeck, Esq., Under-Sheriff of the County of Down, second son of Wm. Caldbeck, Esq. of Lisburn. He was a young man of the highest promise, and was universally and deservedly esteemed by all his friends and acquaintances.

Monday September 29 1858

CALDBECK   September 25, at his residence, De Vesci Terrace, Kingstown, Wm. Caldbeck, Esq., formerly Lisburn, in the County of Antrim.

Wednesday February 2 1870

CALDBECK   January 31, at Eaton Brae, County Dublin, Amy, relict of the late William Caldbeck, formerly of Lisburn, aged 83 years. The funeral will take place at Lisburn, on this (Wednesday) afternoon, at half-past twelve o'clock.

Friday July 23 1847

CAMPBELL   On Tuesday 20th inst. at the house of his brother, Surgeon Campbell, Lisburn, Mr. William Campbell, aged 27 years.

Saturday September 7 1867

CAMPBELL   September 6, at Lisburn, John Campbell, Esq., M.D., County Coroner and Medical Attendant of the Union Workhouse. His remains will be removed from his late residence, Market Square, for interment in Blaris Burial ground, on Monday afternoon next at four o'clock.

Monday January 19 1914

CAMPBELL   January 16, at Island House, Lisburn, Sarah, widow of the late John Campbell, M.D., Lisburn. Funeral private. No flowers.

Tuesday April 7 1818

CARLETON   At Lisburn, on the 29th ult., Cornelius Carleton, Esq. aged 69.

Friday September 24 1824

CARLETON   On the 9th inst., Mrs Carleton, widow of the late Cornelius Carleton Esq. of Lisburn.

Tuesday September 6 1825
CARLETON   At Donaghadee, on 26th ult., in the 43rd year of his age, John Carleton of Lisburn.

Monday January 23 1871
CARR   January 20, at Lisburn, Elizabeth Clarke, wife of T.P. Carr, Esq., R.I.C., eldest daughter of the late William Whitla, Esq., of Lisburn aged 33 Years.

Tuesday January 23 - Friday January 26 1781
CLOSE   Died, a few days ago, at Plantation, near Lisburn, Mr. William Close, of that place, a man of the most unblemished character – whose death is generally lamented, but most feelingly by the poor in his neighbourhood, to whom he was a constant and liberal benefactor.

Friday April 19 1799
CLOSE   On the 11th inst., Mrs Close, relict of the late Wm. Close, of Plantation, near Lisburn, aged 91 years.

Friday June 4 - Tuesday June 8 1790
COULSON   At Lisburn, the 3d inst., sincerely regretted by all her acquaintances, Mrs Ann Coulson, wife of Mr. William Coulson; she was an affectionate wife and tender mother.

Friday August 25 1815
COULSON   At Lisburn, on Tuesday morning, the 15th inst., after a few days illness, occasioned by a severe fall, the Rev. Hill Coulson, Curate of Ballinderry, formerly Curate of Lisburn. It is with unfeigned regret we are called on to record the death of the aimiable young man. Mild unassuming, and unaffected, he engaged the esteem of all who knew him, while his interesting simplicity of manners, his cheerful unobtrusive piety, and his unbounded benevolence commanded their admiration and respect. Ever feelingly alive to the distresses of his suffering fellow-creatures, his chief delight was to visit the lowly cottages to raise the drooping head of its humble inmate, and while he administered the balm of spiritual consolation, to alleviate as much as in his power the pressure of his temporal necessities. In him the poor have lost no *common* benefactor. He will not be soon forgotten- he will long live in the memories of the widow and the orphan.

Tuesday July 1 1834
COULSON   June 27, at 52 Bolton-street, Dublin, after a protracted illness, Anne Coulson, daughter of the late William Coulson, Esq. of Lisburn.

Wednesday August 20 1851
COULSON   On the 18th instant, at Lisburn, Mr. William Coulson. His remains will be removed from his residence, Market Square, for interment in the family burying-ground, Lisburn Church-yard, on Thursday (to-morrow) morning, the 21st instant, at 11 o'clock, forenoon.

Thursday August 9 1860
COULSON   August 7, at his residence, Springfield, Lisburn, Hill Coulson Esq., aged 31 years.

Thursday November 29 1866
COULSON   November 27, at Wilmont Terrace, Belfast, Eleanor, daughter of Mr. Wm. Coulson Esq., Lisburn, aged 27 years.

Monday September 1 1873
COULSON   Aug. 29, at 7, Wilmont Terrace, Belfast, Mrs. Coulson, aged 73 years.

Tuesday March 11 1755

CROMMELIN Last Sunday, died at Lisburn, Mrs. Ann Crommelin, Relict of Mr. Lewis Crommelin, Conductor of the Royal Linen Manufactory of this kingdom, and sister to General Crommelin, late Commander of Gertruydenburg in Holland. She died in the 97th year of her Age, lamented by all who knew her. She was a tender Parent and a faithful Friend; retained her senses perfect to the last and could read and write without spectacles a few Weeks before her Death.

Friday January 4 1805

CROMMELIN On Monday the 31st ult., at the Rev. Dr. Hutchinson's, Donaghadee, Delacherois Crommelin, Esq. in the 80th year of his age. – His mild and aimiable disposition was exerted during a long and useful life, which caused him to be deservedly esteemed and sincerely regretted.

Tuesday March 15 1816

CROSSLEY At his father's house, in Lisburn, on Sunday morning, in the 31st year of his age, Mr. John Crossley, Jun. — To describe the anguish of his Family and Friends at losing a beloved Relative, so warmly affectionate and disinterested in all his conduct would be of little importance to the Public at large, and we must leave to some other pen the task of doing justice to his general Usefulness and Worth.

Friday August 29 1828

CROSSLEY In child-bed, deeply lamented, Hingolee, East Indies, on the 1st of March, Jane Poynte (sic), wife of Major Francis Crossley, of the Hon. East India Company's service, and daughter of William Stewart, Esq. M.D., Lisburn.

Tuesday March 16 1830

CROSSLEY At his house, in Lisburn, on Thursday last, after a short illness, aged 84, Mr. John Crossley – a man of excellent understanding, high integrity, and kind and affectionate heart.

Friday April 27 1838

CROSSLEY On the 20th inst. at Lisburn, Mr. John Crossley, proprietor of the Hertford Arms Hotel, aged 30. His character was marked by much kindness of heart, and a disposition to oblige any of his friends, to a large circle of whom he had endeared himself by unaffected good nature.

Tuesday August 26 1828

CUPPLES At Lisburn, on the 17th inst. in the 67th year of her age, Ellenor, wife of the Rev. Snowden Cupples, D.D. Rector of that parish, and Vicar General of the Diocese of Down & Connor.

Tuesday December 3 1833

CUPPLES At Lisburn, on the 26th of November, in the 49th year of his age, William Cupples, Esq., eldest son of the Rev. Doctor Cupples, Vicar General of Down and Connor. He was a man of many virtues, - a dutiful son, an affectionate brother, and a kind steady friend. To the poor he was an unostentatious benefactor. At an early period of his life, he went out to the East Indies, in the Company's service, where his talents, and facility of acquiring the Asiatic languages placed him at the head of the Cadet Establishment in Bombay, in the management of which he was repeatedly honoured with the approbation and thanks of the local government. Being obliged to return to Europe, with a constitution impaired by the climate, and too intense application to his duties, he was appointed one of the Surveyors of the Irish Post Office, in which situation his urbanity of manners, and thorough knowledge of the business of his department, gave general satisfaction to the public. He died in the faith and hope of a Christian, and in charity with all men, trusting in the merits and mediation of his Redeemer.

Friday October 30 1835
CUPPLES   At Lisburn, on the 22d inst. the Rev. Snowden Cupples D.D. Rector of the parish of Lisburn, alias Blaris, and Vicar General of the united dioceses of Down and Connor, in the 82d year of his age.

Friday October 13 1848
CUPPLES   On the 6th inst. at Lisburn, Charles Cupples, Esq. M.D., Assistant-Surgeon, Royal Artillery, in his 58th year.

Friday November 11 1853
CUPPLES   November 6, at Ballyrashane Glebe, the Rev. Thomas Cupples, Rector of Ballyrashane, son of the late Rev. Snowden Cupples, D.D., Rector of Lisburn, and Vicar General of Down and Connor.

Tuesday November 24 1857
CUPPLES   November 22, at Lisburn, the Rev. Edward Cupples, L.L.B., late Vicar-General of the Diocese of Down and Connor.

Thursday September 30 1869
CUPPLES   September 28, at Lisburn, Frances Cupples, daughter of the late Rev. Snowden Cupples, D.D., Rector of Lisburn and Vicar General of Down and Connor, aged 65 years.

Tuesday June 6 - Friday June 9 1775
DE LA CHEROIS   Died on Monday last, at Donaghadee, Samuel De La Cherois Esq.

Friday December 22 1815
DE LA CHEROIS-CROMMELIN At Lisburn, Mrs De la Cherois Crommelin, in the 58th year of her age.

Friday September 13 1816
DE LA CHEROIS-CROMMELIN At Lisburn, aged 71, Samuel De la Cherois Crommelin, Esq.

Friday February 8 1828
DELACHEROIS   At Lisburn, on Saturday 2d inst. Charlotte, wife of Nicholas Delacherois, Esq.

Tuesday February 3 1829
DE LA CHEROIS   At Lisburn, on the 23d Jan. Nicholas De La Cherois, Esq., in his 92d year.

Monday March 7 - Friday March 11 1796
DILLON   Died, at Lisburn, on the 7th inst., Mr. Wm. Dillon. – A man whose humane and charitable disposition, endeared him to his friends and neighbours, by whom his death is sincerely regretted.

Tuesday November 25 1834
DILLON   At Lisburn, on Saturday last, after a lingering illness, Jane, wife of William Dillon, Esq. deservedly lamented by her numerous friends and acquaintances.

Tuesday December 12 1837
DILLON   At Lisburn, on the 24th ult. in the 65th year of his age, William Dillon Esq., Proctor of the Consistorial Court of Down and Connor. The numerous assembly that followed his remains to the grave testified how much he was respected in life, and how deeply his death is lamented.

Tuesday May 30 - Friday June 2 1775
DOBBS   Sunday last died at Lisburn, advanced in years, the Revd. Doctor Richard Dobbs, Rector of Lisburn.

Monday April 11 - Friday April 22 1796
DOBBS   Died, Mrs Dobbs, relict of the late Doctor Dobbs, of Lisburn.

Tuesday February 16 1802
DOBBS   At Carrickfergus, on the 4th instant, in the 62 year of his age, the Rev. Richard Dobbs, Dean of Connor. –He was promoted to the Deanery in 1776.

Monday January 20 1862
DRAKE   January 18, at Lisburn, Mr. Charles Drake, cattle-dealer, aged 43 years. His remains will be removed from his late residence, for interment in the burial-ground of Lisburn Cathedral, this (Monday) morning, at ten o'clock.

Friday December 18 1812
DUBOURDIEU   At Lisburn, on the 14th inst. in his 96th year, the Rev. Saumarez Dubourdieu, 56 years Minister of the French Church in that town. He was the last of the Huguenots of pure extraction; for though he was born in England, his Father and Mother were natives of France-from whence they went into exile, on the Revocation of the Edict of Nantes, in the latter end of the 17th century.

Thursday February 16 1871
FERGUSON   February 14, at Scotch Street, Downpatrick, Ellen, the beloved wife of Colour-Sergeant John Ferguson. Her remains will be removed from her late residence for interment in the family burying-ground, on this, (Thursday) afternoon, at one o'clock, arriving in Lisburn about 4-30 p.m. Friends will please accept this intimation.

Tuesday November 13 1866
FLYNN   November 11, Elizabeth Cecilia, wife of John Flynn, aged 46 years. Her remains will be removed for interment in the Cathedral Church-yard, Lisburn, on this (Tuesday) afternoon, at three o'clock.

Monday April 15 1895
FLYNN   April 13, at the residence of his son-in-law Hugh McCahey, 16, Bridge Street, Lisburn, John Flynn, aged 76 years. His remains will be removed for interment in the Lisburn Cathedral Burying-ground, this (Monday) afternoon, at three o'clock. No flowers.

Saturday April 15 1876
FORREST   April 14, at Castle Street, Lisburn, Nina, daughter of David and Mary Forrest, aged 8 years.

Friday December 16 - Tuesday December 20 1791
FULTON   At Lisburn on Thursday last, Miss Jane Fulton, her conduct through a tedious illness causes her to be regretted by those who knew her.

Friday February 1 1799
FULTON   On Thursday night last, Mrs Fulton, of Belfast, formerly of Lisburn. -Who in the relations of daughter, sister, wife, mother, neighbour and friend, was an honor and pattern to her sex.

Friday July 24 1812
FULTON   At Lisburn, on Tuesday evening last, Mrs Fulton, wife to Mr. Richard Fulton.

Tuesday June 24 1817
FULTON   In Lisburn, on Saturday morning, James Fulton jun., Esq., aged 25 years.

Tuesday April 8 1823
FULTON   Very suddenly, on Sunday morning, at his house in Castle-street, Lisburn, Joseph Fulton, Esq., aged 88 years.

Tuesday April 22 1823
FULTON   On the 9th instant, at Killinchy, in his 70th year, much and deservedly regretted, Mr. Richard Fulton of Lisburn, merchant.

Friday April 3 1829
FULTON   At Lisburn, on the 17th ult. John Fulton Esq., late Captain in the Hon. East India Company's service, and eldest son of the late James Fulton, Esq.

Tuesday February 2 1830
FULTON   At his house in Upper Harley-street, London, on Friday the 22d ult. aged 60, John Williamson Fulton, Esq. He was a man of great public spirit, as well as private worth; and a sincere lover of this country, Ireland, of which he was a native, having been born in Lisburn. He had resided for a considerable portion of his early life in Calcutta, where he was highly respected as an eminent merchant. During the latter years of his life he transferred his mercantile pursuits to London, having been connected there with a most extensive establishment. In these active avocations he never for a moment omitted to render his best services to his country and his kind, by actions of the most disinterested and devoted generosity. He was distinguished as the zealous friend of civil and religious liberty. His time, it may be said, was spent in seeking out occasions to benefit those who deserved and stood in need of his assistance; in truth, no person could be more entirely free from selfish considerations, and even under the lassitude of disease, he seemed to be invigorated by the performance of benevolent actions. His loss, therefore, is deeply lamented by the extensive circle of those who had the happiness of knowing his great value.

Tuesday June 1 1830
FULTON   At Holywood, on the 6th ult. Mr. Robert Fulton, eldest son of the late Richard Fulton, Esq. of Lisburn.

Tuesday February 19 1833
FULTON   On Tuesday last, Ann, relict of the late Joseph Fulton, Esq., of Lisburn.

Tuesday January 14 1834
FULTON   In Lisburn, on the 5th inst. Ann, relict of the late James Fulton Esq.

Friday September 11 1835
FULTON   In Belfast, on the 24th ult. Mrs. (sic) Eleanor Fulton, daughter of the late John Fulton Esq., of Lisburn, in the 82d year of her age.

Tuesday August 22 1843
FULTON   On the 24th of May, at Dorunah, in the East Indies, aged 27, Lieutenant Joseph Hennessey Fulton, 3d Bengal Native Infantry, son of the late John Williamson Fulton, Esq., of Upper Harley-street, London, and formerly of Lisburn, county of Antrim.

Tuesday June 30 1846
FULTON   At Lisburn, on the 28th instant, Mrs Fulton, widow of the late Lieut. Fulton, of the 6th, or Inniskillen Dragoons, in the 75th year of her age.

Tuesday March 26 1850
FULTON   March 17, at an advanced age, at Clarendon-place, Belfast, Isabella, relict of the late Mr. Andrew Fulton, of Lisburn.

Tuesday November 19 1872
FULTON   Nov. 17, suddenly at Braidujle House, Lisburn, John W. Fulton, Esq., J.P.

Saturday June 28 1879
FULTON   June 26, at The Cottage, Lisburn, Sophia Matilda, wife of William Fulton, District Registrar. Her remains will be removed from her late residence for interment in the Cathedral Burying-ground, this (Saturday) afternoon, at four o'clock. Friends will please accept this intimation.

Wednesday September 7 1881
FULTON   September 5, at The Cottage, Lisburn, William Fulton. His remains will be removed for interment at the Cathedral, Lisburn, to-morrow (Thursday), morning, at half past ten o'clock.

Friday December 3 1869
GARDNER   December 1, at her residence, Bridge Street, Lisburn, Phebe Gardner, wife of John Gardner, aged 71 years. Her remains will be removed for interment in Lisburn churchyard, on to-morrow (Saturday) morning, at ten o'clock. Friends will please accept this intimation.

Tuesday December 19 1820
GELSTON   On Friday morning last, after a short illness, in the 67th year of her age, Mrs Gelston, of Waring-street, formerly of Lisburn.

Friday February 15 1822
GELSTON   On Saturday night last, in the 40th year of his age, Mr. Henry Gelston, of Waring street, formerly of Lisburn.

Saturday February 13 1915
GELSTON   February 12, 1915, at the residence of her brother-in-law, Belvedere, Malone Road, Mary Gelston, younger daughter of the late Samuel Gelston, Belfast. Interment in family burying-ground, Lisburn Cathedral Churchyard. Funeral private.

Tuesday September 19 1826
GILBERT   On Friday last, at Costley's Bridge, near Lisburn, of fever, Mr. Thomas Gilbert, a young man highly esteemed, and, who, for industry, integrity, and strict moral conduct, will be held up as an example to the neighbourhood in which he lived.

Tuesday July 29 1842
GILBERT   On the 4th ult. at Ernestown, Upper Canada, of scarletina, Cornelius C. aged four years, on the 5th, Hannah, aged 12; and on the 9th, William, aged six years, the beloved children of Mr. C.C. Gilbert, formerly of Blaris, near Lisburn.

Friday September 7 1877
GILBERT   September 5, at Market Place, Lisburn, Robert Gilbert, late Quarter Master-Sergeant 61st Regiment, aged 85 years. His remains will be removed for interment in the Cathedral Yard, Lisburn, to-morrow (Saturday) morning, at ten o'clock. Friends will please accept this intimation.

Friday April 11 1884
GILBERT   April 9, at Mountpottinger, Belfast, Sarah, relict of the late John Gilbert, Blaris, aged 74 years.

Monday January 15 1866
GORDON January 13, at his residence, 13, Nile Street, Belfast, Mr. John Gordon.

Thursday July 27 1876
GORDON July 25, at his residence, Flush, near Lisburn, Mr. Nicholas Gordon, aged 85 years. His remains will be removed for interment in Lisburn Cathedral Burying-ground this (Thursday) afternoon at half-past four o'clock. Friends will please accept this intimation.

Saturday December 21 1889
GORDON December 20, at 20, Frederick Street, Belfast, Norris Gordon, aged 62. His remains will be removed for interment in the Cathedral Burying-Ground, Lisburn, to-morrow (Sunday) afternoon at 1 o'clock.

Monday February 19 1865
GRAHAM February 19, at Unicarville, Comber, Eliza, relict of the late Wm. Graham, Esq., of Lisburn.

Monday July 29 1889
GRAHAM July 27, at Lisburn, Wm. Graham, Esq., 62 years. His remains will be removed for interment in the family burying-ground, Drumbo to-morrow (Tuesday) morning at 10:45.

Thursday October 20 1892
GRAHAM October 19, at Unicarvel, Comber, County Down, Anne, daughter of the late William Graham, Esq., of Lisburn, aged 72.

Saturday April 29 1905
GRAHAM April 26, after a short illness, James, Colonel late Bengal Staff Corps of Stonehenge, Killiney, Co. Dublin and Cotswold, Wimbledon, son of the late William Graham, of Lisburn, County Antrim, Esq.

Tuesday April 8 1834
GREGG At Lisburn, on the morning of the 3d inst. Ann F. Gregg, the wife of Wm. Gregg, Esq. and daughter of Wm. Caldbeck, Esq. This lady, who has been thus removed in the very bloom of youth from the social circle, which her virtues were so eminently calculated to adorn, to a nobler sphere of action, was universally esteemed, admired and beloved. Gentleness, affability, benevolence, candour, generosity and genuine piety, were the distinguishing traits which characterised her whole progress through life; and the affliction of her affectionate husband, and the tender regret and sorrow of her relatives and friends, are great indeed, for they are proportionate to the signal merits of the beloved one, of whose society they are deprived, until the appointed time when they shall happily meet in the world of spirits, never more to part.

Friday February 4 1870
GREGG February 2, at his residence, Derryvolgie, Lisburn, William Gregg, Esq., J.P., aged 73 years. His remains will be removed for interment in the Cathedral, Lisburn, on Monday afternoon, 7th inst., at two o'clock.

Friday October 6 1826
HALL Lately, at Bristol, where he went for the recovery of his health, Rowley Hall, Esq., late of Lisburn. – He lived beloved and died lamented.

Tuesday January 31 1826
HAWKSHAW At Lisburn, in the 84th year of her age, Mrs Hawkshaw, the wife of William Hawkshaw, Esq.

Friday December 22 1826
HAWKSHAW At Lisburn, on the 19th inst. William Hawkshaw, Esq., in his 83d year.

Friday July 16 1841
HAWKSHAW On the 12th inst. in Stephen's-green, Dublin, in her 21st year, Emilie, the beloved daughter of Lieut-Colonel Hawkshaw, of Blaris Lodge, county Down.

Friday February 11 1848
HAWKSHAW At Blaris-lodge, on the 10th inst., of typhus fever, Lieut. Colonel Hawkshaw, aged 71.

Friday March 2 1855
HAWKSHAW At Lisburn, suddenly, in the 82nd year of her age, Miss Jane Hawkshaw, daughter of the late Wm. Hawkshaw Esq., of Lisburn, universally respected and regretted.

Saturday August 21 1858
HAWKSHAW At Cheltenham, Lieutenant-Colonel Edward Hawkshaw, aged 78.

Tuesday January 6 - Friday January 9 1778
HERON Died, the 4 inst., at Lisburn, the wife of Mr. Samuel Heron, Attorney at Law.

Tuesday April 7 1807
HERON On Saturday 24th inst. much deservedly lamented by a numerous acquaintance, Mrs Heron, wife of Samuel Heron, of Lisburn, Esq. – She lived the life, and is gone to receive the reward of a truly pious and exemplary Christian.

Friday July 1 1808
HERON At his house, in Lisburn, at an advanced age, on the 19th of June, Samuel Heron, Esq., for many years an eminent and truly respectable Attorney.

Tuesday July 23 1833
HERON At Holywood, on the 11 July, Ann, youngest daughter of Lieut. Ed. Heron, R.N., much regretted by all her friends.

Friday December 2 1836
HERON At Holywood, on the 5th ult. Edward Heron Esq., Lieutenant R.N., aged 56 years.

Tuesday March 6 1849
HERON On the 25th Feb., at Barry's Terrace, Rathmines, Mary, eldest daughter of the late Lieut. Edward Heron R.N., and niece of T.J. Smyth, Esq. of Lisburn.

Thursday February 27 1879
HERON February 24, at Hillsborough, Anne, relict of the late Lieutenant Edward Heron, Royal Navy, aged 90 years. Her remains will leave Hillsborough for interment in the Cathedral Churchyard, Lisburn, this (Thursday) morning, at half-past eleven o'clock.

Friday October 23 1885
HERON October 22, at 15, College South, Belfast, Eliza, widow of the late Samuel Heron, Lieutenant R.N., aged 92 years.

Tuesday July 9 1839
HERRON On the 26th ult. in the 13th year of his age, remarkable during life for a placid temper, moral conduct, and intellectual attainments, both in classical and scientific literature, Master Wallace Herron, son of Samuel Herron, Esq., of Lisburn.

Tuesday February 28 1843

HERRON   At Lisburn, on Thursday morning last, after a protracted illness, Dorothea, the beloved wife of Mr. John Herron, cabinet-manufacturer.

Tuesday June 17 1817

HIGGINSON   At Lisburn, on Sunday the 8th instant, Charles Higginson, Esq. first Lieutenant, on half pay, of His Majesty's royal marines – "Qualis fuit summa dies indicabit."

Friday July 2 1819

HIGGINSON   At his residence in Lisburn, the Rev. T.E. Higginson, aged 51 years.

Friday March 20 1829

HIGGINSON   On the 9th inst. at Glenwood Cottage, near Lisburn, Jane, relict of the late Rev. Thomas E. Higginson.

Tuesday June 22 1869

HIGGINSON   June 20, at his residence, Carnalea House, County Down, Henry Theophilus Higginson J.P. aged 74 years. The funeral will leave Carnalea House for the family vault, Ballinderry, on Thursday morning, the 24th inst., at ten o'clock.

Wednesday June 16 1875

HIGGINSON   June 15, at Carnalea House, County Down, Charlotte, relict of the late Henry Theophilus Higginson, formerly of Lisburn, Co. Antrim, aged 75 years. The funeral shall leave Carnalea House for Ballinderry, on Saturday morning, 19th inst., at nine o'clock.

Tuesday February 7 1832

HODGEN   Suddenly at Lisburn, on the 27th ult., in the 36th year of his age, Mr. William Hodgen, innkeeper. On the day previous to his death he was apparently in his usual good health transacting business, when he suddenly took ill, and in a few fleeting moments was to be found numbered with the dead. He was a man of the most upright and consistent character, and was much respected by everyone within the sphere of his acquaintance.

Tuesday February 5 1884

HODSON   February 3, at the Rectory, Lisburn, the Rev. Hartley Hodson, D.D., Rector of Lisburn and Prebendary of Cairncastle, aged 68.

Friday July 9 1813

HOGG   At Lisburn, a few days ago, at the advanced age of 102, Mrs Hogg, relict of the late Edward Hogg Esq., -In justice to her memory, it may be truly said, that every action of a long and well spent life, declared the native modesty and goodness of her heart. – She was, in an exalted degree, a pious Christian, an affectionate wife, a tender parent, a good neighbour, and a sincere friend.

Tuesday August 17 1824

HOGG   At Lisburn on the 12th inst. William Hogg Esq., aged 70 years.

Tuesday March 4 1856

HOGG   February 28, at her residence, Castle Street, Lisburn, Mrs Hogg, relict of W. Hogg Esq., and mother of Sir J.W. Hogg, Bart, M.P.

Thursday April 15 1858

HUGHES   April 14, in Castle Street, Lisburn, Hariett, the beloved wife of the Rev. James Hughes, Wesleyan Minister. Her remains will be interred in the Cathedral Burying-ground on to-morrow (Friday) morning, at ten o'clock.

Tuesday December 28 1869
HULL   December 26, at James' Street, Lisburn, Joseph Hull. His remains will be removed for interment in the Family Burying-ground, on this (Tuesday) morning, at nine o'clock. Friends will please accept this intimation.

Saturday March 6 1886
HULL   March 5, at her residence, Market Street, Lisburn, Elizabeth, relict of the late Joseph Hull. Her remains will be removed for interment in the Cathedral Graveyard to-morrow (Sunday) afternoon, at four o'clock.

Friday January 24 1913
HULL   January 22, 1913, at her residence, 16, Seymour Street, Jane, only surviving daughter of the late Joseph Hull, of Lisburn, in her 82nd year. Funeral to the Cathedral Burying-ground to-morrow (Saturday) morning at eleven o'clock   A. Victor Waterhouse.

Friday March 4 1814
HUTCHESON   On the 24th ult. in the 57th year of his age, the Rev. Francis Hutcheson, D.D. Vicar of Donaghadee.

Tuesday 17 - Friday 29 March 1778
HUTCHINSON   Suddenly in Cusse-st., Mrs. Hutchinson, widow of the late Francis Hutchinson, Archdeacon of Down.

Tuesday October 5 1830
JACOBSEN   At the house of his father, in this town, on Sunday the 26th ult. universally and deservedly regretted, Mr. James Jacobsen, of Ballymena. His death was extremely premature, and what renders it still more calamitous, he was scarce two months married, and has left a very young and sincerely attached wife to deplore his sudden dissolution.

Wednesday October 3 1855
JEFFERSON   September 29, at his home, Bow Street, Lisburn, Mr. John Jefferson, woollendraper, in the 46th year of his age.

Wednesday May 28 1856
JEFFERSON   May 24, at his residence, Ballymacash, near Lisburn, Mr. John Jefferson, in the 89th year of his age. He was one of the last survivors of the original troop of Cavalry raised by the Marquis of Hertford in 1595 (sic) (1795?), and continued in that troop until its disembodiment, upwards of 20 years afterwards.

Monday December 3 1860
JEFFERSON   November 30, at Lisburn, after a short illness, Ann Jane, relict of the late Mr. John Jefferson, Woollendraper.

Saturday June 4 1864
JEFFERSON   June 2, at Ballymacash, near Lisburn, Ann Jane, relict of the late John Jefferson, aged 86 years.

Monday June 18 1866
JEFFERSON   June 17, at his residence, Market Place, Lisburn, Alexander, second son of the late George Jefferson, aged 19 years. His remains will be removed for interment in the Lisburn Cathedral Burying-ground, on to-morrow (Tuesday) morning at nine o'clock. Friends will please accept this intimation.

Saturday April 5 1879

JEFFERSON   April 4, at her residence, Bow Street, Lisburn, Eliza, wife of Redmond Jefferson, aged 61 years. Her remains will be removed for interment in the Cathedral Burying-ground, on Monday morning, the 7th inst., at half-past ten o'clock. Friends will please accept this intimation.

Tuesday April 10 1888

JEFFERSON   April 9, at Aughnahoe, Lisburn, Robert Jefferson, aged 84 years. Interment in the Cathedral churchyard to-morrow (Wednesday) afternoon at three o'clock.

Tuesday February 2 1892

JEFFERSON   January 30, at his residence, North Circular Road, Lisburn, Redmond Jefferson, aged 76 years. His remains will be removed for interment in the Cathedral Churchyard, this (Tuesday) morning at half-past nine o'clock.

Monday July 20 - Friday July 24 1795

JOHNSON SMYTH   Died at Lisburn, on Monday last, in her 39th year, Mrs Lydia Johnson Smyth, wife to Roger Johnson Smyth Esq. This lady was a native of North America, and came lately to reside in this kingdom. She was a most affectionate wife, a tender mother, and a warm friend – by her death society has sustained a severe loss, as her benevolent heart was at all times ready to relieve her distressed fellow creatures, to the fullest extent of her power.

Tuesday April 9 1816

JOHNSON SMYTH   At Aghnaskeagh, County of Down, on Thursday the 27th ult. Roger Johnson Smyth, Esq. aged 72.

Friday January 12 1838

JOHNSON SMYTH   On the 7th inst. at Lisburn, of typhus fever, Harriet, only daughter of Thomas J. Smyth Esq.

Wednesday April 25 1860

JOHNSON SMYTH   April 22 in Lisburn Thomas Johnson Smyth Esq., J.P., D.L. Aged 78 years.

Monday September 25 1865

JOHNSON SMYTH   September 23, Matthew Johnson Smyth, Esq., third son of the late Thomas Johnson Smyth, Esq., J.P., D.L.

Wednesday August 10 1870

JOHNSON SMYTH   August 8, Madeline, infant daughter of Thomas Johnson Smyth, Esq., J.P., Goremount, Glenavy, County Antrim.

Tuesday April 27 1875

JOHNSON SMYTH   April 25, at Kingstown, Charlotte, relict of the late Thomas Johnson Smyth, Esq., J.P., D.L., Lisburn, aged 83 years. Her remains will arrive for interment in the Cathedral Burying-ground, Lisburn, by the mid-day train from Dublin, on Thursday, 29th inst., at half-past twelve o'clock.

Monday April 3 1876

JOHNSON SMYTH   April 1, at the Glebe, Glenavy, Aemelia, wife of the Rev. E. Johnson Smyth, vicar of Glenavy. Her remains will be removed from the Glebe, for interment in the churchyard of Lisburn Cathedral, on Wednesday morning, the 5th inst. at ten o'clock. Friends will please accept this intimation.

Wednesday April 9 1879

JOHNSON SMYTH   April 8, at Cromwell Terrace, Belfast, Thomas Johnson Smyth, Esq., J.P., elder son of the Rev. E. Johnson Smyth, Vicar of Glenavy, aged 38 years. His remains will be removed for interment in the Cathedral Burying-ground, Lisburn, on Friday morning, at half-past eight o'clock.

Friday August 9 1901

JOHNSON SMYTH   August 8, Matthew Bruce Johnson Smyth, Esq., younger son of the late Matthew Johnson Smyth, of Lisburn, County Antrim, Esq. Funeral private.

Wednesday February 28 1923

JOHNSON SMYTH   February 27, 1923, at Ingram, Lisburn, Co. Antrim, Elizabeth Anne, wife of the late Matthew Johnson Smyth Esq., and daughter of the late Reverend John Corken, of Ingram, and Vicar of Aghalee, in her 90th year. Funeral private.

Tuesday February 28 1826

JOHNSTON At Lisburn, on Saturday, 25th instant, Mr. Arthur Johnston, aged 76 years, much regretted by his acquaintance.

Monday October 16 1871

JOHNSTON October 13 at 3 Cromwell Terrace, Belfast, Kate Frances, wife of Andrew J. Johnston, aged 30 years.

Monday November 6 1871

JOHNSTON November 3, at Wellington Place, Belfast, Andrew John, eldest son of Doctor Johnston, Rotunda Hospital, Dublin.

Friday June 12 1917

JOHNSTON   January 10 1917, at his residence 22, Millbrook Rd., Lisburn, Wm. Johnston. Funeral to family burying ground, Cathedral Churchyard, Lisburn, today, (Friday) at 3 pm.
John and Teresa Johnston, 53, Fort Terrace, Lisburn.

Tuesday November 24 - Friday November 27 1778

JONES   Died at Lisburn, on Saturday 21st inst., Conway Jones, Esq., Doctor of Physick.

Friday December 5 - Tuesday December 9 1788

JONES   Died, on Wednesday last in St. Andrew St., Dublin, Mrs. Wray Jones, relict of the late Conway Jones, of Lisburn, the last of that branch of Sir Cecil Wray and of the ancient family of Harrisons of Magheralave Castle, near Lisburn.

Tuesday February 27 1838

JONES   On the 22d inst. at Rostrevor, Miss Jones of Lisburn, aged 82.

Monday August 19 1872

KELLY   Aug. 17, at his residence, Railway Street, Lisburn, Mr. John Kelly, builder. His remains will be removed for interment in the Cathedral Burying-ground, this (Monday) afternoon, at four o'clock. Friends will please accept this intimation.

Tuesday February 20 1866

KIDD   February 18, at Castle Street, Lisb___n, after a severe and lingering illness, Mr. James Kidd, aged 44 years.

Monday March 4 1878
KIDD   March 3, at 4, Amelia Street (Great Victoria Street), Belfast, Annie, daughter of the late James Kidd, of Castle Street, Lisburn, aged 20 years. Her remains will be removed for interment in the Lisburn Cathedral Burying-ground, on to-morrow (Tuesday) afternoon, at two o'clock, arriving in Lisburn about four. Friends will please accept this intimation.

Wednesday May 30 1866
MACARTNEY   May 29, at Lisburn, Agnes, the beloved wife of Mr. Arthur Macartney, aged 73 years. Her remains will be removed for interment in Lisburn church-yard, on to-morrow (Thursday) morning, at nine o'clock. Friends will please accept this intimation.

Saturday May 30 1874
MACARTNEY   May 28, at the residence of his son-in-law, Ballyholme, Bangor, Arthur Macarty (sic), formerly of Lisburn, in his 71st year. His remains will be removed for interment in Lisburn Churchyard, on Monday morning, June 1, at eight o'clock, arriving in Lisburn about one p.m. Friends will please accept this intimation.

Friday April 27 1877
MACARTNEY   April 24, at Dublin, Arthur, only surviving son of the late Arthur Macartney, Lisburn.

Tuesday May 16 - Friday May 19 1775
MARMION   Died, on the 8th inst., at Lisburn, Alice, second daughter of Henry Marmion, Esq.; Her goodness, innocence, and beauty, were known to, and admired by every body – but herself.

> She's gone, but whither? Home. Nor can we blame
> Her sudden flight to Heaven, from whence she came:
> Kind was her visit; eighteen years and more:
> She sojourn'd with us on this barren more:
> Angels are seldom known so long to stay,
> Who do but shew themselves, - and fly away.

Tuesday August 19 - Friday August 22 1788
MARMION   Died at Lisburn, on Monday last, much lamented, Mrs. Marmion, said wife of Mr. Henry Marmion, son to the late Mr. Henry Marmion, after a tedious illness, which she bore with a becoming resignation to the Divine will. She was a real Christian, a good wife, a tender parent, and a sincere friend.

Tuesday July 19 1814
MARMION   On the morning of the 12th inst. at Lisburn, Mr. Henry Marmion, of consumption.

Tuesday January 20 1829
MARMION   At Lambeg, on Sunday 11 inst. Henry Hamilton Marmion, eldest son of the late Henry Marmion Esq. of Lisburn, much regretted by all who knew him. And in Demerara, a few months ago, Philip Talbot, second son of the late Henry Marmion, Esq.

Tuesday September 17 1833
MARMION   On Friday the 6th inst. at the residence of her mother, Greenwood Cottage, near Lisburn, Margaret, eldest daughter of the late Henry Marmion Esq.

Tuesday January 24 1843
MARMION   On the 15th inst. at her house in Lisburn, Mrs. Eliza Marmion, relict of the late Henry Marmion, Esq. In the demise of this estimable woman, the widow and the orphan will lose a friend.

Tuesday November 1 1870
MATEER   October 31, at his late residence, 125, Hertford Place, Lisburn Road, Mr. Joseph Mateer, aged 79 years. His remains will be removed for interment in Lisburn Church-yard, on to-morrow (Wednesday) morning, at ten o'clock. Friends will please accept this intimation.

Friday July 27 1855
McALESTER   July 23, at the residence of her son, the Rev. C.J. McAlester, Holywood, Eliza, relict of Mr. Charles McAlester, of Belfast, aged 76.

Tuesday March 12 1811
McALLESTER (SIC)   On the 5th instant, Mr. Charles McAllester, of this town, Merchant, aged 44 years, a man of gentle manner, and strict integrity. On his tomb-stone might be engraved with truth – A *Steady Patriot*, and *Earnest* Friend; in a word AN HONEST MAN.

Tuesday May 16 1865
McCLURE   May 13, Agnes, youngest daughter of Adam McClure, Esq., Lisburn.

Monday March 30 1874
McCLURE   March 28, at Lisburn, Adam McClure, aged 76 years. His remains will be removed from his late residence, for interment in the Cathedral Burying-ground, to-morrow (Tuesday) morning at ten o'clock.

Tuesday February 22 1881
McCLURE   February 21, at his mother's residence, Market Square, Lisburn, of bronchitis, Joseph McClure.

Monday December 16 1889
McCLURE   December 14, at The Manse, Saintfield Road, Margaret, the widow of the late Adam McClure, of Lisburn, in her 86th year.

Wednesday July 23 1890
McDOWALL   July 22, at Seymour Street, Lisburn, Eleanor, the widow of the late John McDowall, M.D., Dawson Street, Dublin and daughter of the late George Haynes, Esq., of Stratford-on-Avon, Warwickshire, aged 93 years. Funeral on Friday morning at half past nine o'clock, at the Cathedral Churchyard.

Saturday October 25 1890
McHENRY   October 24, at the residence of her son, 6, Cromac Park Terrace, Belfast, Jane, relict of the late Robert McHenry, in the 76th year of her age. Funeral private.

Thursday January 8 1914
McHENRY   January 6, at his residence, 7, Windsor Gardens, Malone Road, Robert McHenry, Chief Clerk of Petty Sessions. Funeral strictly private.

Wednesday December 29 1920
McHENRY   December 26, 1920, at Rosleigh, 24, Leeds Road, Harrogate, Sarah McMaster, widow of the late Robert McHenry, Windsor Gardens, Belfast. Funeral to-morrow (Thursday) from Heysham Boat, at 10a.m. to Lisburn Cathedral.

Friday February 10 1837
McKEE   At Lisburn, on the 2d inst. of influenza, John McKee, late serjeant in the 89th regiment, much and highly regretted by his friends and acquaintances.

Monday October 7 1861
McKEE October 6, at the Lisburn Union Workhouse, Mr. George McKee, aged 52 years, for upwards of twenty years master of that house. His remains will be removed from thence for interment in the Cathedral Church-yard of that town on Tuesday (to-morrow) morning, at ten o'clock.

Saturday November 2 1867
McKEE October 31, at Market Square, Lisburn, Mr. George McKee, Inland Revenue, in his 23rd year. His remains will be removed for interment in the Cathedral church-yard, on Monday morning next, the 4th inst., at eleven o'clock.

Thursday February 26 1891
McKEE February 25, at 6, Market Square, Lisburn, Eliza, widow of the late George McKee, aged 80 years. Interment in the Cathedral Churchyard, to-morrow (Friday) morning, at 10 o'clock.

Monday December 28 1896
McKEE December 25, at 24 Market Square, Hannah McKee. Interment in the Cathedral Burying-ground this (Monday) morning at half past ten o'clock.

Wednesday March 14 1900
McKEE March 13, at her residence, No. 24, Market Square, Lisburn, Jane McKee. Her remains will be removed for interment in the Cathedral Churchyard, to-morrow (Thursday) morning, at half past ten o'clock.

Thursday March 21 1878
McMULLAN (SIC) March 17, at his residence, Knockmore, Lisburn, James McMullan (sic), aged 61 years.

Tuesday March 12 1811
MERCER On the 7th inst. after a tedious and severe illness which she bore with remarkable piety and resignation, Mrs Ann Mercer of Hill-hall – In her were eminently united the character of a tender wife, affectionate mother, sincere friend and obliging neighbour. She lived a life of faith upon the Son of God and she died in sure and certain hope of a *glorious immortality*.

Tuesday December 8 1863
MOORE December 6, at Warren Cottage, County Antrim, Jane Deborah, eldest daughter of the late Hugh Moore, Esq., Eglantine House, County Down.

Tuesday May 8 1827
MURRAY At Lisburn, on Saturday 5th May inst., in the 24th year of his age, of consumption, William Murray, only son of Mr. Richard Murray. - He bore his long illness with Christian resignation, and died in the faith of the Lord, much regretted by his numerous friends and acquaintances, and deeply lamented by his fond parents, in whose affections his departure has left a blank which can be repaired only by strong and sincere faith in Jesus.

Monday May 19 1851
MURRAY On the 12th instant, at Lisburn, Mr. James Murray, Saddler, aged 79 years.

Wednesday July 2 1856
MURRAY June 28, at her residence, Castle Street, Lisburn, Jane, wife of Richard Murray, aged 87 years.

Friday February 14 1834
MUSGRAVE At Lisburn, on Sunday the 9th inst. Samuel Musgrave Esq. Surgeon, in the 66th year of his age.

Tuesday May 5 1840
MUSGRAVE   On the 1st inst. at the residence of his mother, 26, Upper Arthur-street, Thomas Musgrave, eldest son of the late Surgeon Musgrave, of Lisburn.

Monday June 27 1853
MUSGRAVE   June 23, at the residence of her brother, Lisburn, Jane, eldest daughter of the late Doctor Musgrave, Lisburn.

Monday March 11 1867
MUSGRAVE   March 9, at his residence, Drumglass House, Malone, Belfast, Robert Hamilton Musgrave.

Tuesday May 14 1872
MUSGRAVE   May 12, at 29, Upper Temple Street, Dublin, William Musgrave, Esq., Barrister-at-law, eldest surviving son of the late Dr. Musgrave, of Lisburn. His remains will be removed from Drumglass House, Malone, on to-morrow (Wednesday) morning, at nine o'clock, for interment at Lisburn.

Thursday June 23 1892
MUSGRAVE   June 22, at Drumglass House, Margaret, eldest surviving daughter of the late Doctor Musgrave, of Lisburn. Her remains will be removed for interment in Lisburn Churchyard, on Saturday morning, at nine o'clock. No flowers.

Thursday April 20 1893
MUSGRAVE   April 19, at the residence of his brother, Drumglass House, Belfast, Dr. Samuel Musgrave, J.P., of Lisburn (son of the late Dr. Musgrave). His remains will be removed for interment in Lisburn Churchyard, on Saturday morning, 22nd inst., at nine o'clock. No flowers.

Saturday March 7 1895
MUSGRAVE   On Friday evening, March 29th, at his residence, Drumglass House, Belfast, John R. Musgrave, J.P., D.L., eldest surviving son of the late Doctor Musgrave of Lisburn. His remains will be removed for interment in the Cathedral Burying-ground, Lisburn, on Tuesday morning, 2nd April, at nine o'clock. No flowers.

Wednesday February 24 1904
MUSGRAVE   February 22, at Drumglass House, Belfast, Sir James Musgrave, Bart., D.L., eldest surviving son of the late Dr. Samuel Musgrave, Lisburn. Funeral on Friday morning, 26th inst., at half-past nine o'clock. No flowers.

Tuesday May 14 1912
MUSGRAVE   Died on Sunday night, at his residence, Drumglass House, Belfast, Edgar Musgrave, youngest son of the late Dr. Musgrave, of Lisburn. Funeral private. No flowers.

Wednesday January 4 1922
MUSGRAVE   January 2, at his residence, Drumglass, Belfast, Henry Musgrave D.L., O.B.E. aged 95 years. Funeral private. No flowers.

Friday March 31 1843
MUSSEN   On the 18th inst. at Lisburn, Anna, youngest daughter of Mr. James Mussen.

Wednesday July 16 1851
MUSSEN   On Sunday, the 13th inst., Mr. James Mussen, Market Square, Lisburn, aged 85 years.

Wednesday November 10 1852
MUSSEN   November 8, at his residence, Market Square, Lisburn, Mr. Edward Cupples Mussen, in the 39th year of his age.

Friday March 17 1854
MUSSEN   March 15, at her late residence, Market square, Lisburn, Miss Mary Mussen.

Friday October 5 1838
NEELY   On the 1st inst. at his residence, in Castle-street, Lisburn in the 61st year of his age, Benjamin Neely, Esq. Principal of the Academy.

Friday April 2 1841
NEELY   On the 29th ult. at Lisburn, after a very short illness, Mr. John Boyes Neely, only son of Mr. Erskine Neely, aged 23 years. Few lived more respected, and it is long since the death of so young a man caused such a general feeling of regret as that which was evinced by all classes in his neighbourhood, at his premature dissolution.

Friday May 28 1841
NEELY   On the 25th inst. at Lisburn, aged 58, Mary, relict of Benjamin Neely, Esq., late Principal of the Lisburn Academy.

Monday February 11 1856
NEELY   February 8, at Lisburn, Sarah, wife of Erskine Neely, aged 79 years.

Friday October 7 1864.
NEELY   October 5. At her lodgings Chapel Hill, Lisburn, Mary, eldest daughter of the late Benjamin Neely Esq. Principal of the Lisburn Academy. Her remains will be removed for interment in the burial ground of the Lisburn Cathedral on tomorrow (Saturday) at twelve o'clock.

Tuesday April 9 1872
NEELY   At Augusta, Georgia, U.S., the Rev. John Neely, eldest son of the late Mr. Benjamin Neely, of Lisburn, aged 68 years.

Saturday September 8 1855
NEWBURN   September 4, at Lisburn, Mr. Thomas Newburn, Bridge Street, aged 46 years.

Friday September 26 1856
NEWBURN   September 21, at her late residence, Bridge Street, Lisburn, Mrs Eleanor Newburn, wife of the late Mr. T. Newburn, aged 36 years.

Wednesday October 15 1884
NEWBURN   October 12, at 22 College-street West, Belfast, Mary, the dearly beloved wife of William Newburn. Her remains will be removed from above residence this (Wednesday) afternoon at ten o'clock. Friends will please accept this intimation.

Tuesday December 21 1830
NICHOLSON   On Wednesday last in Dawson-street, Dublin, in the 35th year of his age, Alex. Jaffray Nicholson Esq. M.D., eldest son of the late John Nicholson Esq. of Stramore-House, County Down.

Tuesday January 9 1843
NICHOLSON   Killed in action, on the 3d of Nov. returning through the Kyber Pass, Alexander, son of the late Alexander J. Nicholson Esq. and grandson of the late John Nicholson, Esq., of Stramore House, county of Down.

Friday January 30 1863
NICHOLSON December 18, at Doomree, on his way to join his station, from the effects of a wound received at Delhi, Major Charles Johnson Nicholson, of the Bengal Staff corps, and brother of the late Brigadier-General Nicholson.

Thursday May 28 1863
NICHOLSON May 17, at Cheltenham, Lizzie, widow of Major Charles Johnson Nicholson, of the Bengal Staff Corps, and eldest daughter of Edmond Gilliland, Esq.

Thursday February 19 1874
NICHOLSON Feb, 17, At Lisburn, Clara, relict of the late Alexander Jeffrey (sic) Nicholson, Esq., M.D., in her 86th Year.

Tuesday June 19 1827
O'FLAHERTY At Lisburn, on the 13th inst., after a lingering illness which she bore with christian resignation, Mary, wife of Francis H. O'Flaherty. She died deeply lamented by her numerous acquaintances, and has left her husband, with two infant children, to deplore her loss. She was a tender parent and an affectionate wife, and during her short life she discharged her duties with the most zealous attention.

Tuesday May 7 1844
O'FLAHERTY At Lisburn, on the 30th ult. of consumption, Charlotte Fawnia, only daughter of Mr. Francis H. O'Flaherty, Deputy Registrar of Down and Connor.

Friday August 3 1849
O'FLAHERTY July 17, at Holywood, of Cholera, in the 7th year of his age, John Hale, second son of Mr. Francis O'Flaherty, of Lisburn.

Thursday October 20 1859
O'FLAHERTY October 18, Francis Hale O'Flaherty, Esq., Solicitor. His remains will be removed from his late residence Castle Street, Lisburn, for interment in the burying ground of the Lisburn Cathedral, on Friday (to-morrow) morning at nine o'clock precisely.

Tuesday June 1 1875
O'FLAHERTY May 30, at her residence, Castle Street, Eleanor, widow of the late Francis Hale O'Flaherty. Her remains will be removed for interment in the Cathedral Burying-ground, Lisburn, to-morrow (Wednesday) morning, at ten o'clock.

Monday October 29 1888
O'FLAHERTY October 27, suddenly, at his brother's residence, Ros-a-voe, Cultra, Thomas Alexander O'Flaherty M.D., R.N. His remains will be removed for interment in Cathedral Burying-ground, Lisburn to-morrow (Tuesday) morning at half-past eight o'clock, crossing Queen's Bridge at ten o'clock.

Monday May 6 1901
O'FLAHERTY May 5, at 105, Eglantine Avenue, Belfast, Francis H. O'Flaherty. Funeral private. No flowers, by request.

Monday July 10 1916
O'FLAHERTY Killed in action on July 1 1916, Captain Douglas Hale O'Flaherty, Royal Irish Rifles, son of the late Frank H. O'Flaherty, Belfast. 8, Kincora Avenue, Strandtown.

Tuesday May 1 1877

PARKINSON   April 30, at his residence, Lower Maze, near Hillsborough, Thomas Parkinson. His remains will be removed for interment in the Cathedral Churchyard, Lisburn, to-morrow (Wednesday) afternoon, at three o'clock. Friends will please accept this intimation.

Friday November 6 1829

PELAN   In Lisburn, on the 3d inst. of decline, in the 31st year of his age, Mr. Thos. Pelan, jun.

Tuesday July 22 1834

PELAN   On the 11th inst., Eliza Jane, wife of Mr. Samuel Pelan, of Lisburn, in the 28th year of her age.

Friday July 4 1862

PELAN   At his late residence, No. 41, Frederick Street, Belfast, Mr. Samuel Pelan, formerly of Bridge Street, Lisburn, aged 69 years. His remains will be removed for interment in the Lisburn Cathedral Church-yard this (Friday) morning at ten o'clock. Friends will please accept this notice.

Monday April 5 1875

PELAN   April 3, at his residence, Market Square, Lisburn, Mr. Thomas Rutherford Pelan, aged 42 years. His remains will be removed for interment in Lisburn Churchyard to-morrow (Tuesday) morning, at half-past nine o'clock.

Monday April 23 1923

PELAN   April 21 1923, at the residence of her son, "Belvedere" North Circular Road, Lisburn, Sarah Jane Pelan, widow of the late Thomas R. Pelan. Funeral private.

Wednesday March 4 1874

PENNINGTON   March 3, at Thorn Hill, Lisburn, John Pennington Esq., Solicitor, in his 83rd Year.

Tuesday November 13 1877

PENNINGTON   November 11, at his residence, Railway Street, Lisburn, John Pennington. His remains will be removed for interment in the Cathedral Churchyard, this (Tuesday) morning, at nine o'clock.

Friday September 15 1843

PURDON   On the 11th inst. at Sans Souci, near Belfast, Dr. Purdon, aged 73.

Tuesday May 21 1861

PURDON   May 19, at Lucyville, Whitehouse, Jane Maria, third daughter of C.D. Purdon Esq., M.D.

Thursday January 10 1861

PURDON   January 8, at No 5, Wellington Place, Amelia Georgina, the beloved wife of T.H. Purdon Esq., M.D., in the 45th year of her age.

Monday January 9 1882

PURDON   January 8, at 14, Wellington Place, Belfast, Charles Delacherois Purdon A.M., M.B., T.C.D., F.R.C.S.I., aged 63 years. Funeral to-morrow (Tuesday) morning, at nine o'clock.

Monday August 9 1886

PURDON   August 6, at 5, Wellington Place, Belfast, Thomas Henry Purdon, M.A., M.B., T.C.D., in his 81st year. Funeral strictly private.

Tuesday February 8 1916
PURDON   February 6, at her residence, 56 Eglantine Avenue, in her 94th year, Jane Maria, widow of the late Charles D. Purdon, M.D., F.R.C.S.I.

Tuesday June 24 1828
REID   In Lisburn, on Tuesday evening last, John Reid, aged 21. He was a dutiful son, an affectionate brother, and kind hearted friend.

Friday May 8 1829
REID   In Lisburn, Mrs Reid, relict of the late Doctor Reid, and daughter of the late James Fulton, Esq.

Wednesday September 26 1860
REID   September 24, at the General Hospital, Belfast, Margaret Reid, formerly of Lisburn.

Friday August 11 1865
REID   August 9, at Ardoyne, Belfast, Mary Anne, wife of Mr. Robert Reid. Her remains will be removed for interment in the Cathedral Burying ground, Lisburn, on this day (Friday), at twelve o'clock. Friends will please accept this intimation.

Monday March 18 1867
REID   March 17, at Ardoyne, of comsumption, Matilda, second daughter of Mr. Robert Reid. Her remains will be removed from her late residence for interment in Lisburn cemetery, on to-morrow (Tuesday) morning, at ten o'clock. Friends will please accept this intimation.

Monday November 6 1854
REILLY   November 4, at his residence, Bow Street, Lisburn, Mr. James Reilly, printer.

Monday July 18 1859
REILLY   July 15, at Lisburn, Bridget, relict of the late Mr. J.L. Reilly, aged 83 years. Her remains will be removed for interment in the Cathedral Burying-ground on this day (Monday) the 18th inst., at ten o'clock.

Monday July 3 1922
RIDDAL (SIC)   Friday 30th June, 1922, at his residence, 4, Parkmount, Lisburn, the Rev. E.P. Riddal M.A. Funeral to Lisburn Cemetery today (Monday) 3rd July at 11:30p.m.

Friday September 26 1817
ROGERS   On Saturday morning, 21st inst. at Lisburn, in the 78th year of his age, William Rogers, Esq.

Tuesday October 28 1828
ROGERS   At Lisburn, on the 21st October, aged 78, Mrs Rogers, relict of the late William Rogers, Esq., of Lisburn.

Friday July 29 1831
ROGERS   On Sunday evening last, Mrs. Rogers, wife of Mr. Pat Rogers, of Lisburn.

Tuesday November 24 1835
ROGERS   At Lisburn, on Wednesday last, at the house of his brother, Mr. Thos. Rogers, formerly grocer in that town, and late of Coleraine, aged 32 years.

Friday December 18 1835
SEFTON   On Saturday last, of consumption, Frances Charlotte, wife of Mr. Isaac Sefton, and second daughter of Mr. Richard Murray, Lisburn.

Tuesday September 4 1827
SHANNON   On the 27th ult. of consumption, in the 21st year of his age, deeply and deservedly lamented, Mr. John Shannon, eldest son of Mr. J.B. Shannon, of Belfast.

Tuesday February 18 1834
SHANNON   On the 5th inst. at Lagan Vale, the residence of her son, in the 83d year of her age, Mary, the relict of the late James Shannon Esq. of Dublin.

Friday November 10 1837
SHANNON   On the 3d inst. in the prime of life, James, son of J.B. Shannon, Esq., of this town. Though young in years, yet mature in virtue, and rich in Christian grace; his cheerful temper, his mildness, affability, candour, benevolence, and warmth of heart, rendered him the joy of his parents and delight of the social circle which he adorned. In health it was his chief pleasure to diffuse happiness around him-and in sickness, during the agonies of a protracted disease, which he felt to be mortal no murmur escaped his lips, but he resigned himself, with a pious submission, to the will of God, and a patient endurance of suffering which Christianity alone could have enabled him to support. Already, therefore, as we humbly yet ardently trust, hath his pure and gentle soul become a denizen of Heaven, and mingled in endless felicity with its kindred spirits-the spirits of "just men made perfect." The remains of this excellent young man were accompanied from Belfast to Lisburn, the place of their interment, on the morning of the 6th instant, by an immense assemblage of the most respectable inhabitants of this town and neighbourhood, who, having been thoroughly acquainted with his sterling worth, loved him when living, and now deeply lament his decease, as a common loss to the community.

Friday March 2 1838
SHANNON   On the 23d ult., age 65, Mary, wife of John B. Shannon, Esq., deeply regretted.

Tuesday April 13 1824
SIMON   At Lisburn, on Sunday, the 4th inst. Julia, wife of John Simon, formerly of Mount Pleasant, Co. Down, Esq.

Tuesday April 24 1827
SIMON   At Lisburn, on Saturday the 14th inst,. in his 82d year, John Simon, Esq.

Wednesday September 7 1859
SIMPSON   September 4, at the residence of her husband, near Stoneyford, aged 82 years, the beloved wife of Mr. James Simpson.

Tuesday December 24 1799
SMITH   On the 11th inst., in Donaghadee, John Smith Esq.

Saturday December 31 1870
SMITH   December 20, at Ballylintough, Charlotte, relict of Jas. Smith, Esq.

Tuesday July 30 1822
SMYTH   On the 24th inst. at Lisburn, at the advanced age of 94 years, Mrs. Smyth, relict of the late William Smyth of Ballintoy, Esq.

CATHEDRAL 133   **MOMENTO MORI**

CATHEDRAL 177 & 176   **PENNINGTON**

CATHEDRAL 113   **GIBSON**

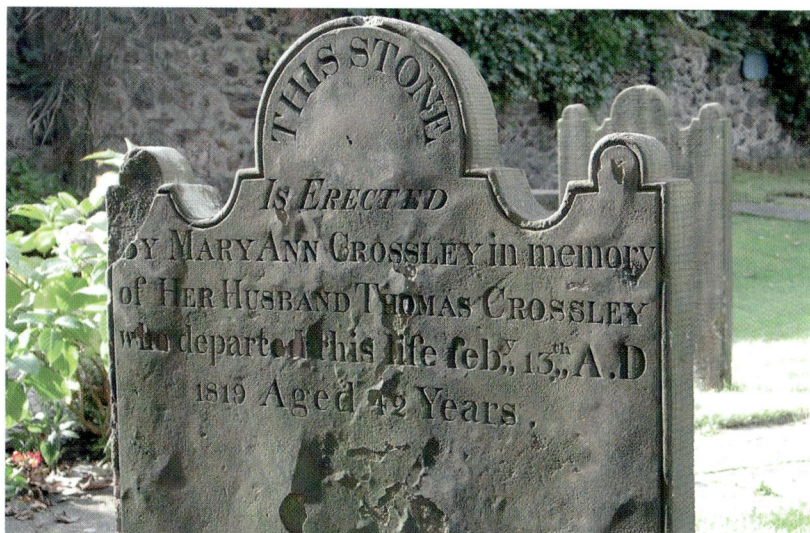

CATHEDRAL 181   **CROSSLEY**

CATHEDRAL 12 &·13 **HOGG, BOLTON AND NICHOLSON**

CATHEDRAL 2 **STANNUS**

CATHEDRAL 67 & 66 **JOHNSON SMYTH AND NEELY**

(Courtesy of Queen's University Belfast Art Collection)
HENRY MUSGRAVE
1826 – 1922

(Courtesy of the Irish Linen Centre & Lisburn Museum)
DR. WILLIAM STEWART
c1768 – 1844

CHRIST CHURCH CATHEDRAL
LISBURN c1920

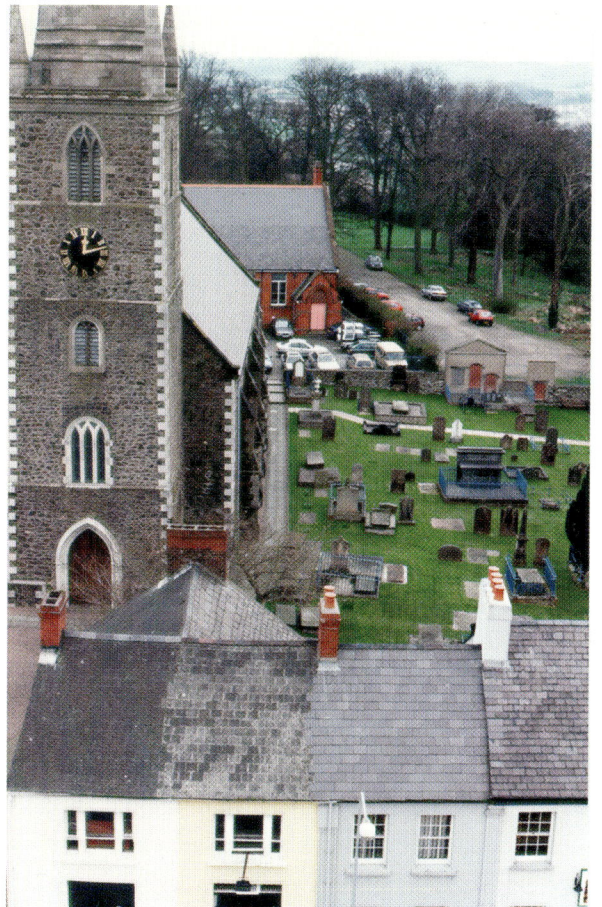

OBLIQUE VIEW OF CATHEDRAL AND
BURYING GROUND 1993

CHRIST CHURCH CATHEDRAL, LISBURN – EAST WINDOW
(Presented in 1950 by Sir John Milne Barbour in memory of his wife, Eliza, and son, John Milne Barbour.
It depicts the four archangels, four Old Testament prophets and saints and martyrs.)

Friday December 5 1823

SMYTH   At his lodgings in Donegall Place, on the 29th November, much lamented, the Rev. James Smyth, of Churchtown Glebe, county of Waterford.

Tuesday September 9 1845

SPROULL   On the 2d inst., in Queen-street, Jane, wife of William H. Sproull, solicitor, and daughter of the late Major Robert Bell Fulton, of the Bengal Artillery, aged 25 years.

Saturday May 19 1860

SPROULL   May 16, at 32, College Street, Mary, daughter of the late Mr. Wm. Sproull, aged 57 years.

Wednesday May 20 1863

SPROULL   May 17, at 32 College Street, Belfast, Mrs. Eleanor Sproull, aged 88 years.

Saturday June 13 1868

SPROULL   June 9, at 32 College Street, Belfast, Eliza Sproull, aged 55 years.

Friday March 12 1830

STANNUS   At Lisburn, on the 9th inst. Elizabeth Harriet, aged 4 years, youngest daughter of the Rev. James Stannus.

Tuesday December 16 1834

STANNUS   At Lisburn, on Wednesday last, of scarletina, Jas. Erasmus, aged 5 years, youngest son of the Dean of Ross.

Thursday May 15 1873

STANNUS   May 14, at Lisburn, in her 81st year, Elizabeth, the beloved wife of the Very Reverend James Stannus, Dean of Ross, and the last surviving daughter of Sir Erasmus Dixon Borrowes, sixth Baronet of Gilltown, Co. Kildare.

Saturday January 29 1876

STANNUS   Jan. 28, at his residence, Castle Street, Lisburn, The Very Rev. James Stannus, Dean of Ross and Rector of Lisburn, aged 88 years.

Wednesday February 22 1893

STANNUS   February 16, at 13 Connaught Square, Hyde Park, London, Harriet Jane Stannus, eldest and last surviving daughter of the late Very Reverend James Stannus, Dean of Ross, and Rector of Lisburn. Funeral at the Cathedral, Lisburn, to-morrow (Thursday) morning, at half past ten o'clock.

Saturday March 2 1895

STANNUS   February 28, in Dublin, suddenly, of congestion of the lungs, Walter Trevor Stannus, D.L., Manor House, Lisburn.

Tuesday November 12 1907

STANNUS   November 8, at Gogmagog Hills, Cambridgeshire, Thomas Robert Stannus, J.P., of Magheraleave, Lisburn, Co. Antrim, eldest son of the late Very Reverend James Stannus, Dean of Ross, aged 89 years. Funeral at Lisburn Cathedral on Wednesday at 10.30 a.m.

Tuesday February 26 - Friday March 1 1782

STEWART   Died, at Lisburn, on Thursday last, aged 92, Mrs. Stewart, relict of Charles Stewart Esq. late Captain of Invalids.

Friday July 26 - Tuesday July 30 1793
STEWART   Died, at Lisburn, Mrs Stewart, wife of Poyntz Stewart Esq.

Tuesday September 7 1824
STEWART   In Lisburn, on the 8th ult. Anne, wife of Major William Stewart and eldest daughter of the late William Rogers of Lisburn, Esq.

Tuesday January 1 1828
STEWART   At his residence at Howrah, near Calcutta, on the 16th of July last, in the 28th year of his age, Doctor Poyntz Stewart, M.D., Civil Assistant Surgeon in the Hon. East India Company's Bengal Service, son to Dr. Stewart M.D., of Lisburn.

Friday June 22 1832
STEWART   At Cheltenham, on the 26th ult. Mary Angelica, wife of Dr. Stewart, of Lisburn.

Friday August 30 1833
STEWART   At Lisburn on the 24th inst. after a tedious illness, in the 23d year of her age, Mary Ann, the fourth daughter of Doctor Stewart, of that town.

Tuesday May 9 1837
STEWART   On the 6th inst. in the 84th year of his age, Mr. Robert Stewart, of Lisburn.

Tuesday April 25 1837
STEWART   At Bath, on Sunday the 9th instant, Major Charles Stewart, brother of Doctor Stewart, of Lisburn. Major Stewart, at an early age, was appointed to a responsible situation in the East India Company's Service, and discharged the duties of it with such talents and integrity, that, on his return to England, he was appointed to an important office in the East India College, which he held for many years, with great credit to himself and benefit to the company. A warm hearted and intelligent Irishman, he was anxious for his country and all belonging to it, and never appeared more happy than when, by his influence and indefatigable exertions, he could promote the interests of the young men from the North of Ireland, for whose welfare and success in life he was ever anxious. His worth, talents, and public sevices, gave him considerable influence; and he never lost an opportunity of doing the kindest actions in the most unassuming manner.

Tuesday February 25, 1840.
STEWART   On the 21st Inst. at Lisburn in the 45th year of her age, Arabella, the wife of Major Wm. Stewart, of the Hon. East India Company's Madras Service.

Monday September 12 1853
STEWART   Sept. 11, at Lisburn, Lucinda the beloved wife of Robert Stewart, Esq., aged 60 years. Her remains will be removed for interment in the Cathedral Church-yard of Lisburn, on Tuesday (to-morrow) morning the 13th instant, at eight o'clock.

Monday September 8 1856
STEWART   September 5, at 15, Clarendon Place, Mr. Richard Stewart, aged 46 years.

Saturday June 5 1858
STEWART   June 4, at his residence, Lisburn, Robert Stewart Esq. aged 75 years. His remains will be removed for interment at Cathedral, Lisburn, on Monday morning at eight o'clock.

Wednesday December 6 1871
STEWART   December 5, at Glenavy Glebe, Magdelene, eldest surviving daughter of the late William Stewart, Esq., M.D., of Lisburn. Her remains will be removed from the Glebe, for interment in Lisburn Cemetery, on Friday morning, the 8th inst., at ten o'clock.

Friday March 17 1876
STEWART   Fell asleep, March 16, at Castle Street, Lisburn, of diptheria, Maria Jackson, the beloved child of Robert and M.J. Stewart, aged 6 years and 6 months.

                "Safe in the arms of Jesus,
                  Safe on His gentle breast."

Monday August 23 1920
SWANZY   August 22, 1920, in Lisburn, Oswald Ross Swanzy, D.I. Royal Irish Constabulary, second and dearly-beloved son of the late James Swanzy, Castleblayney, and Mrs. Swanzy, 31, Railway Street, Lisburn. "The Lord gave and the Lord hath taken away. Blessed be the name of the Lord." Funeral strictly private. No flowers, by special request.

Monday April 14 1823
THOMPSON   On Friday last, deeply lamented, Mrs. Thompson, aged 74, wife of Dr. Thompson, of Lisburn.

Monday September 8 1856
THOMPSON   September 5, at 15, Clarendon Place, Mr. Richard Thompson, aged 46 years.

Monday December 29 1862
THOMPSON   December 26, at Cheltenham, Stewart Thompson, Madras Civil Service, youngest son of W. Thompson, M.D., Lisburn, aged 27 years.

Monday July 10 1882
THOMPSON   July 7, at his father's residence, Lisburn, County Antrim, Colonel William Thompson, late 3rd Madras Cavalry, son of William Thompson, Esq. M.D.

Friday September 23 1882
THOMPSON   September 22, Wm. Thompson Esq. M.D., F.R.C.S.I., of Lisburn, aged 76 years.

Tuesday December 9 1884
THOMPSON   On 8th December at 4, Dunedin Terrace, Belfast, in the 82nd year of her age, Rosina, widow of the late William Thompson, Esq. M.D., of Lisburn, Co. Antrim.

Friday July 6 1894
THOMPSON   July 5, at his father's residence, Bridge Street, Lisburn, Samuel, youngest son of James Thompson, aged 18 years. Funeral to-morrow (Saturday) afternoon, at half past three o'clock.

Saturday July 30 1898
THOMPSON   July 29, at his residence, 49 Bridge Street, Lisburn, James Thompson, aged 68 years. Funeral to-morrow (Sunday) afternoon at three o'clock.

Thursday October 7 1875
TINSLEY   Oct. 6, at 8, Lawrence Street, The Plains, Belfast, Arthur Tinsley. His remains will be removed from his late residence for interment in Lisburn Cathedral Burying-ground to-morrow (Friday) morning, at ten o'clock.

Friday December 2 1910
TINSLEY   December 1st, at her residence, 11, Ulsterville Avenue, Belfast, Mary, widow of the late Arthur Tinsley, formerly of Lisburn. Funeral strictly private.

Saturday September 10 1921

TINSLEY   September 9 (suddenly) at 11, Ulsterville Avenue, David Charles, youngest son of the late Arthur Tinsley, formerly of Lisburn. Funeral strictly private.

Tuesday September 17 1839

TURNER   On the 12th inst., at his residence Seymour–street, Lisburn, aged 44 years, Mr. Stewart Turner, for the last 24 years House Surgeon and Apothecary to the county Antrim Infirmary.

Friday August 20 1869

TURNER   August 18, at Aberdeen, Scotland, James Turner, H M's Customs, eldest son of Francis Turner, Esq., Lisburn, aged 47 years.

Wednesday December 10 1873

TURNER   Dec. 8, at Tonagh, Lisburn, Frs. Turner, aged 77 years. His remains will be removed for interment to-morrow (Thursday) morning at ten o'clock. Friends will please accept this intimation.

Saturday January 30 1875

TURNER   Jan. 26, at Cottingwood, Morpeth, Margaret Ann, third daughter of the late Francis and Ann Turner, Tonagh, Lisburn, Ireland, Matron of the Prisons, Newcastle-on-Tyne.

Thursday April 28 1886

VERNON   April 28, at his residence, Bridge Street, Lisburn, James Vernon, aged 83 years. His remains will be removed for interment in the Cathedral Churchyard on Saturday morning, May 1st, at half-past ten o'clock. Friends will please accept this intimation.

Thursday January 22 1880

WATSON   January 21, at Bridge Street, Lisburn, Henry Watson, aged 58 years. His remains will be removed for interment in the Cathedral Burying Ground, to-morrow (Friday) morning at ten o'clock. Friends will please accept this intimation.

Monday August 9 1880

WATSON   August 8, at Smithfield, Lisburn, Mary Jane, the beloved wife of Robert Watson. Her remains will be removed for interment in the Cathedral-yard, to-morrow (Tuesday) afternoon at three o'clock. Friends will please accept this intimation.

Monday May 4 1903

WATSON   May 3, at her residence, 10 Sea Cliff Terrace, Bangor, Mary Ann, relict of the late Henry Watson, in her 80th year. Interment at Lisburn Cathedral Burying-ground. Funeral private. No flowers.

Tuesday February 12 1839

WETHERED   At Lisburn, on the 3rd inst., Mary, the beloved wife of Mr. Wethered, after a long and severe illness, which she bore with great Christian resignation.

Tuesday September 9 1845

WETHERED   At Bombay, of Malignant Cholera, on the 6th July, Anthony, only child of the late Thomas Wethered M.D., of Lisburn, belonging to the barque Earl of Eglinton.

Tuesday December 21 1830

WHITEFORD   On the 13th inst. at his house in Lisburn, of fever, contracted by his attendance on the patients in the hospital, Hugh Boyd Whiteford M.D. During his professional career in Lisburn, his conduct has been uniformly marked by disinterested philanthropy; and he has now, in the prime of his life, at the early age of 36, fallen a victim to his humanity and benevolence. - So speedy was the progress of the disease, that he was snatched from his friends almost before they could believe the melancholy tidings. Did we require any proof of the high estimation in which he was held by all classes of society, it would be found in the marked demonstrations of respect shown to his memory. During the interment of his remains, which took place at ten o'clock on the morning of Wednesday, almost every shop was closed and business suspended. In addition to a very large number of the respectable inhabitants of the town and neighbourhood, a dense multitude of the poorer classes accompanied the procession, and crowded round the grave to take a last look, and last farewell of their friend and benefactor: - Seldom has a similar event produced such sensations of unfeigned sorrow; and the proofs of this feeling which have been given must be highly gratifying to those who have sustained so severe a loss.

Friday March 30 1821

WHITLA   On the 21st inst. At his father's house Lisburn, John Whitla Esq., aged 25 years.

Tuesday May 24 1831

WHITLA   In Lisburn, on the morning of the 13th instant, George Whitla Esq.

Friday May 18 1842

WHITLA   On the 8th inst. John, third son of William Whitla Esq., Lisburn, aged six years and six months.

Friday December 30 1842

WHITLA   On the 25th inst. at Lisburn, Margaret, relict of the late George Whitla, Esq., aged 71.

Tuesday July 16 1861

WHITLA   July 12, at Lisburn, William Whitla, Esq., aged 68 years.

Wednesday June 2 1886

WHITLA   May 30, at Chepstow Villas, Bayswater, London, Elizabeth, widow of the late William Whitla, of Lisburn, aged 75 years. Interred at Plumstead, Kent, on Ascension Day.

Friday December 18 1801

WIGHTMAN   At Lisburn, on Tuesday the 15th inst., Mr. John Wightman, Merchant. – A gentleman who fulfilled the relative duties of life with exemplary propriety, whose loss is not only sincerely regretted by his numerous connections, but will be severely felt by a numerous class of manufacturing poor, to whom he uniformly evinced himself a warm and steady friend, and to whom he afforded constant and liberal employment.

Friday March 5 1819

WIGHTMAN   In Lisburn, on the 25th ult. in the 68th year of her age, Mrs Wightman, relict of the late Mr. John Wightman.

Friday July 1 1825

WIGHTMAN   On 22nd April, in the prime of life, after a few days illness at Florence, Alabama, United States, Mr. William Wightman, Merchant, formerly of Lisburn.

Tuesday January 31 1843

WIGHTMAN   On the 15th inst. at his residence, Prospect-place, Southampton, at the advanced age of 86, Robert Wightman, Esq., M.D., formerly of Lisburn.

Friday March 28 1845
WIGHTMAN   At Lewistown, Pennsylvania on the 7th Nov. last, James Wightman Esq., formerly of Grove Green, near Lisburn.

Friday June 30 1848
WIGHTMAN   On 25th May, at Ilavana, on board the steamer *Tay*, on her passage from New Orleans to England, Nancy, daughter of the late Mr. J. Wightman, Lisburn.

Saturday November 8 1856
WIGHTMAN   October 14, at St. Louis, Missouri, Magdeline, relict of William Wightman, Esq., formerly of Lisburn, and eldest daughter of the late Isaac Patton, Esq., of Belfast.

Tuesday June 18 1833
WILSON   At Lisburn, on Tuesday last, after a lingering illness, Mr. Adam Wilson, of the same place, aged 48 years.

Tuesday August 4 1835
WILSON   At Lisburn, on the 13th ult. aged 18 years, William, eldest son of the late Adam Wilson, of that town.

Tuesday September 27 1842
WILSON   On the 17th inst. at Ashgrove, near Lisburn, Mr. Thomas Wilson, aged 68 years, late of High-street, Belfast, woollen-draper.

Saturday June 6 1868
WILSON   June 5, at her residence, 4, Upper Queen Street, Belfast, Sarah, youngest daughter of the late Adam Wilson of Lisburn. Her remains will be removed for interment in Lisburn churchyard, on Monday morning, 8th inst., at nine o'clock. Friends will please accept this intimation.

Monday November 19 1877
WILSON   November 18, at his late residence, 46, Upper Queen Street, Robert, only surviving son of the late Adam Wilson, Lisburn. His remains will be removed for interment in the Cathedral Burying ground, Lisburn, on Wednesday morning, the 21st instant, at ten o'clock. Friends will please accept this intimation.

Monday April 15 1878
WILSON   April 13, at his father's residence, Ballymacash, Lisburn, Mr. Thomas Wilson, in the 26th year of his age, beloved and respected by all who knew him. His remains will be removed for interment in the Cathedral Churchyard, Lisburn, this (Monday) morning, at eleven o'clock.

Monday February 25 1884
WILSON   At her residence, 46, Upper Queen Street, Belfast, Susanna, eldest daughter of the late Adam Wilson, Lisburn. Her remains will be removed from the above address, for interment in the Cathedral Burying-ground, Lisburn, to-morrow (Tuesday) morning at half-past nine o'clock. Friends will please accept this intimation.

Friday April 6 1900
WILSON   April 4, at her residence, Ballymacash, Lisburn, Sarah, widow of the late William Wilson. Her remains will be removed from interment in the Cathedral Churchyard, this (Friday) afternoon, at two o'clock. Friends will please accept this (the only) intimation. Robert Wilson

Wednesday February 27 1929
WILSON   February 25, 1929, at her residence, 2 Smithfield, Lisburn, Isabella, second daughter of the late George Wilson (Carrier). Funeral today (Wednesday) at 3:30p.m. to Cathedral churchyard, Lisburn. Friends will please accept this intimation.
Deeply regretted by all.

W.A. and George Wilson.

Wednesday November 7 1877
WOODHOUSE   November 5, at Fintona, County Tyrone, Mary Cairns, the beloved wife of George Woodhouse Esq. Her remains will arrive for interment at Lisburn, by the 10-25 train, to-morrow (Thursday) morning.

Saturday November 29 1890
WOODHOUSE   November 27, at 68 Morehampton Road, Dublin, Catherine Jane, wife of George Woodhouse, Esq., and daughter of the late William Patterson, Esq., J.P., Fivemiletown. Funeral private.

Thursday March 10 1898
WOODHOUSE   March 8, at Bray, Co. Wicklow, George Woodhouse, aged 84 years. Funeral strictly private. No flowers by request.

Friday September 8 1809
WRAY   At his residence Rostrevor, Colonel H. Wray, late of the Hon. East India Company's service.

Tuesday June 5 1849
WRAY   June 1, at Rostrevor, in her 87th year, Mrs Wray, relict of the late Lieut-Colonel Wray.

NORTHERN WHIG
DIED

Tuesday September 1846
CROSSLEY On the 17th inst. Major Francis Crossley, a Magistrate of the County Down.

Thursday June 16 1831
NEELY   On Saturday last, Violet Neely, in her 20th year, and Benjamin Neely Esq., Lieutenant in the Ballymacash Yeomanry, in his 23rd year, the former at 9½ am and the latter at 6½ pm, at the house of their father, Benjamin Neely Esq., Principal of the Lisburn Academy.

Wednesday December 18 1861
NEELY   December 17, at the residence of his son-in-law (Jas. Major Esq., Beaver Hall, Ballymacarett) Mr. Erskine Neely, Lisburn, aged seventy-seven years. [His remains will be removed for interment in the Churchyard of the Cathedral, Lisburn, at half-past ten o'clock on Thursday morning. Friends will please accept this notice.]

Saturday March 6 1849
WOODHOUSE   On the 2d inst. at Lisburn, Margaret, wife of Mr. Geo. Woodhouse.

BELFAST COMMERCIAL CHRONICLE
DIED

Saturday December 24 1836

CLARKE   On the 11th inst. at Shamrockvale Lodge, Lisburn, Mary, wife of Lieutenant Clarke, late Royal Artillery, aged 58, deeply lamented by her husband and family to whom she was an affectionate wife and a fond mother.

Saturday August 6 1836

MARMION   Of consumption at Greenwood Cottage, Lisburn, on Tuesday the 26thult. Eliza, youngest daughter of the late Henry Marmion, Esq.

Wednesday March 23 1836

NEELY   In Lisburn, on the 15th inst. aged 18 years, Miss Eleanor Cupples Neely, daughter of Mr. Neely, Principal of the Academy.

Monday April 14 1823

STEWART   On Wednesday, the 9th instant, at his house in Castle-street, Lisburn, Poyntz Stewart, Esq., aged 87 years.

BANNER OF ULSTER
DIED

Tuesday February 24 1852

HIGGINSON   On the 20th instant, at Fairy Villa, Lisburn, Margaret, aged seventy-five years, last surviving daughter of Philip Talbot Higginson Esq., late of Dublin.

Friday March 16 1849

LECKIE (SIC)   At Lisburn, on Sabbath last, of Cholera, after a very few hours illness, Mr. William Leckie (sic), aged forty-six years. He was twenty-two years in the service of Messrs. Coulson, the eminent damask manufacturers of that town. The best character that can be given of the deceased is, that he was the chief support of a widowed mother.

Friday May 18 1849

MATEER   On the 12th inst., after a long illness, Isabella, wife of Joseph Mateer, of Malone turnpike, aged sixty-four.

Friday October 13 1843

THOMPSON At Ardglass, on Saturday 7th inst., Doctor Thompson, formerly of Lisburn, aged ninety.

Tuesday September13 1842

WETHERED   DEATH OF DOCTOR WETHERED OF LISBURN.— This highly respected gentleman, we deeply regret to state, died on Wednesday evening last, 7th inst., from apoplexy, with which he had been attacked on the preceding day. His loss is sincerely and universally lamented in the circle which he ornamented by his public and private virtues, and benefited by his high professional talents and attainments.

Friday January 28 1853

WHITLA   On the 25th instant, of scarletina, Seymour Conway, son of Wm. Whitla, Esq., Lisburn, aged seven years and five months.

Tuesday March 1 1853

WHITLA   On the 27th ultimo, of scarletina, Sydney, son of William Whitla, Esq., Lisburn, aged 9 years and 7 months.

TYRONE CONSTITUTION
DIED

Friday January 27 1871

CARR   Jan. 20, at Lisburn, Elizabeth Clarke, wife of T.P. Carr, Esq., R.I.C., eldest daughter of the late Wm. Whitla, Esq., Lisburn, aged thirty-three years.

THE IRISH TIMES
DIED

Saturday February 9 1907

HAWKSHAW   On the 7th February 1907, at 1 Wellington road, Dublin, in her 93rd year, Eleanora Frances, last surviving daughter of the Lieutenant-colonel John Stewart Hawkshaw, 31st (Huntingdonshire) Regiment.

LISBURN STANDARD
DIED

Saturday November 12 1887

ALLEN   November 8, at his mother's residence, Bachelor's Walk, Lisburn, Andrew, eldest son of the late James Allen, aged 28 years.

Saturday October 6 1888

CLARKE   September 30, at 115, Lower Baggot Street, Dublin, Marianne Clarke, the very dearly beloved wife of the Rev. Samuel Clarke, late assistant chaplain, Hyeres, France, and third daughter of the late Robert Stewart, Sen., Esq., Lisburn.

Saturday February 19 1887

McCLURE   February 16, at her mother's residence, the Manse, Saintfield Road, Lisburn, Martha, daughter of the late Adam McClure.

Saturday December 2 1911

McKEE   November 28, at a Nursing Home, Belfast, Emily McKee, late of 24 Market Square. Interred on 30th November in the Cathedral Burying-ground, Lisburn.

Saturday February 22 1890

STANNUS   February 13, Caroline M.A. Stannus, second daughter of the late Very Rev. James Stannus, Dean of Ross, and Rector of Lisburn.

Saturday April 2 1887

STEWART   At Sion Hill, Clifton, Bristol, Elizabeth Scott Stewart (Eliza), eldest daughter of the late Robert Stewart, Sen., Lisburn, aged 66 years.

Saturday January 30 1886

TINSLEY   January 26, at 34, Second Street, Connswater, John Tinsley, formerly of Lisburn.

Saturday June 5 1886

WHITLA   At No. 6, Chepstow Villas, Bayswater, London, on Sunday afternoon, the 30th May, 1886, Elizabeth Whitla, widow of the late William Whitla, of Lisburn, County Antrim, Ireland, aged 75 years. Peacefully fell asleep in the arms of Him she loved so well; deeply regretted by her large family and numerous friends.

LISBURN CATHEDRAL WILLS

BLACKBURN

Adam, Lissue, Lisburn, Co. Antrim, Farmer.
Died 19th May 1879.
Probate granted 31st July 1882, Belfast.
Mentions William Blackburn, Lissue, Farmer.

BLACKBURN

Ann, formerly Belfast and late Lissue, Co. Antrim, Widow.
Died 28th February 1882, Lissue.
Probate granted 27th March 1882, Belfast.
Mentions William Blackburn, Lissue, Lisburn, Publican and Farmer.

BLACKBURN

Alexander, Hillview-street Belfast, Publican.
Died 19th September 1891.
Probate granted 13th November 1891, Belfast.
Mentions Jane Anne Blackburn, Hillview-street, Belfast, Widow.

BLACKBURN

William, Lissue, Lisburn, Co. Antrim, Retired Farmer.
Died 8th May 1900.
Probate granted 5th December 1900, Belfast.
Mentions Henry Monroe, Farmer.

BOLTON

James, Lisburn, Co. Antrim, Commander in Royal Navy.
Died 3rd April 1867.
Probate granted 29th May 1867, Principal Registry.
Mentions James Richard Ffennell of Lisburn, surgeon, Rev. Edward Mockler, Magherafelt, Clerk, and William Henry Conn of Lisburn.

BOOMER

Walter C., Knockmore, Co. Antrim.
Died 2nd October 1918.
Probate granted 14th February 1919, Belfast.

CALDBECK

William, De Vesci Terrace, Monkstown, Co. Dublin, Esquire.
Died 25th September 1858.
Probate granted 18th November 1858, Principal Registry.
Mentions Thomas Fulton Caldbeck, Blackrock, Co. Dublin, Esquire.

CAMPBELL

John, late of Lisburn, Co. Antrim, Doctor of Medicine.
Died 6th September 1867.
Probate granted 25th October 1867, Belfast.
Mentions Sarah Campbell, Lisburn, Widow.

CAMPBELL

Sarah, late of Island House, Lisburn, Co. Antrim, Widow.
Died 16th January 1914.
Administration granted 4th March 1914, Belfast.
Mentions Susan D. Campbell, Spinster.

CARR

Elizabeth Clarke, Newport, Co. Mayo.
Died 20th January 1871, Lisburn.
Administration granted 3rd March 1871, Ballina.
Mentions Thomas P. Carr of Newport, husband.

CLARKE	Marianne, (wife of the Reverend Samuel Clarke,) late of 115 Lower Baggot-street, Dublin. Died 30th September 1888 at same place. Probate granted 10th January 1889, Principal Registry. Mentions James Andrew Stewart, Lisburn, County Antrim, Merchant.
COULSON	Hill, Sprucefield, Co. Down, Esquire, Bachelor. Died 7th August 1860. Administration granted 27th August 1860, Belfast. Mentions William Coulson of Lisburn, County Antrim, Esquire, the Brother.
COULSON	Eleanor, formerly Lisburn and late Belfast, Co. Antrim, Spinster. Died 27th November 1866. Probate granted 19th January 1867, Principal Registry. Mentions Rev. Augustine Fitzgerald of the Glebe, Portadown, Co. Armagh, Clerk.
CUPPLES	Reverend Edward, late of Lisburn, County of Antrim, Clerk. Died 22nd November 1857. Probate granted 2nd February 1858, Principal Registry. Mentions Snowden Corken, Ingram, near Lisburn, aforesaid Solictor.
CUPPLES	Frances, Lisburn, Co. Antrim, Spinster. Died 28th September 1869. Probate granted 27th October 1869, Belfast. Mentions Snowden Corken of Ingram, Esq. Lisburn.
FLYNN	John, Bridge-street, Lisburn, Co. Antrim, Rent Agent. Died 13th April 1895. Probate granted 26th June 1895, Belfast. Mentions Hugh McCahey, Grocer and Joseph Connell, Clogmaker, both Bridge-street, Lisburn, and William John Robinson of Mercer-street, Lisburn, Co. Down, Grocer.
FULTON	John Williamson, late of Braidujle, Co. Antrim and Braidujle House, Co. Down, Esquire, J.P. Died 17th November 1872 at Braidujle House. Probate granted 10th February 1873, Belfast. Mentions Matilda Fulton of Braidujle House (Lisburn) aforesaid widow.
FULTON	William, Lisburn, Co. Antrim, Registrar of Births, Deaths and Marriages. Died 5th September 1881. Probate granted 10th October 1881, Belfast. Mentions Eliza Pirrie, Belfast, Spinster.
GORDON	Norris, Belfast, Pawnbroker. Died 20th December 1889. Probate granted 5th February 1890, Belfast. Mentions Thomas Archer Fullerton, Clothier and Postal Receiving Officer and William Nicholas Pratt, Merchant, both of York-street.

GRAHAM	Eliza, Lisburn, Co. Antrim, Widow. Died 19th February 1865, at Unicarvel near Comber, Co. Down. Administration granted 7th April 1865, Belfast. Mentions William Graham, Lisburn, Co. Antrim, Brewer and Merchant, son.
GRAHAM	William, Lisburn, Co. Antrim, Farmer. Died 27th July 1889. Probate granted 4th September 1889, Belfast. Mentions James Graham, 16, Miles-road, Clifton, Bristol, Co. Gloucester, Colonel on Retired List of Her Majesty's Bengal Army.
GRAHAM	Anne, Lisburn, Co. Antrim, Spinster. Died 19th October 1892, Unicarval, Co. Down. Probate granted 7th November 1892, Belfast. Mentions James Graham, 16 Miles-road, Clifton, Bristol, Retired Colonel.
GRAHAM	James, Cotswold, Wimbledon, Co. Surrey, Retired Colonel. Died 26th April 1905. Probate granted 15th September 1905, Dublin. Mentions Louisa M. Graham, the Widow, Donald C. Graham Esquire and William G. Smith, Retired Colonel.
GREGG	William, Derryvolgie, Lisburn, Co. Antrim, Esq. J.P. Died 2nd February 1870. Probate granted 25th March 1870, Belfast. Mentions Edward Fisher, Spring Dale, Huddersfield, England, Elizabeth Rebecca Gregg and Anna Bradshaw Gregg, both of Lisburn.
HAWKSHAW	Sophia Agnes, Blaris, Co. Antrim, Widow. Died 18th December 1859. Administration granted 22nd January 1861, Principal Registry. Mentions Eleanora Frances Hawkshaw, No 7 Belgrave-square, Monkstown, Co. Dublin, Spinster, daughter.
HAWKSHAW	Eleanora (otherwise Eleanor) Frances, 1 Wellington-road and Belgrave-square, Monkstown, both Co. Dublin, Spinster. Died 7th February 1907. Probate granted 1st March 1907, Dublin. Mentions Alfred D. Crawford and Tyndall S. Johns, Solicitors.
HERON	Eliza, Belfast, Widow. Died 22nd October 1885. Probate granted 16th November 1885, Belfast. Mentions John Hind (Junior) 19 College-street, South Belfast, Commission Agent.
HIGGINSON	Henry Theophilus, Carnalea House, Bangor, Co. Down, Esq., J.P. Died 20th June 1869. Probate granted 16th August 1869, Principal Registry. Mentions John McConnell Higginson, District Registrar, Court of Belfast, J.P. and Henry Seeds, Belfast, Solicitor.

HIGGINSON	Charlotte, (otherwise McConnell) Carnalea House, Co. Down, Widow. Died 15th June 1875. Probate granted 12th July 1875, Principal Registry. Mentions John McConnell Higginson, Carnalea House, Esquire, J.P.
HIGGINSON	Theophilus, formerly 23 Camden House Road, Kensington, County Middlesex and Lonsdale, Farnham, County Surrey, C.B. Died 30th August 1903. Probate granted 5th November 1903, London, resealed 8th April 1904, Dublin. Mentions Ada Higginson, Widow and William Whitla.
HODSON	Rev. Hartley, Lisburn, Co. Antrim, Clerk, D.D. Died 3rd February 1884. Probate granted 28th March 1884, Belfast. Mentions Hannah Hodson, Lisburn, Widow.
HULL	Joseph, Lisburn, Co. Antrim, Grocer. Died 26th December 1869. Probate granted 21st January 1870, Belfast. Mentions William Henry Lavery, Lisburn, Grocer.
HULL	Eliza, Lisburn, Co. Antrim, Widow. Died 5th March 1886. Probate granted 2nd July 1886. Belfast. Mentions William Henry Lavery, Lisburn, Grocer.
HULL	Jane, 16 Seymour Street, Lisburn, Co. Antrim, Spinster. Died 22nd January 1913. Probate granted 17th February 1913, Belfast. Mentions Albert Victor Waterhouse, Student and James McClenaghan, Land Steward.
JEFFERSON	Anne Jane, Lisburn, Co. Antrim, Widow. Died 30th November 1860. Administration granted 26th January 1861, Belfast. Mentions Sarah Jane Pelan (wife of Thomas Rutherford Pelan) Lisburn, daughter.
JEFFERSON	Redmond, late of Lisburn, Co. Antrim, Merchant. Died 30th January 1892. Probate granted 1st August 1892, Belfast. Mentions Margaretta Jefferson, Spinster and Redmond Jefferson, Merchant, both of Lisburn.
JEFFERSON	Robert, Aughnamor, Co. Antrim, Farmer. Died 8th April 1888. Probate granted 19th November 1888, Belfast. Mentions Redmond Jefferson (junior), Lisburn, Co. Antrim, Merchant.
JOHNSON SMYTH	Thomas, Lisburn, Co. Antrim, Esquire. Died 22nd April 1860. Probate granted 12th May 1860, Principal Registry. Mentions Matthew Johnson Smyth, Lisburn, Esquire, son.

JOHNSON SMYTH	Matthew, late of Lisburn, County of Antrim, Solicitor.
	Died 23rd September 1865.
	Administration granted 24th November 1865, Belfast.
	Mentions Elizabeth Anne Johnson Smyth of Lisburn, aforesaid Widow.

JOHNSON SMYTH	Armelia, Glanavey (sic), Co. Antrim.
	Died 1st April 1876.
	Administration granted 22nd April 1876, Principal Registry.
	Mentions Edward Johnson Smyth, husband.

JOHNSON SMYTH	Thomas, 14 Cromwell-terrace, Belfast, Esq.
	Died 8th April 1879.
	Administration granted 9th June 1879, Belfast.
	Mentions Matilda Johnson Smyth, Belfast, Widow.

JOHNSON SMYTH	William Stewart, Wyoming-street, Kansas City, U.S.A., Gentleman.
	Died 14th July 1888.
	Administration granted 17th April 1889, Principal Registry.
	Mentions Reverend Edward Johnson Smyth of Fenloe, Palmerston-road, Co. Dublin, Clerk, the father.

JOHNSON SMYTH	William Stewart, Wyoming-street, Kansas City, Missouri, U.S.A.
	Died 14th July 1888.
	Administration granted 28th October 1902, Dublin.
	Mentions Jane Johnson Smyth, Widow.

JOHNSON SMYTH	Thomas Roger, Major Durham Light Infantry.
	Died 5th February 1900, Tugela, South Africa.
	Probate granted 9th November 1900, Dublin.
	Mentions Evernia F.E. Johnson Smyth, Widow.

JOHNSON SMYTH	Matthew Bruce, late of Ingram, Lisburn, Co. Antrim, Solicitor.
	Died 8th August 1901.
	Administration 5th September 1902, Belfast.
	Mentions Elizabeth A. Johnston Smyth, Widow.

JOHNSON SMYTH	Reverend Edward, Fenloe, Palmerston-road, Rathmines, Co. Dublin.
	Died 23rd July 1902.
	Probate granted 7th October 1902, Dublin.
	Mentions Jane Johnson Smyth, the Widow.

JOHNSON SMYTH	Elizabeth Anne, Ingram, Lisburn, County Antrim, Widow.
	Died 27th February 1923.
	Probate granted 24th July 1924, Belfast.
	Mentions Maria Frances McNaughton Johnson Smyth, Spinster.

JOHNSON SMYTH	Roger Henry Ellis, Tonagh Lodge, Lisburn, County Antrim, Retired Farmer.
	Died 7th February 1969.
	Probate granted 21st January 1970, Belfast.

JOHNSTON	Andrew John, Waring-street, Belfast, Commission Agent, Widower. Died 3rd November 1871. Administration 21st December 1871, Belfast. Mentions George Johnston, Rotunda Hospital, Dublin, M.D., Curator of the minor, Daughter of said deceased.
KELLY	Hugh, Railway-street, Lisburn, Co. Antrim, Car owner. Died 3rd April 1869. Probate granted 12th November 1869, Belfast. Mentions James Wilson Bow-street (Grocer), Moses Bullick (Painter), and Eleanor Kelly (Widow) both of Railway-street, Lisburn.
KELLY	John, Lisburn, Co. Antrim, Carpenter, Bachelor. Died 17th August 1872. Administration granted 6th September 1872, Belfast. Mentions Eliza Taylor (wife of Richard Taylor, Saintfield, Co. Down R.I.C.,) a sister.
MACARTNEY	Arthur, formerly Lisburn and of Holywood, Co. Down and late Ballyholm, Bangor, Co. Down, Gentleman. Died 28th May 1874. Probate granted 26th June 1874, Belfast. Mentions Arthur Gamble and Agnes Gamble, his wife, both of Ballyholm, Bangor.
MACARTNEY	Arthur, Lisburn, Co. Antrim, Bachelor. Died 24th April 1877, Dublin. Administration granted 10th October 1877, Belfast. Mentions Agnes Gamble (wife of Arthur Gamble of 53 Strand-road, Sandymount, Co. Dublin, Gentleman) sister.
McCLURE	Adam, Lisburn, Co. Antrim, Publican. Died 28th March 1874. Probate granted 22nd April 1874, Belfast. Mentions Rev. Edmund McClure, 102 Richmond-terrace, Belfast, Clerk.
McDOWALL	Eleanor, Seymour Street, Lisburn, Co. Antrim, Widow. Died 22nd July 1890. Probate granted 5th November 1890, Belfast. Mentions Rev. Pounden and George Haynes Fosbroke, Bedford. Co. Warwick. M.D.
McHENRY	Robert, 7 Windsor Gardens, Belfast, Chief Petty Sessions Clerk. Died 6th January 1914. Administration with will granted 14th October 1914, Belfast. Mentions Sarah McHenry, the Widow.

McKEE	George, Old Warren, Lisburn, Co. Antrim, Master of the Lisburn Union Workhouse. Died 6th October 1861. Probate granted 4th November 1861, Belfast, Mentions George Thompson, Leather Merchant and Bootmaker and John Stevenson, Flour Dealer and Book-keeper, both of Lisburn.
McKEE	Hannah, Croft-place, Bangor, Co. Down, Widow. Died 11th December 1896. Probate granted 6th January 1897, Belfast. Mentions Samuel McKee Barry Fitchie, 50 Glenallen-street, Belfast, Electrician and Hannah Alexander Fitchie, Ballydrain, Comber, Co. Down, Spinster.
McMULLEN	James, Knockmore, Co. Antrim, School Teacher. Died 17th March 1878. Probate granted 26th April 1878, Belfast. Mentions John McBride, Beechfield, Gentleman, and Henry Monro, Lissue, Farmer, Co. Antrim.
MATEER	John, 125 Hertford-place, Dublin-road, Belfast, Gentleman. Died 17th November 1897. Probate granted 18th January 1898, Belfast. Mentions William Mateer, 185, Durham-street, Manager, and William Holmes of Bradbury-place, Carpenter, both of Belfast.
MOORE	Jane Deborah, Warren Cottage, near Lisburn, Co. Antrim. Died 6th December 1863. Administration granted 20th January 1864, Belfast. Mentions Rev. John Robert Moore of Rowallen House, near Saintfield, Co. Down, Clerk, brother.
MUSGRAVE	Robert Hamilton, Drumglass, Belfast, Merchant. Died 9th March 1867. Probate granted 27th September 1867, Belfast. Mentions John Riddel Musgrave and James Musgrave both of Drumglass, Merchants.
MUSGRAVE	Samuel, Drumglass House, Belfast, F.R.C.S. Edin. Died 19th April 1893. Probate granted 10th July 1893, Belfast. Mentions James Musgrave and Henry Musgrave, both of Drumglass House, Esquires.
MUSGRAVE	John Riddel, Drumglass House, Belfast, Esq. Died 30th March 1895. Probate granted 24th January 1896, Belfast. Mentions James Musgrave, Drumglass House, Belfast, Esq.
MUSGRAVE	Sir James, Drumglass House, Belfast. Died 22nd February 1904. Probate granted 8th April 1904, Belfast. Mentions Henry Musgrave and Edgar Musgrave, Merchants.

MUSGRAVE	Edgar, Drumglass House, Belfast, Gentleman. Died 12th May 1913. Probate granted 7th July 1913, Belfast. Mentions Henry Musgrave D.L.
MUSGRAVE	Henry, Drumglass House, Belfast & 69, Ann Street, Belfast, Esquire, D.L. O.B.E. Died 2nd January 1922 at Drumglass. Probate granted 15th May 1922, Belfast.
NEELY	Erskine, Market-square, Lisburn, Co. Antrim, Pawnbroker. Died 27th November 1861 at Beaver Hall, Ballymacarett, County of Down. Probate granted 27th October 1862, Belfast. Mentions James Major, James-street, South Belfast, Merchant.
NEWBURN	William, late of 19 Turin street, Belfast, Superannuated Postman. Died 22nd February 1890. Probate granted 21st March 1890, Belfast. Mentions Robert Shannon, 3, Dickson-street, Moulder and William Burgess, 163, Ormeau Road, Belfast, Inspector of Postmen.
NICHOLSON	Clara, late of Lisburn, Co. Antrim, Widow. Died 17th February 1874. Probate granted 14th April 1874, Principal Registry. Mentions Rev. Edward Maxwell, High Roding, County Essex, clerk, Rev. John Seymour, Newcastle, Co. Down and Rev. William Dawson Pounden, Lisburn (the Sons-in-law) (sic).
O'FLAHERTY	Francis Hale, Lisburn, Co. Antrim, Solicitor. Died 18th October 1859, Lisburn. Probate granted 28th November 1859, Belfast. Mentions Eleanor O'Flaherty, Widow, Thomas Alexander O'Flaherty M.D., both Lisburn and David Hale, Drumnavaddy, Co. Down, Gentleman Farmer.
O'FLAHERTY	Eleanor, Lisburn, Co. Antrim, Widow. Died 30th May 1875. Administration granted 14th July 1875, Belfast. Mentions Francis Hale Hill O'Flaherty, Bangor, Co. Down, Warehouse-man, son.
O'FLAHERTY	Thomas Alexander, 44 Botanic-avenue, Belfast, M.D. and Staff Surgeon R.N. Died 26th October 1888, Cultra, Co. Down. Probate granted 26th November 1888, Belfast. Mentions Francis Hale Hill O'Flaherty, Rosavo, Cultra, Co. Down, Linen Merchant.

O'FLAHERTY	Francis Hale Hill, Eglantine Avenue, and Franklin Street, both Belfast, Handkerchief Manufacturer. Died 5th May 1901. Probate granted 24th June 1901, Belfast. Mentions Harriette E. O'Flaherty, Widow.
O'FLAHERTY	Douglas Hill, Aughnanure, Marlborough Park, Belfast, Captain. Died 1st July 1916 (killed in action in France.) Double probate granted 18th August and 00 January 1916, Belfast. Mentions Robert G. Glenning (Junior) Electrical Engineer and Frederick J. Leitch, Flax Merchant.
PARKINSON	Allice, Beersbridge-road, Ballymacarrett, Belfast, Widow. Died 29th December 1892, at same place. Probate granted 26th June 1893, Belfast. Mentions George Tate 63, Beersbridge-road, Provision Dealer and Robert Neill Howard-street, Artist.
PELAN	Thomas R., Lisburn, Co. Antrim, Pawnbroker. Died 3rd April 1875, Lisburn. Probate granted 7th May 1875, Belfast. Mentions Sarah Jane Pelan, Lisburn, Widow.
PELAN	Sarah Jane, Belvedere, Lisburn, Co. Antrim, Widow. Died 31st August 1923. Probate granted 17th September 1923, Belfast. Mentions James Erskine Pelan, Pawnbroker and William Lindsay Woods, Manufacturer.
PENNINGTON	John, late of Lisnagarvey, near Lisburn, Co. Antrim, Gentleman Atorney-at-Law. Died 3rd March 1874. Probate granted 29th April 1874, Belfast. Mentions John Pennington, Lisnagan, Lisburn.
POUNDEN	Rev. William Dawson, The Rectory, Castle Street, Lisburn, County Antrim, Canon. Died 29th September 1917. Probate granted 19th November 1917, Dublin. Mentions Philippa F. Pounden and Louisa M. Pounden, Spinsters.
PURDON	Charles Nicholas Delacherois, late of Wellington Place, Belfast, Esquire, M.D. Died 8th January 1882. Probate granted 8th February 1882, Belfast. Mentions Elias Hughes Bell and Joseph Bell, both of Belfast, Esquires.
PURDON	Thomas Henry, Wellington Place, Belfast, M.D. Died 6th August 1886. Probate 18th October 1886, Belfast. Mentions Eleanor Grace Purdon, Wellington Place, Belfast, Widow, and William Purdon, Enniskillen, Co. Fermanagh, Esquire C.E.

PURDON	Jane Maria, 27 Hughendon Terrace, Belfast, late of 56, Eglantine Avenue, Belfast, Widow. Died 6th February 1916. Probate granted 25th September 1916, Belfast. Mentions Richard J. Purdon, M.D.
REID	Margaret, Nelson-street, Belfast, Spinster. Died 24th September 1860, Belfast. Administration granted 12th November 1860, Belfast. Mentions Maria Woods of Athol-street, Belfast, Spinster, the cousin, only next of kin.
REID	Samuel, formerly Downpatrick, Co. Down, late Lisburn, Co. Antrim, Gentleman. Died 5th December 1868, Lisburn. Administration granted 7th May 1869, Belfast. Mentions William Reid, Lisburn, Quarter Master Sergeant in Royal Artillery, Son.
RIDDALL	Rev. Edward Parkinson, 4 Parkmount, Lisburn, Co. Antrim, Clerk. Died 30th June 1922. Probate granted 13th October 1922, Belfast. Mentions Henrietta Seward Riddall, Widow.
SPROULL	Eleanor, late College-street, Belfast, County of Antrim, Widow. Died 17th May 1863. Probate granted 18th June 1863, Belfast. Mentions William Henry Sproull of Carrickfergus, Solicitor and Eliza Sproull of College-street, Belfast, Spinster.
SPROULL	Eliza, College-street, Belfast, Co. Antrim, Spinster. Died 9th June 1868. Probate granted 3rd July 1868, Belfast. Mentions William Henry Sproull, Solicitor and Jane Sproull, his wife, both of Carrickfergus, Co. Antrim.
STANNUS	Elizabeth, Lisburn, Co. Antrim (wife of the Very Reverend James Stannus, Dean of Ross) Died 14th May 1873. Administration granted 17th May 1876, Belfast. Mentions Harriet Jane Stannus, Lisburn, Spinster.
STANNUS	Very Reverend James, late of Lisburn, Co. Antrim, Clerk in Holy Orders and Dean of Ross, and Rector of the Parish of Lisburn, otherwise Blaris. Died 28th January 1876. Probate granted 3rd March 1876, Belfast. Mentions Thomas Robert Stannus, Magheralave, Lisburn, Esquire.

STANNUS	Walter Trevor, Manor House, Lisburn, Co. Antrim, Esq. Died 28th February 1895, Dublin. Probate granted 11th April 1895, Belfast. Mentions Honorable Catherine Geraldine Stannus, Manor House, Lisburn, Widow.
STANNUS	Thomas Robert, Magheraleave, Lisburn, Co. Antrim, Esquire. Died 8th November 1907 at Gog Magog Hills, Cambridgeshire, England. Probate granted 24th January 1908, Belfast. Mentions Margaret Elizabeth Stannus, theWidow.
STEWART	Robert, late of Lisburn in the County of Antrim, Mill Owner. Died 4th June 1858. Probate granted 28th November 1862, Belfast. Mentions Robert Stewart Jun., James Andrew Stewart, Flax Spinners, Eliza Stewart, Spinster, all of Lisburn, aforesaid, and William John Johnston, Belfast, aforesaid Merchant, four of the Executors.
STEWART	Magdalene, Glenavy, Co. Antrim, Spinster. Died 5th December 1871. Probate granted 27th January 1872, Principal Registry. Mentions Thomas Fulton Caldbeck, Eaton Brae, Loughlinstown, Co. Dublin, Esquire and Rev. Edward Johnson Smyth, Glenavy, Clerk.
STEWART	Elizabeth, Lisburn, County Antrim, Spinster. Died 25th March 1887 at Zion-hill, Clifton, County Gloucester. Probate granted 29th April 1887, Belfast. Mentions James Andrew Stewart, Lisburn, Merchant.
SWANZY	Oswald Ross, Lisburn. Died 22nd August 1920. Probate granted 20th October 1920, Belfast.
THOMPSON	William, Lisburn, Co. Antrim, Esquire, Doctor of Medicine and Surgeon. Died 22nd September 1882, Dunmurry. Probate granted 13th October 1882, Belfast. Mentions James Bruce, Thorndale, Belfast. Esq.
THOMPSON	Rosina, 4 Dunedin-terrace, Belfast, Widow. Died 8th December 1884. Administration granted 5th January 1885, Belfast. Mentions Mary Hogg Bruce (wife of James Bruce) of Thorndale, Belfast, D.L., the child.
TINSLEY	Matthew, 5 Mount Pleasant, Stranmillis, Belfast, Gentleman. Died 17th February 1949. Probate granted 2nd June 1950, Belfast. Mentions Marianne Tinsley, Spinster.

TINSLEY	Marianne (otherwise Minnie) 5 Mount Pleasant, Stranmillis, Belfast, Spinster. Died 16th July 1951. Probate granted 13th February 1952, Belfast. Mentions George Herbert Leitch and George Herbert Leitch Junior, Solicitors.
WATSON	Henry, Bridge-street, Lisburn, Grocer and Provision Dealer. Died 21st January 1880. Probate granted 16th July 1880, Belfast. Mentions Mary Anne Watson, Bridge-street, Lisburn, Widow.
WHITLA	William, Lisburn, Co. Antrim, Esq. Died 12th July 1861. Probate granted 14th August 1861, Belfast. Mentions Elizabeth Whitla, Widow, George Whitla, Assistant Surgeon Royal Horse Artillery, James Buchanan Whitla, Lieutenant 88th Regiment of Infantry, residing Lisburn.
WILSON	Sarah, 4 Upper Queen-street, Belfast, Spinster. Died 5th June 1868. Administration granted 24th September 1869, Belfast. Mentions Amelia Wilson, 4 Upper Queen-street, Belfast, Spinster, sister.
WOODHOUSE	George, late of 1 Lorretto Villas, Bray, Co. Wicklow. Died 8th March 1898. Administration granted 29th April 1898, Dublin. Mentions Stewart Woodhouse M.D., 41, Northumberland-road, Dublin, and Thomas F. Shillington of Dromart, Belfast, Esquire and The Reverend Benson E., Gentleman of 15 Norman-terrace, Jones-road, Dublin.

VIEW OF OLD CATHEDRAL ENTRANCE TO MARKET PLACE c1924

HISTORY OF THE QUAKERS

George Fox, a weaver's son from Leicestershire, founded the Religious Society of Friends in the seventeenth century. The term "Quakers" was first used in 1650 and the title "Friends" was adopted in 1652. William Edmundson, who had been in Cromwell's army, settled first in Antrim and later in Lurgan. After attending a meeting held by the Quaker Minister, James Naylor, he adopted the Quaker faith and in 1654, in Lurgan, a meeting for worship of the Society of Friends was held. This is believed to be the first in Ireland.

John Shaw became convinced after hearing William Edmundson, and also in 1654 meetings were held at his house at the Broad Oak, near Lisnagarvey. This was the start of Lisburn Meeting. In 1658 these meetings moved to the home of George Gregson, whose house was situated at the corner of Railway Street and Market Square. The present building on this site is now occupied by Shannon's the jewellers and was formerly the Northern Bank. Previous buildings on this site were another Northern Bank building and before that the Hertford Arms Hotel. The Quakers are the second oldest religious congregation in Lisburn.

About 1674 a Meeting House was built in Gregson's back garden. Access to this was by a narrow lane running from Market Square. This Meeting House was about 34 feet by 20 feet. This was one of the few buildings to survive the fire of 1707. In 1795 a new and larger Meeting House was erected on the same site. There was now also an opening onto what was then known as Jackson's Lane. Before 1720 Jackson's Lane was known as School Room Lane, and is now Railway Street. This building was 2 storeys high, built of stone and lime and was slated.

In 1853 the building was again replaced. This building is still standing in Railway Street and was sold in 1995 when another new Meeting House was built at 4 Magheralave Road, Lisburn.

The Burying Ground is beside the old Meeting House in Railway Street, and hidden from view by a stone and lime wall. The original entrance was through a cast iron gate. Quaker principles would not allow clergymen of other religions to conduct burial services, and, as Quakers wanted to conduct their own burials, some Quakers provided a plot of ground on their land. The burial ground in Railway Street is part of Friends' earliest property in Lisburn. The first recorded burial is that of Joseph Patterson in 1780 and the last Mary Jane McCready in 1907. As the ground became full a plot was used in Lisburn Cemetery, Hillsborough Road, from about 1900 until about 1970. The local Friends now use Friends' Burial Ground, Hillsborough.

In 1783 the Ireland Yearly Meeting of the Religious Society of Friends recommended the removal of all gravestones as it was felt there was a danger that memorial stones might become objects of worship. When gravestones were finally allowed again in the mid 1800's rules were drawn up with reference to size and inscriptions so that no distinction was made between persons. The inscription consisted of name and age. Burial notes recording name, age and date of death were prepared and recorded. These regulations were in accordance with the Quaker belief that, in the sight of God, all men and women are equal.

We have included a list of all those recorded as being buried in the Burying Ground in Railway Street, along with a record of the gravestone inscriptions. There may have been other burials which were not recorded. There are twenty-eight gravestones and at least one had cast iron railings surrounding it. Most of these gravestones are of members of the Richardson family. These stones were originally upright, but they are now lying flat.

The Quaker records may be found in the Public Record Office of Northern Ireland under MIC/16/19 and 20.

FRIENDS' BURYING GROUND, RAILWAY STREET, LISBURN

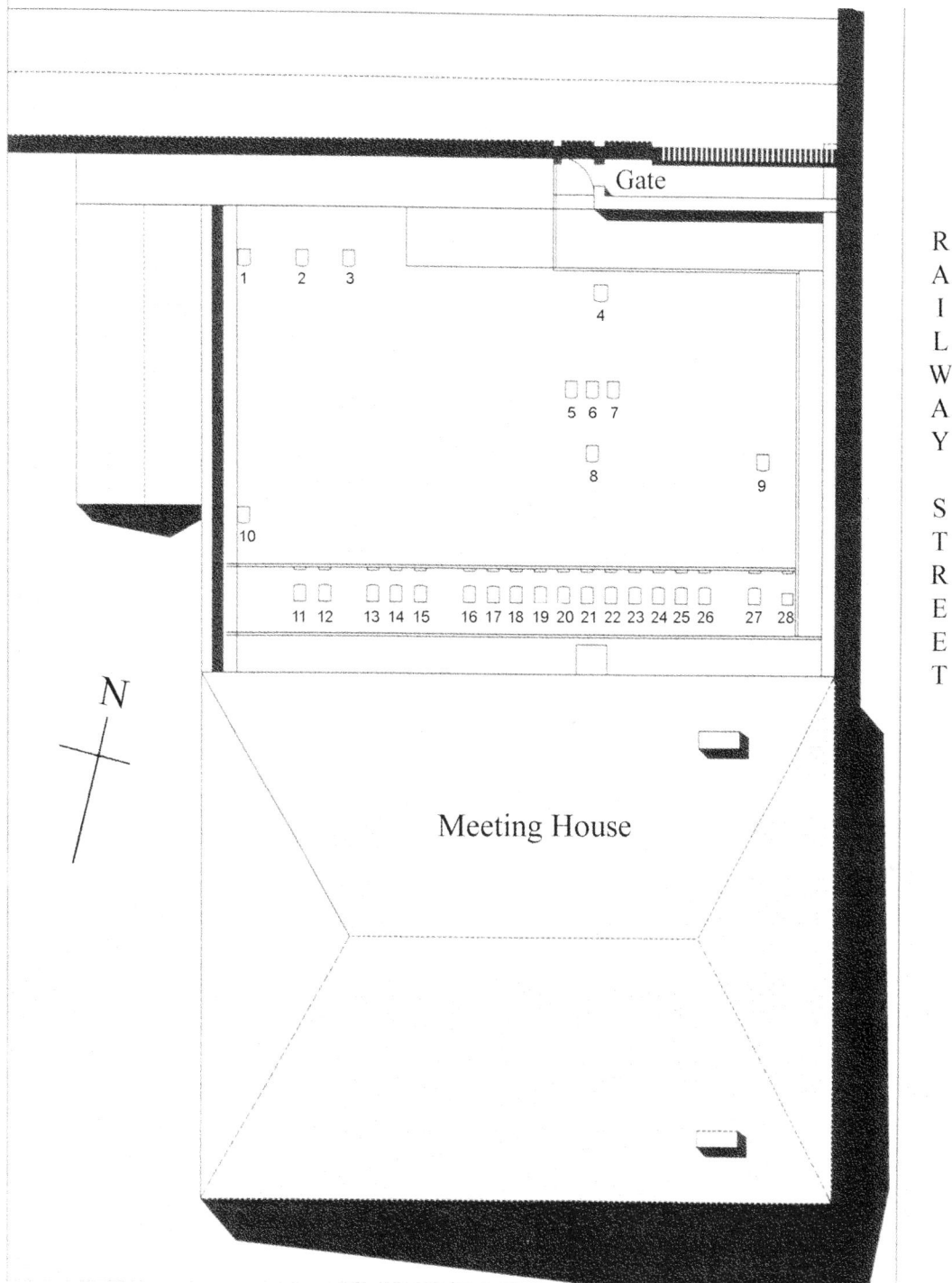

Gate

1 2 3

4

5 6 7

8   9

10

11 12   13 14 15   16 17 18 19 20 21 22 23 24 25 26   27 28

N

Meeting House

RAILWAY STREET

FRIENDS' BURYING GROUND, RAILWAY STREET, LISBURN.

1. PEARSON
2. ROBSON
3. BAILEY
4. GREGG
5. GREGG
6. GREGG
7. GREGG
8. LAMB
9. HANCOCK
10. SMITH
11. RICHARDSON
12. RICHARDSON
13. RICHARDSON
14. RICHARDSON
15. RICHARDSON
16. RICHARDSON
17. MALCOMSON
18. CLIBBORN
19. RICHARDSON
20. RICHARDSON
21. RICHARDSON
22. RICHARDSON
23. RICHARDSON
24. RICHARDSON
25. RICHARDSON
26. RICHARDSON
27. RICHARDSON
28. GOUGH

(Courtesy of PRONI T/2571/6/1/11)

VIEW OF FRIENDS' BURYING GROUND, RAILWAY STREET, LISBURN c1900

FRIENDS' BURYING GROUND INSCRIPTIONS

BAILEY *[small, flat granite stone]* 3

Sarah Jane Bailey.
Died 14th of 4th month 1877,
aged 5 weeks.

Robert Wm. Bailey.
Died 29th of 9th month 1889,
aged 8 years and 10 months.

BARCROFT See **MALCOMSON** 17

CLIBBORN *[small, flat granite stone]* 18

Frederic Clibborn.
Died
6th of 2nd month 1848,
aged 41 years.

His wife,
Ruth Clibborn.
Died 23rd of 11th month 1876,
aged 62 years.

GOUGH *[small, flat slate stone]* 28

John Gough.
Born 1721.
Died 25th 10 Mo 1791.

GREGG *[small, flat granite stone]* 4

Catherine Alicia Gregg.
Born 2nd Mo 25th 1815.
Died 2nd Mo 27th 1879.

Maria Gregg.
Born 9th Mo 12th 1803.
Died 5th Mo 21st 1883.

Anna Bradshaw Gregg.
Born 4th Mo 12th 1812.
Died 3rd Mo 21st 1898.

Daughters of
Dominick and Mary Ann Gregg.

| GREGG | [*small, flat granite stone*] | 5 |

George Gregg.
Died 15th of 6th month 1845,
aged 41 years.

Elizabeth R. Gregg.
Died 29th of 9th month 1876,
aged 67 years.

Son and daughter of
Dominick and Mary Ann Gregg

| GREGG | [*small, flat granite stone*] | 6 |

Samuel Thomas Gregg.
Died 20th of 3rd month 1828,
aged 27 years.

Sarah Gregg.
Died 5th of 3rd month 1876,
aged 81 years.

Son and daughter of Dominick
and Mary Ann Gregg.

| GREGG | [*small, flat granite stone*] | 7 |

Dominick Gregg.
Died 19th of 3rd month 1826,
aged 62 years.

Mary Ann Gregg.
Died 2nd of 12th month 1862,
aged 92 years.

| GRUBB | See **RICHARDSON** | 19 |

| HANCOCK | [*small, flat granite stone*] | 9 |

Emma Hancock.
Died 8th of 9th month 1843,
aged 29 years.

Thomas Hancock.
Died 18th of 4th month 1849,
aged 66 years.

GREGG   [*small, flat granite stone*]   5

George Gregg.
Died 15th of 6th month 1845,
aged 41 years.

Elizabeth R. Gregg.
Died 29th of 9th month 1876,
aged 67 years.

Son and daughter of
Dominick and Mary Ann Gregg

GREGG   [*small, flat granite stone*]   6

Samuel Thomas Gregg.
Died 20th of 3rd month 1828,
aged 27 years.

Sarah Gregg.
Died 5th of 3rd month 1876,
aged 81 years.

Son and daughter of Dominick
and Mary Ann Gregg.

GREGG   [*small, flat granite stone*]   7

Dominick Gregg.
Died 19th of 3rd month 1826,
aged 62 years.

Mary Ann Gregg.
Died 2nd of 12th month 1862,
aged 92 years.

GRUBB   See **RICHARDSON**   19

HANCOCK   [*small, flat granite stone*]   9

Emma Hancock.
Died 8th of 9th month 1843,
aged 29 years.

Thomas Hancock.
Died 18th of 4th month 1849,
aged 66 years.

LAMB	[*small, flat granite stone*]	8

Joshua Lamb.
Died 18th of 12th month
1866,
aged 64 years.

His widow,
Mary Lamb.
Died 15th of 12th month
1881,
aged 75 years.

MALCOMSON	[*small, flat granite stone*]	17

David Malcomson Junr.
Died 9th of 11th month 1840,
aged 29 years.

Sarah Malcomson, his wife.
Died 18th of 5th month 1864,
aged 52 years.

Erected by their daughter
Anna Richardson Barcroft.
1912

PEARSON	[*small, flat granite stone*]	1

Jonathan William Pearson.
Died 5th month 26th 1867,
aged 12 years.

RICHARDSON	[*small, flat granite stone*]	11

John Richardson,
son of
Jonathan Richardson.
Died 27th of 11th month 1866,
aged 84 years.

RICHARDSON	[*small, flat granite stone*]	12

Harriet Richardson,
wife of
John Richardson.
Died 8th of 5th month 1863,
aged 84 years.

Henrietta Richardson,
daughter of above.
Aged 42 years.

RICHARDSON   [*small, flat granite stone*]   13

Henry Richardson.
Born 11th of 3rd month 1821.
Died 7th of 9th month 1843.

Samuel Richardson.
Born 9th of 7th month 1817.
Died 24th of 10th month 1847.

Samuel Richardson Junr.
Born 2nd of 5th month 1852.
Died 20th of 2nd month 1853.

RICHARDSON   [*small, flat granite stone*]   14

Joseph Richardson.
Born 9th of 3rd month 1789.
Died 19th of 4th month 1821.

Jonathan Richardson.
Born 22nd of 6th month 1815.
Died 2nd of 10th month 1876.

RICHARDSON   [*small, flat granite stone*]   15

Mary Richardson.
Born 17th of 11th month 1790.
Died 24th of 3rd month 1855.

Eliza Richardson.
Born 29th of 3rd month 1814.
Died 13th of 8th month 1887.

RICHARDSON   [*small, flat granite stone*]   16

Catherine Richardson.
Died 17th of 2nd month 1842,
aged 27 years.

Her daughter,
Anna Catherine.
Died 13th of 3rd month 1842,
aged 3 months.

RICHARDSON   [*small, flat granite stone*]   19

Anna Richardson,
nee Grubb,
wife of James N. Richardson.
Died 28th of 5th month 1843,
aged 61 years.

Erected by her Grandson
James N. Richardson *of Bessbrook.*

RICHARDSON   [*small, flat granite stone*]   20

Helena Richardson,
wife of
John Grubb Richardson.
Died 7th of 12th month 1849,
aged 30 years.

Erected in Loving Memory
by her son
James N. Richardson
of Bessbrook.

RICHARDSON   [*broken, small, flat granite stone*]   21

James N. Richardson,
of Glenmore,
son of Jonathan Richardson.
Died 13th of 5th month 1847,
aged 66½ years.

Erected by his Grandson
and namesake.

RICHARDSON   [*small, flat granite stone*]   22

Susan Lecky Richardson.
Died
6th of 3rd month 1855,
aged 31 years.
---ooo---
Howard Richardson.
Died
5th of 12th month 1860,
aged 6 years.

| RICHARDSON | [*small, flat granite stone*] | 23 |

Joshua Henry Richardson.
Died
25th of 4th month 1859,
aged 10 years.
---ooo---
Cathn Josephine Richardson.
Died
29th of 11th month 1860,
aged 9 years,

| RICHARDSON | [*small, flat granite stone*] | 24 |

William Richardson.
Died
13th of 12th month 1862,
aged 38 years.
---ooo---
Elizabeth Joseph,
his wife
Died 27th of 9th month 1877,
aged 52 years.

| RICHARDSON | [*small, flat granite stone*] | 25 |

Jonathan Richardson.
Died
2nd of 8th month 1869,
aged 58 years.

| RICHARDSON | [*small, flat granite stone*] | 26 |

Mary Gertrude Richardson.
Died 5th month 23rd 1872,
aged 2 years and 1 month.

| RICHARDSON | [*small, flat granite stone*] | 27 |

Sarah F. Richardson.
Died 1886,
aged 68 years.

| ROBSON | [*small, flat granite stone*] | 2 |

Ellen Robson.
Died 15th of 5th month 1872,
aged 61 years.

| SMITH | [*small, flat slate stone*] | 10 |

John Shaw Smith.
Died 29th of 1st month 1873,
aged 61 years.

BURIALS IN FRIENDS' BURYING GROUND, RAILWAY STREET

3. ✝	BAILEY	Robert William	29/09/1889	9	Son of William John
3. ✝	BAILEY	Sarah Jane	12/04/1877	5 wks.	Dau. of John and Margaret Anne
	BARCROFT	John	30/07/1815	60	Linen Draper
	BARTER	Emma	06/01/1861	19	Governess
	BASTIVILLE	Charles	29/06/1827	18	
	BASTIVILLE	William	31/01/1828	24	
	BELL	Sarah	16/07/1863	80	A minister
	BLACK	Joseph	23/05/1850	22	Teacher at Provincial School
	BOADLE	Mary	24/02/1833	82	
	BOHUMIAN	James	07/12/1864	84	
	BOYD	Joseph	10/10/1817	70	
	BOYD	Joseph	19/12/1825	33	
	BRAGG	Anna	05/12/1820	22	Brookfield, dau. of Henry and Mary
	BRAGG	Henry	31/01/1837	77	
	BRAGG	Jane	02/09/1819	23	Prospect Hill, dau. of Henry and Mary
	BRAGG	Mary	07/04/1848	87	Widow of Henry
	CLARKE	Ann	09/02/1863	84	Formerly Lower Grange
	CLARKE	Thomas	03/05/1835	51	Tailor
	CLEGG	Samuel H.	21/07/1819	16	
18. ✝	CLIBBORN	Frederic	06/02/1848	41	
18. ✝	CLIBBORNE	Ruth	23/11/1876	62	Widow of Frederick
	CONRAN	John	16/06/1827	87	
	DOUGLAS	Anne	05/01/1815	5	Prospect Hill, dau. of Samuel
	DOUGLAS	Eliza	07/09/1823	9	
	DOUGLAS	Samuel	31/10/1856	82	
	DOUGLAS	Samuel Jnr.	26/01/1844	30	Son of Samuel and Sarah
	DOUGLAS	Sarah	05/04/1855	82	Wife of Samuel
	DOUGLAS	William D.	10/02/1848	18 mts	Son of William and Mary
	DUNCAN	John	15/01/1834	35	Shopkeeper
	FAWCETT	Mary	29/06/1862	68	Wife of Thomas
	FAWCETT	Thomas	30/11/1868	86	Formerly of Antrim
	GARRET	Jackson	26/12/1827	4	
	GARRET	James	03/05/1832	47	Drowned in aqueduct-Tyrone Merchant
28. ✝	GOUGH	John	25/10/1791	70	
	GRAHAM	Eleanor	10/01/1838	16	Dau. of Robert and Eleanor
	GRAHAM	Robert	11/05/1845	15	Son of Robert and Eleanor
	GRAHAM	Robert	26/01/1879	89	Widower
4. ✝	GREGG	Anna Bradshaw	21/03/1898	85	Dau. of Dominick and Mary Jane
7. ✝	GREGG	Dominick	19/03/1826	63	
5. ✝	GREGG	Elizabeth Rebecca	29/09/1876	67	Dau. of Dominick and Mary Anne
5. ✝	GREGG	George	15/06/1845	41	Son of Dominick and Mary Ann
4. ✝	GREGG	Katherine Alicia	27/02/1879	64	Spinster
4. ✝	GREGG	Maria	21/05/1883	79	Dau. of Dominick and Mary Anne
7. ✝	GREGG	Mary Ann	02/12/1862	93	Widow of Dominick

6. †	GREGG	Samuel Thomas	20/03/1828	27	Doctor
6. †	GREGG	Sarah	05/03/1876	81	Dau. of Dominick and Mary Anne
	HANCOCK	Anna	12/12/1820	28	Dau. of Jacob and Elizabeth
	HANCOCK	Elizabeth	05/07/1832	86	
	HANCOCK	Elizabeth Jun.	07/02/1832	54	
9. †	HANCOCK	Emma	08/09/1843	29	Dau. of Thomas and H.
	HANCOCK	Jacob	12/01/1818	75	
	HANCOCK	Jacob	13/01/1828	47	
	HANCOCK	John	24/09/1823	61	
	HANCOCK	Mary	17/10/1812	66	Wife of Jacob Linen Draper
	HANCOCK	Sarah Anne	10/03/1870	80	Widow of Jacob
9. †	HANCOCK	Thomas	16/04/1849	65	Doctor of Medicine
	HANCOCK	William	07/11/1819	31	
	HAUGHTON	George Fennell	23/03/1859	4 mts.	Son of Thomas
	HILL	Samuel	21/04/1827	84	
	HOBSON	Rebecca	08/11/1851	11	U.P.S. dau. of William & Mary, Moy
	HOGG	James	09/05/1847	92	
	HOGG	Mary	07/08/1818	78	Widow of James
	HOGG	Mary	13/06/1828	54	
	HOGG	Wakefield	22/03/1834	56	
	HUNTER	Jonathan	10/08/1835	54	
	JACOB	Richard	14/02/1828	36	Merchant
	JOHNSON	Elizabeth	30/03/1828	39	
8. †	LAMB	Joshua	18/12/1866	64	Farmer
8. †	LAMB	Mary	15/12/1883	75	Widow of Joshua
	LOCKART	Abner	03/04/1784		
	LOCKART	John	01/07/1802		
	LOCKART	Sarah	21/07/1786		
	LYNESS	Dorathea	10/06/1851	3 wks	Dau. of Robert
	LYNESS	Mary	02/05/1863	70	Widow
	LYNESS	Mary	13/02/1894	53	Wife of Robert
17. †	MALCOMSON	David Jun.	09/11/1840	29	Son of C. and M.
17. †	MALCOMSON	Sarah D.	18/05/1864	52	Relict of David
	MASON	Mary Ann	08/10/1822	25	Prospect Hill
	McCLURE	Robert S.W.	16/02/1848	37	Woollen Draper
	McCLURE	Susanna	15/01/1848	43	Wife of Robert S.W.
	McCREADY	Joseph	23/05/1879	25	Son of Joseph and Mary Jane
	McCREADY	Mary Jane	02/01/1907	83	Widow of Joseph
	McCREADY	Rachel	19/02/1894	33	Dau. of Joseph and Mary Jane
	McINTIRE	Jane	06/01/1838	54	
	McINTIRE	John	19/06/1873	60	Carpenter
	McINTYRE	Sarah	15/01/1860	40	Wife of John
	MURPHY	Margaret	06/03/1815	15	
	MURRAY	Timothy	09/04/1816	61	Chandler
	PATTERSON	Joseph	28/10/1780		
1. †	PEARSON	Jonathan William	26/06/1867	12	U.P.S., son of Jonathan, Moyallon

	PIM	Sarah	21/05/1836	71	
19. ✝	**RICHARDSON**	Anna	28/05/1843	61	Wife of James Nicholson
16. ✝	**RICHARDSON**	Anna Catherine	13/03/1842	11 wks	Dau. of Joshua Pim and Catherine
16. ✝	**RICHARDSON**	Catherine	17/02/1842	27	Wife of Joshua Pim
23. ✝	**RICHARDSON**	Catherine Josephine	29/11/1860	10	Dau. of Joshua Pim & Susanna Leckey
	RICHARDSON	Charlotte	11/11/1834	17	
	RICHARDSON	Edmund Leckey	26/03/1855	5 wks	Son of Joshua Pim & Susanna Leckey
15. ✝	**RICHARDSON**	Eliza	13/06/1887	74	Widow of Jonathan Joseph
	RICHARDSON	Eliza Jane	18/10/1813	3	Dau of Jonathan Linen Merchant
	RICHARDSON	Elizabeth	25/09/1824	2	
24. ✝	**RICHARDSON**	Elizabeth Joseph	27/09/1877	61	Widow of William
12. ✝	**RICHARDSON**	Harriet	08/05/1863	84	Wife of John
20. ✝	**RICHARDSON**	Helena	07/12/1849	30	Wife of Jonathan Grubb
12. ✝	**RICHARDSON**	Henrietta	05/09/1862	42	Dau. of John
13. ✝	**RICHARDSON**	Henry	07/09/1843	22	Son of Joseph and Mary
22. ✝	**RICHARDSON**	Howard	05/12/1860	6	Son of Joshua Pim & Susanna Leckey
21. ✝	**RICHARDSON**	James Nicholson	13/05/1847	66	Linen Merchant
11. ✝	**RICHARDSON**	John	27/11/1866	84	
	RICHARDSON	Jonathan	22/06/1817	62	Linen Draper
25. ✝	**RICHARDSON**	Jonathan	02/08/1869	58	Linen Merchant
14. ✝	**RICHARDSON**	Jonathan Joseph	02/10/1876	61	Son of Joseph and Mary
14. ✝	**RICHARDSON**	Joseph	19/04/1821	32	Linen Merchant
23. ✝	**RICHARDSON**	Joshua Henry	25/04/1859	10	Son of Joshua Pim & Susanna Leckey
	RICHARDSON	Lucia	23/10/1813	8mts.	Dau. of Johnathan Linen Merchant
	RICHARDSON	Mary	10/06/1814	60	Widow of Jonathan
15. ✝	**RICHARDSON**	Mary	24/05/1855	64	Widow of Joseph
26. ✝	**RICHARDSON**	Mary Gertrude	23/05/1872	2	Dau. of Joseph
	RICHARDSON	Richard Grubb	01/02/1848	2 wks	Son of John Grubb and Helena
	RICHARDSON	Ruth	07/08/1817	98	
13. ✝	**RICHARDSON**	Samuel	20/02/1853	10 mts.	Son of Jonathan Joseph and Elizabeth
13. ✝	**RICHARDSON**	Samuel L.	24/10/1847	30	Flax Spinner
27. ✝	**RICHARDSON**	Sarah Fennell	06/01/1886	69	Widow of James Nicholson
22. ✝	**RICHARDSON**	Susanna Leckey	06/03/1855	31	Wife of Joshua Pim
24. ✝	**RICHARDSON**	William	13/12/1862	38	Linen Merchant
2. ✝	**ROBSON**	Ellen	15/05/1872	61	
	ROGERS	Abigail	20/01/1804		
	ROGERS	Abigail	20/10/1818	16	Dau. of John and E.
	ROGERS	Elizabeth	10/10/1830	72	
	ROGERS	John	01/01/1834	61	Shopkeeper
	ROGERS	William	10/02/1789	51	
	SEDGEWICK	Mary	02/09/1832	90	
	SILCOCK	Matilda	16/12/1872	2 wks.	
10. ✝	**SMITH**	John Shaw	29/01/1873	62	Gentleman
	SMYTH	Mary Jane	13/06/1851	16	Brookfield School
	STRANGMAN	Isabella	24/03/1843	14	Dau. of Joseph and H., Waterford
	THOMPSON	Ann	19/03/1866	71	Wife of Robert

THOMPSON	Armstrong	04/11/1843	9	
THOMPSON	James	30/05/1855	38	Son of Robert and Anne
THOMPSON	Jane	18/05/1844	2	Dau. of Robert and Eleanor
THOMPSON	Jane	23/03/1851	22	Dau. of Robert
THOMPSON	Robert	30/12/1871	76	School Master
THOMPSON	Sarah Ann	28/12/1855	3 mts	Dau. of Robert and Elizabeth
THOMPSON	William	31/10/1842	20	Son of William
VALENTINE	George Jun.	22/08/1828	20	
VALENTINE	Hannah	07/06/1824	4	
VALENTINE	James	21/08/1831	24	
VALENTINE	Mary	18/10/1831	48	
VALENTINE	Susanna	06/12/1824	6 mts	
WETHERALD	George Valentine	06/09/1834	2¼	
WETHERALD	William	04/12/1834	41	
WHITFIELD	Jane	14/11/1843	78	
WOODS	Isabella	02/12/1827	60	

FRIENDS' 11   **RICHARDSON**

FRIENDS' 16   **RICHARDSON**

192

QUAKER DEATH NOTICES
BELFAST NEWS LETTER
DIED

Friday April 13 1877
BAILEY   April 12, at Bow Street, Lisburn, Sarah Jane, youngest daughter of W.J. Bailey. Her remains will be removed for interment in the Friends' Burying-ground, Railway Street, Lisburn, this (Friday) morning at eleven o'clock. Friends will please accept this intimation.

Tuesday October 1 1889
BAILEY   9th month, 29, at British Workman, Bow Street, Lisburn, Robert William, second son of W.J. Bailey. His remains will be removed for interment in The Friends' Burying-Ground, Railway St., on 3rd day (Tuesday), 10th month, 1st, at three o'clock. Friends will please accept this intimation.

Tuesday February 19 1828
BASTIVILLE   In Rosemary-street, on the 31st ult. in his 24th year, Wm. Bastiville; a promising young man, for usefulness in society deservedly esteemed and loved by his friends and acquaintances.

Wednesday February 11 1863
CLARK   February 9, at the residence of her brother-in-law, Thomas Fawcett, Long Stone, Lisburn, Anne Clark, of Grange, aged 84 years. Her remains will be removed for interment in Friends' Burying-ground, Lisburn, on to-morrow (Thursday) morning, at half-past nine o'clock. Friends will please accept this notice.

Friday February 11 1848
CLIBBORN On the 6th inst., at Myrtle-hill, near Lisburn, Frederic Clibborn, son of the late William Cooper Clibborn of Moate, county Westmeath, in his 41st year.

Friday November 24 1876
CLIBBORN November 23, at Aberdelghy, near Lisburn, Ruth, widow of the late Frederic Clibborn, aged 62 years. Her remains are intended to be removed for interment in the Friends' Burying-ground Lisburn, on Monday afternoon, the 27th inst., at half-past one o'clock.

Friday February 2 1844
DOUGLAS On Friday morning, the 26th ult. at his father's residence in Lisburn, Samuel Douglas, jun. late of Donegall-street, Belfast, aged 29 years. He was a steady member of the "Society of Friends," and though young in years was old in Christian experience. That fell and delusive disease consumption, seized upon him when in the midst of his health and vigour; and, in the brief space of four months, the ruddy cheek and agile limb of him who expected to have had the pleasure of being the support and solace of his dear parents in their declining years, were cold in the embrace of death. So great was his patience and resignation under extreme suffering, that a murmur did not escape his lips; and so calm and peaceful was his end, that his weeping relatives, who were by his bedside, could scarcely determine the moment his happy spirit took its flight to bliss.

> And thou art gone my brother dear,
> The flood of death triumphant pass'd!
> Shall mem'ry drop a pious tear,
> That one so lov'd should fade so fast?
>
> Without a struggle or a groan,
> His happy spirit took its flight
> With angels to surround the throne,
> In amaranthine scenes of light!

Monday April 9 1855
DOUGLAS   April 3, at Lurgan, Sarah Douglas, late of Lisburn, aged 82 years.

Monday November 3 1856
DOUGLAS   Oct. 31, at Lurgan, Samuel Douglas, late of Lisburn, in his 83rd year.

Tuesday December 1 1868
FAWCETT   November 30, at the residence of his son-in-law, James A. Stewart, Bow Street, Lisburn, Thomas Fawcett, aged 86 years. His remains will be removed for interment in Friends' Burying Ground, Lisburn, on to-morrow (Wednesday) morning at eleven o'clock. Friends will please accept this intimation.

Friday May 11 1832
GARRETT   On the 2^d inst. whilst on a visit at the house of his brother, 8, Corn-market, James Garrett, Esq. of Farlough, Co. Tyrone, (member of the Society of Friends.) He was a gentleman of most amiable character, charitable disposition, and unassuming though engaging manners; and is much deservedly regretted by a numerous circle of relatives and friends.

Friday October 28 to Tuesday November 1 1791
GOUGH   At Prospect Hill, near Lisburn, on the 25 instant John Gough, one of the people called Quakers.

Tuesday March 28 1826
GREGG   At Lisburn, on Sunday the 19th inst. Dominick Gregg, Esq., a member of the Society of Friends, in the 63d year of his age.

Tuesday March 25 1828
GREGG   At Lisburn, on the 20th inst. Samuel Thomas Gregg Esq., M.D. in his 26th year.

Tuesday June 24 1845
GREGG   At his residence in Bedford-street, Liverpool, on Sunday, the 15th inst. after a few days illness, universally regretted, George Gregg Esq. of the firm of Messrs. H. & G. Gregg, Liverpool.

Thursday December 4 1862
GREGG   December 2, Mary Anne, the beloved wife of the late Dominick Gregg, Esq., of Lisburn, aged 93 years.

Tuesday March 7 1876
GREGG   March 5, at Derryvolgie, Sarah, eldest daughter of the late Dominick Gregg, Lisburn.

Monday October 2 1876
GREGG   September 29, at her residence, Derryvolgie, Lisburn, Elizabeth R. Gregg, daughter of the late Dominick Gregg, Esq., Lisburn.

Monday March 24 1898
GREGG   March 21, at her residence, Derryvolgie, Lisburn, Anna Bradshaw Gregg, aged 85.

Friday December 3 1756
HANCOCK   On Monday last died at Lisburn, Mr. John Hancock, an eminent Linen Draper and one of the people called Quakers.

Friday October 5 1764

HANCOCK Last Sunday died, greatly lamented, Mr. John Hancock of Lisburn, an eminent Linen Draper; one of the people called Quakers; A gentleman remarkably distinguished for a generous and charitable Disposition, and a liberal publick Spirit; As a last Evidence whereof, he has left One Thousand Pounds for the Support of a School in the Town of Lisburn for the Education of poor Children. Yet, however considerable the Bequest may appear, it makes but a small Compensation for the Loss the Publick has sustained by the Death of so Valuable a member of Society.

Tuesday January 20 1818

HANCOCK On the 12th inst. Jacob Hancock, sen. Esq. in the 75th year of his age.

Friday November 12 1819

HANCOCK On the 7th inst. in Corn-market, Lisburn, William Hancock, son of the late Jacob Hancock, of that town.

Tuesday September 30 1823

HANCOCK At Lisburn, on the 25d inst. John Hancock Esq. aged 61.

Tuesday September 12 1843

HANCOCK On the 8th inst. of a rapid decline, Emma, eldest daughter of Thomas Hancock, M.D. of Lisburn.

Friday April 20 1849

HANCOCK On the 16th of the fourth month, at his house in Lisburn, Thomas Hancock, M.D., aged 66.

Monday July 7 1851

HANCOCK June 24, at Birkenhead, Cheshire, Elizabeth, eldest surviving daughter of the late Thomas Hancock, M.D., of Lisburn, County Antrim.

Tuesday March 15 1870

HANCOCK March 10, at her residence, Railway Street, Lisburn, Sarah, relict of the late Jacob Hancock, Esq., at a very advanced age.

Tuesday May 11 1847

HOGG At his residence, Castle-street, Lisburn, on the 9th inst., James Hogg Esq., aged 93 years. His remains will be removed for interment in the Friends' Burying-ground, on Wednesday, the 12th inst., at half-past 12 o'clock.

Friday February 22 1828

JACOB On the 13th instant, Mr. Richard Jacob, of the town, merchant: a man whose kind benevolent, candid and honourable disposition, had exceedingly endeared him to his numerous friends, and, indeed, to all who were acquainted with the benevolence of his heart, and his inherent love of truth. –The more intimately he was known, the more highly he was esteemed, and the more deeply his decease lamented.

Thursday December 20 1866

LAMB December 18, at Pear Tree Hill, near Lisburn, Joshua Lamb, aged 64 years. The interment is intended to take place on the seventh day (Saturday) the 22nd inst., at Lisburn. The funeral to leave Pear Tree Hill at eleven o'clock a.m.

Thursday February 15 1894
LYNESS   At her residence, 42, Bow Street, Lisburn, Mary R., the beloved wife of Robert Lyness. Her remains will be removed for interment in Friends' Burying-Ground at eleven o'clock. Friends will please accept this intimation.

Friday November 13 1840
MALCOMSON   On the 9th inst. at Glenmore, near Lisburn, at the house of his father-in-law (James N. Richardson), David Malcomson, jun. son of David Malcomson, Melview, Clonmel.

Thursday May 19 1864
MALCOMSON   May 18, at Lisnegarvy (sic), Sarah, relict of the late David Malcomson, jun., and daughter of the late James N. Richardson, Glenmore, Lisburn.

Tuesday February 22 1848
McCLURE   On the 16th inst., at his residence, Market-square, Lisburn, Mr. Robert McClure, woollendraper.

Friday January 4 1907
McCREADY   January 2, at the residence of her brother, Robert Lyness, Bow Street, Lisburn, Mary Jane, widow of the late Joseph McCready. The remains of my beloved sister will be removed for interment in the Friends' Burying ground, Railway Street, Lisburn, to-morrow (Saturday) afternoon at two o'clock.   Robert Lyness

Friday April 19 1816
MURRAY   At his house in Arthur-street on Tuesday, 9th instant, after a tedious illness, Timothy Murray, of the Society of Friends, in whose death his family have sustained a real loss, and who through life bore the character of an honest upright man.

Thursday June 27 1867
PEARSON   June 26, at Friends' School, Lisburn, Jonathan William, youngest son of Mr. Jonathan Pearson, of Drumlin Hill, Gilford, aged 12 years and 8 months.

Tuesday May 1 1821
RICHARDSON   On the 9th (sic) inst. at his house in Lisburn, Joseph Richardson Esq., one of the Society of Friends.

Tuesday May 30 1843
RICHARDSON   At Glenmore, near Lisburn, the 28th day of the fifth month, in her 61st year, Anna, wife of James N. Richardson.

Friday September 15 1843
RICHARDSON   On the night of the 7th inst. at Penzance, Cornwall, of consumption, Henry Richardson M.D. aged 22 years, youngest son of the late Joseph Richardson, of Lisburn.

Friday May 18 1847
RICHARDSON   On the 13th inst., at his residence, Glenmore, near Lisburn, James Nicholson Richardson, in the 67th year of his age.

Friday October 29 1847
RICHARDSON   On the 27th inst. at his residence, the Island, Lisburn, Samuel Richardson, aged 30 years.

Tuesday December 11 1849
RICHARDSON   Dec. 7, at College-square North, Helena, wife of John G. Richardson, Esq.

Friday May 25 1855
RICHARDSON   May 24, at Lisburn, Mary Richardson.

Monday December 15 1862
RICHARDSON   December 13, at Brooklands, near Belfast, William Richardson, aged 38 years. His remains will be removed for interment in Lisburn, on to-morrow (Tuesday), at half-past nine o'clock.

Friday November 30 1866
RICHARDSON   November 27, at the residence of his son, Trew Mount, near Moy, John Richardson, of Lisburn, aged 85 years. His remains are intended to be interred at Friends' Burying-ground, Lisburn, on the 7th day, the 1st of the 12th month, leaving Lisburn station at eleven o'clock a.m.

Tuesday August 3 1869
RICHARDSON   August 2, at Craigdarragh, Jonathan Richardson, Esq., of Glenmore, Lisburn, in the 59th year of his age. The funeral is intended to leave Craigdarragh at eight o'clock on Thursday morning, arriving at Friends' Burying ground, Lisburn, about half-past twelve o'clock.

Friday May 24 1872
RICHARDSON   May 23, at Springfield, near Lisburn, Mary Gertrude, youngest child of Joseph Richardson, aged 2 years.

Thursday October 5 1876
RICHARDSON   Oct. 2, at Westcliff, Tramore, County Waterford, Jonathan Joseph Richardson Esq., J.P., Kircassock, Lurgan, aged 61 years.

Friday September 28 1877
RICHARDSON   September 27, at Windsor, Belfast, Elizabeth J. Richardson, wife of the late William Richardson, of Brooklands, Belfast.

Friday February 13 to Tuesday February 17 1789
ROGERS   Died at Lisburn, Mr. William Rogers;- being in health to appearance the 9th, was taken ill same night, and departed this life next morning, much regretted by a great number of friends.

Tuesday October 19 1830
ROGERS   On the 10th inst. after an illness of nearly two years, Elizabeth, wife of Mr. John Rogers, Market-square, Lisburn.

Tuesday January 7 1834
ROGERS   Suddenly, at Lisburn, on the 1st instant, Mr. John Rogers, formerly of the Society of Friends.

Friday March 31 1843
STRANGMAN   On the 24th inst. in Lisburn, at the house of her aunt, Mary Richardson, Isabella, daughter of Mr. Joshua Strangman of Waterford, aged 14 years.

Wednesday March 26 1851
THOMPSON   March 23, at the residence of her brother, Castle-street, Belfast, Jane, second daughter of Robert Thompson, Castle-street, Lisburn.

Friday June 1 1855
THOMPSON   May 30, at the residence of his father, in Lisburn, James Thompson, formerly of Castle Street, Belfast.

Tuesday March 20 1866
THOMPSON   On the 19th of the 3rd month, at 25 Castle Street, Lisburn, Ann, wife of Robert Thompson. Her remains are intended to be removed for interment in Friends' Burying ground, Railway Street, on the fifth day (Thursday) morning, the 22nd inst., at half-past nine o'clock.

Monday January 1 1872
THOMPSON   Dec. 30, at his residence, No. 25 Castle Street, Lisburn, Robert Thompson. His remains will be removed for interment in Friends' Burying ground, on to-morrow (Tuesday) morning, at ten o'clock.

Friday August 26 1831
VALENTINE   On the 21st inst. after a short illness, at the house of his father, Mr. James Valentine, of Belfast. The mild unassuming manners and amiable disposition of this talented young man gained him esteem and friendship of a large circle of aquaintance, by whom his premature death (being only in his 25th year) will be long and deeply lamented.

Tuesday December 16 1834
WETHERELD   On the 14th inst. in the 41st year of his age, William Wethereld, of Donegall-street, one of the Society of Friends. A number of friends and acquaintances of the deceased have been introduced into considerable feelings of sorrow at the rather unexpected removal of this unassuming and upright individual.

LISBURN STANDARD
DEATHS

Saturday January 9 1886
RICHARDSON   January 6, at Lissue, Lisburn, Sarah F., beloved wife of James N. Richardson, aged nearly 69 years. The funeral is intended to leave at Ten o'clock on the 9th inst. for Friends' Burial Ground, Lisburn.

Saturday June 18 1887
RICHARDSON   June 13, at Kircassock, Lurgan, Eliza, widow of the late Jonathan Joseph Richardson, formerly M.P. for Lisburn, aged 74 years.

BELFAST COMMERCIAL CHRONICLE
DEATHS
Wednesday June 26 1817
RICHARDSON   At Lisburn on the 22d ult., Jonathan Richardson, Esq., one of the Society of Friends, aged nearly 62 years.

QUAKER WILLS

LAMB Joshua, Pear Tree Hill, County Antrim, Farmer.
Died 18th December 1866.
Probate granted 10th January 1867, Belfast.
Mentions Thomas Lamb of Pear Tree Hill, Lisburn, Farmer and Samuel Douglas Lamb of Bessbrook (Newry) County Armagh, Linen Manufacturer.

LYNESS Mary, Lisburn, County Antrim.
Died 13th February 1894.
Administration granted 7th September 1894, Belfast.
Mentions Robert Lyness, of Lisburn, Grocer, Husband.

RICHARDSON William, late of Brooklands and Belfast, both in the County of Antrim, Merchant.
Died 13th December 1862, Brooklands.
Probate granted 5th May 1863, Principal Registry.
Mentions Joseph Richardson of Belfast, Merchant and James Nicholson Richardson, of Lisburn in the County of Antrim, Gentleman.

RICHARDSON John, formerly of Lisburn, County Antrim, and late of Trewmount in the Barony of Dungannon, County Tyrone, Esquire.
Died 27th November 1866 at Trewmount.
Probate granted 24th December 1866, Armagh.
Mentions James Greer Richardson of Trewmount, Esquire.

RICHARDSON Jonathan, Glenmore, near Lisburn, County Antrim, Merchant.
Died 3rd August 1869 at Craigdarragh, County Down.
Probate granted 23rd December 1869, Belfast.
Mentions James Nicholson Richardson, Lissue and Joseph Richardson of Springfield, both in Lisburn, County Antrim, Merchants.

RICHARDSON Jonathan Joseph, late of Kircassock, County Dublin, Esq., J.P.
Died 2nd October 1876 at Tramore, County Waterford.
Probate granted 6th November 1876, Principal Registry.
Mentions Eliza Richardson, Kircassock, Widow, and Wakefield Christy 35, Gracechurch-street, London, Esq.

RICHARDSON Eliza, Kircassock, County Down, Widow.
Died 13th June 1887.
Probate granted 11th August 1887, Principal Registry.
Mentions Wakefield Christy, 29 Collinglane-road, South Kensington, Esq., and Thomas Tighe Mecredy of 28, Westmoreland-street, Dublin, Solicitor.

SMITH John Shaw, late of No. 57 Fitzwilliam-square, Dublin, Esq.
Died 29th January 1873.
Probate granted 24th February 1873, Principal Registry.
Mentions John Augustus Smith Esq. and Mary Henrietta Florence, Spinster, both of Fitzwilliam-square.

THOMPSON Robert, Lisburn, County Antrim, Gentleman.
Died 30th December 1871.
Probate granted 12th February 1872, Belfast.
Mentions Robert Thompson, Belfast, Merchant and Eliza Ann Thompson and Maria Thompson, both Lisburn, Spinsters.

FAMILY INFORMATION

ALLEN

CATHEDRAL 53

James Allen (1831-1873), the first named on this stone, was the son of **George Allen** and his wife, who was formerly **Thompson**. James Allen was a Shoe-maker of Bow Street, Lisburn, as was his brother, **David**. James was married to **Mary Short**, whose mother, **Mary Elizabeth Short**, is also buried in the grave. James and Mary Allen had a family of at least four sons and two daughters. One son, **Andrew**, who was a clerk in William Barbour & Sons, and two daughters, **Mary Elizabeth** and **Margaret**, are buried in the grave. The other sons were **George** (31st December 1860-9th July 1938), an agent for Lord Downshire, **James** (died 14th April 1940), a chemist, and **Joseph** (9th February 1864-12th March 1939) a solicitor in Lisburn. George was a J.P. and was married with one son. Joseph was first in partnership with F.W. Charley, then with John Dorman and then with his own son **Millar Allen**. He was a very keen local historian and was very knowledgeable on the history of Lisburn. Joseph was married and as well as his son, Millar, he had two daughters. Both George and Joseph were buried in Hillsborough Churchyard. [Joseph Allen is mentioned in THG Vol. 1 page 151 where a photograph of him may also be seen.]

[*Linen Hall Library - Blackwood Pedigrees.*]

BLACKBURN

CATHEDRAL 49, 82, 84, and 85

Five separate Blackburn headstones have been noted in the Cathedral Graveyard. Of these one cannot now be located, one gives only one name and another one is very worn and almost illegible. It is not known if they are all related to each other. Some of the Blackburns were farmers at Lissue, Ballymacash and Laurel Hill. In June 1860 the Belfast News Letter had the reports of a boating tragedy on Belfast Lough. One of the two men to die was **James Blackburn**, and, although his name is not now recorded on a headstone, the burial is recorded in the Cathedral records.

The accident happened on the evening of Saturday June 16th 1860 when three young men went out boating. Only one survived, and over three days there were various reports in the paper, concluding with the report of the inquest on James Blackburn which was held on Wednesday June 22nd 1860. James Blackburn was the nephew of the late **Jas. McNamara Esq. J.P.**:-

(*Extract from the report.*)

BELFAST NEWS LETTER
THURSDAY JUNE 23 1860

THE LATE ACCIDENT ON THE LOUGH

Yesterday morning, at seven o'clock, an inquest was held by J.K. Jackson, Esq., Coroner, on the body of Mr. James Blackburne (sic), one of the young gentlemen who were drowned in the Lough last Saturday. The inquest was held in the house of Mr. William Blackburne, brother of the deceased residing in the west division of Carrickfergus (Greenisland).

Alexander McCullough Bell, who was assisted in, being in a very weak state, was examined by the Coroner - I was in the boat on Saturday, when the accident occurred. We went out at two o'clock, and the accident occurred at five o'clock. I had been at the helm during the day. I know something about boating. The others knew something about it also. When the accident happened I had gone forward in the boat, and left Mr. Steen at the helm. I could not say how the accident happened. I think it must have been caused by the ballast shifting. We were all three in the water together. I could swim, and I spoke to them and told them what to do, but they did not speak. Mr. Steen got hold of an oar. Mr. Blackburne was holding on by a life-belt, but he was the first who sank. Mr. Steen had only gone down a couple of minutes before Mr. Usher reached me. I got off my coat in the water, and put on the life-belt. The life-belt had been lying in the boat before the accident. After Mr. Steen went down I took off my coat, and put on the belt. We were all perfectly sober, though we had taken some drink on the boat. I believe I could have reached the shore without the life-belt. I found no difficulty in taking off my coat. I was very well while in the water. It was after I was taken out of the water I became so nervous.

This closed the evidence, and the jury immediately returned a verdict of death by accidental drowning.

LISBURN STANDARD
MAY 12 1900

DEATH OF MR. WILLIAM BLACKBURN, LISSUE

The death was announced on Tuesday last of Mr. William Blackburn, Lissue, at the residence of his brother-in-law, Mr. Henry Monroe. The deceased, who was 69 years of age, has been for many years a prominent figure in Lisburn and the surrounding district, and the announcement of his death will be received with sincere regret by many. He was one of the oldest and most prominent members of the Killultagh and Derryvolgie Farming Society in days gone by, and was a hearty supporter of the Lisburn Horticultural Society, frequently acting as judge in the vegetable classes. For many years he carried on the business of a licensed merchant at Lissue, but of late went in extensively for farming pursuits. He was a staunch Unionist, and regarded as the oldest member of the Watson Loyal Orange Lodge. His loss will be keenly felt in many ways. The funeral took place on Thursday morning, and was attended by a large number of the leading residents of Lisburn and neighbourhood. The place of interment was the Cathedral Graveyard, and prior to interment a short service was held in the Cathedral, where the Rev. Canon Pounden and the Rev. John Leslie (Broomhedge) officiated. The same gentlemen conducted the closing portion of the burial service at the graveside. Mr. John Magill carried out the funeral arrangements in his usual satisfactory manner.

BRACEGIRDEL

CATHEDRAL 178
This stone is very badly weathered. Only part of the inscription survives. **Sarah Bracegirdel** was the daughter of **Samuel** and **Jane Bracegirdel**. She was baptised in Lisburn Cathedral on 5th May 1799. She had a brother, **Charles**, who was baptised in St. Anne's Parish Church, Belfast, on 27th December 1810. Charles married **Elizabeth Wilson McGowan** on 18th March 1848, and he died 25th February 1895. It is probable that Samuel Bracegirdel was a brother to **Matthew Bracegirdel** of Belfast.

CALDBECK

CATHEDRAL 1
The only inscription on the memorial stone for Caldbeck is "The Burying Ground of W. Caldbeck", and so a brief family history of the family has been put together from Cathedral records, newspaper entries, directories and Calendar of Wills.

It would appear that several generations of the family were Barristers. From the abstract of a will of 1803, found in the Registry of Deeds, it seems that **William Caldbeck**, a Barrister of Clondalkin, Dublin, was the grandfather of **William Caldbeck** of Lisburn. William Caldbeck, of Dublin, probably had three sons, **William Eaton**, **Frederick John** and **Harry** and two daughters, **Sarah** and **Ann**. William Eaton pre-deceased his father. His wife was **Dora Graham**, sister of **Anne Graham**, who married **Joseph Fulton**, [see Fulton Cathedral No.109 and page 221]. William and Dora had at least two sons, William and **Francis Cope**. It is William, the son, who is named on the stone attached to the wall of the Cathedral graveyard. This William married his cousin, **Amy Boyd Fulton**, and they had a family of three sons and four daughters.

Descendants of William Caldbeck

This is not a complete Family Tree.

Cathedral No. 1

?

William Caldbeck
b: abt. 1733
d: Sept. 6 1803
Married
Ann Keatinge
b: abt 1745
d: June 21 1821

Joyce Caldbeck
Married
? Townsend

William Eaton Caldbeck
Married
Dora Graham

Frederick John Caldbeck
Married
Eliza Pearson
Issue

Harry Caldbeck

Sarah Caldbeck
Married
? Langley

Ann Caldbeck
Married
? Warren

Francis Cope Caldbeck
Married
Anne Curran
Issue

William Eaton Caldbeck
bap: May 4 1787
d: Sept. 25 1858
Buried Lisb. Cath.
Married March 4 1808

Amelia (Amy) Boyd Fulton
bap: May 1787
d: January 31 1870
Buried Lisb. Cath.
(See Fulton)

Anne Fulton Caldbeck
bap.: July 29 1811
d: April 3 1834
Buried Lisburn Cath.
Married
William Gregg
b: 1796
d: February 2 1870
Buried Lisb. Cath.
(See Gregg)

Dorothea (Dora) Caldbeck
b: abt 1814
d: April 21 1827
Buried Lisb. Cath.

William Eaton Caldbeck
bap: August 8 1815
d: September 21 1855

Joseph Fulton Caldbeck
bap.: June 4 1819
d: August 1 1840
Buried Lisb. Cath.

Thomas Fulton Caldbeck J.P.
bap.: July 11 1821
d: June 20 1891
Married April 10 1851
Charlotte Stewart
b: May 20 1812
d: February 2 1897
(See Stewart)

Emily Caldbeck
bap.: January 18 1823
d: 1909
Married Feb. 26 1851
Capt. Charles William Thompson
d: Dec. 30 1881
Issue

Elizabeth Caldbeck
b: July 26 1826
d: April 7 1835
Buried Lisb. Cath.

William Eaton Caldbeck
b: abt. 1854
d: April 25 1896
Married 1890
Sara Watkins
b: Abt. 1862
d: March 31 1946

Charlotte Hannah Caldbeck
b: Sept. 14 1891

Sarah Frances Caldbeck
b: Sept. 2 1892

Thomas Fulton Caldbeck
b: Aug. 9 1894
d: April 8 1910

Capt. William Eaton Caldbeck
b: May 24 1896
d: March 6 1938

202

In 1812 William was a Churchwarden of the Cathedral, is described as a "Gent, of Belfast Gate" in an 1819 Directory, and in an 1824 Directory he was living in Castle Street, Lisburn. In 1838 two of the original subscribers to the Lisburn Newsroom were William and **Jos. Caldbeck**. By 1840 a William Caldbeck is a Guardian of the Lisburn Poor House. When William died in 1858 he was living in Dublin. In 1851 William wanted a Caldbeck residence near Dublin for his sons, so he purchased an estate at Shankill, Dublin, and built a house, which he named "Eaton Brae". Unfortunately he and his son, William, died before the house was completed.

Of his sons, **Thomas Fulton Caldbeck, J.P.**, who in 1843/44 was the Under Sheriff for County Down, married **Charlotte**, daughter of **Dr. Stewart**, [See Stewart Cathedral No.19 and page 269], and his home was at Eaton Brae, Shankill, Dublin. He was High Sheriff of Co. Dublin in 1871. Thomas Fulton, his wife, Charlotte, their son, **William Eaton**, his wife, **Sara**, and their two sons, **Thomas Fulton** and **Capt. William Eaton**, are all buried in Dean's Grange Cemetery, Blackrock, Co. Dublin, the largest cemetery in south Co. Dublin. This cemetery was opened in 1865. Another son, **William Eaton**, was a Barrister in Dublin, and a third son, Joseph Fulton, was Under Sheriff of Co. Down when he died in 1840.

Of the daughters of William Caldbeck, **Anne Fulton** married **William Gregg**, Seneschal, [See Gregg Cathedral No. 147 and page 228], and **Emily** married, in 1851, **Capt. Charles William Thompson**, of the 58th Regiment, son of **Lt. Colonel Charles Thompson** of the 27th Regiment.

CARLETON

CATHEDRAL 44 AND 47

There are only two headstones in the name of Carleton in the Cathedral Graveyard. This family had been in the Lisburn area, and connected with Lisburn Cathedral, for quite some time. There is a burial record of a **Capt. Cornelius Carleton** of Blaris on 7th November 1726. He had been a churchwarden in 1695 and there is also mention of other Carletons being churchwardens of the Cathedral. Because of the large gaps in the Cathedral records it is not possible to establish fully all the family connections, but there are many mentions of the name Carleton and they married into many other families in the area.

Number 44 is for two brothers, **Edward** and **Cornelius Carleton** of Blaris, and their respective wives, **Sarah** and **Mary**. Their exact relationship to the family of Cornelius Carleton of number 47 is not known.

Cornelius Carleton (c1750-29th March 1818) of No. 47, was "of Lisburn". It is likely he was married twice. About 1780 he married **Elizabeth Casement** (c1752-9th September 1824). His daughter, **Eleanor**, (c1775-17th May 1863), mentioned on the stone, married **William Sproull** (c1772-1817) of Dungannon, Co. Tyrone, on 27th June 1797. They had two sons, **Robert** and **William Henry**, and three daughters. The daughters were **Frances Carleton**, who married **William Holmes** in 1822, **Mary** and **Elizabeth**. The last two are mentioned on the stone. The son, **William Henry Sproull** (1812-1883), an attorney in Belfast, married **Jane Fulton** (1819-1845) in 1839. [See Fulton Cathedral Number 137 and page 221.] After she died he went on to marry three more times. His wives were **Sarah Ferguson**, **Bonella McDowal** and **Jane Birney**. In total he had fifteen children, but not all survived infancy.

Cornelius had at least three other daughters, **Frances**, who married **Samuel Davidson** on 7th November 1801, **Elizabeth** (c1791-c1887) who married **Thomas Harden Carleton**, probably a relative, and **Mary** (c1792-17th February 1869), who first married **Charles Casement** (c1791/2-13th July 1832) and then **John Shaw Carleton**. John Shaw Carleton (c1801-2nd July 1844) was the son of **Cornelius Carleton** of Blaris. John Shaw Carleton and Mary Carleton Casement married in Lisburn Cathedral on 31st December 1839. They lived in Roseville, Lisburn, and are buried in Blaris Graveyard.

Cornelius Carleton had at least two sons. One of these was the **Rev. Hugh Casement Carleton** (c1784-April 1860). He was rector of Arrow in Warwickshire, England. The other son was **John** (c1783-26th August 1825). He married **Margaret Joyce** on 3rd November 1818. Although his name is not now recorded on a stone he is in the Cathedral records as being buried in the graveyard. His wife married secondly, on 15th January 1830, **John Legge Jun.** of Carrickfergus.

An earlier **John Carleton** is probably buried in the graveyard. He was an innkeeper in Lisburn and died about March 1779. His wife was **Mary Maphet** and they had a family of at least six sons and three daughters. A **Rev. John Carleton** was also a rector of Arrow. He died unmarried in 1818 and left a bequest of £2,000 to Lisburn Cathedral. The interest was to be distributed each St. Thomas' Day among the poor householders of all denominations.
[*P.R.O.N.I. D/2489/3 and T/2578/1*]

COULSON

CATHEDRAL 72

This memorial is a box tomb, surrounded by tall iron railings. The Coulson family have been in Lisburn since about 1669. In 1764 it is believed that **William Coulson** first established his linen business near the old County Down bridge across the Lagan, with a small number of linen looms, and, in 1766, he then had his factory built on a site granted by the Earl of Hertford. This site was in Linenhall Street. Here eventually he had 24 damask looms, and other diaper looms, with a workforce in excess of 200 people.

William and his wife, **Ann**, had a family of at least five sons and three daughters. All the sons, except for one, **John**, are named on the stone. Four of the sons, John (born c1770), **William** (c1774-1851), **James** (1779-1854) and **Walter** (c1783-1836), were in the linen business. **Hill** (1777-1815) became a Church of Ireland clergyman and was first a curate in Lisburn Cathedral, and was curate in Ballinderry when he died from injuries received in a riding accident. Most of his brothers were churchwardens in Lisburn Cathedral at various times. The daughters were **Mary** (b.1770), **Jane** (b.1771) and **Ann** (c1787-1834). Only Ann is named on the stone.

After the death of their father, in 1801, John and William ran the family business and were joined in partnership by Walter in 1810, and by James some time later. On July 10th 1811 the firm received a Royal Warrant, or patent, from the Prince Regent appointing them "Table Linen Manufacturers to His Royal Highness the Prince of Wales." Coulsons were among the earlier linen damask manufacturers to weave national emblems, heraldic designs, ornamental borders and mottoes etc. Their cliental was international and in the years 1818 to 1820, as their fame grew, several notable people of that time visited Coulson's factory. These included Archduke Michael of Russia, the Crown Prince of Sweden, the Duke of Wellington and Lord John Russell.

About 1816 the factory was extended to take in the adjacent disused Yeomanry barracks. By 1834 the firm was employing about 500 people in the factory as well as having "out" workers i.e. people working in their homes. There was also a bleach green at Sprucefield. After the death of Walter, in 1836, a wall was built across the factory to divide the business into two firms i.e. William Coulson & Sons and James Coulson & Co. As can be seen from their obituaries, the brothers were very skilled in their work and well known for their care of their workers and for their involvement with other deserving causes in Lisburn. One memorial stone in the Cathedral grounds, that of William Leckey (No. 58), was erected by William Coulson & Sons.

Later William Coulson & Sons was bought by the Belfast Damask and Linen Company and survived, still using Jacquard handlooms, until the closure of the thatched building in the mid 1950's. A powerloom factory in Barrack Lane continued with table linen until 1968.

William Coulson married **Catherine Casement** (1800-1873), of Harryville House, Ballymena, Co. Antrim, on the 8ᵗʰ April 1825 and had a family of at least four sons and five daughters. His daughter, **Catherine** (1830-1924), married **Rev. Augustine Fitzgerald**. William, his wife, Catherine, his son, **Hill** (c1828-1860), and daughters **Ann Jane** (1826-1830), **Jane** (1835-1840) and **Eleanor** (1839-1866) are all buried in No. 72, although not all the names are on the stone.

John Coulson is known to have married and to have had a daughter, **Elizabeth**. John continued as a partner in the firm all his life and may have been involved in the sales side of the business as he lived mainly in Dublin and latterly in Paris. It is thought that he died and was buried in Paris.

The Coulsons were related to the Fulton family by marriage. [See Fulton page 221.]

BELFAST NEWS LETTER
TUESDAY FEBRUARY 23 1836

DEATH OF WALTER COULSON ESQ.

At the family residence, in Lisburn, on the evening of Wednesday the 17ᵗʰ inst. WALTER COULSON, Esq., departed this life, aged 51 years. As one of the proprietors of the far-famed Damask Manufactory of that town, he was eminently distinguished for an acute understanding; and it was greatly owing to his genius in the mechanical department, his felicitous conception in planning designs, and his ability in putting them into execution, that the peculiar and splendid portion of the linen business, in which he and his brothers were engaged, has arrived at its present elevated position in the history of scientific improvement, by any similar establishment in the world. As a citizen, Mr. Coulson was a gentleman in the widest sense of the term; and as a master, those who only knew him in that capacity could fully appreciate his character: the happiness of his workmen was his delight - it was his pride to encourage industry. In him the poor of Lisburn have lost a steady and liberal benefactor; and towards the objects of his charity, he always mingled courtesy with kindness. To the local institutions of Lisburn he was a large contributor; and many of his private acts of benevolence will only come to light, now that he is removed to that land where no good deed is forgotten.

BANNER OF ULSTER
FRIDAY AUGUST 22 1851

THE LATE MR. WILLIAM COULSON, ESQ.

(Extract from obituary.)

As a merchant engaged in the manufacture of textile fabrics, which demand a greater degree of skill and ingenuity than perhaps any other human pursuit, Mr. Coulson possessed talents rarely met with, and much of the perfection to which the art of damask-weaving has arisen in the northern districts of Ulster may be attributed to his genius. The patterns of those beautiful table-cloths shown by Mr. William Coulson in the Industrial Exhibition were designed solely by himself, as were also many of the magnificent specimens of damask which at present adorn the tables, not alone of the British Monarch, but several of the most celebrated of the Continental kings and European nobles. In his capacity as an employer, he was remarkable for his attention to the wants and the comforts of his work-people, and, as was stated of his late brother, Walter Coulson, Esq., he was the *friend* as well as the master of those engaged at his manufactory. To all the charitable institutions of his native town he was ever among the most liberal contributors, and his acts of private benevolence were ample, and confined neither to sect nor party.

Mr. W. Coulson held the rank of captain in the Lisburn corps of yeomanry, and for more than a quarter of a century supported, at his own expense, the excellent band attached to that company.

BELFAST NEWS LETTER
WEDNESDAY MARCH 29 1854

THE LATE JAMES COULSON ESQ., OF LISBURN.

(Extract from obituary.)

From an early period up to the date of his demise, Mr. Coulson was identified with the celebrated Damask Factory at Lisburn. He was for many years junior partner in the firm of John, William, Walter and James Coulson, sons of the Mr. Coulson whose enterprise, under the auspices of the Marquis of Hertford, established the Damask Factory, and brought it into fame. With extraordinary perseverance and energy, Mr. James Coulson applied himself to business — visiting the Continent and every part of the United Kingdom to forward its interests. At the dissolution of the partnership between himself and his brothers, with an arbour unabated, he adhered to his favourite pursuit, and continued to carry on the trade under the name of James Coulson & Co. Of his well merited success, a judgment may be formed by considering some of the many distinguished prizes assigned to his fabric, on account of its peculiar excellence. The Royal Dublin Society awarded to him its gold medal, at the two triennial exhibitions, when damask was admitted for competition - namely, in 1847 and 1850. The Royal Society of Arts in London conferred on him its medal, in 1850. The Commissioners of the Great Exhibition in the Crystal Palace, Hyde Park, London, in 1851, adjudged to him a prize medal. At the Dublin Exhibition last year, his specimens of damask were greatly and deservedly admired, while his own off-hand frankness and generosity won the plaudits of Mr. Dargan himself. So anxious was Mr. Coulson for the welfare of his workmen, and the preservation of the trade in their hands and in his native town, that he has left special instructions in his will that the firm of James Coulson & Co. shall be maintained in vigour, in the prosecution of its trade. It was a great consolation to the deceased that the senior partner of the old firm, his brother John, was permitted to be by him in his last days, to cheer his dying moments by his presence, as he had all along animated and encouraged him and his partner in their arduous and honourable undertakings. Mr. John Coulson, the last of the four brothers who were for a lengthened period in happy partnership, will, no doubt, cherish a deep interest in the success and prosperity of the firm of James Coulson & Company, from which his brother is snatched away.

CROMMELIN

CATHEDRAL 166, 162, 161

The Huguenot surname which is probably best known in connection with Lisburn Cathedral Burying Ground is that of Crommelin. This family of Crommelins had been in the linen business from the sixteenth century and branches of the family lived in Northern France and Holland. Their families were large and there was also some intermarriage with cousins, which continued with the branch of the family who came to Ireland. This was probably to protect family wealth and position. **Louis Crommelin**, born 1625, married **Marie Metayer** and had a family of eight children. One of these children was **Louis Crommelin**, born in 1652 in St. Quentin, Picardy, France, who, in April 1680, married his second cousin, **Anne Crommelin**, daughter of **Samuel Crommelin** and **Madeleine Testart**. After the revocation of the Edict of Nantes in 1685 Louis and Anne moved to Amsterdam, Holland, for several years. In 1697 Louis was asked by King William III to come to Ireland as Overseer of the Royal Linen Manufacture. He came to Lisburn about 1698 and established a factory at the foot of Bridge Street, Lisburn, near the wooden bridge, and a bleach-green at Hilden. He brought over French artisans and he and his business associates also promised to invest £10,000 of their own money in machinery, looms and in giving instruction. The Huguenot contribution to the linen industry has, perhaps, been overestimated as the linen industry was already established in the Lisburn area before this time, but Louis did play a part in promoting this industry and he provided leadership to the Huguenot colony.

Louis brought with him his wife, his two children, **Louis** and **Mary Madeleine**, two of his brothers, **Samuel** and **William**, and his sisters, **Jeanne**, **Anne** and **Marie**, and several cousins. Along with them were also several friends and business associates with their own incomes. After Louis

Descendants of Crommelin

Cathedral Nos. 161, 162 & 166

First Cousins

↑ ↓

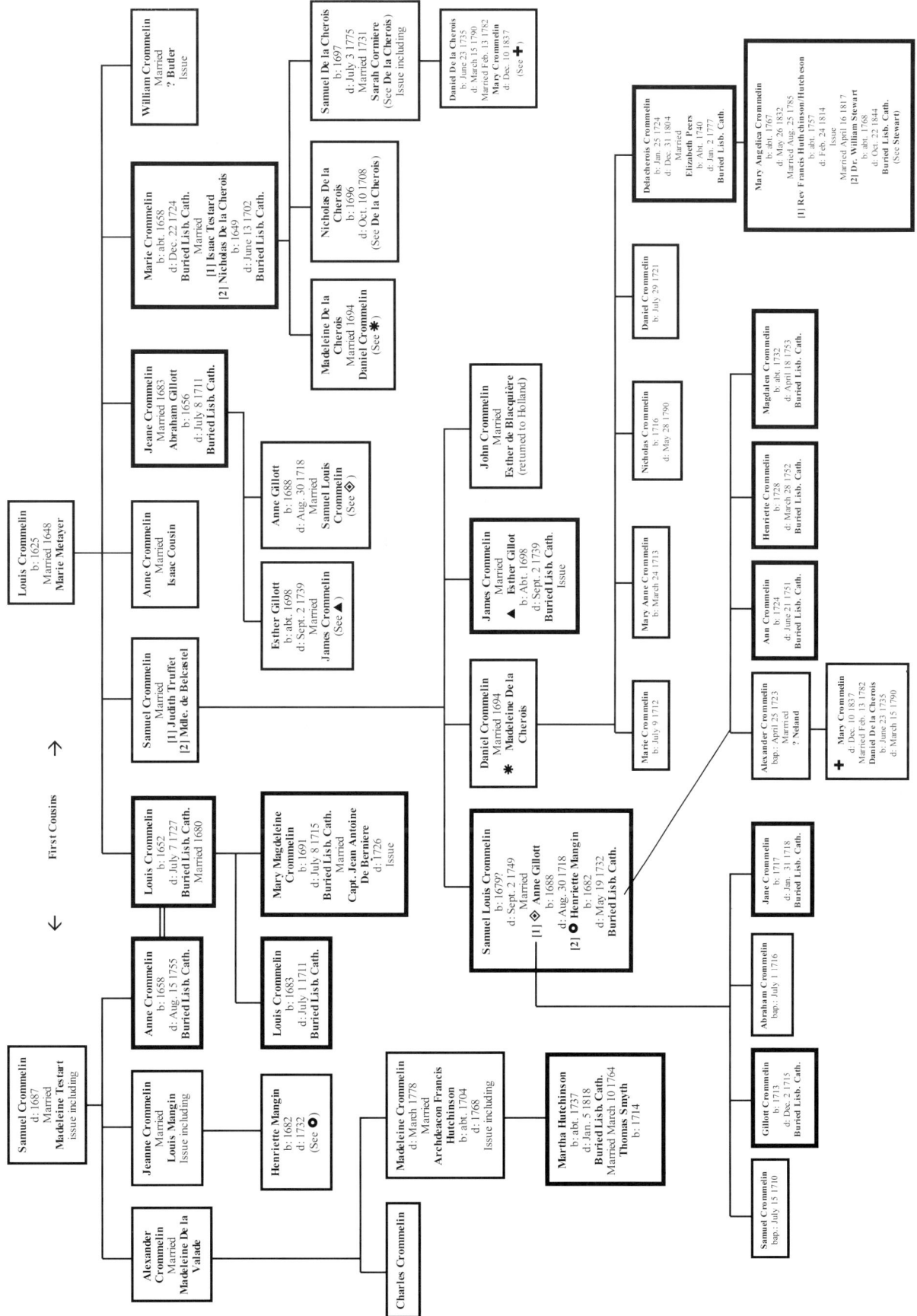

207

Crommelin's death his brother Samuel, and his family, continued in the linen business. His brother, William, did not stay long in Lisburn, but moved on to Waterford.

Louis Crommelin's son, Louis, was born in 1683 and died in Lisburn 1st July 1711. His daughter, Mary Madeleine, who was born 1691 and died 8th July 1715, married **Captain John De Berniere**. A descendant of theirs, **Catherine**, was the first wife of **John Smith** [see De la Cherois page 213.] Louis and Anne Crommelin, their son, Louis, and daughter, Mary Madeleine Berniere, Catherine, John, and his second wife, **Judith Smith** are buried in Cathedral No. 162.

Louis's brother, Samuel, married first **Judith Truefet** and second **Mlle. De Belcastel**. They had four sons, **Samuel Louis**, **Daniel**, **James** and **John**. Samuel Louis's first marriage was to his cousin, **Anne Gillott**, and they had at least three sons, **Samuel**, **Gillott** and **Abraham**, and a daughter, **Jane**. He then married **Henriette Mangin** and had at least three daughters, **Ann**, **Henriette**, and **Magdalen,** and a son, **Alexander.** Alexander married a **Miss Neland** and had a daughter, **Mary**, who, in 1782, married her second cousin, **Daniel De la Cherois**, son of **Samuel De la Cherois** [see De la Cherois page 213.] Samuel Louis Crommelin, his two wives, Anne and Henriette, his son, Gillott, his daughters, Jane, Ann, Henriette and Magdalen are all buried in Cathedral No. 161. His son, **Abraham Crommelin** was a churchwarden of the Cathedral in 1749.

James Crommelin, son of Samuel Crommelin, Louis's brother, married his cousin, **Esther Gillott** and she is buried in Cathedral No. 161. **Daniel**, also a son of Samuel, married his cousin **Madeleine De la Cherois** [see De la Cherois page 213.]

Esther and Anne Gillott, who had married their cousins, were the daughters of Louis Crommelin's sister Jeanne, who had married **Abraham Gillott**. Abraham Gillott is also buried in Cathedral No. 161. Another of Louis's sisters, Marie, married **Isaac Testard de Blois** and then **Nicholas De la Cherois** [see De la Cherois page 213.] A third sister, Anne, married **Isaac Cousin de Meaux**.

Alexander Crommelin (a brother of Anne Crommelin, Louis Crommelin's wife) married **Madeleine De la Valade**, sister of **Charles De la Valade**, the first Huguenot pastor in the French church in Lisburn. They had a son, **Charles**, and a daughter, **Madeleine**. Madeleine married **Rev. Francis Hutchinson** (1704-1768). He was Archdeacon of Down and Connor and was nephew of the **Rev. Francis Hutchinson**, Bishop of Down, who is named on the Memorial window in the south nave of the Cathedral. Madeleine and Francis had a son, **Samuel Hill Hutchinson**, and three daughters, **Sophia**, **Martha** and **Frances**. Martha was the third wife of **Thomas Smyth**, of Drumcree. They married on 10th March 1764 and had at least one son, **Thomas Hutchinson Smyth**. Martha Smyth is buried in Cathedral No. 164. Frances married **Rev. William Browne** in 1757.

Through the passage of time the inscriptions on the headstones of the Crommelin family became worn so they were copied onto a bronze plaque, which was attached to the tall iron railings surrounding the family graves. This was unveiled in August 1964.

CROSSLEY

There are three separate headstones in the name of Crossley. It is not known if these families are related to each other.

Number 180 is for **John Crossley**, Proprietor of the Hertford Arms, Market Square, who died in 1838. The stone was erected by his widow, **Sarah**, who had formerly been Sarah **Moore**. On 31st May 1841 she married **John Oswald Head**, Captain of the "Reindeer" Steam Packet.

Number 181 is for **Thomas Crossley**, who would appear to have been a publican from Bridge Street, and died in 1819. His wife, **Mary Ann**, then married **George Davis** of Culcavy.

More is known about the Crossley family of Number 41. They are descended from the Crossleys of Scaitcliffe, Co. Lancaster. The first of these Crossleys to come to Ireland was **Anthony Crossley** of Further Scaitcliffe and Dromore, who fought at the Battle of the Boyne 1690 and died in August 1757. His son was **Anthony** and his grandson was **John Crossley**, who was baptised 29th January 1746 and died 11th March 1830. John married **Elizabeth Alcott** and had at least two sons, **John** and **Francis**, and a daughter, **Margaret**, who was baptised 15th January 1772. He also had a brother, **William**, baptised 7th April 1745, who married **Margaret Johnston**, and had a family. It is the father, John, and the son, John, who are named on the gravestone.

John Crossley junior was born about 1786. On the 29th May 1810 John and Rev. Thomas Cupples, son of the Rev. Snowden Cupples, [see Cupples No. 3 and page 211], had opened the Lisburn Male Free School based on the Bell and Lancaster system of teaching. A simple explanation of this is that it was a system of teaching children with the help of monitors, who were chosen from among the brighter children, to help instruct others. This system was called after Rev. Dr. Andrew Bell and Joseph Lancaster, a Quaker.

The school was originally held in the Court House in Castle Street. A description of the school appeared in the Belfast News Letter of 21st August 1810:-

SCHOOL FOR POOR CHILDREN

It is pleasing to record acts of benevolence and institutions to promote the benefits of education. Two young men, John Crossley and Thomas Cupples have most benevolently devoted two hours in the morning and as much of the evening in each day to the education of a number of poor boys in the town of Lisburn. They have adopted the plans of Bell and Lancaster, and instruct about seventy boys after the manner introduced by them. The boys are taught in classes from lessons posted upon the walls, and they write on sand laid smoothly on a board fitted for the purpose, previously to using slates in their future progress. Much of the expense of schools on the usual plan, in books, paper, quills, &c. is thus saved. The labour of teaching, which they undertake themselves, is facilitated by the assistance of monitors chosen from the children, who while they instruct others are also benefited in their turn. A record of the merits and demerits is kept, and once a week the deserving are rewarded by some small premium, and those who are marked in the black book are tried by a jury of their peers, chosen from the other children, and receive punishment according to their misdeeds. It is observed that even during the short time which has elapsed since the opening of the school, the morals of the boys have been considerably improved by a steady execution of this system.

Unfortunately John Crossley died of consumption on 10th March 1816, but the school was kept going by public subscription and a committee was formed to run it. A new school building was built in 1821 in Market Place, opposite to where Lisburn Square is now. Money for the school was donated by the inhabitants of Lisburn and included a donation from the Marquis of Hertford. The site of the schoolhouse, the master's house and the grounds were also a gift from the Marquis of Hertford. A description of the building is given in the Ordnance Survey Memoirs of 1837. This said it was one storey high, 41 feet by 24 feet, and 15 feet high, made of brick and lime and was slated. There was a small cupola, with a bell, which was presented by Rowley Hall in 1822. The master's house was built in 1830. In 1837 there were 263 pupils and the master was William McCann. He had been appointed in 1820, and at one time the school was commonly called "McCann's School." As well as the yearly subscriptions there was also the interest from a legacy left to the school by Rowley Hall and the interest from £100 left by George Whitla.

The inscription on the stone on the front of the building was :- "This free school commenced A.D. 1810, under the directions of the late John Crooley <Crossley> Junior. The inhabitants of Lisburn, to perpetuate his benefits, have erected this schoolhouse, 1821, on a site allotted for it by the most honourable, the Marquis of Hertford."

In 1816 the committee consisted of Rev. Dr. Cupples, Rev. Andrew Craig, Rev. T. Higginson, Mr. Charles Higginson, Joseph Fulton, Dr. Thompson, Thomas Cupples, William Wightman and John Crossley, father to the principal founder of the school. In 1837 the committee was Rev. Dean Stannus, Rev. Thomas Cupples, Rev. Ralph Bridge, Dr. Thompson Sen., William Whitla and Francis Crossley, brother of the founder of the school.

Francis, John Crossley's brother, was born about 1787. The story is told that in the winter of 1804 Robert Owenson, a dramatist and actor, came to Lisburn with his company of strolling players. He also had with him his two daughters, Sydney and Olivia. It would appear that Francis Crossley fell in love with Sydney Owenson, but at that time he did not have the means to support himself and a wife. Perhaps under the patronage of the Marquis of Hertford, Francis managed to get a position with the East India Company. First he was in the Madras Infantry and then he obtained an appointment in the Civil Service. He progressed well, but unfortunately his letters home to Sydney, with money to pay her passage to India, arrived too late. Sydney had become a celebrated authoress and in August 1812 at Baronscourt, Co. Tyrone, she married Sir Charles Morgan M.D., an aged medical man.

Francis returned home in 1824. By now he was a Captain, and on the 20th August 1824 he married **Jane Poyntz Stewart**, daughter of **Dr. William Stewart**, Castle Street, [see Stewart page 269.] Unfortunately she died in childbirth on 1st March 1828. In 1835 Francis Crossley was back in Ireland, now a Major, and he was living at Glenburn in Dunmurry. He then married **Elizabeth Helen Irwin** on 20th April 1837 and had three sons and a daughter. The daughter, **Emmeline**, was born 30th March 1842 and died 25th December 1917. She married **Alexander McLaren** on 13th September 1871. Major Francis' eldest son was **Francis William**, born 27th November 1839 and died 1st June 1897. He married **Emily Kerr** in 1871. They had four sons and a daughter. Major Francis' second son, **William John**, born 22nd April 1844, became M.P. for Altrincham, Cheshire from 1906-1910 and was made a baronet in 1909. In 1876 he married **Mabel Gordon Anderson**, daughter of **Francis Anderson** and grand-daughter of **Drummond Anderson** and Margaret Crossley, and had three sons and two daughters. The firm of Crossley Brothers was set up in 1867, in Manchester, by the two eldest sons of Major Francis, Francis and William Crossley. Francis, with the help of his uncle, bought the engineering works of John M. Dunlop. This firm made pumps, presses and small steam engines. William concentrated on the business side and Francis on the engineering. Over the years they developed gas fuelled engines, "oil" engines and Diesel engines. These were eventually used in motorcars. They introduced the "production line" and are supposed to have influenced Henry Ford. Crossley Motors Ltd. was first registered in 1906. The business expanded into many other areas, but later was in financial difficulties and has now been taken over by other firms. Sir William was also one of the original directors of the Manchester Ship Canal. He took an active part in philanthropic works in the Manchester area. He died 12th October 1911 and his wife died in 1943. The third son, **Thomas Hastings Henry**, born in August 1846 and died 23rd March 1926, became Professor of Greek at Queen's College, Belfast and Bristol University. He married **Agnes Irwin** and had one son.

Major Francis Crossley died on 17th September 1846 and is buried in Lisburn Cathedral Graveyard. His wife, Elizabeth, died 9th February 1891.

John Crossley (1785-1816) and Major Francis Crossley's sister, Margaret, was baptised 15th January 1772 and died 1861. She married Drummond Anderson, editor of the Belfast Commercial Chronicle, in Lisburn Cathedral on 23rd April 1810. They had at least two sons, **John Crossley Anderson**, baptised 20th February 1812, and **Francis Anderson**, baptised 13th December 1813.
[P.R.O.N.I. D/1725/1]

(This is an extract from a lengthy obituary on John Crossley (1786-1816).

NEWS LETTER
MARCH 19 1816

The late Mr. John Crossley Jun.

"This young man, at an early period of life, had attained the characteristics of "honourable age," and filled up a portion of usefulness which will cause his loss to be severely felt and lamented in his native town. He embarked early in the cause of the Education of the Poor, and in the year 1810, in conjunction with another young man, the companion of his labours, he established a School for boys, to which he has ever since dedicated his attention. At this period Schools of this nature were not so common as they have since become. Thus he had not only the merit of being among the first in the highly praiseworthy attempts "to cause ignorance to see," but he gratuitously engaged with that enthusiastic ardour which enabled him to overcome difficulties, and to persevere in his unwearied exertions to benefit the offspring of the poorer classes of the community, even at the risque of his health, and frequently under the pressure of a considerable degree of pain, as the closeness of the School room must have often increased an asthmatic complaint, from which he had greatly suffered. The affectionate and sorrowful deportment of the children of the various religious denominations, and the often repeated benedictions of their parents, at his interment, were the best attestations of his substantial merits.

"His death has occasioned a vacancy, which will not be easily filled up. The School may still continue to be supported by Subscription, but who will fill the place of this indefatigable disinterested instructor, who dedicated his time to the service of his country? He felt a most earnest and parental care towards the children, whom he instructed not only in school-learning but in the principles of Religion and Virtue. Nor were his good deeds solely confined to his care of the school – he gave many other proofs of possessing a feeling and benevolent heart.

CUPPLES

CATHEDRAL 3 AND MEMORIAL
The gravestone in the Cathedral grounds, near the Market Square entrance to the Churchyard, is to the **Rev. Dr. Snowden Cupples** and some members of his family. Rev. Snowden Cupples was Curate of Carrickfergus 1781-1796 and the Rector of Lisburn Cathedral from 1796 until his death in 1835. He was Vicar General of Down and Connor in 1809 and Seneschal of the Manor of Killultagh and Derryvolgie 1812–1834. His wife was **Elinor Ross**, and inside the Cathedral building there is also a memorial to her, her Ross relatives and two of her children. The Rev. Cupples was Rector during the unrest during the 1798 Rebellion. It is believed that Snowden was the grandson of **Thomas Cupples** (1650-1715) of Scarvagh, Co. Down, and son of **William Cupples** (1693-1783), and **Eleanor** (c.1720-1765), of Prospect House, Millahead, Co. Armagh. William had a brother, **Capt. Alexander**, who died in 1729 and is thought to have made a fortune in the slave trade.

Snowden Cupples had at least nine children, five boys and four girls. The eldest son, **William**, born about 1785 and died 26th November 1833, started off in the Bombay Army, became a Lieutenant and

REV. DR. SNOWDEN CUPPLES
(c1753 - 1835)

an expert in Asiatic languages, before returning to Lisburn because of ill health. He then became a Surveyor of the Irish Post Office. Another son, **Charles**, was baptised 18th July 1791 and died 6th October 1824. He became a surgeon in the Royal Artillery and married **Antonia Legg** on 31st August 1824.

Two sons became Church of Ireland clergymen. The **Rev. Edward Cupples**, baptised 2nd August 1785 and died 22nd November 1857, was Vicar of Glenavy 1813–1845 and Vicar General of Down and Connor. The **Rev. Thomas Cupples**, baptised 25th September 1789 and died 6th November 1853, was Curate of Lisburn 1824 and Rector of Ballyrashane, Co. Londonderry 1826–1853. The Rev. Thomas, with John Crossley, was one of the founders of the Lisburn Male Free School, [see Crossley page 209.] Rev. Thomas Cupples is buried in Ballyrashane, where inside the church is a memorial to him erected by his parishioners and friends:-

To the Memory of
The Rev. Thomas Cupples, A.B.,
Rector of Ballyrashane.
His life was one unwearied course of duties
performed with scrupulous regard to his ministerial engagements
His acts of Charity
to his poor brethren were limited only by his means.
The humility of an honest and good heart
was manifest in the easy courtesy of his cheerful manners,
which were also distinguished by Godly simplicity
and Christian moderation.
"There is laid up for him a Crown of righteousness."
He died at Ballyrashane, on the VIth day of November MDCCCL III,
in the LXVth year of his age, and the XXVIIth of his Incumbency.
Erected by His Parishioners and Friends.

In the Ballyrashane graveyard he is buried in the same grave as his niece, **Frances Jane McNaghten**, and her husband, **Lt. Alexander McNaghten R.N.**

The fifth son was **Ezekiel Davys Wilson Cupples** baptised 9th March 1795. He died unmarried. Of the four daughters, two died young. They were **Maria**, born about 1788 and died 24th March 1796 and **Elinor**, baptised 1799 and died 1803. Another daughter was **Frances**, baptised 3rd October 1803 died 28th September 1869. The only daughter to marry was **Maria Cupples**, born 13th April 1797 and died 1st May 1888. She married **Rev. John Corken** on 16th August 1819. He was born about 1798 and died 30th April 1834 and was vicar of Aghalee 1830-1834. They had a family of three sons and three daughters. The sons were **William John** (c1821-1869), **Thomas T.** (c1822-7th July 1841), and **Snowden** (c1825-25th September 1871). The daughters were **Elinor**, (baptised 11th May 1827-19th March 1904), Frances Jane (baptised 1st January 1829-3rd July 1853), who married, on 17th May 1849, Lt. Alexander McNaghten R.N. and Coastguard of Portrush (c1816-29th October 1852), and **Elizabeth Anne**, baptised 9th March 1833 and died 27th February 1923, who married **Matthew Johnson Smyth** [see Johnson Smyth page 243.]

The Rev. Snowden Cupples had a brother, **Thomas** (8th June 1756-6th August 1801) who was a doctor in Newry. His daughter, **Elizabeth**, married **Henry Ellis** on 15th December 1810.

DE LA CHEROIS AND DE LA CHEROIS–CROMMELIN
CATHEDRAL 16, 162, 167, 163, 17 AND 165

Several of the Huguenot families who were closely related to each other are buried together in the south part of the Cathedral burying ground, near to the east wall. This area has been renovated at least once over the years and is surrounded by tall iron railings. Several of these stones are for the De la Cherois family.

This De la Cherois family were originally from Ham, Picardy in France. There were three brothers, **Nicholas, Daniel** and **Bourjonval**, and four sisters, **Louise, Judith, Anthoinette** and **Marie**. Nicholas and Bourjonval had been in the army of King Louis XIV, but after the revocation of the Edict of Nantes, in 1685, they fled to Holland, where they were joined by their brother, Daniel. All three joined the army of William, Prince of Orange, later King William III. Nicholas eventually becoming a major, Daniel a captain and Bourjonval a lieutenant. All three were in Ireland fighting for King William, but unfortunately Bourjonval died at Dungannon in 1690.

Daniel was the first of the De la Cherois family to come to live in Lisburn, probably coming to join Louis Crommelin about 1699. He was then followed by his brother, Major Nicholas, and later by two of his sisters, Louise and Judith. Louise is thought to have died about 1723 and Judith about 1762, aged about 113.

Major Nicholas De la Cherois (c1649-13th June 1702) was married to **Marie Crommelin** (c1658-22nd December 1724), a sister of Louis Crommelin. Her first husband was **Isaac Testard de Blois**. Nicholas and Marie De la Cherois had at least three children, **Madeleine** (born c1694), who married her cousin, **Daniel Crommelin**, **Nicholas** (c1696-22nd October 1708) and **Samuel** (c1697-June 1775), who in 1731 married another Huguenot, **Sarah Cormière** (died 1748). Major Nicholas, his wife, Marie, and son, Nicholas are buried in Cathedral No. 163.

Captain Daniel De la Cherois (died 1732), the first of the De la Cherois family to reside in Lisburn, had, in London in 1699, married **Marie Angélique Crommelin** (c1663-1708), a cousin of Louis Crommelin, [see Crommelin page 206]. He came to Lisburn shortly afterwards, living in Castle Street, and was in business partnership with Louis Crommelin. They had one child, **Marie Angélique** (1700-May 1771), who, in the autumn of 1719, married **Philip Grueber**, a merchant of Faversham Park, Kent, England. He died in May 1723. Marie Angélique then married, in 1725, **Hon. Thomas Montgomery**, of Mount Alexander, near Comber, Co. Down, and lived there and at Donaghadee. In 1744 he became the fifth and last **Earl of Mount Alexander** and died in 1757. Countess Mount Alexander had no family and when she died in 1771 she willed her property to her cousin, Samuel De la Cherois, and to **Nicholas Crommelin**, son of her cousin, Madeleine Crommelin, as well as making bequests to other cousins. She is buried in Newtownards Priory, Co. Down.

Madeleine De la Cherois, daughter of Major Nicholas, who had married Daniel Crommelin, son of Samuel Crommelin and nephew of Louis Crommelin, had at least three sons, **Nicholas** (1716-28th May 1790), **Daniel** (born 1721) and **Delacherois**, and two daughters, **Marie** and **Mary Anne** (or **Nancy**). Delacherois Crommelin (25th January 1724-31st December 1804) married **Elizabeth Peers** (c1747-2nd January 1777). They had a daughter, **Mary Angelica** (c1767-26th May 1832) who on 25th August 1785 married **Rev. Francis Hutchinson** (or **Hutcheson**), vicar of Donaghadee, and had two sons, **Francis Crommelin** and **Nicholas Crommelin** and a daughter, **Elizabeth**. The Rev. Hutchinson died 24th February 1814 and Mary Angelica then married **Dr. William Stewart**, [see Stewart Cathedral No. 19 and page 269]. Delacherois and Mary Crommelin and the Rev. Hutchinson are buried in Cathedral No. 166. Mary Angelica Stewart is also buried in the Cathedral grounds, but, although there is a written copy of it, the actual inscription cannot now be found.

Samuel, son of Major Nicholas De la Cherois, and his wife, Sarah, had three sons, **Daniel**, **Captain Nicholas** and **Samuel**, and a daughter, **Judith**. Daniel, on 13th February 1782, married **Mary Crommelin**, daughter of **Alexander Crommelin,** [see Crommelin page 206], and eventually went to live in the Manor House, Donaghadee, Co. Down. They are buried in Donaghadee Graveyard with other members of their family. Captain Nicholas (1736-23rd January 1829), on 11th June 1787, married **Charlotte Higginson**, [see Higginson page 233], and had no family. They are buried in Cathedral No. 167. Samuel, on 16th April 1776, married **Maria Dobbs,** [see Cathedral Nos. 16 & 17 and Dobbs and Purdon page 214]. He was made heir of his cousin, Nicholas Crommelin (1716-28th May 1790). Nicholas hadn't married and made the stipulation in his will that Samuel should take the additional surname Crommelin. This was done officially in 1808, this branch of the family now becoming De la Cherois-Crommelin. Samuel and Maria had at least one son, **Nicholas**, and two daughters, **Ann** and **Sarah**. Nicholas (10th June 1783-28th March 1863), son of Samuel and Maria De la Cherois-Crommelin, on 17th December 1810, married **Elizabeth Mullins** (c1783-12th April 1820), daughter of the second **Lord Ventry**. They lived at Carrowdore, Co. Down, and are buried in the graveyard there. Anne married **Dr. Henry Purdon** and they are buried in Cathedral No. 16, [see Purdon page 214]. Sarah married, on 20th January 1807, **William Irwin** (1769-1848) of Mount Irwin and had at least four sons and a daughter. The daughter, **Elizabeth Helen**, married **Major Francis Crossley**, on 20th April 1837, as his second wife, [see Crossley page 209].

Judith (c1747-22nd August 1824), daughter of Major Nicholas and Sarah De la Cherois, married **John Smith** (c1745-11th December 1799) a linen draper, as his second wife. They had at least two sons, **Captain Samuel Delacherois Smith** (1774-1829) and **Daniel Crommelin Smith**. Judith and John Smith are buried in Cathedral No. 162 and their son, Captain Samuel Delacherois Smith in Cathedral No. 165. John Smith's first wife was **Catherine De Bernier**, a descendant of **John De Bernier** and Louis Crommelin. She died 6th December 1781 and is also buried in No. 162.

DOBBS AND PURDON

CATHEDRAL 16, 17 AND MEMORIAL
There are two headstones for the related Dobbs, De la Cherois-Crommelin and Purdon family. They are lying side by side on the north side of the Cathedral, close to the wall of the car park and the Vestry door. Inside the Cathedral there is a very fine memorial to **Lt. William Dobbs R.N.**

REV. RICHARD DOBBS
(c1741 – 1802)

On the first headstone, No. 17, the first named **Rev. Richard Dobbs** was Rector of Lisburn from 1743 until his death in 1775. He was a descendant of **John Dobbs**, who, it is thought, came from England about 1596. The Dobbs lived at Castle Dobbs, Co. Antrim. Richard's father was **Capt. Richard Dobbs**, High Sheriff of Co. Antrim in 1720 and M.P. for Carrickfergus from 1727 to 1760. Richard's brother, **Arthur** (1689-1765) was Engineer in Chief and Surveyor General of Ireland and late in life was appointed Governor of North Carolina, U.S.A. (1753-1765). Richard's uncle, **John**, became a Quaker and a doctor, and was disinherited by the family.

Rev. Richard married **Mary Young**, widow of **Cornet McMannus**, and they had a family of at least four sons and one daughter. Two sons, **John** and **Richard**, became clergymen. Rev. John is mentioned on the stone and died quite young. Only the first wife of Rev. Richard Dobbs Jun. (1741-1802) is buried in the grave. She was **Harriett Lambert**, the widow of **Ralph Lambert**, and daughter of the **Rev. John Welsh**, who had been born in Lisburn in 1693 and Rector of Lisburn 1741-1743, and his wife, **Mary Peers**. Rev. Richard was curate to his father in Lisburn and then Rector of Carrickfergus and Dean of Connor in 1775. His second wife was **Mary Craig**.

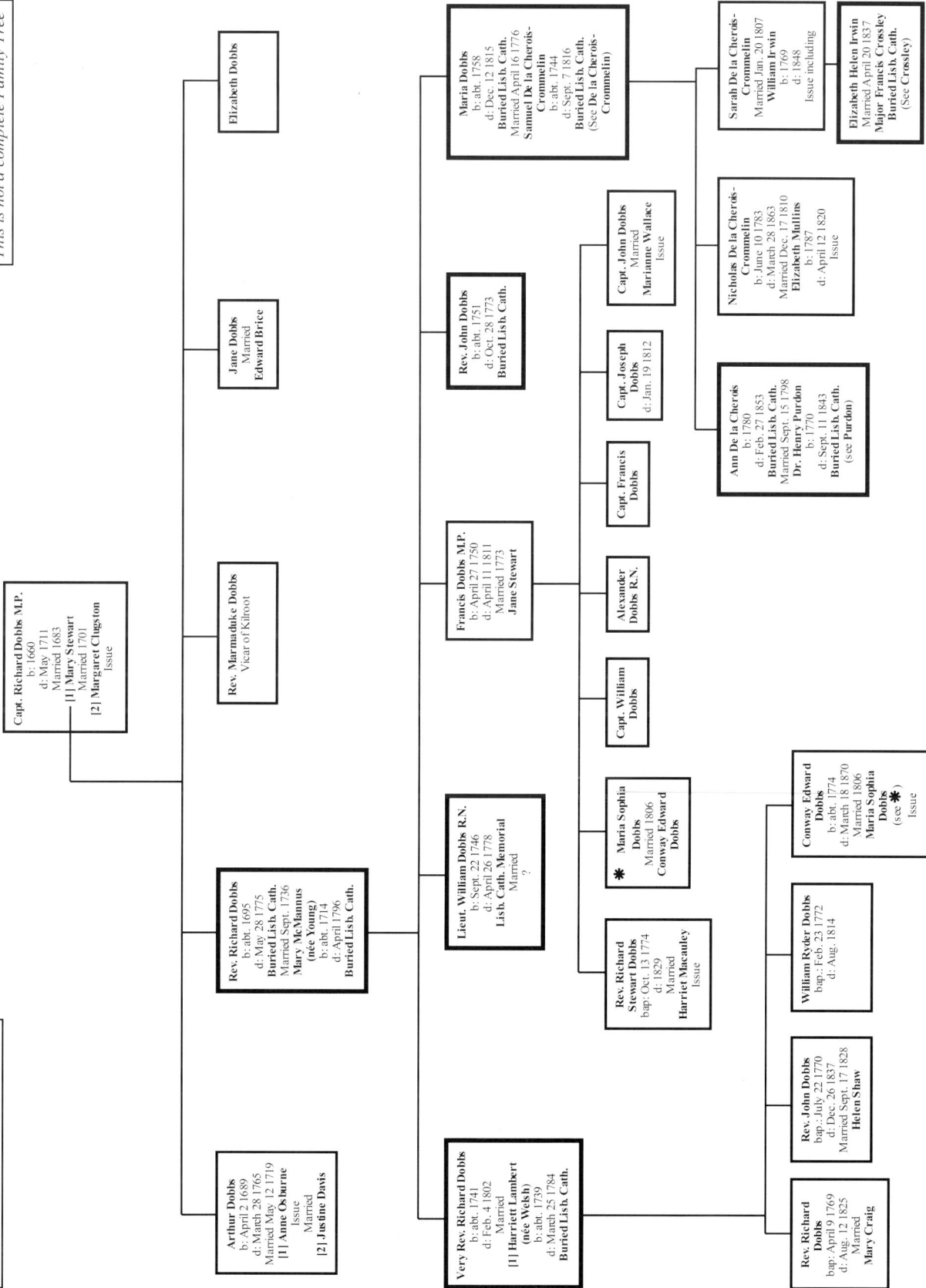

Descendants of Capt. Richard Dobbs

This is not a complete Family Tree

Capt. Richard Dobbs M.P.
b: 1660
d: May 1711
Married 1683
[1] Mary Stewart
Married 1701
[2] Margaret Clugston
Issue

Elizabeth Dobbs

Jane Dobbs
Married
Edward Brice

Rev. Marmaduke Dobbs
Vicar of Kilroot

Arthur Dobbs
b: April 2 1689
d: March 28 1765
Married May 12 1719
[1] Anne Osburne
Issue
Married
[2] Justine Davis

Rev. Richard Dobbs
b: abt. 1695
d: May 28 1775
Buried Lisb. Cath.
Married Sept. 1736
Mary McManus
(née Young)
b: abt. 1714
d: April 1796
Buried Lisb. Cath.

Maria Dobbs
b: abt. 1758
d: Dec. 12 1815
Buried Lisb. Cath.
Married April 16 1776
Samuel De la Cherois-
Crommelin
b: abt. 1744
d: Sept. 7 1816
Buried Lisb. Cath.
(See De la Cherois-
Crommelin)

Rev. John Dobbs
b: abt. 1751
d: Oct. 28 1773
Buried Lish. Cath.

Francis Dobbs M.P.
b: April 27 1750
d: April 11 1811
Married 1773
Jane Stewart

Lieut. William Dobbs R.N.
b: Sept. 22 1746
d: April 26 1778
Lish. Cath. Memorial
Married
?

Very Rev. Richard Dobbs
b: abt. 1741
d: Feb. 4 1802
Married
[1] Harriet Lambert
(née Welsh)
b: abt. 1739
d: March 25 1784
Buried Lisb. Cath.

**Sarah De la Cherois-
Crommelin**
Married Jan. 20 1807
William Irwin
b: 1769
d: 1848
Issue including

Capt. John Dobbs
Married
Marianne Wallace
Issue

**Nicholas De la Cherois-
Crommelin**
b: June 10 1783
d: March 28 1863
Married Dec. 17 1810
Elizabeth Mullins
b: 1787
d: April 12 1820
Issue

Elizabeth Helen Irwin
Married April 20 1837
Major Francis Crossley
Buried Lisb. Cath.
(See Crossley)

Capt. Joseph Dobbs
d: Jan. 19 1812

Capt. Francis Dobbs

Capt. William Dobbs

Alexander Dobbs R.N.

Ann De la Cherois
b: 1780
d: Feb. 27 1853
Buried Lish. Cath.
Married Sept. 15 1798
Dr. Henry Purdon
b: 1770
d: Sept. 11 1843
Buried Lish. Cath.
(see Purdon)

✱ **Maria Sophia Dobbs**
Married 1806
Conway Edward Dobbs

Conway Edward Dobbs
b: abt. 1774
d: March 18 1870
Married 1806
Maria Sophia Dobbs
(see ✱)
Issue

Rev. Richard Stewart Dobbs
bap: Oct. 13 1774
d: 1829
Married
Harriet Macauley
Issue

William Ryder Dobbs
bap: Feb. 23 1772
d: Aug. 1814

Rev. John Dobbs
bap: July 22 1770
d: Dec. 26 1837
Married Sept. 17 1828
Helen Shaw

Rev. Richard Dobbs
bap: April 9 1769
d: Aug. 12 1825
Married
Mary Craig

Another son of Rev. Richards's was Lieutenant William Dobbs R.N. There is a memorial to him in the Cathedral. William was born in Lisburn 22nd September 1746. In 1778 he was at Castle Dobbs having just been married, when he got news that the American Privateer ship, the "Ranger", under the command of Paul Jones, was in the area. The sloop of war "Drake" had lost its First Lieutenant and Boatswain, and Lt. William volunteered his services. In the fighting that ensued Dobbs was fatally wounded and died 26th April 1778.

THOMAS HENRY PURDON
(c1806 – 1886)

Rev. Richard Dobbs's daughter, **Maria**, married **Samuel De la Cherois-Crommelin** on 16th April 1776. They had a least two daughters, **Ann** and **Sarah**, and a son, **Nicholas**. [See De la Cherois-Crommelin page 206.] Their daughter, **Ann De la Cherois-Crommelin**, married **Dr. Henry Purdon** on 15th September 1798. He was from Rathwire, Co. Westmeath and was descended from **James Purdon** of Cumberland, England, who settled at Lurgan Race, Co. Louth, about seven generations previous to Henry Purdon. Henry and Ann had a family of six sons and six daughters, although some of the family died young. Three of the sons are buried in Cathedral No. 16 along with the wives of two of them and a grand-daughter and her husband. Dr. Henry Purdon (1770-1843) was a surgeon in Belfast and lived in Sans Souci, Belfast. Three of his sons were doctors. They were **Drs. Thomas Henry** (1806-1886), **William** (died 1908) and **Charles Nicholas De la Cherois Purdon** (1818-1882). Several grandchildren and great grandchildren were also in the medical profession. Some of the family were connected with St. George's Church, Belfast.

BELFAST COMMERCIAL CHRONICLE
WEDNESDAY SEPTEMBER 13 1843

Death of Dr. Purdon, Sen. – It is our melancholy duty this day to announce the death of one of our oldest and most respected townsmen, Dr. Purdon, Sen., who up to last Monday, was in his accustomed health, and yet, painful as is the statement, his demise took place on the night of that day, after a few minutes illness, we believe by disease of the heart. There are few within the circle of our acquaintance whose removal from among us will cause a more deep and wide regret, than that of this truly excellent man and accomplished physician.

(Extract from obituary)

BELFAST NEWS LETTER
MONDAY JANUARY 9 1882

DEATH OF DR. CHARLES D. PURDON, M.B., F.R.C.S.I.

By the death of Dr. Charles Delacherois Purdon, which took place yesterday, an honoured name has been removed from the burgess-roll of Belfast, and a distinguished practitioner from the register of the medical profession. His death was quite unexpected, the illness which yesterday afternoon terminated fatally having only set in on Thursday last. Dr. Purdon belonged to a family long connected with Belfast, and scarcely less identified with the medical profession. He was the son of Dr. Henry Purdon, whom the older residents of the town will remember as one of the foremost surgeons of the tome. Dr. Charles D. Purdon having received his education at the Royal Academical Institution, where among his school fellows were many who rose to eminence in professional, political, and commercial life, proceeded to Trinity College, Dublin, from which he received the degrees of Master of Arts and Bachelor of Medicine in 1841. The Royal College of Surgeons was closely connected with Trinity College, and by this connection students who had graduated in arts were eligible for admission to the more distinctly medical school, to fellowship of which Dr. Purdon was admitted in 1842. He began to

Descendants of Dr. Henry Purdon

This is not a complete Family Tree

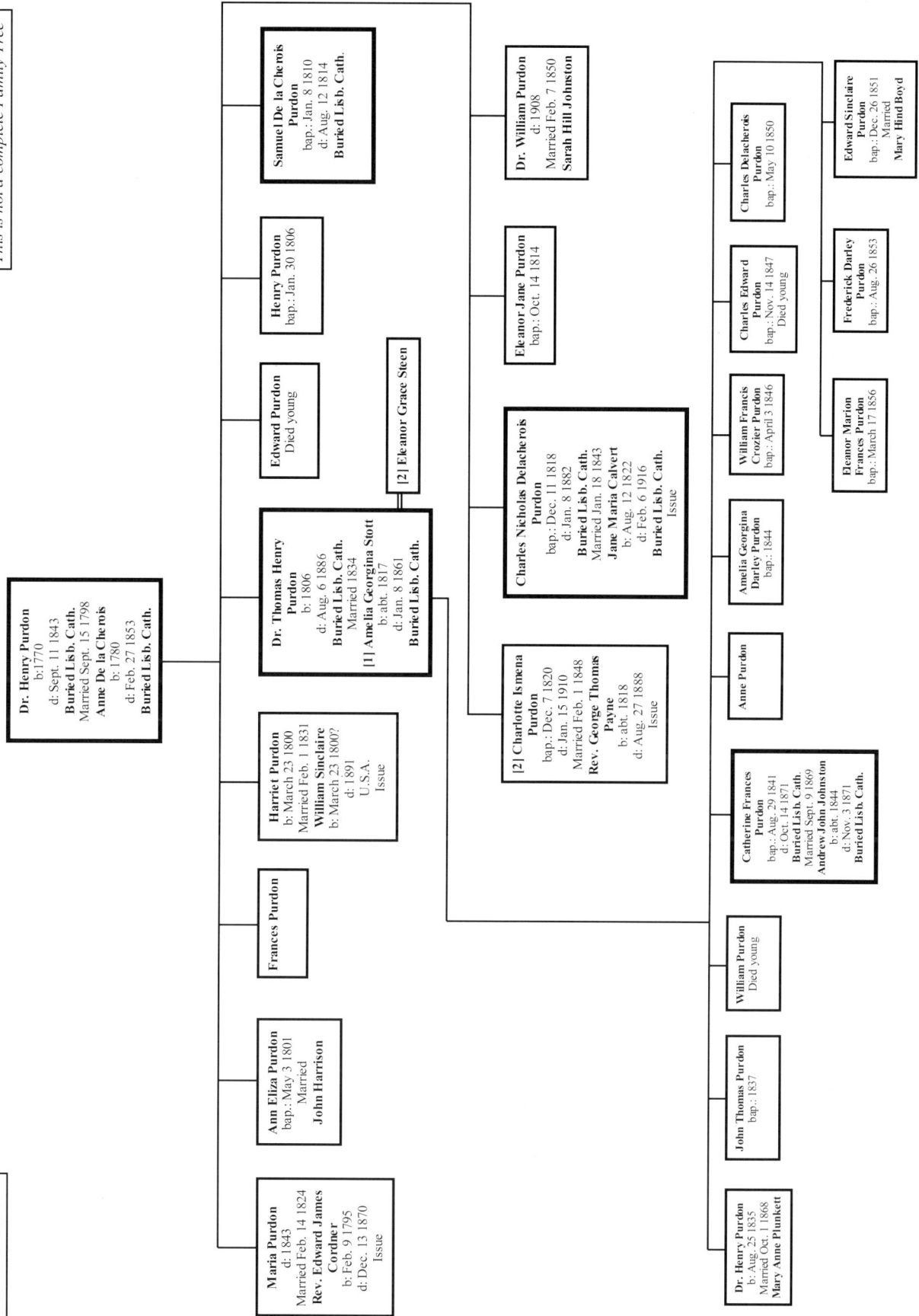

Dr. Henry Purdon
b:1770
d: Sept. 11 1843
Buried Lisb. Cath.
Married Sept. 15 1798
Anne De la Cherois
b: 1780
d: Feb. 27 1853
Buried Lisb. Cath.

Maria Purdon
d: 1843
Married Feb. 14 1824
Rev. Edward James Cordner
b: Feb. 9 1795
d: Dec. 13 1870
Issue

Ann Eliza Purdon
bap.: May 3 1801
Married
John Harrison

Frances Purdon

Harriet Purdon
b: March 23 1800
Married Feb. 1 1831
William Sinclaire
b: March 23 1800?
d: 1891
U.S.A.
Issue

Edward Purdon
Died young

Henry Purdon
bap.: Jan. 30 1806

Samuel De la Cherois Purdon
bap.: Jan. 8 1810
d: Aug. 12 1814
Buried Lisb. Cath.

Dr. Thomas Henry Purdon
b: 1806
d: Aug. 6 1886
Buried Lisb. Cath.
Married 1834
[1] **Amelia Georgina Stott**
b: abt. 1817
d: Jan. 8 1861
Buried Lisb. Cath.

[2] **Eleanor Grace Steen**

Charles Nicholas Delacherois Purdon
bap.: Dec. 11 1818
d: Jan. 8 1882
Buried Lisb. Cath.
Married Jan. 18 1843
Jane Maria Calvert
b: Aug. 12 1822
d: Feb. 6 1916
Buried Lisb. Cath.
Issue

Eleanor Jane Purdon
bap.: Oct. 14 1814

Dr. William Purdon
d: 1908
Married Feb. 7 1850
Sarah Hill Johnston

[2] Charlotte Ismena Purdon
bap.: Dec. 7 1820
d: Jan. 15 1910
Married Feb. 1 1848
Rev. George Thomas Payne
b: abt. 1818
d: Aug. 27 1888
Issue

Anne Purdon

Amelia Georgina Darley Purdon
bap.: 1844

William Francis Crozier Purdon
bap.: April 3 1846

Charles Edward Purdon
bap.: Nov. 14 1847
Died young

Charles Delacherois Purdon
bap.: May 10 1850

Eleanor Marion Frances Purdon
bap.: March 17 1856

Frederick Darley Purdon
bap.: Aug .26 1853

Edward Sinclaire Purdon
bap.: Dec. 26 1851
Married
Mary Hind Boyd

Catherine Frances Purdon
bap.: Aug. 29 1841
d: Oct. 14 1871
Buried Lish. Cath.
Married Sept. 9 1869
Andrew John Johnston
b: abt. 1844
d: Nov. 3 1871
Buried Lish. Cath.

William Purdon
Died young

John Thomas Purdon
bap.: 1837

Dr. Henry Purdon
b: Aug. 25 1835
Married Oct. 1 1868
Mary Anne Plunkett

practice in Belfast, in which his elder and surviving brother, Dr. Thomas H. Purdon had already taken a high place, and opened a promising career. He achieved a considerable amount of success in his profession. He became honorary medical officer of the Belfast Charitable Society, and for nearly twenty years was the physician of the Deaf and Dumb Institution. He received the appointment of certifying surgeon under the Factories Acts, and in that capacity gave very general satisfaction. The Medical Society of Ulster also honoured him by making him vice-president. While applying himself to the duties of a growing practice he also took a deep interest in literary and scientific subjects, and was connected with various local societies for the advancement of science and art. His tastes were antiquarian, and in the gratification of these he collected many interesting works relative to history, genealogy, and archaeology. His experience and attainments eminently qualified him for the position of secretary for Ulster of the Royal Archaeological Society of Ireland. On the occasion of the visit of the society to Belfast, a few years ago, Dr. Purdon took the deepest interest in the proceedings, and largely contributed to one of the most enjoyable gatherings of antiquarians ever held in Ireland. It is somewhat interesting that upon that occasion the Benn collection of antiquities, the gift of a gentleman whose death also we have this morning to record, was opened. He had devoted particular attention to the study of the history of Huguenot settlers in Ireland, and on several occasions delivered most instructive lectures on the history of those families whom French persecution had driven to this country. He was all his life connected with S. George's Church, and for many years was a member of the select vestry. The confidence with which he was regarded, and the esteem in which he was held, were shown by his appointment as representative of S. George's at the Diocesan Synod.

BELFAST NEWS LETTER
MONDAY AUGUST 9TH 1886

DEATH OF DR. T.H. PURDON

We deeply regret to have to record the death of this distinguished medical practitioner and highly esteemed gentleman, which occurred at his residence, Wellington Place, late on Friday night. Dr. Thomas Henry Purdon, who was in his 81st year, was the chief representative of an old Huguenot family which settled in Ireland during the reign of Queen Elizabeth. That family has given to the world many men eminent in the medical and other professions, and the members of it have long been distinguished not only for their ability and high attainments, but for their benevolence, and for the efforts which they have made to relieve the sufferings of all who came within their reach. The deceased gentleman was the eldest son of the late Dr. Henry Purdon, staff surgeon, who was well known to all the elder inhabitants of Belfast, and as highly respected as he was well known. Dr. Thomas Henry Purdon had two brothers in the medical profession-the late Dr. Wm. Purdon, who was in the Army Medical Department; and the late Dr. Charles Purdon, whose death we noticed a little more than four years ago. The deceased gentleman had one son in the medical profession (Dr. Henry Purdon), who was lost at sea; and three nephews at present in extensive medical practice in Belfast-Dr. H.S. Purdon, Dr. R.J. Purdon, and Dr. Joseph A. Purdon. The deceased was born in Chichester Street, Belfast, and was educated at the Royal School, Armagh. After leaving school he matriculated in Trinity College, Dublin, at the age of thirteen. After a distinguished university career he took the degrees of M.A. and M.B. in the year 1828, but prior to that - in 1826 - he was elected a Fellow of the Royal College of Surgeons. Dr. Purdon also received part of his medical education in the Edinburgh Medical School. He was for many years the father of the profession in this town, having been engaged in active practice for the last sixty years. Even before he had completed his medical education his ability was so well recognised that he was employed to assist several eminent doctors then resident in Belfast; and while living in Dublin and attending the university he was prosector and demonstrator for the celebrated Dr. Harrison, of that city. In 1832 he was actively engaged during the cholera epidemic, and rendered much valuable assistance at that distressing period. He was formerly senior surgeon to the Royal Hospital and latterly consulting surgeon to the same institution. He was also consulting surgeon to the Ophthalmic Hospital and consulting physician to the Belfast Hospital for Consumption. Among the other professional appointments which he held were those of medical officer to the County Antrim Prison, to the Deaf and Dumb Institution, to the Ulster Magdalene

Asylum, and to the infirmary and poorhouse. He was permanent president of the Belfast branch of the Royal Medical Benevolent Fund Society of Ireland. .... He performed the first cases of tracheotomy in Ireland, the subject of which lived for thirty-six years afterwards. He was much respected by his professional brethren as a consultant on account of his great skill, ripe experience, and his honourable and upright professional conduct. .... Dr. Purdon was twice married, first to a daughter of the late Mr. John Stott, Belmont; and after her death to the only daughter of the late Mr. Steen, Skegoneil, who survives him. He leaves behind him four sons and two daughters. In politics the deceased gentleman was a Conservative, but never took any active part in the management of political affairs. His death will be widely regretted, as well by the members of his profession as by the general public.

[*Dobbs P.R.O.N.I. D/162   Linen Hall Library – Purdon - Blackwood Pedigrees*]

DUBOURDIEU

CATHEDRAL MEMORIAL

In the Cathedral Chancel is the memorial to **Rev. Saumarez Dubourdieu**. This originally had the bust of the Rev. Saumarez Dubourdieu attached to the wall at the top of the memorial, but in 1987 it fell off the wall and so for safety reasons the bust is now sitting on the window sill. The Dubourdieus are a Huguenot family. The Rev. Saumarez's grandfather was **James Dubourdieu** (c1640-1683) and his great uncle was **Rev. Jean Dubourdieu** (c1644-1722), who served as the Duke of Schomberg's chaplain during the winter of 1689. James and Jean were the sons of **Rev. Isaac Dubourdieu**, who was pastor in Montpellier, France and then London. James Dubourdieu married a sister of **Charles De la Valade**, later to become Minister of the French Church in Lisburn. James had a son, **Rev. Jean Armand Dubourdieu** (1683-1723) who married **Charlotte Massey**, **Countess D'Esponage**. Rev. Jean Armand fled from France to England and became minister to the Savoy Chapel in London and Chaplain to the Duke of Richmond and Lennox. He had two sons, one of them being Saumarez (1717-1812).

REV. SAUMAREZ DUBOURDIEU
(1717 – 1812)

Rev. Jean Armand died when Saumarez was six years old. Saumarez was then sent to Dublin to be educated and graduated from Trinity College, Dublin. He founded a school at Hillsboro, Co. Dublin. He married **Mary**, daughter of the **Rev. Shem Thompson** and came to Lisburn in 1756. His great-uncle, Charles, was by then chaplain in the Huguenot church in Castle Street, Lisburn. Saumarez opened a Classical school in Bow Street, Lisburn, and it was later known as Lisburn Academy. When Charles De la Valade died Saumarez became the last chaplain to the Huguenot church. In 1768 he became Curate in Perpetuity of Lambeg, Co. Antrim, and in 1780 Vicar of Glenavy. He had five children, three sons and two daughters. One son, **Rev. John Saumarez**, was born in Dublin in 1755. He became Rector of Annahilt, Co. Down, died in 1844, and is buried at Soldierstown, Co. Antrim. On 28th March 1780 he married **Margaret Sampson**. The other sons were **Shem** and **Saumarez**. It is believed they became surgeons. The daughters were **Charlotte** and **Anne.**

Rev. Saumarez's school was very well known and some of his pupils became famous. These included the first Marquis of Hastings, Hon. William Saurin and Rev. George Vaughan Sampson.

After Rev. Saumarez's death on 14th December 1812 he was buried in Lambeg Graveyard. Because of the high regard his former pupils had for him two memorials were erected to him. One of these is the very fine memorial in Lisburn Cathedral, with its Latin inscription, erected in 1814. This was the work of John Smyth (c1773 – 1840), son of Edward Smyth, Montgomery Street, Dublin. The second is the gravestone in Lambeg Graveyard. The inscription on this is now illegible but the wording was very similar to that on the Lisburn Cathedral memorial.

FIRST WORLD WAR

MEMORIAL
On the First World War Memorial are recorded the names of forty-nine men from Lisburn Cathedral who died during the war. Listed below are brief details on the background of some of these men.

Walter Charter Boomer M.C.   Killed in action 2nd October 1918. Only son of Richard W. Boomer and Mrs Boomer, Knockmore, Lisburn. Awarded the Military Cross for conspicuous gallantry and devotion to duty in command of his company.

David Boyd   Rifleman. Died 1st July 1916. Lived with widowed mother at Millbrook, worked in Glenmore, and was organ blower in Lisburn Cathedral.

Robert John Corken   M.G.C., Corporal, Ulster Division. Third son of Mr and Mrs James Corken, Antrim Road, Lisburn. Employed by Messrs. Abraham Neill and Co. Castalia Mills, Belfast, as a Book-keeper, severely wounded 1st July 1916 and tried to make it back alone to the Dressing Station.

Henry Corkin   Sgt., drowned accidentally in France on 17th May 1916. Son of Henry Corkin, 83 Gregg St., Lisburn. Member of Lisburn Temperance Silver Band.

Albert Griffen   R.I.R., Lewis Gun Section. Died in Germany, reported missing 21st March 1918.

George Henry Hull   Machine Gun section, Lance Corporal. Reported dead August 1916.

Frederick Cross King   2nd Lieut., M.G.C., killed 23rd October 1916, son of the late Mrs Alex. King of Cultra, architect, married Anne J Wilson, daughter of the late Robert Wilson, Courtrai, Belgium and Mrs Wilson, 23 Seymour Street, Lisburn.

William Leathem   Rifleman, killed 24th June 1916, eldest son of Wm. Leathem, 22 Young St., Lisburn. He was a plasterer aged 21 years and a member of the Orange Order.

Edward Martin   Rifleman, killed 1st September 1916. Husband of Mrs Martin, Millbrook. He had a young family.

John Mulligan   Lance Corporal R.I.R., killed in action. Went to front with the Ulster Division in 1915. Shoemaker by trade. Died 11th April 1918.

Samuel Patterson   Rifleman, killed 8th August 1917, eldest son of the late Mr Rainey Patterson and Mrs Patterson, 26 Old Hillsborough Road, Lisburn.

Robert Porter   Corporal (YCV) husband of Mrs Porter, East Down View, Low Road, Lisburn, had two young children and was killed in his first action. He was a reserve man with nine years service. He was servant to Lieut. Colonel McCammond. Died 15th August 1917.

George F. Walker   Lance Corporal, killed 1st July 1916. He kept goals for Ashmount Football Club and was a member of LOL 207 and UVF. He lived at Sloan Street.

Alex. Colvin Welch   son of Mr T. Welch, Dublin Road, Lisburn. He worked at Glenmore. Died 1st July 1916.

This report on the death of Robert Heron is a typical example of newspaper reports of military deaths in World War One.

LISBURN STANDARD
AUGUST 24 1917

Rifleman Robert Heron R.I.R. Lisburn.
Killed in Belgium.

Rifleman Robert Heron, son of Mr William Heron, Barnsley's Row, Lisburn. He was gassed on 1st September last year. Prior to the war he worked in Messrs. Robert Stewart and Sons Mill. A brother, Corporal Wm. Heron, of the same battalion, was wounded in the same offensive. Prior to receiving his wounds he was present at the burial of his brother. The father of these two volunteers was in his day also a good soldier, and fought under Lord Roberts in the Afghanistan War, rising from the rank of private to sergeant during that campaign.

FLYNN

CATHEDRAL 9
John Flynn was the son of **Charles Flynn** who lived at Piper's Hill, Lisburn.

LISBURN STANDARD
APRIL 1895

DEATH OF MR. JOHN FLYNN

At a ripe old age, Mr. John Flynn, so well known and so deservedly esteemed in Lisburn, has laid life's burdens down, and passed away at the residence of his son-in-law, Mr. Hugh McCahey, Bridge Street, to the rest that remaineth for the people of God. Deceased was a native of Lisburn, and for some years, like tens of thousands in Ulster, was a hand-loom weaver. Afterwards he carried on an extensive trade in linen remnants, having customers in many parts of the North of Ireland, and also in England and Scotland. Of late years Mr. Flynn acted as an agent for house property. All through his long career, he proved himself to be an upright and sterling man, whose word was as good as his bond. He originally worshipped in the old Wesleyan Methodist Church in Market Street, but recently he was connected with the Salem New Connexion Church. It will be seen by advertisement that the Rev. J. Lee Fox will hold a memorial service in the latter church on Sunday evening. "The memory of the just is blessed."

FULTON

CATHEDRAL 71, 119, 109, 112, 137, 32 and MEMORIAL
The ancestors of the various Fulton family branches are believed to have come from northern Ayreshire, Scotland, in the first half of the 17th century, and to have first settled on a large farm at Belsize, in the parish of Derriaghy. Mention of the family is to be found in the records of Lisburn Cathedral, Christ Church, Derriaghy, and First Lisburn Presbyterian Church. Some of the family were churchwardens in the Church of Ireland churches. Because of the gaps in all these church records, exact relationships are hard to establish and verify.

A **James Fulton** is believed to have married **Ann Coulson** about 1720. They had two sons and four daughters. One of the sons, **Robert Coulson Fulton** (1723-1762) married **Ann Forrest** in Lisburn Cathedral in 1751. They had at least a son and a daughter.

Cathedral Nos. 71 and 119 are for one branch of the Fulton family. **Richard Fulton**, (1752-1823) on 3rd March 1774 married **Elizabeth Shanks** (1752-1812). He was a prosperous draper and haberdasher. From 1798 until 1806 he lived at Ballyhomra and then sold the lease to Edward Gayer. Richard then probably lived in the Bridge Street area of Lisburn. Richard had a family of five sons and eight daughters. The sons were **Robert** (1777-1830), **Andrew** (1779-1822), **Lt. Col. James Forrest** (1780-1854), **Capt. Richard** (1788-1827) and **John Forrest** (1790-1790). The daughters were **Margaret** (1775-1819), **Ann** (or **Fanny**) (1776-1799), **Eliza** (1778-1805), **Jane** (1782-1840), **Mary Ann** (1783-1850's), **Grace** (1784-1865), **Sarah** (1785-1802) and **Ellen** (1787-1864). It was Lt.-Col. James Fulton who had the stone erected to the memory of his parents and some of his brothers and sisters, although not all those mentioned are actually buried here. The youngest son, John Forrest, died soon after birth and his death is not recorded on the stone.

The eldest son, Robert, had a flour mill, married **Jane** (abt. 1768-1831) and had at least three sons and a daughter. Robert is mentioned on Cathedral No. 71, but his wife, Jane, and three of the children, **Joseph** (1795-1831), **James** and **Elizabeth Anne** (born 1805), are buried in Cathedral No. 119. There was another child called **Robert** born in 1807.

The second son, Andrew, was a woollen draper with a shop at the top of Bridge Street and was married to **Isabella** (abt. 1780-1850). They had three sons and two daughters. **William** (1806-1881), one of the sons, married **Sophia Matilda Bolton** in 1856. She was a daughter of **John** and **Abigail Bolton** [see Cathedral No. 12 and Hogg and Bolton page 239]. **Mary Jane Fulton**, wife of **Robert Watson**, was William Fulton's daughter. She was born about 1850, married Robert Watson on the 21st November 1878 and died in 1880. It is believed that William had emigrated to America, and later returned, leaving several of his family in America, so Sophia Bolton is probably his second wife. William was the Registrar of Births, Marriages and Deaths when he died in Lisburn in 1881. Andrew and Isabella's daughter, **Eliza** (1800-1888), was the second wife of **John Barbour** (abt. 1796-1831) and she and her husband are buried in the Barbour grave Kilrush No. 23 [see THG Vol. 1 pages 147-149]. Andrew, Isabella and their three sons, **Richard** (1802-1810), **Andrew** (1804-1808), and William, William's wife, Sophia and daughter, Mary Jane Watson, are buried in Cathedral No. 71. There was another daughter called **Isabella** who was baptised on 23rd December 1807.

The third son, Lt. Col. James Forrest Fulton (1780-1854) was the son responsible for headstone No. 71. After a career in the army he retired in 1824, settled in Belgium, married twice and had in total a family of five sons and three daughters. He married **Penelope Frances Bowyer** in 1807 and **Fanny Goodrich Jessop** in 1828. He died 12th December 1854, while on a visit to Downpatrick, and is buried there. His youngest son, **Sir James Forrest Fulton M.P.** (born 1846), was Recorder for London in 1900.

The fourth son, **Capt. Richard** (1788-1827), was in the Dragoon Guards and the Prince of Wales' Regt. of Light Dragoons. He retired on half pay in 1816 and appears to have lived at Killinchy, Co. Down.

The eldest daughter, Margaret, married **James Wightman** in 1803. She died on 30th March 1819. She and James had five daughters [see Wightman page 278]. The third daughter, Eliza, was the first wife of **James Ward** (who died 1847). They married in 1802 and had a son, **Thomas**. After Eliza died James then married **Margaret Craig** in 1814, [see Craig THG Vol. 1 page 151]. The fourth daughter, Jane, married **Francis Abbott Thompson** in 1805 [see Thompson Cathedral No. 42 and page 274]. Jane and Francis are buried at Hillhall Presbyterian Church. Two daughters of Richard and Elizabeth Fulton, Ann (Fanny) and Sarah, are named on the stone. The other three daughters, Mary Ann, Grace and Ellen, were living in Bangor when they died and are buried there.

Cathedral Nos. 109, 112, 137 and a memorial belong to another branch of the Fulton family. The exact relationship to the first Fulton branch is not certain. **John Fulton**, who may have been born in the early 18th century, died at sea 26th July 1803, on his way home from Calcutta, India. He married **Ann Wade** and had a family of three sons and three daughters. Ann Wade is possibly related to the **Atkinson/Wade** family of Cathedral No. 110. This stone is lying flat in front of Fulton No. 109. John's sons were **Joseph**, **James** and **John Williamson**, and the daughters were **Eleanor**, **Ann** and **Eliza**. They lived in Bow Lane, Lisburn. In 1780 John was appointed Assistant Registrar of the High Court of Calcutta, but because of a shipwreck it took him eighteen months to get to India, by which time the post had been filled, so he then followed a mercantile pursuit and is supposed to have amassed a large fortune.

The eldest son, Joseph (1751-1823), a linen merchant, solicitor and land agent, in 1777, married **Ann Graham**, daughter of **Francis Graham** and a sister of **Dora Graham**, who married **William Caldbeck** [see Caldbeck Cathedral No. 1 and page 201]. In 1792 Joseph was appointed Commissioner for taking affidavits in the King's Bench and in 1816 was on the committee of the Lisburn Male Free School. Joseph and Ann had a family of four sons and three daughters. The sons were **Francis, Capt. Thomas, Lieut. Nicholas Graham** and **Dr. Henry**. Francis was a merchant in Calcutta and was lost at sea on his voyage home in 1809. Thomas was in military service and in 1799 married **Lydia Johnson**. He was also a J.P. for counties Armagh and Antrim. Lieut. Nicholas Graham was in the Bengal army and was killed in action in 1804. Dr. Henry was briefly in the Bengal Medical Service and then settled in Dublin and was twice married. The daughters were **Anne Elizabeth** and **Amelia Boyd**. Anne Fulton in 1799 married **Christopher Henry Barry Meade**.

Descendants of John Fulton

Cathedral Nos. 109, 112, 137, & Memorial

This is not a complete Family Tree.

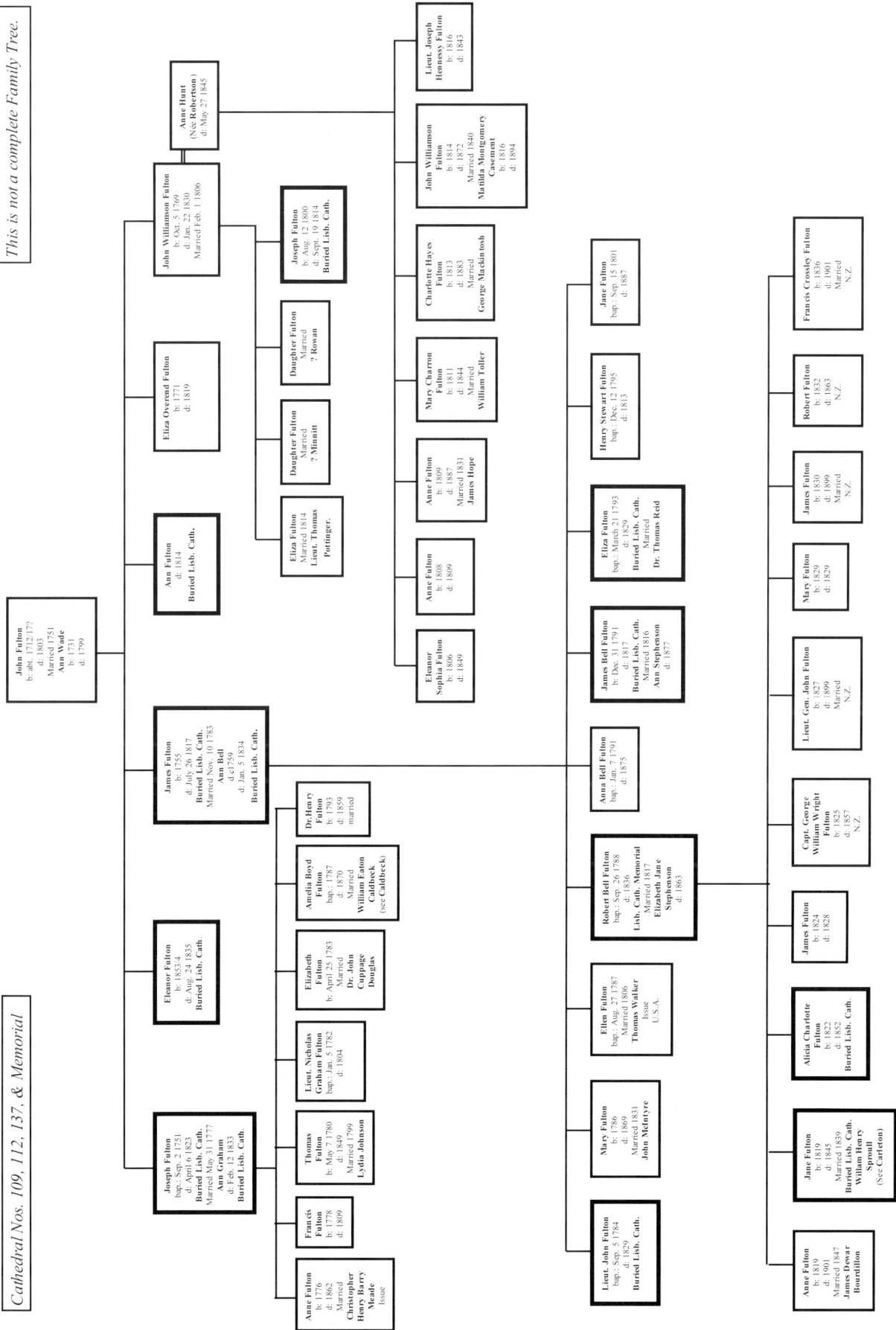

John Fulton
b: abt. 1712/17?
d: 1803
Married 1751
Ann Wade
b: 1731
d: 1799

Anne Hunt
(Née Robertson)
d: May 27 1845

John Williamson Fulton
b: Oct. 5 1769
d: Jan. 22 1830
Married Feb. 1 1806

Eliza Overend Fulton
b: 1771
d: 1819

Ann Fulton
d: 1814
Buried Lisb. Cath.

Joseph Fulton
b: Aug. 12 1800
d: Sept. 19 1814
Buried Lisb. Cath.

Lieut. Joseph Hennessy Fulton
b: 1816
d: 1843

John Williamson Fulton
b: 1814
d: 1872
Married 1840
Matilda Montgomery Casement
b: 1816
d: 1894

Charlotte Hayes Fulton
b: 1813
d: 1883
Married
George Mackintosh

Mary Charron Fulton
b: 1811
d: 1844
Married
William Toller

Daughter Fulton
Married
? Rowan

Daughter Fulton
Married
? Minnitt

Eliza Fulton
Married 1814
Lieut. Thomas Pottinger.

Anne Fulton
b: 1809
d: 1887
Married 1831
James Hope

Anne Fulton
b: 1808
d: 1809

Eleanor Sophia Fulton
b: 1806
d: 1849

Jane Fulton
bap: Sep. 15 1801
d: 1887

Henry Stewart Fulton
bap: Dec. 12 1795
d: 1813

Eliza Fulton
bap: March 21 1793
d: 1829
Buried Lisb. Cath.
Married
Dr. Thomas Reid

James Bell Fulton
b: Dec. 31 1791
d: 1817
Buried Lisb. Cath.
Married 1816
Ann Stephenson
d: 1877

Anna Bell Fulton
bap: Jan. 7 1791
d: 1875

James Fulton
b: 1755
d: July 26 1817
Buried Lisb. Cath.
Married Nov. 10 1783
Ann Bell
d c1759
d: Jan. 5 1834
Buried Lisb. Cath.

Eleanor Fulton
b: 1853/4
d: Aug. 24 1835
Buried Lisb. Cath.

Dr. Henry Fulton
b: 1793
d: 1859
married

Amelia Boyd Fulton
bap: 1787
d: 1870
Married
William Eaton Caldbeck
(see Caldbeck)

Elizabeth Fulton
b: April 25 1783
Married
Dr. John Cuppage Douglas

Lieut. Nicholas Graham Fulton
bap: Jan. 5 1782
d: 1804

Thomas Fulton
b: May 7 1780
d: 1849
Married 1799
Lydia Johnson

Francis Fulton
b: 1778
d: 1809

Joseph Fulton
bap: Sep. 2 1751
d: April 6 1823
Buried Lisb. Cath.
Married May 31 1777
Ann Graham
d: Feb. 12 1833
Buried Lisb. Cath.

Anne Fulton
b: 1776
d: 1862
Married
Christopher Henry Barry
Issue

Robert Bell Fulton
bap: Sep. 26 1788
d: 1836
Lisb. Cath. Memorial
Married 1817
Elizabeth Jane Stephenson
d: 1863

Ellen Fulton
bap: Aug. 27 1787
Married 1806
Thomas Walker
Issue
U.S.A.

Mary Fulton
b: 1786
d: 1869
Married 1831
John McIntyre

Lieut. John Fulton
bap: Sep. 5 1784
d: 1829
Buried Lisb. Cath.

Francis Crossley Fulton
b: 1836
d: 1901
Married
N.Z.

Robert Fulton
b: 1832
d: 1863
N.Z.

James Fulton
b: 1830
d: 1899
Married
N.Z.

Mary Fulton
b: 1829
d: 1829

Lieut. Gen. John Fulton
b: 1827
d: 1899
Married
N.Z.

Capt. George William Wright Fulton
b: 1825
d: 1857
N.Z.

James Fulton
b: 1824
d: 1828

Alicia Charlotte Fulton
b: 1822
d: 1852
Buried Lisb. Cath.

Jane Fulton
b: 1819
d: 1845
Married 1839
Buried Lisb. Cath.
William Henry Sproull
(See Carleton)

Anne Fulton
b: 1819
d: 1901
Married 1847
James Dewar Bourdillon

223

There is a **Mary Barry Meade** buried in Kilrush No. 25 [see THG Vol. 1]. Elizabeth married **Dr. John Cuppage Douglas** and Amelia Boyd married her cousin, **William Eaton Caldbeck** [see Caldbeck page 201]. The parents, Joseph and Ann Fulton, are buried in Cathedral No. 109.

Joseph's brother, James (1755-1817), was probably in the same line of business as his brother and was Sub-sheriff for Counties Armagh, Antrim and Down, as well as a Lieutenant in the Lisburn Yeomanry Cavalry. He married **Ann Bell**, daughter of **Henry Bell**, Lambeg. They had four sons and five daughters. The eldest son, **John**, was a captain in the Bengal Army, where he died in 1829. The second son was **Robert Bell**. The third son, **James Bell**, a lawyer, married **Anne Stephenson,** of York, and died in Lisburn in 1817 at the early age of 26, just a year after his marriage. The fourth, and youngest son, **Henry Stewart**, died in 1813, while out hunting near Dublin. The daughters were **Mary**, who married **John McIntyre** in 1831, **Ellen**, who married **Thomas Walker,** in 1806, and emigrated to the United States of America and **Eliza**, who, on 27th February 1823, married **Thomas Reid,** a surgeon, who died at Demerara on 22nd June 1826. Eliza died 27th April 1829. Daughters **Anna Bell**, who died in 1875 and **Jane,** who died in 1887 were unmarried and both are buried in Nunehead Cemetery, Blackheath, Kent, England.

The second son, Robert Bell, who rose to the rank of major in the Bengal Artillery, married **Elizabeth Jane Stephenson,** daughter of the agent to the Downshire Estate, while home from India in 1817. They were married twice, first at Gretna Green, Scotland, and later at Hillsborough, Co. Down. Robert and Elizabeth returned to India where Robert died 11th May 1836. The memorial in the Cathedral is to Robert Bell Fulton's memory. Robert and Elizabeth had six sons and four daughters. Of these **James,** the eldest son, and **Mary** died young in India. Elizabeth and her family returned from India to Chapel Hill, Lisburn, in 1838. After a few years the family moved to England. One daughter, **Jane,** married **William Henry Sproull** in 1839 [see Carleton page 203], and had a son and a daughter. Another daughter, **Anne**, married **James Dewar Bourdillon** in 1847. In 1848 two of the sons, **James** and **Robert Fulton**, emigrated to New Zealand and in 1852 another son, **Francis Fulton**, and their widowed mother, Elizabeth Fulton, joined them. Another daughter, **Alicia Charlotte**, was on a return visit to England, in 1852, and died while visiting the Caldbeck family. The second son, **George**, was in the Bengal Army engineers and died during the siege of Lucknow, in 1857, where he was in charge of the fortifications. The third son, **John**, was in the Bengal Artillery, was present at the siege of Delhi during the Mutiny of 1857 and later rose to the rank of Lieut.-General. After his retirement he too emigrated to New Zealand and settled at Dunedin and later Christchurch. For more information on this branch see Lisburn Historical Society's Journal, Volume 4 December 1982.

James Fulton (1755-1817) his wife, Ann Bell, his sons, John and James Bell, his daughter, Eliza Reid, and his grand-daughters, Jane Sproull and Alicia Charlotte Fulton, are remembered on Cathedral 137.

The third son of John Fulton, John Williamson Fulton (1769-1830), joined his father in India in 1787. This John became very prosperous. He was a merchant, storekeeper, commission agent, administrator of estates of deceased officers, Assistant Accountant to the Board of Revenue, Bengal and mayor of Calcutta in 1816. He was connected with India for thirty-three years. He had a first family of perhaps two sons and four daughters. It is a son, **Joseph** (1800-1814), and possibly John's sister, Ann (died 10th October 1814), who are buried in Cathedral No. 112. The eldest daughter, **Eliza**, married **Lieut. Thomas Pottinger**, as his second wife, in Calcutta in June 1814. John Williamson Fulton married **Ann Hunt** (née **Robertson**) on 1st February 1806 and they had two sons and five daughters. It was while he was in India that about 1819 he collected £1192:3:2 for the Irish Harp Society [see THG Vol. 1 page 161]. He also contributed one hundred guineas to the foundation of Royal Belfast Academical Institution. John Williamson returned from India with a substantial fortune and settled in London in Upper Harley Street. He died 22nd January 1830 and is buried in Trinity Church, St. Marylebone, London. On summer visits home to Lisburn he rented Glenmore at Lambeg.

His elder son from his marriage to Anne, **John Williamson Fulton** (1814-1872), was a barrister. He went to Calcutta in 1841, with his wife, **Matilda Montgomery Casement**. They had married 25th

June 1840 in Larne. [She is a connection of the Casements who married into the Carleton and Higginson families. See pages 203 and 233]. When John Williamson's mother died in 1845, the family returned to London and then lived in Rugby for a few years, before returning to Calcutta for a couple of years. He then returned to Ireland. In 1851 he bought property near Broughshane, Co. Antrim, from the Commissioners of Encumbered Estates, which he named Braidujle. About 1854 he bought a house near Drumbo, Co. Down, near Lisburn, which he named Braidujle House. He became a J.P. for counties Antrim and Down. He had a family of four sons and a daughter. He died 10th November 1872 and his wife on 27th February 1894 and both are buried in Drumbo Church of Ireland Graveyard. The only daughter, **Josephine Mary McGildowney Fulton**, married her first cousin, **Sir Theodore Cracraft Hope** of the Bombay Civil Service and it is Sir Theodore Hope who wrote the book "The Memoirs of the Fultons of Lisburn" published 1903. He died 4th July 1915 and is buried in Highgate Cemetery, London.

John Williamson Fulton's younger son was **Lieut. Joseph Hennessy** (1816-1843) of the Bengal Infantry. He died 24th May 1843 at Dorunda, Chuta, Nagpore, East Indies. His brother officers erected a tablet to his memory in Trinity Church, St. Marylebone, London, where his father had been buried. The daughters of John Williamson and Anne Fulton were **Eleanor Sophia**, **Anne**, who was Sir Theodore Hope's mother, **Mary Charron** and **Charlotte Hayes**. Another daughter, **Anne**, died young.

Cathedral No. 32 is the odd one out of the Fulton gravestones. **Ellen Fulton** appears to be the husband of **Lieut. William Fulton**, and it is not known how or if he is related to the other Fulton families. Ellen's surname may have been **Garrett** and a relative may have been **Alice**, wife of **Thomas Carleton**.

(*Extracts from obituary*)

BELFAST NEWS LETTER
FRIDAY NOVEMBER 22 1872

DEATH OF J.W.FULTON, ESQ., J.P. OF BRAIDUJLE.

The sudden and unexpected death of this gentleman will be heard of with sincere regret in a very wide circle of society at home and abroad. John Williamson Fulton returned from India about fifteen years ago with an ample fortune. He was one of the ablest and most successful practitioners at the Bar of the Court of Calcutta, and on several occasions had been highly complimented by the Judges who presided over that tribunal. Early in the present century the father of the deceased was appointed, through the influence of the second Marquis of Hertford, to a lucrative situation in the East. During his residence in India the elder Mr. Fulton did not forget his native town, Lisburn. He contributed liberally to its local institutions, and he was one of the most munificent patrons of the Belfast Harp Society. ………. At one period the different branches of the Fulton family took a high place among the gentry and merchants of Lisburn. In the Governmental Department of India the name of Fulton may still be found in that long list of names to which Lisburn had contributed so largely: and down to the present day many of the leading men, both in the Civil and Military Departments of the Presidencies of Bombay and Bengal, are natives of the same town. We have said that the late John Williamson Fulton had gained a prominent place among the legal practitioners of India. Some time after his return home he went to reside on his handsome property in the next county, and of which Braidujle was the mansion-house. In his capacity as magistrate he held commissions for Down and Antrim. Mr. Fulton was well known as an upright and impartial judge; and, in his adjudications, he was able to bring to bear on each case a thorough knowledge of law, and what, in many instances, is still more important-a good stock of common sense. ……….. He was an excellent landlord, and took as much interest in the well-being of his tenants as if each of them had been a member of his own family. ………. He was nearly the last of a long line of ancestry, and now, with one or two exceptions, there is not a single representative of the Fulton family in the ancient borough of Lisburn.

GOUGH

FRIENDS' BURYING GROUND 28

In the Friends' Burying Ground, Railway Street, Lisburn, is a headstone for **John Gough**, first headmaster of the Ulster Provincial School, Lisburn (Friends' School, Lisburn), which was opened in 1774. John Gough was born in Kendal, Co. Westmoreland on 21st March 1721. He was an assistant at a Friends' school in Wiltshire, England, until 1750, and then became headmaster of the Chief School, Dame Street, Dublin, for twenty-four years. In the spring of 1774 he was appointed "Teacher-in-chief" of Friends' School, Prospect Hill, Lisburn. He published a book entitled "Teacher of Arithmetic" which for many years was a standard text book in Irish schools. He also published, in 1789, "A History of the People called Quakers," in four volumes. He died 25th October 1791. After his death there was no stone to mark his burial site and the stone in the Burying Ground has been erected much later.

GRAHAM

CATHEDRAL MEMORIALS

There are two memorials to the Graham family in Lisburn Cathedral. One is for **William Graham** and his wife, **Elizabeth,** and two of their children, **William** and **Anne,** who are all buried in Drumbo Presbyterian Burying Ground. This memorial was erected by **Colonel James Graham**, another son of William and Elizabeth. The other memorial is for Colonel James Graham and was erected by his widow and children. The Grahams were in the Drumbo area from the seventeenth century and at the townland of Lisnastrain, Co. Down from the early eighteenth century.

William Graham (c1693-1773) and his wife, **Margaret Carlisle** (c1698-1777) had a family of three sons and one daughter. One of the sons, also **William** (1750-1842), married **Phoebe Norwood** (c1751-1829) and they had a family of sixteen children, although several of them died young. One of William and Phoebe's sons, another William (1785-1850), married **Elizabeth Beatty** (1787-1865) on November 30th 1810. She was married in her father's drawing room by the Rev. Snowden Cupples. This is the William Graham from the memorial. He lived in Market Square, was a merchant, tanner and brewer and in 1839 was the Deputy Vice-chairman of the Lisburn Board of Guardians. His wife's family were also tanners in Bow Street, Lisburn. His wife was the daughter of **Thomas Beatty** and **Elizabeth Higginson,** [see THG Vol. 1 Kilrush No. 97 and pages 149 and 150]. William's sister, **Rachel Graham**, married Elizabeth's brother, **Samuel Beatty**. William and Elizabeth Graham had a family of eight daughters and four sons. Anne and William, their children named on the memorial, were not married. William, the son, was also a tanner and brewer and also lived in Market Square.

Colonel James Graham (1830-1905), William and Elizabeth's son, who had the memorial erected, was in the 14th Regiment of Native Infantry in India. He married, on 14th September 1865, **Louisa Maria Joy**. Their three sons were **William George** (born 1866), **Allan Gordon** (born 1870) and **Donald Charles** (born 1874), and their daughter was **Grace Elizabeth MacDougall** (born 1867). Colonel Graham was buried in Putney Cemetery, London.

Several of William and Elizabeth's other children were married. One of these was **Henrietta**, who married **Rev. Stuart Smith** of Co. Cavan. There is a memorial window to two of their sons in Christ Church, Lisburn. There is also a Graham family connection with Legacurry Presbyterian Church.

Another connection with India was William Graham's brother, **James** (1796-1857), who was a doctor in the Honourable East India Company. Three of his sons were in military service in the Honourable East India Company.

Graham Gardens in Lisburn is named after this Graham family, who were owners of property there. Tan Yard Lane was originally a cul-de-sac running off Bow Street and is now a continuation of Graham Gardens.
[*P.R.O.N.I. T/1289*]

(Extract from obituary.)

BANNER OF ULSTER
TUESDAY AUGUST 27 1850

DEATH OF WILLIAM GRAHAM, ESQ., LISBURN.-It is with much regret we have to-day to record this melancholy event, which has cast a general gloom over society in Lisburn, and the whole neighbourhood. We understand that the afflictive visitation was very sudden; that, on the morning of the 23rd instant, the fatal attack was experienced, and that, in an alarmingly brief period, the mournful scene of the sick chamber was closed in death. Mr. Graham was a man of activity, energy, and great integrity as a merchant; highly esteemed by those with whom he mingled in business habits and transactions, and beloved, and venerated by multitudes among whom he freely circulated the means of comfortable subsistence. He was a man of quiet, practical benevolence; without any display or ostentation, he dispensed benefits in a wide circle. Yesterday his interment took place at Drumbo, to which an extremely large funeral concourse followed his remains.

(Extract from obituary.)

LISBURN STANDARD
SATURDAY MAY 13 1905

THE LATE COL. JAMES GRAHAM

The deceased was the son of the late William Graham, of Lisburn and Lisnastrain, County Antrim (sic), and was educated at Dungannon School, County Tyrone. At the age of 18 he received a commission in the East India Company's forces, and on his arrival in India joined the 14th Regiment of Native Infantry, being attached to that regiment till it mutinied in 1857. As senior commissariat officer he served under Major-General Sir James Outram, G.C.B., at the capture of Lucknow, and also in a similar capacity under Sir J. Hope Grant, K.C.B., during the campaign in Oude in 1858. He was present at various engagements, including Nawabqunge, re-occupation of Fyzabad, at the crossing of the Gogra, in November, 1858. He was mentioned in Sir Hope Grant's despatches and received medal and clasp. In 1874 he was placed at the disposal of the Department of Agriculture and Commerce, in connection with the famine at that time, and at the close of the relief operations received the thanks of the Government of India for his services. In 1875 he was gazetted lieutenant-colonel, and retired in 1879 with the honorary rank of colonel. In 1892 he accepted the offer of a seat on the Board of the Delhi and London Bank, which he held to the time of his death. After his retirement he lived at Killiney, County Dublin, and at Cotswold, Wimbledon. He leaves a widow, one daughter, and three sons.

GREGG

There are four headstones to the Gregg family in Friends' Burying Ground, Railway Street. These are for **Dominick Gregg**, his wife **Mary Anne Hancock**, daughter of **Jacob Hancock** and **Sarah Grubb** [see Hancock page 229], and most of their family. There is one memorial in the Cathedral Grounds. This is for Dominick and Mary Anne's son, **William**. Dominick Gregg (c1764-19th March 1826) was a linen merchant and Quaker, of Castle Street, Lisburn and Coleraine, Co. Londonderry. He was a friend of John Hancock. In 1817 a Spinning Institution was established in Lisburn with John Hancock, Dominick Gregg and William Coulson on the committee of the school.

Dominick and his wife, Mary Anne (24th February 1770-2nd December 1862), married on 21st November 1793 and had a family of six sons and four daughters. It would seem that five of the daughters are buried in Railway Street and none of these five married. They were **Sarah** (1794-5th March 1876), **Maria** (12th September 1803-27th May 1883), **Elizabeth Rebecca** (1809-29th September 1876), **Anna Bradshaw** (12th April 1812-21st March 1898), and **Catherine Alicia** (25th February 1815-27th February 1879). The other daughter was **Jane**, born 1806, who married **Edward Fisher**. She lived in Huddersfield and had at least three sons and three daughters. One of her sons, **Charles Edward Gregg Fisher** married **Mary Phillipa Philipps**. In 1876 he changed his surname to **Philipps** and was created a knight in 1887.

Of Dominick Gregg's sons, it is probable that two of them, **Hancock**, born 1798, and **George** (1804-15th June 1845), were in business in Liverpool, as this is where George died. Another son, **Dr. Samuel Thomas** (1800-20th March 1823) died in Lisburn. The eldest son, William, (1796-2nd February 1870) left the Quakers. On 2nd April 1831 he married **Anne Fulton Caldbeck** in Lisburn Cathedral [see Caldbeck page 201]. She died in 1834 and a very fine monument was erected to her in the Cathedral Burying Ground and is mentioned in the Ordnance Survey Memoirs of 1835.

William Gregg was one of Lord Hertford's agents. In 1843 he was Seneschal, a post which was appointed by Lord Hertford, and Chief Magistrate, with an office in Castle Street. About 1835 he built Derryvolgie House at Lambeg. He was very involved with various affairs in Lisburn. In 1837 he was in the Killultagh Hunting Club, subscribed to the Newsroom, was on the committee of the Fever Hospital and was a governor of the Infirmary. Later he became a Town Commissioner. He is buried with his wife in Cathedral No. 147.

BELFAST NEWS LETTER
THURSDAY FEBRUARY 3 1870

DEATH OF WILLIAM GREGG, Esq, J.P., of DERRIEVOLGIE (sic) HOUSE LISBURN. –The demise of this highly-respected gentleman will be heard of with regret by all who knew him, but especially by those who, from more intimate knowledge of the amiability and kindliness of his disposition, are best able to form a correct judgment on that subject. The deceased was son of the late Dominick Gregg, one of the old linen merchants of Lisburn, and who, in conjunction with his friend, John Hancock, and other members of the trade, led the way in getting up the movement which resulted in the repeal of the law which made bleach green robbery a capital offence. In the early part of his days, the late Mr. Gregg held a confidential situation in the Hertford Office, in Lisburn; and during the long period of his connection with that estate he was ever the friend of the industrious tenant, while, at the same time, he never forgot the legitimate rights of the landlord. On his retiring from that situation the tenantry and other friends presented him with a valuable service of plate, in token of their respect for his character, and of the kindly and considerate course he had pursued while engaged in the affairs of the Hertford Office. On the death of the Rev. Dr. Cupples, Mr. Gregg was appointed Seneschal of the Manors of Killultagh and Derrievolgie; and, when the Bill was passed for the sweeping away of Manor Courts, he received a life-pension in consideration of the loss of that department of his office. For upwards of thirty years he had been in the Commission of the Peace; and in the whole of his active life, whether on the Bench or elsewhere, he was never known to make an overstretch of power in his magisterial capacity. For several years past his health had been giving way, and he had ceased to take any prominent part in public affairs; but, although confined to his room, little idea was entertained by those around him that death was so close at hand. On Monday last he appeared much worse than usual, and he gradually sank until yesterday morning, when his spirit passed away as peacefully as had been the even tenor of his life.

LISBURN STANDARD
MARCH 26 1898
THE LATE MISS GREGG OF DERRYVOLGIE

By the death of Miss Anna B. Gregg on Monday 21st inst., Lisburn has lost one of its oldest and most respected inhabitants. This amiable lady was a life-long member of the Society of Friends. She was born in 1812, and was a younger daughter of Dominick Gregg, and was the last survivor of a large family. Her brother, William Gregg, was for many years Seneschal of Lisburn, and one of the most active magistrates in the district. He built and laid out the beautifully situated residence of Derryvolgie, and at his decease left it to his unmarried sisters. One sister is married to Mr. Fisher, of Spring Dale, Huddersfield, whose sons and grandsons have this day followed the remains as chief mourners. Miss Gregg was a lady of high intellectual taste, and only a few years ago commenced the study of the Greek Testament. She had strong sympathies with everything that was good, without respect to denominational distinctions. The gardens of Derryvolgie were renowned for their excellence, and their yearly contributions to the Lisburn Horticultural Society were always looked for. Amongst the gentry of the country Miss Gregg was well-known and highly esteemed. And her name was not unknown to the poor, who at all times had her warmest sympathies. She was ill only for a few weeks, a gentle break-up of Nature closing the end of a peaceful life. She died in perfect peace, and with bright and unclouded faculties committed herself into the arms of her loving Saviour. The chief mourners were Sir Charles Phillips, Bart.; Mr. Sharples Fisher, and Mr. George Fisher, nephews; and Mr. Henry Phillips, and Mr. Lindesay Fisher, great-nephews of the deceased. The general public attended in large numbers, thus showing their respect for the deceased lady. The wreaths sent to Derryvolgie were numerous and beautiful.

HANCOCK

FRIENDS' BURYING GROUND 9

There have been members of the Hancock, or Handcock, family in the Lisburn area for almost four hundred years. There is a **William Hancock** mentioned in the Hearthmoney Roll of 1669, and he may have been one of about 300 men who came to the Lisburn area with Conway. Many of the Hancock family were Quakers, but some later belonged to the Church of Ireland.

William Hancock and his wife, **Margaret**, had at least three sons, **John**, who married **Deborah Webb** in 1683, **William**, who died in 1684 in Dublin, and **Jacob**, of Market Square, Lurgan, who in 1691 married **Isabel Calvert**. Jacob and Isabel had a family of at least four sons, **Joseph**, **John**, **Jacob** and **Thomas**. Of these sons, John (died about 1757) married twice. His first wife was **Mary Forbes** and they had a son, **John**, and a daughter, **Anna**. John's second wife was **Sarah Bradshaw** and they also had one daughter, **Sarah**, and one son, **Jacob Jun**. John's brother, Jacob (died 1763) married **Mary Richardson,** in 1732, and had a son, **Jacob Sen.** (born about 1743 and died 1818). The other two sons of Jacob and Isabel, Joseph and Thomas, lived in Dublin. Joseph (died 1729), a merchant, married **Anna Forbes** in 1724 and had two sons and a daughter. Thomas (born 1703), in 1733/4 married **Sarah Forbes**, (1714-1776), and had two sons and two daughters.

John Hancock, son of John Hancock and Mary Forbes, married twice. The surname of the first wife may have been **Hogg**. He then married **Elizabeth Hunter** in 1761. They had two children, **John**, born 1762, and **Jacob**, born in 1764 and died 1769. John Hancock died September 1764 when his son, John, was two. By his will he left property to his sons and directed how they were to be

Descendants of William Henry Hancock

This is not a complete Family Tree.

William Henry Hancock
Married
Margaret

William Hancock
d. Oct. 7 1684

John Hancock
Married April 6 1683
Deborah Webb

Jacob Hancock
Married Aug. 8 1691
Isabel Calvert

Thomas Hancock
b. June 30 1703
Married Dec. 1 1733-34
Sarah Forbes
b. July 10 1714
d. Jan. 1 1776
Issue

Jacob Hancock
b. 1732
Married 1732
Mary Richardson

Jacob Hancock Sen.
b. abt. 1743
d. Jan. 12 1818
Buried Friends'
[1] Sarah Grubb
Married Feb. 7 1765
d. Oct. 29 1772
[2] Mary Gregg
b. abt. 1744
d. Oct. 17 1812
Buried Friends'

William Hancock
b. Dec. 12 1785
d. Nov. 7 1819
Buried Friends'

Susannah Hancock
b. March 17 1783
Married Nov. 16
1806
George Horford

Jacob Hancock
b. Jan. 28 1781
Married May 4 1818
Sarah Ann Boyd
b. 1790
d. March 3 1870
Buried Friends'

Catherine Hancock
b. March 22 1780
Married Jan. 12 1809
Francis Horner

Isabella Hancock
b. March 22 1780
d. April 2 1780

Alice Hancock
b. Jan. 26 1778

Jacob Hancock
b. Aug. 24 1776

Jane Hancock
b. Jan. 17 1775
Married
Samuel Gatchell

Joseph Hancock
d. 1729
Married May 14 1724
Anna Forbes
b. April 29 1708
Issue

John Hancock
d. abt. 1756
Married
[1] Mary Forbes
Married
[2] Sarah Bradshaw

Sarah Hancock
Married June 7 1769
William Middleton

Jacob Hancock Jun.
d. Jan. 15 1793
Married Oct. 13 1771
Elizabeth Phelps
d. Aug. 5 1832
Buried Friends'

Dr. Thomas Hancock
b. March 24 1783
d. April 16 1849
Buried Friends'
Married
Hannah Wakefield
Strangman
d. 1828

Hannah Hancock
b. June 22 1784
d. Sept. 18 1789

Anna Hancock
Married June 7 1753
William Neville

Celia Hancock
b. Aug. 26 1774
d. March 19 1777

Thomas Hancock
b. Oct. 4 1781
d. May 7 1782

Elizabeth Hancock
b. 1777
d. June 24 1851

Isabella Hancock
b. Feb. 12 1786
d. Aug. 5 1872
Married Feb. 27 1807
William Steele Nicholson
Issue

John Hancock
b. 1764
d. 1769

Sarah Hancock
b. Dec. 12 1772
d. March 5 1847
Married Jan. 21 1796
Samuel Greer
Issue

Elizabeth Hancock
b. Oct. 26 1777
d. Feb. 7 1832
Buried Friends'

John Hancock
b. Sept. 16 1779

George Hancock
Married Oct. 16 1850
Rachel Barrott

Jacob Hancock
b. Sept. 16 1788

John Hancock
Married June 7 1753
[1] "Hogg"
Married Oct. 18 1801
Sarah Greer
[2] Elizabeth Hunter

John Hancock Jun.
b. Aug. 12 1762
d. Sept. 25 1823
Buried Friends'
Married June 16 1794
Sarah Greer
d. Dec. 21 1794

Jacob Hancock
b. 1764
d. 1769

Sarah Hancock
b. 1765
Married April 10 1817
Samuel Haughton

Thomas Hancock
b. Nov. 9 1780
d. May 26 1781

Mary Hancock
b. Oct. 9 1773
d. June 13 1828
Married Oct. 3 1822
James Hogg
b. 1756
d. May 9 1847
Buried Friends'

Emma Hancock
b. abt. 1814
d. Sept. 8 1843
Buried Friends'

Hannah Wakefield
Hancock
Married Dec. 20 1862
Wm. James Barcroft
Issue

Joseph Hancock
b. April 5 1767
d. Feb. 5 1795

Robert Hancock
b. Jan. 11 1790

William John Hancock
b. Sept. 15 1791
d. Aug. 29 1848
Married July 22 1816
Mary Neilson
Issue

Elizabeth Hancock
b. May. 9 1793

Anna Hancock
b. Feb. 18 1791
d. Dec. 18 1820
Buried Friends'

John Hancock
b. 1794
d. April 1896

Mary Anne Hancock
b. Feb. 24 1770
d. Dec. 21 1862
Married Nov. 21 1793
Dominick Gregg
b. abt. 1764
d. March 19 1826
Buried Friends'

Sarah Hancock
b. Oct. 6 1771
d. Nov. 26 1852
Married Jan. 21 1799
James Gatchell

Margaret Hancock
b. Oct. 17 1772
d. Oct. 17 1772

Isabella Hancock
b. Oct. 17 1772
d. Dec. 18 1772

Catherine Alicia Gregg
b. Feb. 25 1815
d. Feb. 27 1879
Buried Friends'

Anna Brabshaw Gregg
b. Apr. 12 1812
d. Mar. 21 1898
Buried Friends'

Elizabeth Rebecca
Gregg
b. 1809
d. Sept. 29 1876
Buried Friends'

Jane Gregg
b. 1806
Married
Edward Fisher
Issue

George Gregg
b. June 15 1845
Buried Friends'

Dr. Samuel Thomas
Gregg
b. 1800
d. Mar. 20 1828
Buried Friends'

Maria Gregg
b. Sept. 12 1803
d. May 24 1883
Buried Friends'

Hancock Gregg
b. 1798

William Gregg
b. 1796
d. Feb. 2 1870
Married April 2 1831
Anne Fulton Caldbeck
bap. July 29 1811
d. April 13 1834
Buried Estb. Cath.

Sarah Gregg
d. Mar. 5 1876
Buried Friends'

230

educated. Most importantly for Lisburn he also left £1,000 for the purchase of land in or near Lisburn on which to build a school for the education of the children of members of the Society of Friends. The setting up of the school was brought about by two of the trustees, Thomas Greer and **William Nevill** (who was a brother-in-law of John Hancock, having married John's sister Anna Hancock in 1753.) Twenty acres of land were leased from the Earl of Hertford at Prospect Hill, Lisburn, on June 9th 1766, at a cost of £500. Subscriptions of £1,300 were raised for the building of the original building. The school was opened as a boarding school in 1774, was known as the Ulster Provincial School - the name was later changed to Friends'School - and had John Gough as its first headmaster, [see Gough page 226].

John Hancock (1762-1823), the son, became an extensive linen merchant and owned a large bleaching concern at Lambeg, which later was owned by Messrs. Richardson, Sons & Owden. He also had a bakery in Market Square. In 1800, a famine year, he imported 200 tons of Indian Meal from Philadelphia, the first time a sample of this grain was seen in Ulster, and 500 barrels of American flour. He sold these at cost price to the needy people of the Lisburn area. In 1811 his bleach green at Lambeg was broken into and 3 webs of linen were stolen. He refused to prosecute the accused, as he knew the penalty would be death. Later, with the help of other linen merchants, they were able to have the M.P., Sir Samuel Romily, bring about a bill for the milder punishment of bleachgreen robbers. In 1817, in another period of famine, along with John Rogers, he purchased wheels for spinning flax with both hands and opened a school, which proved to be unsuccessful, for training girls and women to operate these wheels, and prepared flax for spinners who were in need and guaranteed the purchase of their work. John married **Sarah Greer** (1760-1794) in 1784 and had four sons and two daughters, although one son died young. The surviving children were **John** (born 1785), **Robert** (born 1790), **William John** (born 1791), **Sarah** (born 1787) and **Elizabeth** (born 1793). John died in 1823 and although he had left the Quakers in 1801 he is buried in Friends' Burying Ground. His daughter, Sarah, married **Samuel Haughton** in Lisburn Cathedral in 1817. His son, **William John**, married **Mary Neilson**, daughter of Samuel Neilson, of Belfast, and had issue.

Jacob Hancock Jun., half brother of John Hancock (died 1764), and son of John Hancock of Lisburn, married **Elizabeth Phelps**, of Dublin, in October 1771. They had a family of four sons and seven daughters. Some of these children died young. The sixth of their daughters, **Isabella** (1786-1872), married **William Steele-Nicholson** in Lisburn Cathedral on February 1807 and had issue. One of the sons, **Thomas** (born 1783) studied medicine in Dublin and Edinburgh. In 1810 he settled in London and married **Hannah Strangman**. After her death in 1828 he moved to Liverpool, and six years later he returned to Lisburn, where he died in 1849. He lived at Stannus Place in Lisburn and wrote several books on medicine and the Society of Friends. Dr. Thomas, his daughter, **Emma** (c1814-1843), and his sister, **Anna** (1791-1820), are buried in Friends' Burying Ground. Another daughter, **Hannah Wakefield Hancock** married **William James Barcroft** in 1862 and had two daughters. A son, **George,** married **Rachel Barrott** in 1850.

Another daughter of Jacob Hancock Jun.'s, **Mary** (1773-1828) married **James Hogg** (1756-1847) in 1822 and they are both buried in Friends' Burying Ground, [see Hogg and Bolton page 239], along with Mary's mother, Elizabeth, who died August 5th 1832. Jacob Jun. died on January 15th 1793 and he may be buried in Friends' Burying Ground, although there is no written record.

Jacob Hancock Sen., a cousin of John Hancock (who died 1764), was born about 1743 and died in 1818. His first marriage was to **Sarah Grubb** (1747-1772) in 1765. They had a family of four daughters and one son, but some of the children died young. One of the daughters, **Mary Anne**, married **Dominick Gregg** in 1793, [see Gregg page 228]. Jacob's second marriage was to **Mary Gregg**, of Coleraine, in 1773. There was a family of five daughters and three sons by this marriage and again some of the children died young. Jacob, his second wife, Mary, who died in 1812, two sons, **Jacob** (1781-1828), and **William** (1785-1819), and a daughter-in-law, **Sarah Ann** (died 1870), who was son Jacob's wife, are all buried in Friends' Burying Ground.

NEWS LETTER
TUESDAY SEPTEMBER 30 1823

FUNERAL OF JOHN HANCOCK
(From the Commercial Chronicle)

This very valuable man was buried on Sunday, in the Quakers' burying-ground in Lisburn. His remains were followed to the tomb by a large concourse of people of all denominations. The most respectable inhabitants of Lisburn and its vicinity assembled to pay their respect to a fellow townsman, whose solid and substantial qualities they had long admired. The poor, with the sincerity which generally characterizes them, followed the remains of their friend and protector. They called to their recollection those sad and calamitous days when nobody almost was to be found at the bedside of the dying victim to the Typhus Fever but the inestimable individual whose loss they had to lament. Protestants, Presbyterians, and Catholics, felt it a duty they owed to this inflexible advocate of public justice, to pay him the last sad honours of the grave. — When the body had arrived at its destined abode, Doctor Tennent, one of the most intimate and confidential friends of the deceased, addressed the surrounding multitude.

HAWKSHAW

CATHEDRAL 149 AND MEMORIAL
As well as the two stones in the graveyard, there is also one surviving memorial in the Cathedral, and the record of a memorial that cannot now be located.

The small flat stone records the death of **William Hawkshaw J.P.**, (1744-1826), of Divernagh, Co. Armagh, and Castle Street, Lisburn, and his wife **Eleanor Johnston** (1742-1826). They married in 1768 and had a family of at least two sons and probably two daughters. One daughter, **Jane**, is remembered on the small flat stone and the memorial in the Cathedral. Jane is believed to have established the Lisburn Female School in 1821 and supported the school with donations. She was still on the committee in 1836. George Whitla had also bequeathed £100 to this school, [see Whitla page 275]. **Elizabeth** may be another daughter. She married **William Darby** in 1799. The larger upright stone is in memory of one of the sons, **Lt. Col. John Stewart Hawkshaw**, of the 31st Huntingdonshire Regiment and 91st Argyll and Sutherland Highlanders. He lived at Divernagh, Co. Armagh and Blaris Lodge, and had fought in Holland, the West Indies, Peninsular War and at Waterloo. He died of typhus in 1848. He married **Sophia Agnes Lawrence** on 13th December 1815 and they had a family of at least four daughters and a son. The son, **William**, died young, **Emilie**, one of the daughters, died in 1841, aged 20, and **Eleanor Frances** died in Dublin in 1907, at the age of 92. The other two daughters were **Anna**, baptised in 1816, and **Eliza**, baptised in 1822. Sophia died in 1859. There is also in the Cathedral records a **Charles Hawkshaw**, son of John Hawkshaw, baptised 12th January 1808.

John Stewart's brother, **Edward**, was also a Lt. Col. and served in HM 31st Regt. and 7th Portuguese Cacadores. He married **Lucy Irwin Chetwood** in 1820. The marriage notice in the newspaper said he was the youngest son. He died in Cheltenham in 1858. His only son was **Rev. Edward Burdett Hawkshaw**. His mother was **Hester Pratt** and Rev. Edward was born in 1815. In 1845 he married **Catherine Mary Jane Hoskyns**. Their son, **Edward Crichton Hawkshaw**, was one of the mourners at Eleanora Frances Hawkshaw's funeral in 1907.

LISBURN STANDARD
FEBRUARY 23 1907

THE LATE MISS HAWKSHAW

A link with the past has been severed by the death on the 7th inst., in her 93rd year, at 1, Wellington Road, Dublin, of Miss Eleanor Francis Hawkshaw, youngest daughter of the late Lieutenant-Colonel John Stewart Hawkshaw, 31st (Huntingdonshire) Regiment and 91st (Argyll and Sutherland) Highlanders, late of Divernagh and Blaris Lodge, County Armagh (sic), a veteran of the campaigns in Holland, West Indies, Peninsular, and Waterloo. Miss Hawkshaw had for many years resided in Dublin, deservedly loved for herself and her charity. She was laid to rest in the family vault at Lisburn Cathedral on the 9th February, those attending being Major Edward Crichton Hawkshaw, R.A. (retired), Colonel William Dashwood, commanding 1st Northumberland Fusiliers (chief mourners), Miss Willis (her maid), Mr. Tyndall Johns, and Mr. A.D. Crawford. The service was read by Canon Pounden.

HERON
CATHEDRAL 125

Samuel Heron, who was an attorney, died 19th June 1808. This is probably the Samuel Heron, who had a house in Castle Street. A **Mrs. Jane Heron**, wife of Samuel Heron, Attorney at Law, was buried in the Cathedral grounds 5th January 1778, and a **Mrs. Heron**, wife of Samuel Heron, died in 1807. Samuel Heron appears to have had at least two sons, **Edward** and **Samuel**, who were Lieutenants in the Royal Navy. An Edward Heron became a Lieutenant on 22nd September 1806 and a Samuel on 24th March 1809. Only the death of Samuel is recorded on the stone. Samuel, who died on 18th May 1840, married **Elizabeth Wallis** and they had a son, **Samuel Wallis**, also mentioned on the stone. He was baptised 12th October 1825 and died in 25th June 1839. There was also a daughter, **Gertrude Elizabeth**, baptised 3rd August 1823.

Edward was baptised in Lisburn Cathedral 16th June 1781. He married **Anne Johnson Smyth**, daughter of **Roger Johnson Smyth**, [see Johnson Smyth Cathedral No. 67 and page 243]. She is named on the stone. They probably had three daughters. The two mentioned on the stone are **Mary**, who died 25th February 1849 and **Charlotte**, baptised 4th June 1818, who, on 1st January 1852 in Dublin, married **James Smyth** of Ballylintough House, Annahilt, and died 20th December 1870. A Lieutenant Edward Heron, who died 5th November 1836, aged 56, is buried in Holywood graveyard, Co. Down, along with his daughter, **Ann**, who died 11th July 1833, aged 13 years.

In 1824 both Lieut. Edward Heron and Samuel Heron were living in Castle Street, Lisburn.

HIGGINSON AND MARMION
CATHEDRAL 88 AND MEMORIAL

The Higginson family, which can be traced back to Warwickshire, England, have been in Ireland since the 17th century and in the Lisburn and Ballinderry area since the late 17th century, and so there is an extensive Higginson family to be found in this part of the North of Ireland. Many of them have been clergymen, some served in the navy and some served in the army. Many of them are buried in Ballinderry.

There is not now a Higginson headstone in the Lisburn Cathedral graveyard, although the family have been connected with Lisburn and the Cathedral. There are two memorials in the Cathedral and two of the Higginsons are buried in the Marmion grave [see Cathedral No. 88]. The **Rev. Thomas Higginson** (1722-1789) was rector of Lisburn, 1775-81, before becoming vicar of Ballinderry, 1782-89. His son, the **Rev. Thomas Edward Higginson**, (c1767-1819) was curate of Lisburn 1817-1819,

233

Descendants of Col. Edward Higginson (1)

Cathedral No. 88 & Memorial

This is not a complete Family Tree

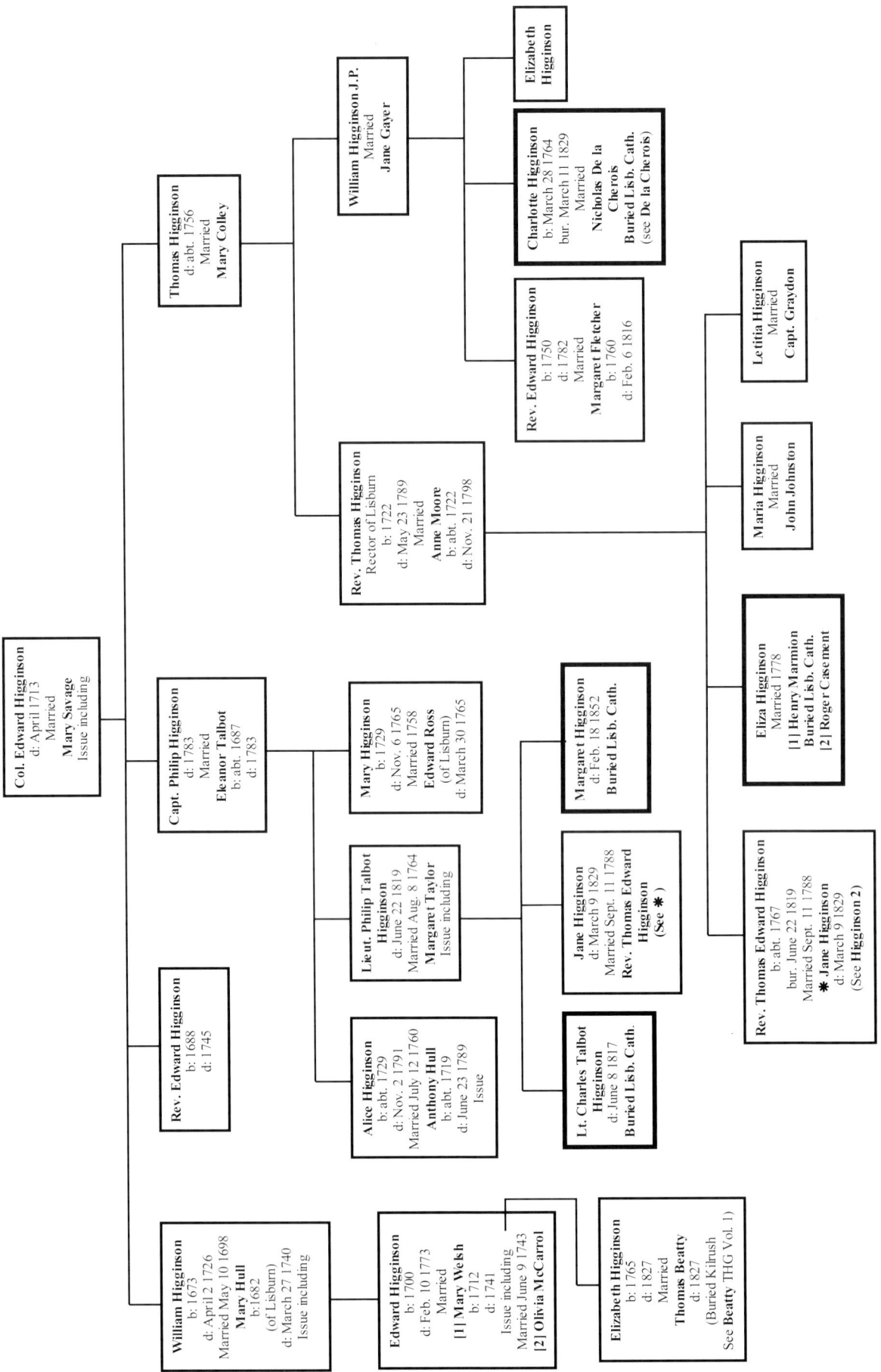

Col. Edward Higginson
d: April 1713
Married
Mary Savage
Issue including

Thomas Higginson
d: abt. 1756
Married
Mary Colley

William Higginson J.P.
Married
Jane Gayer

Elizabeth Higginson

Charlotte Higginson
b: March 28 1764
bur. March 11 1829
Married
Nicholas De la Cherois
Buried Lisb. Cath.
(see De la Cherois)

Rev. Edward Higginson
b: 1750
d: 1782
Married
Margaret Fletcher
b: 1760
d: Feb. 6 1816

Rev. Thomas Higginson
Rector of Lisburn
b: 1722
d: May 23 1789
Married
Anne Moore
b: abt. 1722
d: Nov. 21 1798

Letitia Higginson
Married
Capt. Graydon

Maria Higginson
Married
John Johnston

Capt. Philip Higginson
d: 1783
Married
Eleanor Talbot
b: abt. 1687
d: 1783

Rev. Edward Higginson
b: 1688
d: 1745

Mary Higginson
b: 1729
d: Nov. 6 1765
Married 1758
Edward Ross
(of Lisburn)
d: March 30 1765

Margaret Higginson
d: Feb. 18 1852
Buried Lisb. Cath.

Eliza Higginson
Married 1778
[1] **Henry Marmion**
Buried Lisb. Cath.
[2] **Roger Casement**

Lieut. Philip Talbot Higginson
d: June 22 1819
Married Aug. 8 1764
Margaret Taylor
Issue including

Alice Higginson
b: abt. 1729
d: Nov. 2 1791
Married July 12 1760
Anthony Hull
b: abt. 1719
d: June 23 1789
Issue

Jane Higginson
d: March 9 1829
Married Sept. 11 1788
Rev. Thomas Edward Higginson
(See ✱)

Lt. Charles Talbot Higginson
d: June 8 1817
Buried Lisb. Cath.

Rev. Thomas Edward Higginson
b: abt. 1767
bur. June 22 1819
Married Sept. 11 1788
✱ **Jane Higginson**
d: March 9 1829
(See **Higginson 2**)

William Higginson
b: 1673
d: April 2 1726
Married May 10 1698
Mary Hull
b:1682
(of Lisburn)
d: March 27 1740
Issue including

Edward Higginson
b: 1700
d: Feb. 10 1773
Married
[1] **Mary Welsh**
b: 1712
d: 1741
Issue including
Married June 9 1743
[2] **Olivia McCarrol**

Elizabeth Higginson
b: 1765
d: 1827
Married
Thomas Beatty
d: 1827
(Buried Kilrush)
See **Beatty** THG Vol. 1)

234

previously having been in Ballinderry and Lambeg. One of the memorials in the Cathedral is to his son, **Henry Theophilus Higginson** (1798-1869), his wife, **Charlotte McConnell** (c1800-1875) and two of their sons, **Thomas Edward** and **Charles Henry**. A third son, **Col. Theophilus** (1839-1903) is mentioned on the second memorial and his wife, **Ada Whitla**, (1846-1919) is mentioned on the Whitla memorial [see Whitla page 275]. Both Rev. Thomas and his son, Rev. Thomas Edward, are buried at Ballinderry.

As well as being curate of Lisburn the Rev. Thomas E. Higginson had been appointed Registrar for the Dioceses of Down and Connor in 1810. This was the Registry Office for the records of the diocese. He was succeeded by his son, Henry Theophilus Higginson, in 1819. The purpose of this office was to try the validity of wills, enforce payment of legacies, cause distribution of intestate's estates and matrimonial causes and grant probate of wills and letters of administration. The following description of Higginson's Tower in Lisburn at the time of Queen Victoria's coronation in 1838 appeared in the Lisburn Standard on August 6th 1892:-

A SKETCH OF AN HISTORIC PILE

Young and old of the Lisburn people, as well as passengers on their way by Bachelor's Walk to the railway station, will miss the Higginson Tower, that for more than half-a-century presented its quaint architecture and peaked parapets to passers-by. In clearing off the ground for the erection of additional houses on the north-west side of the Walk the builder has, of course, been obliged to take down the Tower erected there in 1838 by the late H.T. Higginson, J.P., a native of Lisburn, but who, for the last thirty years of his life, resided at Carnalea House, near Bangor. That gentleman was the first manager of the Northern Bank. He had for many years before held the important position of District Registrar of Wills, and resided in Bow Street, nearly opposite to the entrance to Hillsborough Road, and in 1836 removed to the large building, the lower part of which now forms the office of the local branch of the Ulster Bank. At that time the sites of the row of houses now standing on that side of the Bachelor's Walk was grazing land, and when the road was laid out as the Antrim Street way towards the ground selected for the Ulster Railway Station, Mr. Higginson built a wall to enclose the field, which he improved and added an orchard to the old garden of his new dwelling house. One of the parlours of the house he converted into a Registry Office, and the dining-room was transferred into the business place of the Northern Bank, of which he continued manager. The garden Tower, which presented the appearance of a tiny fortress, was finished early in June, 1838, and a prominent feature of its architecture was a port hole, from which protruded the muzzle of a small cannon. The evening of the day of Queen Victoria's Coronation was made a time of rejoicing in Lisburn, as it was in nearly all other centres of population throughout Ulster. Mr. Higginson, who had ever been famed for hospitality, had a number of friends with him on that occasion to celebrate the great event, and a host of hangers-on assembled in the Tower, where considerable quantities of powder had been provided to charge the cannon, and as each shot was fired, the loud boom re-echoed from the Chapel Hill to Seymour Street. Vast numbers of people, attracted by the cannonade, assembled near the Tower, and the ringing cheers for "The Queen" from the men inside were duly taken up by the outsiders, giving increased spirit to the celebration. For the refreshment of the men appointed to look after the cannon, an ample supply of the wine of the country was provided, and full justice was done to the beverage. It was nearly eleven o'clock before the proceedings closed, when the people outside dispersed, and the people left the Tower. It happened, however, that an eccentric mason, well known as an expert in the use of the trowel and hammer, had remained in the orchard. He had fallen asleep there, overcome by repeated potations. As the sun began to rise next morning he awoke, and thought he would try his hand at a shot from the cannon. There remained some of the powder, and, determined to have a loud report, the mason put in an ample charge, and then sought a match to apply to the priming. It happened, unfortunately, that the cannon had been left fully charged, and the explosion was so powerful as to blow out part of the walls. Billy Close, sergeant of the night watch, hearing the dread noise, rushed to the spot, and with some assistance forced open the orchard door, and, on entering, found the mason lying half

Descendants of Rev. Thomas Edward Higginson (2)

This is not a complete Family Tree

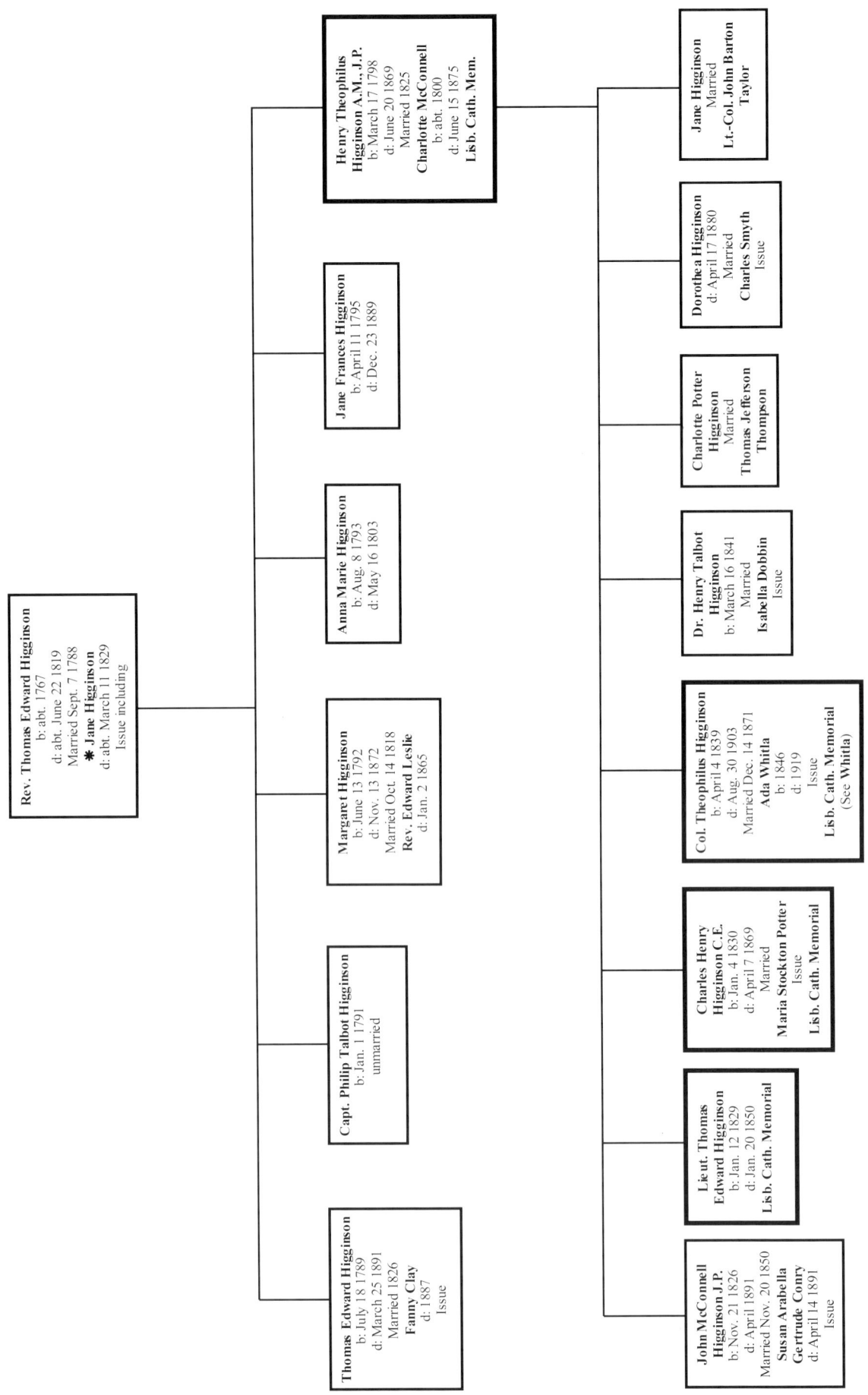

Rev. Thomas Edward Higginson
b: abt. 1767
d: abt. June 22 1819
Married Sept. 7 1788
✳ **Jane Higginson**
d: abt. March 11 1829
Issue including

Thomas Edward Higginson
b: July 18 1789
d: March 25 1891
Married 1826
Fanny Clay
d: 1887
Issue

Capt. Philip Talbot Higginson
b: Jan. 1 1791
unmarried

Margaret Higginson
b: June 13 1792
d: Nov. 13 1872
Married Oct. 14 1818
Rev. Edward Leslie
d: Jan. 2 1865

Anna Marie Higginson
b: Aug. 8 1793
d: May 16 1803

Jane Frances Higginson
b: April 11 1795
d: Dec. 23 1889

Henry Theophilus Higginson A.M., J.P.
b: March 17 1798
d: June 20 1869
Married 1825
Charlotte McConnell
b: abt. 1800
d: June 15 1875
Lisb. Cath. Mem.

John McConnell Higginson J.P.
b: Nov. 21 1826
d: April 1891
Married Nov. 20 1850
Susan Arabella Gertrude Conry
d: April 14 1891
Issue

Lieut. Thomas Edward Higginson
b: Jan. 12 1829
d: Jan. 20 1850
Lisb. Cath. Memorial

Charles Henry Higginson C.E.
b: Jan. 4 1830
d: April 7 1869
Married
Maria Stockton Potter
Issue
Lisb. Cath. Memorial

Col. Theophilus Higginson
b: April 4 1839
d: Aug. 30 1903
Married Dec. 14 1871
Ada Whitla
b: 1846
d: 1919
Issue
Lisb. Cath. Memorial
(See Whitla)

Dr. Henry Talbot Higginson
b: March 16 1841
Married
Isabella Dobbin
Issue

Charlotte Potter Higginson
Married
Thomas Jefferson Thompson

Dorothea Higginson
d: April 17 1880
Married
Charles Smyth
Issue

Jane Higginson
Married
Lt.-Col. John Barton Taylor

236

unconscious beyond the scattered bricks of the wall. After some time the experimenter of cannon-firing was able to go to his home, and so ended the celebration at the Higginson Tower.

The headstone for the Marmion family reveals little information on this family, as no dates are given. The Cathedral records and newspaper notices give some more information, but it is difficult to give the exact relationships owing to gaps in the records. There were at least four **Henry Marmions**, probably sons of each other. In 1762 the Trustees of the Third Division of the Turnpike Board appointed Henry Marmion as Registration Clerk and Treasurer and in 1780 a Henry Marmion was the churchwarden of the Cathedral. A Henry Marmion married **Eliza Higginson**, daughter of the Rev. Thomas Higginson, in 1778. An Eliza Marmion married **Richard Waring**, an attorney, on 3rd November 1804. A **Sarah Jane Marmion,** only surviving daughter of Henry Hamilton Marmion, married **Robert Potter**, of Killlinchy, on 27th November 1844.

Captain Philip Higginson and **Eleanor Talbot** were the grandparents of **Lieut. Charles Talbot Higginson** and **Margaret Higginson**, whose names are on the Marmion headstone. Captain Philip Higginson and his wife are buried in Carrickfergus Old Graveyard along with other relatives.
[*P.R.O.N.I. T/1289/15*]

(*Extract from obituary.*)

THE BELFAST NEWS LETTER
TUESDAY JUNE 22 1869

DEATH OF HENRY HIGGINSON, ESQ., J.P.

It is with extreme regret we announce the death of this most estimable gentleman, which took place at his residence, Carnalea House, County Down, on Sunday-evening, the 20th inst. Mr. Higginson had arrived at a very ripe age, being upwards of 70 years; but notwithstanding this fact and the circumstance that for some time past he had been in declining health, his decease will be learned by a community where he was loved and honoured with that affectionate regret which is amongst the highest tributes reserved for the memories of good men. In various ways he was brought into intimate relations with the people of this extensive district. For the long period of fifty years he was Registrar of the United Diocese of Down and Connor and Dromore, having succeeded an equally amiable and efficient relative in that office. Recently, he resigned this position in favour of his son, who, we are glad to say, inherits the qualities which endeared his lamented father to all with whom, in social or business relations, he came in contact. For thirty years preceding his death, Mr. Higginson was a magistrate for the Counties of Antrim and Down, and in this, and in every other position which he was called upon to occupy, he deserved and enjoyed the good-will and high respect of all who knew him. ……... His social virtues - what Lord Derby would not inaptly call "the sweet civilities of life" – found frequent and congenial outlet in the charities and the re-unions of the Masonic body. In the proceedings which resulted in the erection of the Gillespie Masonic Monument at Comber he took a leading part; and upon other occasions he equally evinced the reality of his fraternal attachment. Throughout the Province of Ulster, and especially in the town of Lisburn, Mr. Higginson was well known and unreservedly esteemed. We understand that he is succeeded by his son, J.M. Higginson, Esq., J.P., the present Registrar of the diocese. The funeral is to take place on Thursday morning.

HILL

The Lisburn Standard of Saturday May 6th 1911 contained a notice referring to the closure of Lisburn Cathedral and Kilrush Burying Grounds, [see page 4], and giving a list of people who had rights of interment in the two places. **Joseph Hill** was one of the people mentioned in the Cathedral list.

LISBURN STANDARD
FEBRUARY 23 1917

MR. JOSEPH HILL

Our obituary column would not be complete to-day without some reference to the passing of Mr. Joseph Hill, Smithfield. The late Mr. Hill, while probably not so well-known as others mentioned, had a host of real friends who sincerely regret his death. Pneumonia followed close on the heels of a bad cold, and the best medical skill proved of no avail. Deceased, like his grandfather and father before him, was a shoemaker to trade. He was a member of the Cathedral congregation, and was one of the few who retained rights of interment in the Cathedral Churchyard, where he was laid to rest on Tuesday in the presence of many mournful friends.

HODSON

CATHEDRAL MEMORIAL

On the north wall of the nave is a memorial to **Canon Hartley Hodson**. His parents were **William Hartley Hodson,** of Old Connaught, Bray, and **Eliza Duell**. His birth date is uncertain but is thought to be about 1815 and he died on the 3rd February 1884. He was ordained in 1841, was Curate of Derriaghy from 1841-1846, and Curate of Lisburn 1846-1862, with sole charge of Christ Church. Then he was appointed Rector of Derrykeighan and Canon of Cairncastle in 1862 and finally Rector of Lisburn from 1876. On the 2nd May 1850 he married **Hannah Gregory** and had three sons and two daughters. The sons were **William Gregory**, **Hartley Richard** and **John Robert**. The daughters were **Mary** and **Hannah**. He is buried in Lisburn Cemetery, Hillsborough Road, Lisburn.

(Extract from obituary)

BELFAST NEWS LETTER
TUESDAY FEBRUARY 5 1884

DEATH OF CANON HODSON, D.D.,
RECTOR OF LISBURN

We regret to announce the demise of this highly respected dignitary of the Episcopal Church.

The late Canon Hodson was appointed to the incumbency of the New Church in Lisburn in 1845, three years after the erection of that sacred edifice. His kindly disposition, and the special attention he paid to the working ranks, visiting them in their homes and cheering them on in the path of industry, gave him the utmost popularity with that section of his congregation; and the powers he displayed in the pulpit, his great facility of expression and impromptu reference to passing events drew around him a large and respectable class of hearers. During what was known as the Revival of 1859 the church became so crowded Sunday after Sunday that sitting room could not be had; and in the course of the following summer a considerable addition was made to the original building, the members of the congregation, those of the Cathedral, and other friends contributing liberally to the cost of the new erection. As secretary of the Diocesan Curate's Aid Society, the late canon took an active part in the work then carried on, and in the raising of the handsome church at Broomhedge he was an effective auxiliary. He discharged the duties of this office with great zeal and ability, to the advantage of the Church at large, and to the satisfaction of the Lord Bishop and clergy of the diocese, by whom he was much respected and esteemed. He was also an ardent supporter of the cause of Scriptural education, as maintained by the Church Education Society, and for many years he was a member of the Diocesan Society, whose work he supported by his consistent advocacy, his influence and means. Early in 1863 Bishop Knox appointed him to the living of Derrykeighan, in this county, where the same disposition that made him so many friends in Lisburn created a host of admirers, not the least of these being members of the Presbyterian Church. We have already noticed that after the death of Dean Stannus the Rev. Hartley Hodson was presented to the important living of Lisburn. Some little opposition had been raised on the occasion, but the geniality of disposition and the hearty spirit of Christian charity that can look beyond social warfare which marked the whole history of the minister, gradually disarmed hostility, and for the years past some of the most generous of his supporters were of those who, in the spring of 1876, had been among the new rector's foemen. Under Canon Hodson's reign over Lisburn parish, the number of pupils attending the cathedral school had largely increased. Some time ago Sir Richard Wallace purchased, at a cost of £700, a valuable site, situate in the Castle Street of that town, on which he erected schools for the parish church, in addition to which the respected baronet gave an exceedingly handsome subscription towards the cost of the erection. A very picturesque plan for the proposed building had been adopted, and all the natural enthusiasm of the late rector had been aroused on the carrying out of that project. But although Canon Hodson has left the scene of his labours-sacred and secular-before one brick of the school building has been laid, we may be permitted to hope that, in honour of his memory, the good work will be finished in the style which seemed to him so worthy as a training school for the future worshippers of the Lisburn Cathedral.

HOGG AND BOLTON
CATHEDRAL 12 AND 13 AND FRIENDS' BURYING GROUND

The Hogg families of the Cathedral and Friends' Burying Ground descend from a **William Hogg** who settled in the Lisburn area at the end of the 17th century. William's son, also **William**, married **Abigail Higginbothom** and had at least three sons and a daughter. One of his sons, **Edward Hogg** (1722-1809) married **Rose O'Neill**, daughter of the **Rev. John O'Neill**, of Largy, in 1752. Edward and Rose Hogg had a family of at least two sons and two daughters. All these four children married, but only two of them had families. These were daughter, **Abigail** (1757-1846), who married **John Bolton** of "The Island", Co. Wexford, and son, **William** (1754-1824), who married **Mary Dickey** of Dunmore, Co. Antrim, on 31st December 1783. The other son, **James**, (1756-1847), a linen merchant, married, **Mary**, daughter of **Jacob Hancock Jun.**, on 3rd October 1822, [see Hancock page 229]. She died 13th June 1828. James and Mary are buried in Friends' Burying Ground, Railway Street. The other daughter, **Mary** (1764-1856), married **John Barnett**.

Abigail and John Bolton had a family of at least three sons and two daughters. Two of the sons, **Edward Hogg Bolton** and **Captain James Bolton**, and one daughter, **Dorothea**, are buried with their mother, Abigail, and grandparents, Edward and Rose, in Cathedral No. 12. The other daughter, **Sophia Matilda Bolton**, married **William Fulton** on 27th November 1856, and is buried in the Fulton grave [see Cathedral No. 71 and Fulton page 221], along with her husband.

James Bolton joined the Royal Navy when he was fourteen. He retired in 1830 and eventually came to live with his uncle, James Hogg (1756-1847), the linen merchant, in Castle Street, Lisburn. When his uncle died James Bolton inherited his property. Before and after his uncle's death James Bolton was generous with his gifts to help others. In 1842 he obtained a plot of land on the Hillhall Road from the Marquis of Hertford. Here he had a school erected, which was known locally as "Bolton's School". He contributed to the expenses for the furniture, equipment and salaries of the teachers. When Captain Bolton died the Hertford Estate Office took over the building and placed it under the National Board of Education in 1870. It then became Largymore National School. Captain Bolton was connected with Christ Church, Lisburn, and there is a memorial to him there.

Abigail Bolton's brother, William Hogg (1754-1824), and his wife, Mary Dickey, had two sons and four daughters. The eldest son was **Sir James Weir Hogg**, born on 7th September 1790. He was in

Descendants of William Hogg

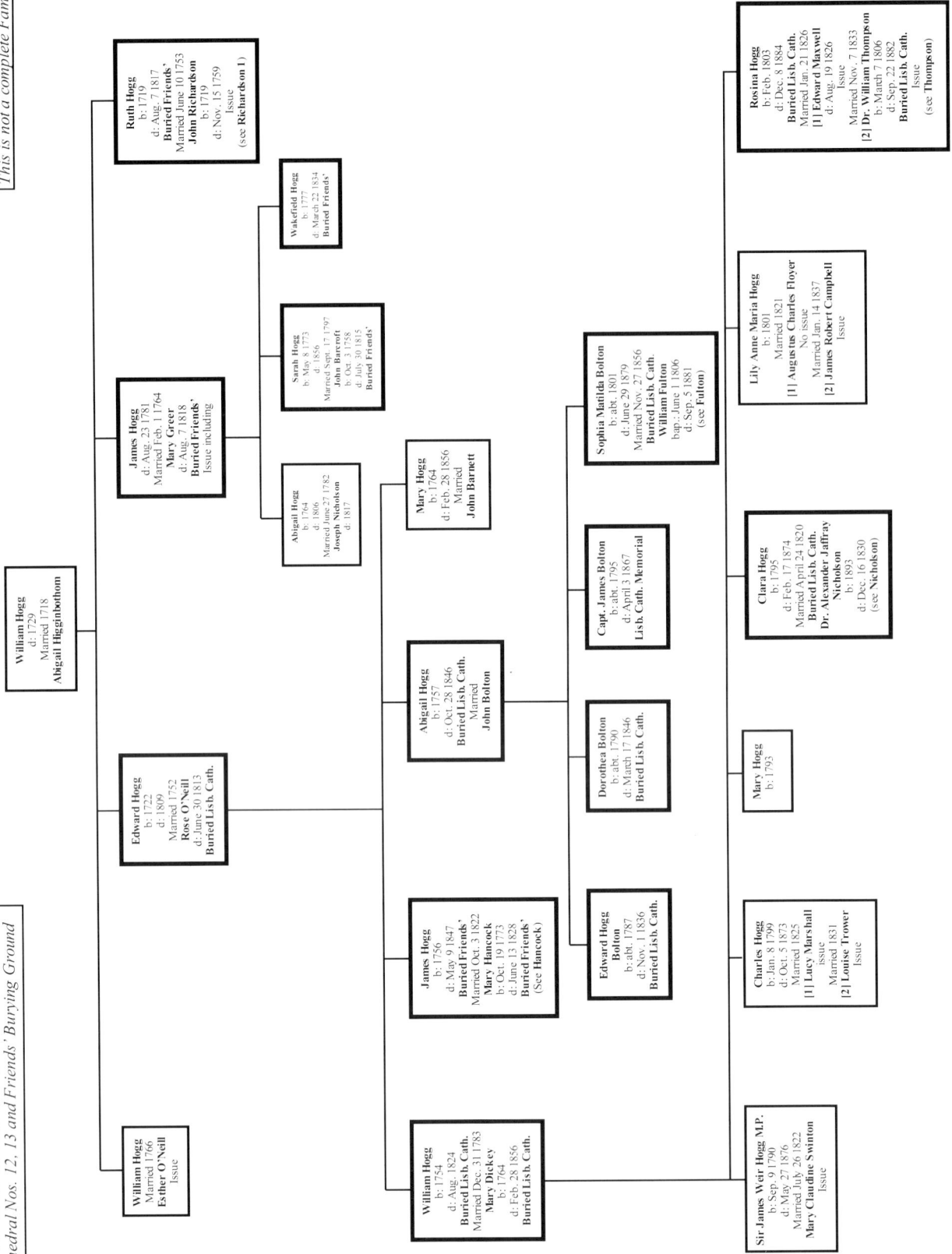

William Hogg
d: 1729
Married 1718
Abigail Higginbothom

William Hogg
Married 1766
Esther O'Neill
Issue

Edward Hogg
b: 1722
d: 1809
Married 1752
Rose O'Neill
d: June 30 1813
Buried Lish. Cath.

Ruth Hogg
b: 1719
d: Aug. 7 1817
Buried Friends'
Married June 10 1753
John Richardson
b: 1719
d: Nov. 15 1759
Issue
(see **Richardson 1**)

James Hogg
d: Feb. 23 1781
Married Feb. 1 1764
Mary Greer
d: Aug. 7 1818
Buried Friends'
Issue including

Wakefield Hogg
b: 1777
d: March 22 1834
Buried Friends'

Sarah Hogg
b: May 8 1773
d: 1856
Married Sept. 17 1797
John Barcroft
b: Oct. 3 1758
d: July 30 1815
Buried Friends'

Abigail Hogg
b: 1764
d: 1806
Married June 27 1782
Joseph Nicholson
d: 1817

Mary Hogg
b: 1764
d: Feb. 28 1856
Married
John Barnett

James Hogg
b: 1756
d: May 9 1847
Buried Lish. Cath.
Married Oct. 3 1822
Mary Hancock
b: Oct. 19 1773
d: June 13 1828
Buried Friends'
(See **Hancock**)

Abigail Hogg
b: 1757
d: Oct. 28 1846
Buried Lish. Cath.
Married
John Bolton

Edward Hogg
Bolton
b: abt. 1787
d: Nov. 1 1836
Buried Lish. Cath.

Dorothea Bolton
b: abt. 1790
d: March 17 1846
Buried Lish. Cath.

Capt. James Bolton
b: abt. 1795
d: April 3 1867
Lish. Cath. Memorial

Sophia Matilda Bolton
b: abt. 1801
d: June 29 1879
Married Nov. 27 1856
Buried Lish. Cath.
William Fulton
bap.: June 1 1806
d: Sep. 5 1881
(see **Fulton**)

William Hogg
b: 1754
d: Aug. 1824
Buried Lish. Cath.
Married Dec. 31 1783
Mary Dickey
b: 1764
d: Feb. 28 1856
Buried Lish. Cath.

Mary Hogg
b: 1793

Charles Hogg
b: Jan. 8 1799
d: Oct. 5 1873
Buried Lish. Cath.
Married 1825
[1] **Lucy Marshall**
issue
Married 1831
[2] **Louise Trower**
Issue

Clara Hogg
b: 1795
d: Feb. 17 1874
Married April 24 1820
Buried Lish. Cath.
Dr. Alexander Jaffray
Nicholson
b: 1893
d: Dec. 16 1830
(see **Nicholson**)

Lily Anne Maria Hogg
b: 1801
Married 1821
[1] **Augustus Charles Floyer**
No issue
Married Jan. 14 1837
[2] **James Robert Campbell**
Issue

Rosina Hogg
b: Feb. 1803
d: Dec. 8 1884
Buried Lish. Cath.
Married Jan. 21 1826
[1] **Edward Maxwell**
d: Aug. 19 1826
Issue
Married Nov. 7 1833
[2] **Dr. William Thompson**
b: March 7 1806
d: Sep. 22 1882
Buried Lish. Cath.
(see **Thompson**)

Sir James Weir Hogg M.P.
b: Sep. 9 1790
d: May 27 1876
Married July 26 1822
Mary Claudine Swinton
Issue

240

the Civil Service of the Honourable East India Company as Barrister-at-law in the Bengal Bar. He became Registrar and Judge of the Supreme Court of Calcutta. He returned to England in 1833 and was M.P. for Beverley 1834-47 and Honiton 1847-57. He was elected a Director of the East India Company in 1839 and Chairman in 1846. He was created a Baronet on 20th July 1846. He married twice and had seven sons and seven daughters. His eldest son, **James Macnaghten Hogg** (1823-90), was created 1st Baron Magheramorne in 1887, and was M.P. for Bath 1865-68, Truro 1871-85 and Hornsey, Middlesex, 1885-87. Sir James Weir Hogg's youngest son, **Quintin** (1845-1903), was the father of **Douglas McGarel Hogg,** who was created 1st Viscount Hailsham. His son was **Quintin McGarel Hogg** (1907-2001), who was elected M.P. for Oxford city in 1938 and was Lord High Chancellor from 1970-1983.

Sir James Weir Hogg's sisters were **Mary** (born 1793), who didn't marry, **Clara** (1795-1874) who married **Dr. Alexander Jaffray Nicholson** in 1820 [see Nicholson page 254], **Lily Anna Maria** (1801) who married firstly, in 1821, **Augustus Charles Floyer** of the Bengal Civil Service and secondly **James Robert Campbell**, and **Rosina** (1803-1884), who married firstly, in 1826, **Edward Maxwell**, of the Bengal Civil Service, and then secondly, in 1833, **Dr. William Thompson** of Lisburn [see Thompson page 274]. Sir James Weir Hogg's brother was **Charles** (1799-1873) who was also a lawyer and in commerce in India and China. He also married twice. His wives were **Lucy Marshall** and **Louise Trower**.

James Hogg (d.1781) was the brother of Edward Hogg (1722-1809). On 1st February 1764 James married **Mary Greer**. They were Quakers and had a family of six sons and seven daughters. Some of the family died young. James Hogg was buried at Magaberry, Co. Antrim, but his wife, Mary, his son, **Wakefield**, and his son-in-law, **John Barcroft** are all buried in Railway Street. Edward Hogg's other brother, **William**, married **Esther,** daughter of Rev. John O'Neill, in 1766, and had a family. Edward's sister, **Ruth**, married **John Richardson** [see Richardson page 258], in 1753, and they are buried in Railway Street.

NEWS LETTER
FRIDAY APRIL 5 1867

DEATH OF CAPTAIN BOLTON R.N.

The announcement of the death of Captain Bolton, which took place at his residence in Lisburn on Wednesday morning will be read with extreme regret. The lamented gentleman, who was widely known and greatly esteemed in the North of Ireland, was an uncompromising supporter of our Protestant institutions, and was remarkable for his kindness of heart, as well as for his liberal support of every philanthropic and religious object. The deceased entered the Royal Navy when only fourteen years of age, and after having been present at numerous engagements, he retired on half-pay about thirty years ago. Captain Bolton lived in Armagh for some time, and while there he devoted much of his leisure to the performance of works of benevolence. He afterwards resided with his uncle, the late Mr. James Hogg, of Lisburn, and at that gentleman's death he inherited considerable property, which he disbursed with a generous hand. The poor and the friendless have lost a real friend by the death of the lamented Captain, who always distributed his wealth without regard to denominational prejudices. In his own unostentatious way he did much good, and his name will long be gratefully remembered in the neighbourhood of Lisburn.

JEFFERSON

CATHEDRAL 35 AND 36

There are two headstones, close to each other, for the Jefferson family. The Jefferson name appears in the Lisburn Cathedral records from 1683. They first lived in the Maze area and then a branch of the family, headed by **Ralph Jefferson**, move to the Derriaghy area. Ralph had a large family of sons and one of these was **John**. John Jefferson, of Aughnahoe, and his wife, **Anne Jane Belshaw**, had a family of at least five sons. Four of these sons were **Robert**, **Richard**, **John** and **Redmond**. Richard and John set up a grocery and fancy delf business and Redmond also joined them in this concern, later becoming the sole owner. The shop in Bow Street became well known as Redmond Jeffersons. In an 1852 street directory the shop was described as a grocer, leather, hardware and timber merchants. Later it expanded and concentrated on the hardware side of the business. It was in existence in Bow Street until the 1980's. John Jefferson, his wife, Anne Jane, and one son, Robert, are buried in Cathedral No. 36.

John's son, Redmond Jefferson, married **Eliza McCall** on 5th May 1841 [see THG Vol. 1 McCall page 160], and had at least two sons, **Redmond** and **John**, and a daughter who married **John McKee**. There were four children who died young. Members of this family are buried in Cathedral No. 35.

There is also a **John Jefferson**, woollen draper, who married **Anne Jane Neely**, [see Neely page 253], buried in the Neely grave (Cathedral No. 66) who may be John's son.

LISBURN STANDARD
SATURDAY FEBRUARY 6TH 1892

THE LATE MR. REDMOND JEFFERSON

For some years past one after another of the old commercialists of this town have been joining the majority, and on Saturday last he who may have been called Father of the local traders died at his residence, Massereene Villa. The deceased was the youngest of five brothers. His father, Mr. John Jefferson, was a large landholder in the Aughnahoe district of the Hertford Estate, and also carried on the burning of lime very extensively. In 1834 his brothers, Richard and John, commenced the grocery and fancy delf business in the concern, opposite Market Street, which for many years past has been occupied by Dr. Ward as a branch of his Medical Hall. Some years afterwards the brothers purchased from Mr. James N. Richardson the premises in Bow Street, and removed their business there, which they extended by the timber, hardware, and iron trades. The late Mr. Redmond Jefferson had become assistant in the concern, and ultimately succeeded as proprietor. For a considerable period he devoted his entire attention to the details of commerce, and very successful were his energetic abilities displayed in every department. It was not, however, until matters outside mere business affairs began to claim his attention that the subject of this obituary notice put forth those mental powers which in time gave him great influence as a leader in politics. In the campaign for electoral freedom in November, 1852, he exercised a powerful influence, and his speeches had a great effect in giving the victory on that occasion to the Independent party. He possessed the peculiar power of adapting his language to the audience he addressed, and that never failed in being effective. In more recent times, the illness under which he suffered caused him to retire from the active duties of mercantile life. These he gave over to his son, and the once political feeling in public affairs, cooled down into the utmost quietude on all subjects. As an effective member of the Town Board, and a very influential administrator in the Select Vestry of the New Church, the deceased has left behind him a worthy record of social duties, ably and conscientiously performed.

THE FUNERAL

On Tuesday morning, at nine o'clock, the tolling of the cathedral bell reminded the townspeople that the mortal remains of one of Lisburn's worthiest merchants were about to be placed in the "narrow house" in the ancient graveyard; and at half-past nine a large number of the principal inhabitants had assembled at Massereene Villa, the late residence of the deceased. Rev. A.J. Moore having conducted a short service in the house, the coffin-of solid oak, richly mounted, and covered with beautiful wreaths-was carried for some distance, and then placed in the hearse. The chief mourners were:- Mr. Redmond Jefferson, son; Mr. John McKee, son-in-law; Messrs. James and Edmund McKee, grandsons; and Dr. James G. Jefferson, nephew. The general cortege was one of the most respectful and at the same time representative seen in Lisburn for many years. Along the route almost every shop had shutters up, and the blinds were drawn in many private residences houses as a mark of respect for the deceased. At the entrance to the grounds of the Cathedral, Rev. A.J. Moore met those who were bearing the coffin, and slowly repeated the appointed texts. The coffin was carried into the cathedral by near relatives, and placed on tressels (sic).

JOHNSON SMYTH

CATHEDRAL 67, 18 AND MEMORIALS

There are two graves for the Johnson Smyth family in the Graveyard. One is a box tomb at the front door of the Cathedral, which is damaged and has parts of the inscription becoming illegible, the other, flat sandstone, set in cement, below the wall memorial stone to the Stewarts. Inside the Cathedral there are four memorials.

The Johnson Smyth family was originally Johnson, and added the Smyth surname after the death of their relative, **Edward Smyth**. It is believed that Edward's great grandfather was **Ralph Smyth** of Ballymacash, who died at the Battle of the Boyne in 1690. Although Edward had several brothers and sisters it would appear that only three sisters survived to adulthood. Edward Smyth appears to have been educated in Lisburn by a Mr. Clarke and to have graduated from Trinity College, Dublin, in 1721, with a degree in law. He was M.P. for Lisburn from 1743 until 1760. During his life he held many other posts. He was twice High Sheriff of Antrim, in 1747 and 1756, Commissioner for the Militia in 1756, for Antrim and Down, held the office of Attorney at Law for the Diocese of Connor and was register for schools for the dioceses of Down and Connor.

He had one daughter, **Anne**, who, in 1765, married **James Carroll** of Aghagallon. Edward died 2nd February 1788 and his will of 29th February 1787 survives in the Registry of Deeds, Dublin. In his will he left property and money to his nephews and sisters and he stated that he wanted his three Johnson nephews to take the additional surname of Smyth. These three Johnson nephews were **Roger**, **Lieutenant Matthew** and **Rev. Philip Johnson**, children of Edward Smyth's sister, **Mary**, and her husband, the **Rev. Thomas Johnson**, who was curate of Lisburn, master of the Latin School 1731-1739, and vicar of Magheragall 1742-1757. The Johnson and Johnson Smyth family produced several clergymen, military men, a Member of Parliament, Justices of the Peace, a Deputy Lieutenant and a solicitor. Edward's other sisters were **Ann** (born 1713) who married **Edward Jones** and **Frances** (born 1714) who married **Edward Obre**.

Roger Johnson Smyth (1744-1816) appears to have lived in Halifax, Nova Scotia, at sometime and, according to her death notice, his wife was an American. Two of his brothers were **Rev. Edward Johnson**, vicar of Magheragall, who died in 1765, and Rev. Philip Johnson, curate of Lisburn and vicar of Derriaghy 1772-1823. Rev. Philip married **Frances Maria Smyth** of Drumcree, Co. Westmeath, (a distant cousin). His sister, **Henrietta**, married **Rev. Henry Reynett**, vicar of Magheragall 1765-1777 and Glenavy 1777-1782. Roger's third brother, Matthew, was Lieutenant Colonel of His Majesty's 69th Regiment of Foot and lived in Cavendish Square in London at the time of his death. He also appears to have been a Gentleman Usher to His Majesty's Privy Chamber at St. James's. That would probably have been to King George III.

Roger Johnson Smyth had at least two sons and at least four daughters. A daughter, **Anne**, married **Lieutenant Edward Heron** and had at least three daughters, [see Heron Cathedral No.125 and page 233]. Another daughter, **Mary**, married **Lt. Stephen Aveling**, of the 45th Regiment of Foot, about October 1799, but she was dead by 1816. A third daughter, **Lydia**, was married to **John Johnson**.

Descendants of John Johnson

This is not a complete Family Tree.

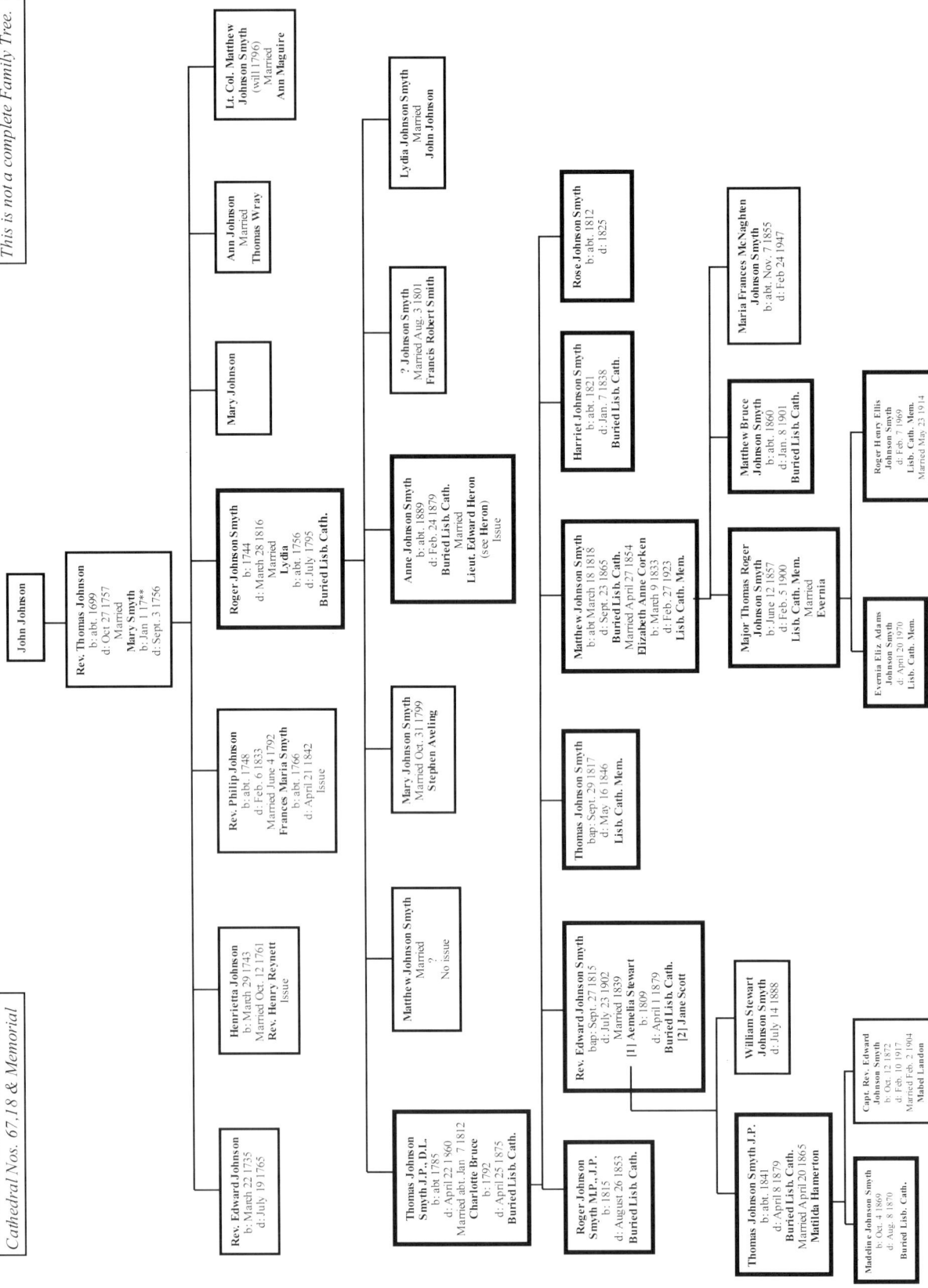

Cathedral Nos. 67, 18 & Memorial

John Johnson

Rev. Thomas Johnson
b: abt. 1699
d: Oct 27 1757
Married
Mary Smyth
b: Jan 1 17**
d: Sept. 3 1756

Lt. Col. Matthew Johnson Smyth
(will 1796)
Married
Ann Maguire

Ann Johnson
Married
Thomas Wray

Mary Johnson

Roger Johnson Smyth
b: 1744
d: March 28 1816
Married
Lydia
b: abt. 1756
d: July 1795
Buried Lish. Cath.

Rev. Philip Johnson
b: abt. 1748
d: Feb. 6 1833
Married June 4 1792
Frances Maria Smyth
b: abt. 1766
d: April 21 1842
Issue

Henrietta Johnson
b: March 29 1743
Married Oct. 12 1761
Rev. Henry Reynett
Issue

Rev. Edward Johnson
b: March 22 1735
d: July 19 1765

Lydia Johnson Smyth
Married
John Johnson

? Johnson Smyth
Married Aug. 3 1801
Francis Robert Smith

Anne Johnson Smyth
b: abt. 1889
d: Feb. 24 1879
Buried Lish. Cath.
Married
Lieut. Edward Heron
(see Heron)
Issue

Mary Johnson Smyth
Married Oct. 31 1799
Stephen Aveling

Matthew Johnson Smyth
Married
?
No issue

Thomas Johnson Smyth J.P., D.L.
b: abt 1785
d: April 22 1860
Married abt. Jan 1 1812
Charlotte Bruce
b: 1792
d: April 25 1875
Buried Lish. Cath.

Rose Johnson Smyth
b: abt. 1812
d: 1825

Harriet Johnson Smyth
b: abt. 1821
d: Jan. 7 1838
Buried Lish. Cath.

Matthew Johnson Smyth
b: abt March 18 1818
d: Sept. 23 1865
Buried Lish. Cath.
Married April 27 1854
Elizabeth Anne Corken
b: March 9 1833
d: Feb. 27 1923
Lish. Cath. Mem.

Thomas Johnson Smyth
bap: Sept. 29 1817
d: May 16 1846
Lish. Cath. Mem.

Rev. Edward Johnson Smyth
bap: Sept. 27 1815
d: July 23 1902
Married 1839
[1] **Aemelia Stewart**
b: 1809
d: April 1 1879
Buried Lish. Cath.
[2] **Jane Scott**

Roger Johnson Smyth M.P., J.P.
b: 1815
d: August 26 1853
Buried Lish. Cath.

William Stewart Johnson Smyth
d: July 14 1888

Thomas Johnson Smyth J.P.
b: abt. 1841
d: April 8 1879
Buried Lish. Cath.
Married April 20 1865
Matilda Hamerton

Maria Frances McNaghten Johnson Smyth
b: abt. Nov. 7 1855
d: Feb 24 1947

Matthew Bruce Johnson Smyth
b: abt. 1860
d: Jan. 8 1901
Buried Lish. Cath.

Major Thomas Roger Johnson Smyth
b: June 12 1857
d: Feb. 5 1900
Lish. Cath. Mem.
Married
Evernia

Roger Henry Ellis Johnson Smyth
d: Feb. 7 1969
Lish. Cath. Mem.
Married May 23 1914

Evernia Eliz Adams Johnson Smyth
d: April 20 1970
Lish. Cath. Mem.

Capt. Rev. Edward Johnson Smyth
b: Oct. 12 1872
d: Feb. 10 1917
Married Feb. 2 1904
Mabel Landon

Madeline Johnson Smyth
b: Oct. 4 1869
d: Aug. 8 1870
Buried Lish. Cath.

On the 3rd August 1801 a **Miss Johnson Smyth**, daughter of Roger Johnson Smyth Esq., married **Mr. Francis Robert Smith**.

The elder son, **Thomas**, was a Deputy Lieutenant for Co. Down and a J.P. He married **Charlotte Bruce** of Kilroot, Co. Antrim, and had a least four sons and two daughters, most of whom are mentioned on the box tomb. His eldest son, **Roger**, was elected M.P. for Lisburn in December 1852. This was in the days before secret ballots, and you had to publicly declare your preference. It had been the policy of the Agent of the Hertford Estate to keep the tenants so dependent that they had either the choice of voting for the Hertford nominated candidate, or losing their farm or holding. By 1852 some of the electors of Lisburn decided they wanted to secure the independence of the borough. Lord Hertford's nomination was John Inglis, the Lord Advocate of Scotland, who had just been defeated at Orkney. The independent electors in Lisburn decided to nominate Roger Johnson Smyth of Castle Street. He was proposed by Jonathan Joseph Richardson, of The Island, and seconded by Redmond Jefferson. Mr. Inglis was proposed by Jonathan Richardson, of Ingram, and seconded by James Coulson. The political opinions of the two candidates were similar, both Conservatives, and in the voting Johnson Smyth had 99 votes and Inglis 87, so Johnson Smyth won by a majority of 12. After the victory a banquet was held in the Queen's Arms Hotel on December 29th 1852, and about 160 sat down to dinner. Unfortunately Roger Johnson Smyth was only to be M.P. for a short time as he died suddenly in August 1853, aged 39 years. In October 1853 Jonathan Joseph Richardson was elected as his successor [see Richardson page 258].

Another son of Thomas Johnson Smyth was **Rev. Edward Johnson Smyth**, vicar of Glenavy 1852-1885. He married **Aemelia Stewart**, daughter of **Dr. William Stewart** [see Stewart Cathedral No. 19 and page 269]. They had two sons, **Thomas**, who was a J.P. and lived at Goremont, Glenavy, Co. Antrim, and **William Stewart**, who died in Kansas, U.S.A. Thomas married **Matilda (Maud) Hamerton**. They had a son, **Capt. Rev. Edward**, and a daughter, **Madeline**, who died young. Edward was killed in the First World War and is buried at St. Sever Cemetery, Rouen, France.

A third son of Thomas (1785-1860), also named **Thomas**, has a memorial erected to his memory inside the Cathedral. He had entered the Royal Navy in November 1829. He was made Lieutenant in 1842 and was appointed to the Frigate "Juno" November 1845, and the ship was "fitting" for the Pacific, where he died off California in May 1846.

A fourth son, **Matthew**, was a solicitor. He married **Elizabeth Anne Corken**, daughter of **Rev. John Corken,** Vicar of Aghalee 1830-1834, and **Maria Cupples**, daughter of **Snowden Cupples**, [see Cupples Cathedral No. 3 and page 211]. They had at least two sons and a daughter. The eldest son, **Thomas Roger**, became Major in the 68th Regt. Durham Light Infantry, and died at Vaal Kranz, Natal, S. Africa, during the Boer War. As well as being remembered on the box tomb (Cathedral No. 67), he is also remembered on a memorial inside the Cathedral. At the time of his death a poem specially written about him was published in the Lisburn Standard. The younger son was **Matthew Bruce**, a solicitor.

Major Thomas Roger Johnson Smyth had a son and daughter, **Roger Henry Ellis** and **Evernia Elizabeth Adams**, and although they are mentioned on memorials in Lisburn Cathedral, they are actually buried in Derriaghy Parish Church Graveyard. Some Johnson and Johnson Smyth family members are buried at Magheragall, Co. Antrim.

[P.R.O.N.I. T/1035/3]

MATEER

CATHEDRAL 139

The flat memorial stone to **Joseph Mateer** and his wife **Isabella** gives no indication that Joseph Mateer was the toll gate keeper of the turnpike between Belfast and Hillsborough. In the Cathedral records there is a marriage of Joseph Mateer and Isabella **Blackburn** on 1ˢᵗ January 1828. When Isabella Mateer died in 1849 she was living at the Malone Turnpike in Bradbury Place, Belfast. This quaint building was a landmark from about 1819, when the Lisburn Road in Belfast was opened, until the house was demolished in 1964. When Queen Victoria visited Belfast in 1849 she passed through the Malone Turnpike gate on her way to visit Queen's College. When Joseph died in 1870 the Mateers were living at Hertford Place, Belfast. **John Mateer**, of Hertford Place, died 17ᵗʰ November 1894 aged 81. His burial is recorded in the Cathedral records, but his name is not recorded on a stone. In his will John mentions his nephews **William Mateer**, and **John**, **William** and **Joseph Culbert**.

The tolls collected at the turnpike gates went towards the upkeep of the roads. In the Ordnance Survey Memoirs of 1837 the Blackburn family is also mentioned as being connected with the turnpike roads, [see Blackburn page 200]. The tolls were abolished in 1857.

BELFAST NEWS LETTER
TUESDAY NOVEMBER 1 1870

DEATH OF AN OLD PUBLIC OFFICER. - Amongst our obituary notices this morning will be found recorded the death of an old and much respected citizen, who for a long term of years occupied a position which brought him into close contact with a very considerable number of inhabitants of this town and a wide extent of the surrounding country. We refer to the demise of Mr. Joseph Mateer, which occurred yesterday morning, at an early hour, at his residence, 125 Hertford Place, Lisburn Road, having attained the ripe age of seventy-nine years. Deceased was lessee for a period of about a quarter of a century of the turnpikes between Belfast and Hillsborough; which he held under the Commissioners at the time of the abolition of the Trust, about twelve years ago; he also filled the office of Postmaster for the Malone sub district for several years - in both of which capacities he succeeded in winning the esteem and respect of all with whom he had intercourse.

McKEE

CATHEDRAL 138

The stone for this McKee family has been badly damaged and the inscription no longer remains. **George McKee** was the Master of the Lisburn Union Workhouse and his wife, **Eliza**, was the Matron. Lisburn Union Workhouse was opened 11ᵗʰ February 1841. The first master was Thomas Carleton. By April 1841 he was ill, and he was replaced, in May 1841, by Sergt. George McKee of the constabulary. In March 1842 George McKee made a request for his wife and four children to be allowed to live with him in the workhouse. The McKee family later lived in 24 Market Square, Lisburn and the **Misses J. & H. McKee** had a shop described as a Drapers in 1888 and a Haberdasher in 1897. In 1859 an **Eliza McKee**, second daughter of George McKee, married a **John Stevenson**.

BANNER OF ULSTER
TUESDAY OCTOBER 8 1861

DEATH OF MR. Mᶜ KEE OF THE LISBURN WORKHOUSE. – The very unexpected death of this respected official has been greatly regretted by those who knew his worth. About twenty years ago he was appointed to the responsible situation of Master in the Union Workhouse at Lisburn, and the remarkable efficiency shown by him in all departments of the establishment gave him a high position in the opinion of the Guardians. So much as he respected by them that he was permitted to act in many cases just as he pleased, the members of the Board-room feeling well assured that he would do all that was possible to be done in each case, and on the best terms for the union at large. Mr. McKee had been in his usual good health until within a few days of his death, when he caught fever, and the

(Courtesy of the Irish Linen Centre & Lisburn Museum)
LISBURN UNION WORKHOUSE

disease rapidly assuming a dangerous type, he lingered till the morning of the 6th, when his spirit passed away without the slightest evidence of struggle. Thirty years ago the deceased joined the Methodist Society, and to the day of his death he continued in connection with that body. As a public man Mr. McKee had few equals: he was an upright citizen of the world, and performed his duties in his official capacity with the zeal of a true Christian.

**LISBURN STANDARD
SATURDAY MARCH 17 1900**

DEATH OF MISS McKEE

During the past week the hand of death has fallen heavily upon the community of Lisburn and the neighbourhood, and the loss of none will be more keenly felt than that of Miss McKee, of Market Square, who died on Tuesday last. The deceased lady had been ailing for some time past, but nevertheless the blow occasioned by her demise is deeply felt by her many relatives and a large circle of friends. She was a devout Christian lady, and a faithful member and supporter of the Methodist cause in the town, worshipping at Seymour Street Church. As a business woman she was of upright character, and successful in her dealings. To all who knew her she was a true, kind-hearted friend, and her death leaves a vacant place in the hearts of many. The interment of her mortal remains took place at the Cathedral Church-yard on Thursday morning, the funeral being largely attended. At the graveside a very impressive service was conducted by the Revs. Robert Jamison, R.E. Sherwood (Belfast), and Joseph Mathers.
[P.R.O.N.I. BG/19/A]

MONRO

Many people will have heard of **Henry Monro**, or **Munro**, the United Irishman who was hanged in Market Square, Lisburn, in 1798. The location of his grave has never been established, although it is likely to have been an unmarked grave in the Cathedral Graveyard. The burial records for that period do not survive. Henry Monro was born in Lisburn about 1758, the son of a Presbyterian father and a Church of Ireland mother. He attended services in Lisburn Cathedral, and would have been educated in Lisburn. Although he served his apprenticeship with a woollen draper he also learned about the linen business and later had a draper's shop in Market Square, where he dealt in linen, purchasing brown linen webs for two of the area's leading bleachers, William McCance and John Hancock [see Hancock page 229]. He would have been well known in the north of Ireland, as he would have attended the local linen markets. In 1795 Henry married **Margaret Johnston**, the fourth daughter of **Robert Johnston**, a bleacher from Seymour Hill, Dunmurry. Henry Monro also had a sister called **Margaret**.

In 1778, because of fear of an invasion by the French, companies of Volunteers were raised in Ireland. There were eight companies formed in the Lisburn area. Henry Monro joined the Lisburn Volunteers. In October 1782 the Lisburn and Lambeg Volunteers were reviewed in Lisburn, and this event was recorded in a painting by John Carey done about 1890. The government in Dublin had the old Volunteers disbanded 11th March 1793.

The Society of United Irishmen had been formed in Belfast in 1791, and several Lisburn men were eventually to join this organisation, including Napper Tandy and Charles and Bartholomew Teeling. Henry Monro joined in 1795. It was their intention to rebel against the Dublin Authorities and the King and Constitution. After several months of unrest the rebellion finally started in early June 1798 when there were uprisings in the north of Ireland. These were in Antrim on the 7th and Saintfield on the 9th. As the insurgents in Down were without a leader, Monro was appointed the rebel general. The Battle of Ballynahinch was fought on Tuesday and Wednesday, the 12th and 13th of June, and the rebels were defeated. The rebels, including Monro, fled for their lives. Monro found refuge somewhere near Dromara, with a farmer called William Holmes, who promptly, perhaps because he feared for his life, revealed Monro's hiding place to the Yeomanry. On the 14th June Monro was captured and taken to Dromore, and then to Lisburn, where he was imprisoned in Castle Street. Here he was given a clean set of clothes by George Whitla, [see Whitla page 275], and had meals provided by Rev. Snowden Cupples, [see Cupples page 211].

At a Court-martial on Saturday 16th June he was charged with treason and rebellion. Three witnesses spoke against him. They were Charles Kinnon, Robert Fullerton and John Johnston. Monro admitted his guilt and so he was found guilty and sentenced to death, the hanging to be at four o'clock that day.

A temporary gallows was set up in Market Square, close to Monro's home. On his way to the Square he received his last communion from the Rev. Cupples. Before being hanged, Henry Monro sent for his shop books and settled some of his accounts. The last one to be settled was a dispute he had had with Poyntz Stewart, Captain of the Derriaghy Yeomanry [see Stewart page 269]. After a few prayers he started up the ladder, but two rungs broke, and he had to ascend the ladder again. His last words are said to be "Tell my country I deserved better of her." About a couple of hours after his death his body was taken down and his head was cut off and displayed on a pike at one corner of the Market House. Heads of three other men who had been executed were also displayed at the other three corners of the Market House. They were Richard Vincent, George Crabbe and Tom Armstrong.

Henry's wife, Margaret, lived until 1840 and is believed to be buried in Derriaghy graveyard. His mother had a shop in Bow Lane and lived until 1815.

MOORE

CATHEDRAL MEMORIAL

Jane Deborah Moore was the eldest daughter of **Hugh Moore**, Eglantine and Mount Panther, Dundrum, Co. Down, and his wife, **Priscilla Cecilia**. Her brother was the **Rev. John Robert Moore**, of Rowallen House, Saintfield, Co. Down, and her sister was **Countess Annesley**. Countess Annesley's name was also **Priscilla Cecilia** and when she married in 1828 she became the second wife of the 3rd Earl of Annesley. Her baptism is recorded in the Cathedral records on 1st September 1808.

Rosevale House, Moira Road, Lisburn, was founded by Miss Moore of Warren Cottage, Lisburn, in 1862. It was a "Home of Rescue for Women." It had at first been supported by voluntary contributions, but by 1906 was almost self-supporting as a laundry.

BELFAST NEWS LETTER
TUESDAY DECEMBER 8 1863

DEATH OF MISS MOORE:-We deeply regret to announce the death of Miss Moore, of Warren Cottage, County Antrim, daughter of the late Hugh Moore, Esq., of Eglantine, County Down, and sister of the Countess Annesley. The name and exertions of Miss Moore were well known in connection with many religious and philanthropic objects. Her whole life was devoted to the work of practical benevolence, and it might be truly said of her that she never wearied of well doing. A few years ago Miss Moore succeeded in collecting funds sufficient for the erection of a church, parsonage, and school-house at Moyrus, in Connemara; and the sacred edifice now stands as an enduring monument of her labours in the centre of a large district previously unsupplied with any Protestant building for religious purposes. Her name is also known in connection with the "Home" for the reformation of females, an establishment in the neighbourhood of Lisburn. It was in returning from that establishment, which latterly claimed her unremitting care, that Miss Moore caught a cold, from the effects of which she died on Sunday afternoon, amid the regret of all who knew her. She was, in the best sense of the word, a Christian, and one of whom, it might truly be said, that "ever looking unto Jesus, and always abounding in the work of the Lord," her end was "perfect peace."

MOREWOOD

CATHEDRAL 86

The stone for Morewood has just the names of **Jane** and **George Morewood** and their year of death. Jane Morewood died 26th June 1820, aged 80 years. The Cathedral records do not record George Morewood's death in 1828. A George Morewood was churchwarden in 1789/80, and in 1824 George Morewood, Esq. was living in Castle Street, Lisburn. George and Jane Morewood had a son, **George Alexander,** baptised 30th January 1780 and a son, **Rev. James Morewood**, born in 1781. Rev. James was a perpetual curate of Lambeg from 1810-1826 and vicar of Dunluce, Bushmills, Co. Antrim, from 1826-1849. While at Lambeg he obtained a lease of 14 acres from Lord Hertford and built a rectory for Lambeg. He died 6th August 1849 and there is a tombstone and mural in Dunluce Church of Ireland. He married **Mary Mahallen** and they had three daughters and a son. **Mary** died 16th February 1838 and is buried in Lambeg Burying Ground. The daughters were **Henrietta Mary** (1805-1884), **Mary** (1808-1903) and **Jane** (born 1810). The son, **John**, was born in 1807 and only lived a few days. Jane married **Com. Edward Hervey R.N.** on 5th April 1836. Edward Hervey was the son of the **Rev. Edward Hervey** (1772-1848), rector of Coleraine, and his wife, **Rebecca Young**.

The will of **Henrietta Stewart**, of Lisburn, found in the Registry of Deeds, Dublin, which was proved 19th September 1807, mentions her brother-in-law, George Morewood, her sister, Jane, and her nephews, George Alexander and Rev. James Morewood.

MURRAY

CATHEDRAL 106

William Murray was baptised in Lisburn Cathedral on the 17th June 1804 and **Frances Charlotte** was baptised on the 4th July 1809. Both brother and sister, the children of **Richard** and **Jane Murray** of Lisnastrain, died of consumption. Frances Charlotte, who died on the 18th December 1835, had married **Isaac Sefton** on the 28th June 1832, and left two young children. The son, **William Sefton**, who was baptised May 1833, married **Sarah Celia Martin** in America. They are thought to have had at least six daughters and one son, who was named **William M. Sefton**. William Sefton became a colonel in the USA army and visited Lisburn at least five times. The Lisburn Standard of 23rd May 1896 records:-

> "Mr. Wm. M. Sefton, of the Adjutant General's Office, War Department, Washington, D.C., U.S. of America, is visiting his sister, Mrs. Alex. Mackenzie. This is the fifth visit Mr. Sefton has made to his native town, Lisburn. He is accompanied by his son Master Wm. M. Sefton. He still has the military bearing of the officer and soldier that characterised him on previous visits. Colonel Sefton is a prominent member of the Grand Army of the Republic, and has been Adjutant of the Department and is now Junior Vice-Commander of the "James A. Garfield Post". The post was named in honour and remembrance of President Garfield."

The daughter, **Jane Sefton**, who was baptised 31st May 1835, married **Alexander MacKenzie** on the 25th April 1885 at St. Anne's, Belfast, and was living at 4, Castle Street, Lisburn at the time of the 1901 census.

CATHEDRAL 103

The Musgrave memorial is the largest memorial in the Cathedral Graveyard and is surrounded by tall iron railings. On it there is not now a record of the names of those who are buried there. It is the memorial to **Dr. Samuel Musgrave** and his family. Dr. Musgrave, the son of **John Musgrave** of Saintfield (c1730-1808), married **Mary Riddel**, daughter of **William Riddel**, a Comber merchant, and his wife **Jane Hamilton**, who was daughter of **Robert Hamilton**, New Comber House. The Riddels are related to the Charley and Barbour families.

Dr. Samuel and Mary Musgrave had a family of three girls and nine boys. One child died young, the rest of the family had an average age at death of seventy. None of them married. For many years Dr. Samuel was a surgeon and apothecary in Lisburn, probably living in Market Square. It is believed that in the 1790's, because of his beliefs, he was held in custody in Dublin Castle for a short time.

All of Dr. Samuel's family were born in Lisburn and were baptised in First Lisburn Presbyterian Church, but, after the old doctor's death, the family had eventually moved to 26 Upper Arthur Street in Belfast, except for his son, **Dr. Samuel Musgrave**, who was the only member of the family to go into the medical profession. In 1839 he had returned to Lisburn where first of all he worked with Dr. William Thompson at the County Antrim Infirmary, and then, in 1841, was the junior practitioner of Lisburn in Market Square. He became medical officer of the Lisburn Workhouse in September 1867, lived in Castle Street and retired in 1891. He was also a magistrate. After his retirement he moved to live with the rest of his family in Drumglass House, Lisburn Road, Belfast. This house had been built by the Musgraves in 1854-56 and is now part of Victoria College, Belfast.

All the other sons went into business in Belfast, except for **William**, who was a barrister in Belfast and Dublin, where he died. **John**, **Robert** and **James** formed Musgrave Brothers, who were iron founders and engineers. Robert died in 1867. John had estates in Knockbrack and Carrick (Glencolumcille) Co. Donegal and was a J.P. and Deputy Lieutenant for Co. Donegal. James retired from the business and was elected a commissioner of the Belfast Harbour Board, a position he held for twenty-eight years, seventeen of them as chairman. During his time on the Harbour Board the port of Belfast was greatly developed and enlarged with a new deep-water channel being made and called the Musgrave Channel. He received a baronetcy in the New Year's Honour's List of 1897 and in 1901 he donated the Musgrave Chair of Pathology to Queen's College, Belfast.

SIR JAMES MUSGRAVE
(1823-1904)

The youngest two brothers, **Henry** and **Edgar**, about 1850, formed the firm of H & E Musgrave Ltd., Wholesale Tea and Sugar Merchants, which was situated at the corner of Ann Street and Musgrave Street, Belfast. Edgar was also a director of Messrs. Riddel, Ltd. Hardware Merchants and Manufacturing Iron Mongers, Donegall Place, and Messrs. John Riddel & Son, Ann Street, Belfast.

After the death of Edgar, Henry was the sole survivor of this Musgrave family and continued with the family tradition of generous donations to education and science in Belfast. He was elected an honorary Burgess of Belfast and Deputy Lieutenant of Belfast and Donegal. He donated £10,000 for the endowment of a Chair for the teaching of Russia, but this was later changed to Spanish. He contributed to the Queen's University's memorial for those who died in World War 1. His friends subscribed to a portrait of Henry that now hangs in the Great Hall at Queen's University, Belfast. Money left over from the donations for the painting was used for the "Musgrave" prizes for pathology. In 1920 Henry presented the grounds in Stockman's Lane, Belfast, now known as Musgrave Park, to the Belfast Corporation for the use of the people of Belfast. The Musgrave Park

This is not a complete Family Tree.

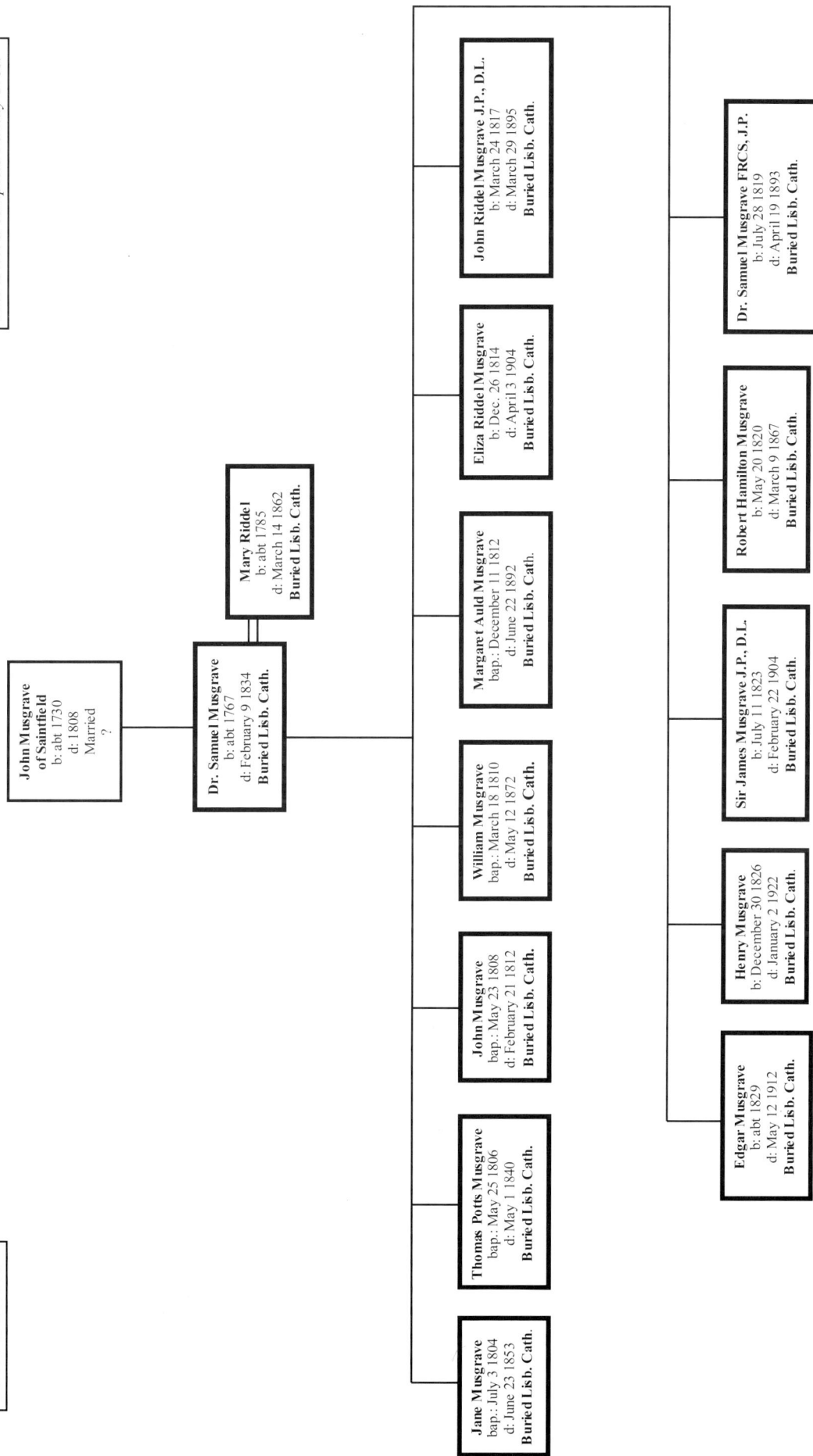

Cathedral No. 103

John Musgrave
of Saintfield
b: abt 1730
d: 1808
Married
?

Dr. Samuel Musgrave
b: abt 1767
d: February 9 1834
Buried Lisb. Cath.

Mary Riddel
b: abt 1785
d: March 14 1862
Buried Lisb. Cath.

Jane Musgrave
bap.: July 3 1804
d: June 23 1853
Buried Lisb. Cath.

Thomas Potts Musgrave
bap.: May 25 1806
d: May 1 1840
Buried Lisb. Cath.

John Musgrave
bap.: May 23 1808
d: February 21 1812
Buried Lisb. Cath.

William Musgrave
bap.: March 18 1810
d: May 12 1872
Buried Lisb. Cath.

Margaret Auld Musgrave
bap.: December 11 1812
d: June 22 1892
Buried Lisb. Cath.

Eliza Riddel Musgrave
b: Dec. 26 1814
d: April 3 1904
Buried Lisb. Cath.

John Riddel Musgrave J.P., D.L.
b: March 24 1817
d: March 29 1895
Buried Lisb. Cath.

Edgar Musgrave
b: abt 1829
d: May 12 1912
Buried Lisb. Cath.

Henry Musgrave
b: December 30 1826
d: January 2 1922
Buried Lisb. Cath.

Sir James Musgrave J.P., D.L.
b: July 11 1823
d: February 22 1904
Buried Lisb. Cath.

Robert Hamilton Musgrave
b: May 20 1820
d: March 9 1867
Buried Lisb. Cath.

Dr. Samuel Musgrave FRCS, J.P.
b: July 28 1819
d: April 19 1893
Buried Lisb. Cath.

251

Hospital was formerly the District National Model Agricultural School and the original building had been completed about 1859.

In 1907, with his brother, Edgar, Henry presented a very fine stained-glass window, depicting the Good Samaritan, to First Lisburn Presbyterian Church. This was in memory of their parents Dr. Samuel and Mary Musgrave. Perhaps one of his best-known gifts to Lisburn is the statue of Brigadier-General John Nicholson in Market Square, [see Nicholson page 254]. It had been Henry's desire to see a fitting memorial to John Nicholson erected in Lisburn, so Mr. F.W. Pomeroy R.A. was commissioned to do a sculpture. This took about two years to complete. Unfortunately, Henry did not live to see the statue officially unveiled, but his last visit was to see how the work was progressing. Henry died 2nd January 1922 and the statue was unveiled on 19th January. Henry had particularly asked for Sir Henry Wilson K.C.B., D.S.O. to perform the ceremony. The statue, in bronze, is nine foot and six inches in height, with two bas-relief bronze panels depicting incidents in the Indian Mutiny. The pedestal is of grey Aberdeen granite and the whole monument is twenty feet in height.

LISBURN STANDARD
SATURDAY APRIL 22 1893

DEATH OF DR. MUSGRAVE, J.P.

It is with extreme regret we to-day announce the death of Dr. Samuel Musgrave, so well known and so widely respected in Lisburn, which was his native place. The sad event took place on Wednesday morning at Drumglass House, the residence of his brother, Mr. James Musgrave, D.L. It was known to many in this town that Dr, Musgrave had been in failing health for some time past, but it was hoped that the distinguished physician might be spared for some years to come. The deceased was a son of the late Dr. Musgrave, whose professional advice was in much request in the town and neighbourhood. After a very successful collegiate course at the Glasgow University, and during which he obtained many honours as a medical student, he returned to Lisburn, and had two years' experience in surgical practice under Doctor Thompson at the County Infirmary. He then obtained all the necessary qualifications to commence practice, and in the autumn of 1841 Dr. Musgrave started as the junior practitioner of Lisburn in a house which has recently been added to the concern of Messrs. Geo. Duncan & Sons. The members of the profession then located in this town were Dr. Thompson, Dr. Wethered, Dr. Kelso, Dr. Hall, and Dr. Macdonald. Dr. Campbell commenced practice in October, 1842. Comparatively slow was Dr. Musgrave's progress for the first two years; still he went on his way. The geniality of his disposition and the hopeful spirit with which he entered on his professional duties gained for him many friends. The population of Lisburn was then little more than half of what it is at present, and the number of operatives engaged at the Hilden, the Island, and the Lisburn Mills did not exceed one for every four of the aggregate employed in later days. Throughout the whole course of his practice, for nearly half-a-century, Dr. Musgrave lived on the best terms with his professional brethren, and when a juvenile member came into the field he seemed to act with something like paternal care over him. This was the case especially when the late Dr. Sloan commenced practice in town, and very promising was this kind-hearted young gentleman's career while his health enabled him to attend an increasing demand on his vocation. Dr. Musgrave paid him marked attention, and had Dr. Sloan lived and enjoyed physical power equal to his professional ability, he would have made a high name for himself in Lisburn. After the death of Dr. Campbell, an exceedingly popular member of the profession, the position of medical officer of the Lisburn Workhouse was conferred on Dr. Musgrave. That was in September, 1867, and from that time until he resigned the office, about two years ago, he conducted his duties with great success, and always managed details greatly to the gratification of the Board of Guardians. As a magistrate, he upheld the dignity of the Bench, while he independently maintained his own. He had succeeded to a large practice before the death of Dr. Thompson, and, as senior medical man, he afterwards obtained a large proportion of the high-class practice of that eminent professionalist. His death has caused a universal feeling of regret in Lisburn, and neighbourhood, where, owing to his kindly disposition and generosity, a strong feeling of respect and affection for him exists. He had made hosts of attached friends for himself, not only among the families of which, for two generations, he was medical attendant, but in many other circles outside his professional range.

[P.R.O.N.I. D/1725]

NEELY

There are two gravestones to Neely families in the Cathedral Graveyard. It is not known if they are related to each other.

The box tomb, No. 66, is to the family of **Erskine Neely**, who was married October 23rd 1811 to **Sarah McCullough**. They had at least two daughters, **Anne Jane** and **Elizabeth**, and a son, **John Boyes**, born about 1818 and died March 29th 1841. Erskine Neely was a Pawnbroker in Market Square. In 1819 he was also described as a school teacher. He was on the committee of Lisburn Charitable Society. His younger daughter, Elizabeth, married **James Major** and is buried in Kilrush, Lisburn [see THG Vol.1 Kilrush No. 40 and page 157]. His elder daughter, Anne Jane, born about 1813 and died November 30th 1869, was first married in August 5th 1830 to **James Jacobsen** of Ballymena and had a daughter, **Sarah Jane Jacobsen**, who died April 21st 1923 aged 94 years. James Jacobsen died on 26th September 1830, a very short time after his marriage. Sarah Jane Jacobsen married June 10th 1857 **Thomas Rutherford Pelan**, a pawnbroker. They had at least two children, **James Erskine Pelan** and **Sarah Neely Pelan**. Sarah Neely was married June 1st 1887 to **Hugh Mulholland**, a solicitor, [see THG Vol. 1 Kilrush No. 94 and page 163].

Anne Jane Neely married secondly, December 24th 1841, **John Jefferson**, a woollen draper of Bow Street. He was born about 1809 and died September 29th 1855. They had a son, **John Neely Jefferson**, born in 1846 and died in 1849.

The other Neely headstone, No. 159, is attached to the east wall of the graveyard. The top of this stone is now broken off and is missing, but parts of the inscription had been recorded earlier. This is the stone of **John Neely** (c1755-1823), his wife, **Mary** (c1758-1829), their son **Benjamin** (c1777-1838), his wife, **Mary Boyd** (c1783-1841), and their family.

Benjamin Neely was Principal of the Lisburn Academy, a boarding and day school, that was established May 6th 1800 and was situated in Castle Street. This was a three storey house, which had been built by the Marquis of Hertford. There were two schoolrooms, and English and Classics were taught. The dwelling house for the Principal joined the academy on the east side, and it contained a room for "young ladies." In 1837, according to the Ordnance Survey Memoirs, the Classical teacher was **Mr. Robert Fulton Neely**, Sizar, T.C.D., the ushers were **William Mills Neely** and **Margaret Craig Neely**, two of Benjamin's children, and there were forty males and sixteen females. Some of the pupils to attend the school included Thomas Spence, writing master, Royal Belfast Academical Institution, A.T. Stewart, Sergeant Armstrong, General John Nicholson, Major Crossley, Surgeon General James Graham and Colonel Joseph Beatty.

Benjamin Neely married Mary Boyd on September 5th 1802 and had a family of at least six sons and six daughters. The sons were **Rev. John** (c1805-1873), **Benjamin** (c1808-1831), **Rev. Andrew Craig** (bap. 1809), William Mills (1816-1864), **Snowden Cupples** (1820-1820) and **Alexander** (1823-1879). The daughters were **Mary** (died 1803) **Mary** (c1806-1864), **Violet** (1812-1831), Margaret Craig (1813-1871), **Jane** (died 1816) and **Eleanor Cupples** (1818-1836). Tragedy struck the family as four of the children died young, and sadly two other children, Benjamin and Violet, died on the same day in 1831. Two of the sons were ministers. Rev. Andrew Craig Neely was Curate of Lisburn from 1843 until 1847, before going to West Hackney, London, and Ashton, Peterborough. The eldest son, Rev. John Neely went to Augusta, Georgia, U.S.A. Two other children also appear to have gone to America, and one went to Australia.

NICHOLSON

There are two very fine memorials in the Cathedral to three members of the Nicholson family. They are for **Brigadier-General John Nicholson**, one of his brothers, **Major Charles Johnson Nicholson**, and **Elizabeth Gillilan**, wife of Major Charles Nicholson. In the graveyard is the gravestone to their mother, **Clara Nicholson**, who is buried with her parents, **William** and **Mary Hogg,** [see Hogg page 239]. General Nicholson's statue is in Market Square, Lisburn, [see Musgrave page 250], and the Nicholson Memorial Schools were built in 1864.

This Nicholson family are descended from a **Rev. William Nicholson** who arrived in Co. Armagh from Cumberland, England about 1589. His grandson was known as **"William the Quaker"**. Descended from him was **John Nicholson** (c1760-1825) of Stramore House, near Gilford, Co. Down, who in 1785 married **Isabella Wakefield** (c1763/68-1838). They had a family of sixteen children. Their eldest son, **Alexander Jaffray** (1893-16th December 1830) qualified as a doctor from Trinity College, Dublin, and on 24th April 1820, when he married **Clara Hogg** (c1795-17th February 1874), he married "out" of the Quaker religion. He was a doctor in Dublin, and he and his wife had a family of five boys and two girls. The children were **Mary Hogg** (baptised 14th November 1821), **John** (born 11th December 1822), **Alexander Jaffray** (born about 1824), **Lilly Anna Floyer** (baptised 12th March 1826), **James Weir** (baptised 14th March 1827), **William Maxwell** (born about 1829) and **Charles Johnson** (born about 1829). At least three of the children were baptised in Lisburn Cathedral. Unfortunately Dr. Alexander died at the early age of thirty-seven, after contracting a fever from a patient. Clara brought her young family back to Lisburn to live with her mother, Mary Hogg, for a year before going to Delgany, Co. Wicklow. In 1835 John was sent to the Royal School, Dungannon, Co. Tyrone, for four years, and then, through the influence of his uncle, **James Weir Hogg**, he was able to obtain a cadetship in the Bengal Infantry and set sail for India in February 1839.

John was not to see home again until 1850, by which time he had made a name for himself in India, and with his courage and leadership qualities, he had reached the rank of Major. During this time he had fought in the Afghan War and 1st and 2nd Sikh Wars. In 1847 he became an Assistant to Sir Henry Lawrence, Resident at Lahore. In 1849 he was deified, by a Hindu devotee, as a reincarnation of Brahma. This sect was known as "Nikalsaini" and the numbers of his followers grew steadily, much to Nicholson's annoyance.

He, and his family, were also to know sorrow during these years. At home, in 1840, his brother James died, aged fourteen. His other three brothers, Charles, Alexander and William, were all eventually to be in the employment of the Honourable East India Company. On 3rd November 1842, during the Afghan War, while riding through the Khyber Pass, he found the body of his brother Alexander, who had been murdered. William was in the Bombay Army and at Sukkur, Scinde, on 1st June 1849 his body was found in suspicious circumstances. In January 1850 John set out on his visit home, having served over ten years in India, and to comfort his bereaved mother.

On his return to India in 1852 he was made Deputy Commissioner for Bannu, a district which was between the Afghan Border and the Indus River. His name became a legend and he brought peace to the area. In 1856 he was appointed Deputy Commissioner of Peshawar and was now a Colonel. It was here that he was when the Indian Mutiny broke out in May 1857.

In June 1857 Nicholson was promoted to Brigadier-General and was appointed to command the Movable Column. By this time Delhi had been taken by the mutineers. The Column set out towards Delhi, followed by a siege train, to deal with the mutineers. The walls surrounding Delhi had been breached at the Kashmir Gate, and it was on September 14th 1857, as they were approaching the Lahore Gate, that Nicholson received his mortal wound. Nicholson was eventually taken to a Field Hospital and, as he was waiting to be examined, his brother, Charles, was brought in with a shattered right arm, which had to be amputated. It was another nine days before Nicholson died on the 23rd September, by which time the whole of the city of Delhi was taken. The capture of Delhi was the turning point in the Indian Mutiny, although the Mutiny did not end until 1859. Nicholson, the "Hero of Delhi", has been described as being a born soldier and administrator, with a commanding and distinguished presence - He was six feet two inches tall with a black beard.

STATUE OF
BRIGADIER-GENERAL JOHN NICHOLSON
DUNGANNON ROYAL SCHOOL, CO. TYRONE

He was buried at Ludlow Castle, facing the Kashmir Gate, along with other soldiers who died in their attempt to capture Delhi. The inscription on his marble gravestone is:- "The grave of Brigadier-General John Nicholson, who led the assault at Delhi, but fell in the hour of victory, mortally wounded, and died September 23 1857, aged 35 (sic)." Today the cemetery is neglected. From the East India Company Clara Nicholson received a pension of £500 per year.

His friends wanted to put up a memorial to him in the Cathedral in Lisburn, where his mother still lived, but she wanted to do it at her own cost. This work of art was by J.H. Foley R.A., with the wording of the inscription by Sir Herbert Edwardes. It was placed in the Cathedral in the Spring of 1862.

In 1890 on the crest of the Margalla Pass, where he saw service in 1848, his friends erected a plain obelisk, with an inscription, to his memory. In the church in Bannu, where he ruled for four years, there is a tablet to his memory. Through the generosity of Henry Musgrave a bronze statue of John Nicholson was erected in Market Square, Lisburn, in 1922. Another bronze statue of him is now at the Royal School, Dungannon, Co. Tyrone. This statue once stood in Nicholson Gardens, near the Kashmir Gate, Delhi, but was removed to Dungannon and unveiled by Earl Mountbatten of Burma in 1960.

More tragedy was to strike Clara's family. Charles left India in 1858, on sick leave and in 1859 visited the United States where on 20th October 1859, at Staten Island, New York, he married Elizabeth Gillilan, a distant cousin. Unfortunately his lungs had been affected by the amputation of his arm, but by the summer of 1862 he seems to have been well enough to accept the command of a Gurkha regiment in Northern India. He and his wife reached Calcutta on December 12th 1862 but a few days later at Doomree he died from a broken blood vessel. He is buried at Raniganj. His wife returned home and five months later she died in Cheltenham, England. These two are remembered on the second memorial in the Cathedral.

In 1864, as a memorial to her children, Clara Nicholson had the Nicholson Memorial Endowed School built beside Christ Church, Dublin Road. This was originally used as a Sunday school. By 1887, when the Trustees of the school were Rev. James Stannus, Magdalene Stewart and Rev. W.D. Pounden, there was a proposal to have it turned into a day school, and so in 1889 it became a National School. Lisburn Central Primary School was opened in November 1934 and the pupils of both the Nicholson Memorial and the Market Square schools were transferred to the new school.

Dr. Alexander and Clara's daughter, Mary, married, on 13th February 1845, **Rev. Edward Maxwell**, who was a Minister in Barnsley and Leeds, Yorkshire, England. They had at least one son, **Dr. Theodore Maxwell**. The second daughter, Lilly Anna Floyer, married, on 16th May 1856, **Rev. John Hobart Seymour** (31st August 1820-29th March 1897), and had a daughter, **Clara**, and a son, **Dr. John Nicholson R.N**. (who died 16th January 1933). Lilly died 14th January 1862.

Clara died in Lisburn on 17th February 1874. The only one of her children to survive Clara Nicholson was Mary Maxwell, who died in 1889.

O'FLAHERTY

CATHEDRAL 69

There is just one gravestone for the O'Flaherty family in the Lisburn Cathedral Burying Ground. This is for the family of **Francis Hale O'Flaherty**. He was a proctor from Castle Street, Lisburn and appears to have also had an office in Arthur Street, Belfast. At the time of the Ordnance Survey Memoirs he was the clerk of petty sessions, district apparitor of the consistorial court and registrar of the consistorial office of Down and Connor. His first marriage was to **Mary Wolfenden** on 29th September 1823. They had one child, **Francis**, baptised 15th September 1826, and a second child, name unknown. Mary died 13th June 1827 and it is not known where she is buried. Francis Hale then married **Eleanor Hill** on 11th May 1836. They had at least four sons and two daughters. At least three of the children died young, **John Greaves**, **Charlotte Fawnia** and **John Hale**. Another daughter, named **Charlotte Eleanor,** was baptised 15th October 1845. On 3rd December 1868 she married **William Richard McCall**, eldest son of **Hugh McCall**. They had a family of one son and five daughters (see THG Vol. 1 Kilrush No.77 and page 159 and Cathedral memorial). Francis Hale O'Flaherty died 8th October 1859 and his wife, Eleanor, 30th May 1875.

The eldest surviving son was **Dr. Thomas Alexander O'Flaherty R.N.**, born about 1837. He had to retire early from the Royal Navy and died 26th October 1888. His brother was **Francis Hale Hill O'Flaherty**. He was born in 1847 and died 5th May 1901. Francis H.H. was in business in Belfast. He became a partner in the firm of Glass & O'Flaherty. They were manufacturers and bleachers of linens and handkerchiefs, with an address at 5, Bedford Street, Belfast. They had a factory in Lurgan and exported goods to the United States and the Continent. When Mr. James Glass retired the firm became known as F.H. O'Flaherty & Co. Francis married **Harriette Isabella (Isa) Felton**, of Rathgar, Dublin, on 29th July 1879, and had three children. One of these was **Capt. Douglas Hill O'Flaherty** of the Royal Irish Rifles, who died in World War One on the 1st July 1916. He was married to **Beatrice Ewing** of Belfast and had formerely worked for John Shaw Brown & Co., Limited. Isa Felton's sister was married to **Arthur Mussen** of Lisburn.

(Extract from obituary.)

BELFAST NEWS LETTER
MONDAY OCTOBER 29 1888

SAD DEATH OF DR. O'FLAHERTY, R.N.

There was a widespread feeling of regret when it became known on Saturday afternoon that the body of Dr. T.A. O'Flaherty, late of the Royal Navy, had been found dead on the strand at Cultra. The deceased who was a member of a family highly popular in the North of Ireland, retired from her Majesty's service some ten years ago, owing to physical disability, and since that time has lived quietly in Belfast, having almost ceased to practice his profession. As to how he came to the place where the body was found is more or less a matter of speculation. It is known at all events that on last Friday evening he travelled by the half-past six train to Holywood, with the object of visiting his brother, Mr. F.H.H. O'Flaherty, who lives at Cultra. Leaving the station he proceeded along the shore, and his hat blowing off, he went down on the sand to regain it, and while making for the steps just opposite his brother's house he had an epileptic seizure, and falling on his face was suffocated. The body was discovered on Saturday afternoon about one o'clock by a girl passing along the road, and on examination no marks of violence of any kind were visible. The deceased was a gentleman of genial disposition, and exceedingly popular. Great sympathy is felt for his relatives owing to the peculiar manner of his death and the abrupt termination of a highly creditable career at the comparatively early age of fifty-one.

POUNDEN

The brass plaque, in the chancel of the Cathedral, to the **Rev. William Dawson Pounden** was to commemorate sixty years of his ministry. It is believed the Pounden family resided in Liege, Belgium, before coming to Ireland. An ancestor of the Rev. William Dawson Pounden was **John Pounden** (born 1765) who, in 1786, married **Alice**, only daughter of **John Colley** of Ballywalter House, Co. Wexford. They had at least two children, the **Rev. Patrick Pounden**, Vicar of Westport, Parish of Tuam, Co. Mayo, and **Jane Maria**, who died 17th December 1878, aged 84, and is buried in Lisburn Cemetery, Hillsborough Road. John Pounden died in the Rebellion of 1798. On 5th November 1822 Rev. Patrick Pounden married **Elizabeth Dawson**, daughter of the **Rev. William Dawson**, Rector of Clontibret, Co. Monaghan, and his wife, **Rosanna Hall**. They had two sons, **John Colley** and the Rev. William Dawson Pounden, and a daughter, **Rosanna**.

John Colley Pounden was born in 1827, and in 1852 married **Betanna Catherine Batterby**. They had three sons and eleven daughters. Two of the daughters, **Alice Betanna Catherine** and **Jane Wilhelmina** married respectively brothers **Major-General Robert Beatty**, Madras Native Infantry, and **Thomas Beatty C.E.** [see THG Vo. 1 Beatty Page 150].

The Rev. William Dawson Pounden was born 7th September 1830 in Ballinasloe, Co. Galway. He graduated from Trinity College, Dublin in 1854 and was eventually appointed Rector of Lisburn in 1884. He died on 29th September 1917, two years after the brass plaque was erected, and is buried in Lisburn Cemetery, Hillsborough Road. Buried with him are his aunt, Jane Maria Pounden (born about 1794 and died 17th December 1878), and his niece, **Philippa Fanny Pounden**, who was born in 1855 and died 10th November 1918. Another relative was **Frances Pounden Aubin** [see THG Vol. 1 Kilrush No. 90 and page 147]. Two other nieces had connections with the Lisburn area. They were **Elizabeth Dawson Pounden**, who married **Rev. George Patton Mitchell**, Rector of Drumbo, and **Thomasina**, who married the **Rev. George Robert Bell** of Lisburn.

REV. CANON WILLIAM DAWSON POUNDEN
(1830 – 1917)

RAWDON

On the wall of the north nave is a diamond shaped brass plaque which was originally on the floor of the old chancel. This plaque is to commemorate **Sir George** and **Sir Arthur Rawdon**. Below the old chancel was a hollow space with a burial chamber containing two coffins. These were found when old tiles were being removed from the floor and it is believed the coffins are those of Sir George Rawdon and his son, Sir Arthur Rawdon.

George was the only son of **Sir Francis Rawdon** of Rawdon Hall, Leeds and **Dorothy Aldborough**. George went to Court about the end of the reign of James I and became Private Secretary to Edward, Lord Conway, Secretary of State. In 1631, after Lord Conway's death, his son, **Edward**, appointed Rawdon as his Land Agent in Ireland. In 1639 Rawdon was the Belfast member of the Irish Parliament and in 1641 Lord Conway's troops under George Rawdon's leadership, defeated the "Rebels" at the Battle of Lisburn.

As well as his concerns with Lisnagarvey, he had a house at Brookhill, and he also was very much involved with the development of Ballynahinch and Moira. He had first married, in 1639, **Ursula Stafford**, who was the widow of **Francis Hill** of Hill Hall, and had no surviving children. In 1654 he married his second wife, **Dorothy**, eldest daughter of **Viscount Conway**. They had at least six sons and three daughters, only three of whom grew to adulthood. A list of the baptisms of their children is given in the Cathedral records.

An article by Francis Joseph Bigger, which was published in the Belfast Newsletter of Saturday September 19, 1925, gives the following description of Sir George's Funeral in 1684:-

> The body had lain in state at Moira Castle for ten days in its heavily-padded velvet coffin, studded with brass nails, skulls, crossbones, cherubs, and hour-glasses, according to the fashion of the times. A purple pall enswathed it, and tall candles in man-high candlestands flickered in the darkened room, for there were no sweet flowers at the tomb in those days, only palls and urns and paid mutes, cloaked and scarfed. The old warrior's charger was there, a good strain of Spanish blood in him, with his "Morocco saddle covered with red velvet and silver lace, with suitable holsters and a leatherne cover," for Rawdon stables were rich in such trappings, including "a morocco saddle covered with russet leather, to be used when colts were "backed." Had not my Lord Conway sent prancing stallions from Spain to enrich his studs at Lisburn, Moira, and Portmore. Pennons would hang limp that warm August day when the old road from Moira through Broomhedge and along the winding stretches of the Lagan water to Lisburn town, for George Rawdon was a knight and a baronet, "a valiant and worthy patriot and captain."

George had been created a baronet of England on 20th May 1665. His son, Sir Arthur, succeeded him. It is believed Arthur died on 17th October 1695 and was succeeded by his son, **Sir John**, who was an M.P. for Co. Down. He, in turn, was succeeded by his son, **Sir John**, who on 9th April 1750 became **Baron Rawdon of Moira**, Co. Down, and then **Earl of Moira** on 30th January 1762.

RICHARDSON

FRIENDS' BURYING GROUND

Of the twenty-eight headstones in Friends' Burying Ground, Railway Street, Lisburn, eighteen of them are connected to the Richardson family. The Richardsons can trace their family back to **Rev. John Richardson**, Rector of Warmington, Warwickshire, England. Two of his sons settled in Loughgall, Co. Armagh, the **Rev. John**, Rector of Loughgall, and **Zachery**. It is thought that Zachery's son, **Jonathan**, may have been the first to become a Quaker. Most of the Quakers closely followed the rule of marrying inside their religion, and this the Richardsons did for several generations by marrying into the Nicholson, Hogg, Grubb, Greer, Smith, Wakefield, Houghton, Malcomson, Clibborn, Fennel, Pim, Strangman and Bell families.

Jonathan's grandson, also **Jonathan** (1681-1737), married **Elizabeth Nicholson**, and his son **John** (1719–1759) married **Ruth Hogg** of Lisburn. The Hoggs were involved in the linen trade and John served his time also in this business [see Hogg page 239]. John and Ruth Richardson lived in Castle Street, Lisburn. Their son **Jonathan Richardson** (1756–1817) acquired a bleach green at Glenmore, Lambeg, and later purchased an adjoining bleach green from the Hancocks, [see Hancock page 229]. Jonathan's first wife was **Sarah Nicholson** and they had three sons and two daughters. The three sons **James Nicholson**, **John** and **Joseph** all went on to expand the Richardson's linen businesses. James Nicholson Richardson (1781–1847) and his wife **Anna Grubb** had a large family of seven sons and three daughters. This family founded the firm of J.N. Richardson, Sons & Owden Ltd. and it expanded to have spinning mills, weaving factories, bleach greens and beetle finishing works with premises at Millbrook, Lisburn, Glenmore, Lambeg, Bessbrook, Co. Armagh, Lurgan and Newry, Co. Down, among others, and a fine warehouse in Donegall Square North, Belfast, which was built in 1869. This building now houses part of Marks and Spencer's Belfast store. When first built this warehouse would have been almost opposite the White Linen Hall. The firm prospered and had offices in many parts of the world. Some of the goods they produced were linen cambric, damask table linen and embroidered handkerchiefs. Their symbol was a rampant lion, a crest of the

Richardson Family Tree 1

Friends' Burying Ground

This is not a complete Family Tree.

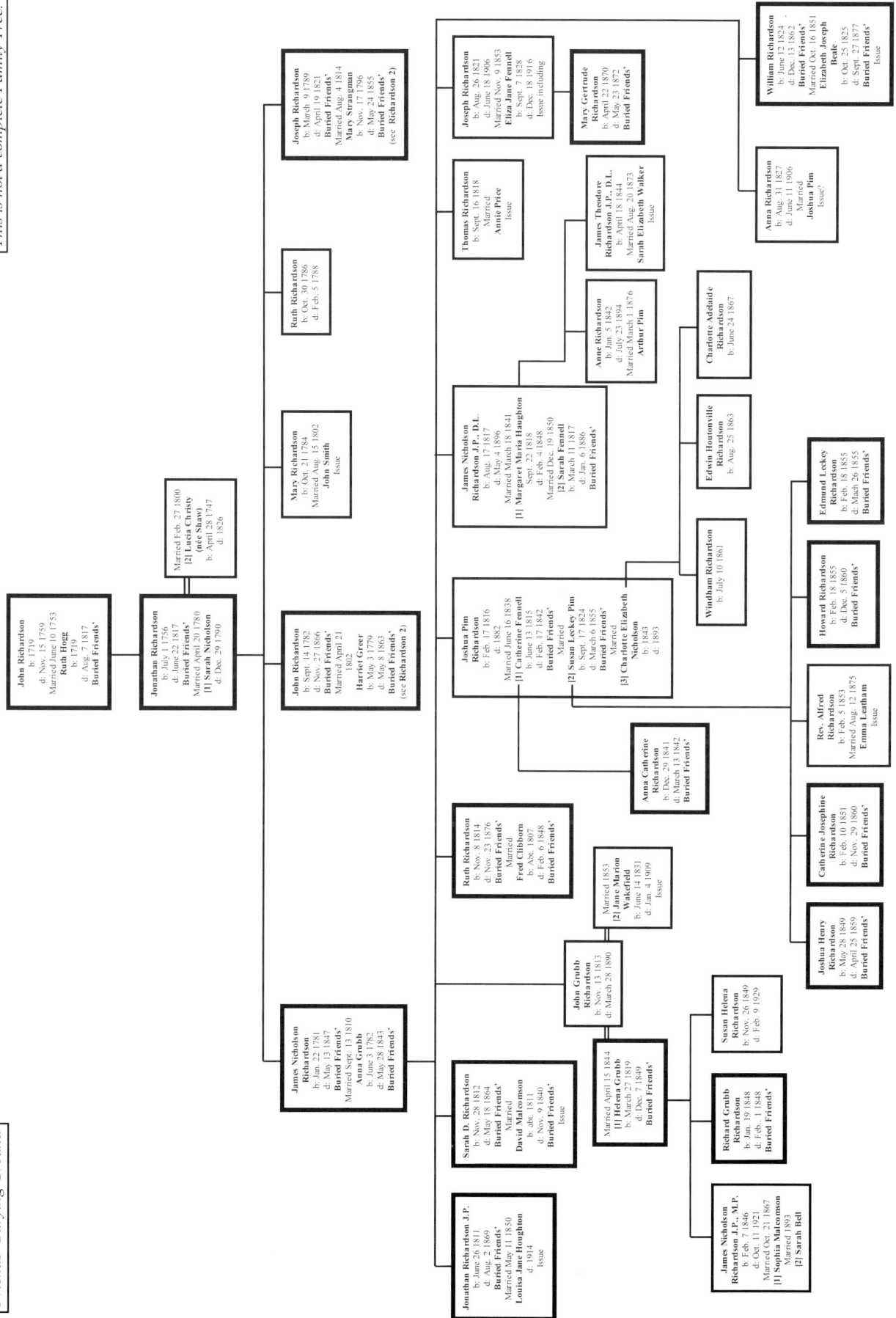

John Richardson
b: 1719
d: Nov. 15 1759
Married June 10 1753
Ruth Hogg
b: 1719
d: Aug. 7 1817
Buried Friends'

Jonathan Richardson
b: July 1 1756
d: June 22 1817
Buried Friends'
Married April 20 1780
[1] Sarah Nicholson
d: Dec. 29 1790

Married Feb. 27 1800
[2] Lucia Christy
(née Shaw)
b: April 28 1747
d: 1826

Joseph Richardson
b: March 9 1789
d: April 19 1821
Buried Friends'
Married Aug. 4 1814
Mary Strangman
b: Nov. 17 1796
d: May 24 1855
Buried Friends'
(see Richardson 2)

Ruth Richardson
b: Oct. 30 1786
d: Feb. 5 1788

Mary Richardson
b: Oct. 21 1784
Married Aug. 15 1802
John Smith
Issue

John Richardson
b: Sept. 14 1782
d: Nov. 27 1866
Buried Friends'
Married April 21 1802
Harriet Greer
b: May 3 1779
d: May 8 1863
Buried Friends'
(see Richardson 2)

James Nicholson Richardson
b: Jan. 22 1781
d: May 13 1847
Buried Friends'
Married Sept. 13 1810
Anna Grubb
b: June 3 1782
d: May 28 1843
Buried Friends'

Joseph Richardson
b: Aug. 26 1821
d: June 18 1906
Married Nov. 9 1853
Eliza Jane Fennell
b: Sept. 7 1828
d: Dec. 18 1916
Issue including

Mary Gertrude Richardson
b: April 22 1870
d: May 23 1872
Buried Friends'

William Richardson
b: June 12 1824
d: Dec. 13 1862
Buried Friends'
Married Oct. 16 1851
Elizabeth Joseph
Beale
b: Oct. 25 1825
d: Sept. 27 1877
Buried Friends'
Issue

Thomas Richardson
b: Sept. 16 1818
Married
Annie Price
Issue

James Theodore Richardson J.P., D.L.
b: April 18 1844
Married Aug. 20 1873
Sarah Elizabeth Walker
Issue

Anna Richardson
b: Aug. 31 1827
d: June 11 1906
Married
Joshua Pim
Issue?

Anne Richardson
b: Jan. 5 1842
d: July 23 1894
Married March 1 1876
Arthur Pim

Charlotte Adelaide Richardson
b: June 24 1867

James Nicholson Richardson J.P., D.L.
b: Aug. 17 1817
d: May 4 1896
Married March 18 1841
[1] Margaret Maria Haughton
b: Sept. 22 1818
d: June 4 1848
Married Dec. 19 1850
[2] Sarah Fennell
b: March 11 1817
d: Jan. 6 1886
Buried Friends'

Edwin Houtonville Richardson
b: Aug. 25 1863

Windham Richardson
b: July 10 1861

Joshua Pim Richardson
b: Feb. 17 1816
d: 1882
Married June 16 1838
[1] Catherine Fennell
b: June 13 1815
d: Feb. 17 1842
Buried Friends'
Married
[2] Susan Leckey Pim
b: Sept. 17 1824
d: March 6 1855
Buried Friends'
Married
[3] Charlotte Elizabeth Nicholson
b: 1843
d: 1893

Anna Catherine Richardson
b: Dec. 29 1841
d: March 13 1842
Buried Friends'

Ruth Richardson
b: Nov. 8 1814
d: Nov. 23 1876
Buried Friends'
Married
Fred Clibborn
b: Abt. 1807
d: Feb. 6 1848
Buried Friends'

Edmund Leckey Richardson
b: Feb. 18 1855
d: Mach 26 1855
Buried Friends'

Howard Richardson
b: Feb. 18 1855
d: Dec. 5 1860
Buried Friends'

Rev. Alfred Richardson
b: Feb. 5 1853
Married Aug. 12 1875
Emma Leatham
Issue

Catherine Josephine Richardson
b: Feb. 10 1851
d: Nov. 29 1860
Buried Friends'

Joshua Henry Richardson
b: May 28 1849
d: April 25 1859
Buried Friends'

John Grubb Richardson
b: Nov. 13 1813
d: March 28 1890
Married April 15 1844
[1] Helena Grubb
b: March 27 1819
d: Dec. 7 1849
Buried Friends'
Married 1853
[2] Jane Marion Wakefield
b: June 14 1831
d: Jan. 4 1909
Issue

Sarah D. Richardson
b: Nov. 28 1812
d: May 18 1864
Buried Friends'
Married
David Malcomson
b: abt. 1811
d: Nov. 9 1840
Buried Friends'

Susan Helena Richardson
b: Nov. 26 1849
d: Feb. 9 1929

Richard Grubb Richardson
b: Jan. 19 1848
d: Feb. 1 1848
Buried Friends'

Jonathan Richardson J.P.
b: June 26 1811
d: Aug. 2 1869
Buried Friends'
Married May 11 1850
Louisa Jane Houghton
d: 1914
Issue

James Nicholson Richardson J.P., M.P.
b: Feb. 7 1846
d: Oct. 11 1921
Married Oct. 21 1867
[1] Sophia Malcomson
Married 1893
[2] Sarah Bell

259

Richardson family. They won many prizes between 1845 and 1883, and at one time employed about seven thousand people.

Three of James Nicholson Richardson's sons **John Grubb**, **James Nicholson** and **Joseph** founded Richardson Bros. & Co., Linen Yarn Merchants, in 1840. They opened an office in Liverpool for the import of flax, grain etc. and export of linen yarn and cloth, and were involved with the Inman Shipping Line for a time. Another son, **Thomas**, settled in America.

James Nicholson Richardson's brother, John (1782-1866), was the owner of the Lambeg Bleaching and Dyeing and Finishing Co. Ltd. At one time he lived in Castle Street, Lisburn. His son **Jonathan** (1804-1894) succeeded his father as owner of this firm. He was Lisburn's Member of Parliament from 1857-63. He left the Quakers and joined the Church of Ireland and was one of the founders of Christ Church, Lisburn. He appears to have spent some time on the island of Elba, but when he died he was living in Killeaton House, Dunmurry. He is buried at Lambeg. A second son of John's was **James Greer Richardson,** who lived at Trew Mount, near Moy, Co. Tyrone.

James Nicholson's third brother, Joseph, married **Mary Strangman** and had four sons. The youngest son, **Harry**, was a doctor and died of consumption in Penzance. The island, where Lisburn's Civic Centre is now situated, was formerly known as "Vitriol Island." In 1840, a flax spinning mill was built on the island by Joseph Richardson's son, **Samuel**. When Samuel died in 1847 his brother, **Jonathan Joseph**, took over the mill and enlarged it. On the death of Roger Johnson Smyth M.P. [see Johnson Smyth page 243], Jonathan Joseph Richardson succeeded him as Member of Parliament for Lisburn. He held this position from 1853 until 1857, when he resigned his seat. This business was bought from J.J. Richardson in 1867 and renamed the Island Spinning Co. Ltd. Again it was increased in size with the addition of a weaving factory. In 1888 Joseph Richardson, of Richardson Bros. & Co., was the chairman of the company.

Several of the large houses in the Lisburn area were lived in by members of the Richardson family. These include Ingram, Aberdelghy, Glenmore, Lisnagarvey House, Killeaton, Lissue and Springfield at Magheragall.

As well as the Richardson burials in Railway Street there are several members of the family buried in the Quaker section in Lisburn Cemetery, Hillsborough Road, Lisburn.

The Richardson family were generous in giving to worthy causes. One of these was contributing to the costs of building the Lisburn Temperance Institute at the corner of Railway Street and the Magheralave Road. This building was opened in 1890 and is now the Bridge Community Centre.

BELFAST NEWSLETTER
FRIDAY MAY 21 1847

DEATH OF JAMES NICHOLSON RICHARDSON.-It falls to our lot to-day to record the removal by death (on 13th inst.) of another of the most valued and extensively useful members of the community; namely the excellent James N. Richardson, Esq., of Glenmore, near Lisburn. The peculiarly peaceful religious society to which he belonged - the Society of Friends - habitually shrinks from public eulogium. Nevertheless, we feel it our honest duty to allude, in terms of high respect and admiration, to the character of one whose memory will be long revered and cherished. As an honourable and upright merchant, he was prospered beyond the attainment of most men, and lived to be the head of truly noble establishments in this country, in England, and in America. The scenery of Lambeg, beautified by its flourishing bleachfields, and the busy and thronged splendid factory at Bessbrook, beside this town, bear ample testimony to the enterprise over which Mr. Richardson presided; while Belfast, and Liverpool, and New York regarded his name, in several mercantile concerns with which he was identified, as the surest guarantee of sterling integrity. His genuine and unaffected benevolence, united with quiet, manly decision, and independence, secured to him the esteem of all

Richardson Family Tree 2

This is not a complete Family Tree.

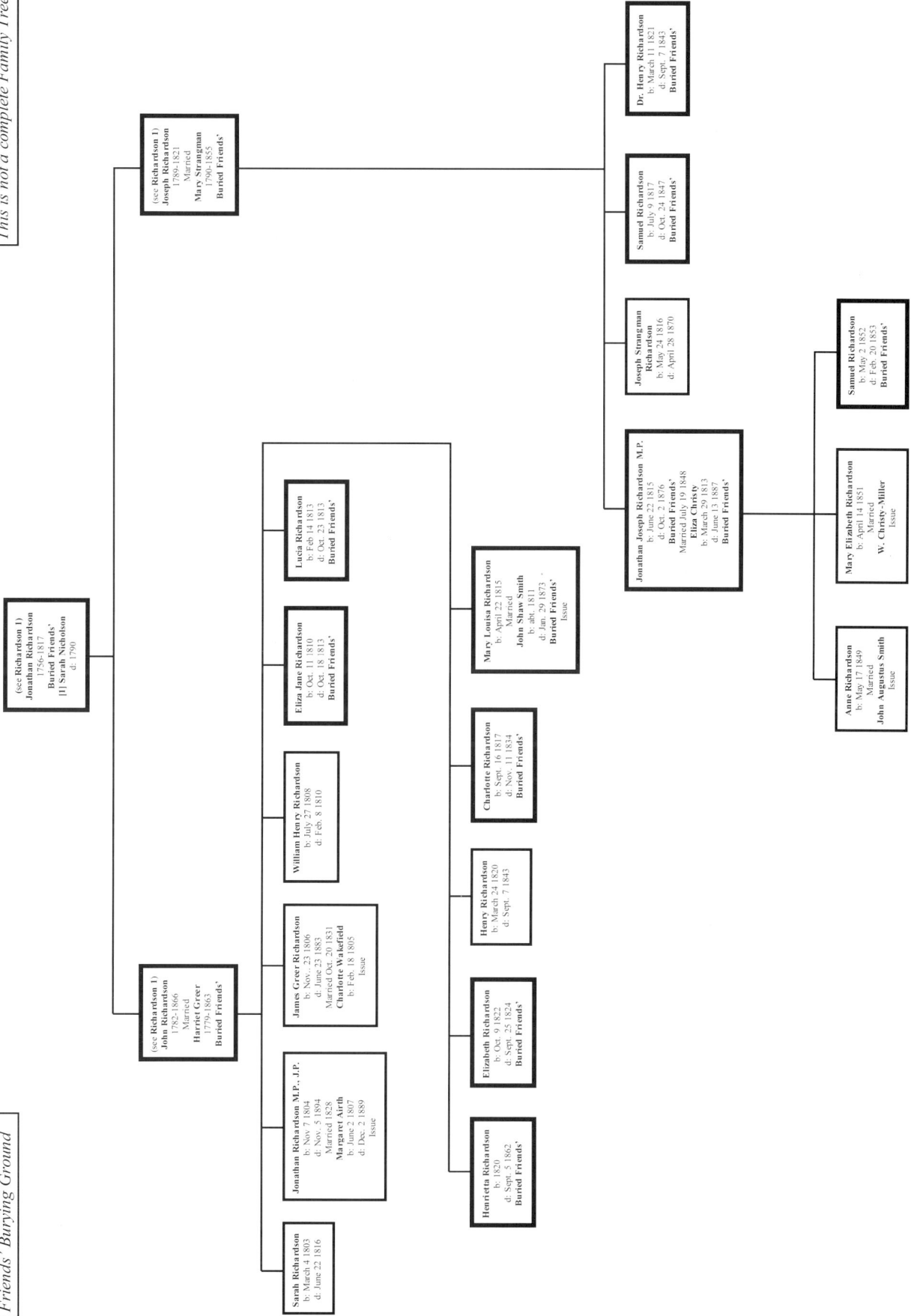

(see Richardson 1)
Jonathan Richardson
1756-1817
Buried Friends'
[1] Sarah Nicholson
d: 1790

(see Richardson 1)
Joseph Richardson
1789-1821
Married
Mary Strangman
1790-1855
Buried Friends'

Dr. Henry Richardson
b: March 11 1821
d: Sept. 7 1843
Buried Friends'

Samuel Richardson
b: July 9 1817
d: Oct. 24 1847
Buried Friends'

Joseph Strangman Richardson
b: May 24 1816
d: April 28 1870

Jonathan Joseph Richardson M.P.
b: June 22 1815
d: Oct. 2 1876
Buried Friends'
Married July 19 1848
Eliza Christy
b: March 29 1813
d: June 13 1887
Buried Friends'

Samuel Richardson
b: May 2 1852
d: Feb. 20 1853
Buried Friends'

Mary Elizabeth Richardson
b: March 11 1851
Married
W. Christy-Miller
Issue

Anne Richardson
b: May 17 1849
Married
John Augustus Smith
Issue

(see Richardson 1)
John Richardson
1782-1866
Married
Harriet Greer
1779-1863
Buried Friends'

Sarah Richardson
b: March 4 1803
d: June 22 1816

Jonathan Richardson M.P., J.P.
b: Nov 7 1804
d: Nov. 5 1894
Married 1828
Margaret Airth
b: June 2 1807
d: Dec. 2 1889
Issue

James Greer Richardson
b: Nov...23 1806
d: June 23 1883
Married Oct. 20 1831
Charlotte Wakefield
b: Feb. 18 1805
Issue

William Henry Richardson
b: July 27 1808
d: Feb. 8 1810

Eliza Jane Richardson
b: Oct. 11 1810
d: Oct. 18 1813
Buried Friends'

Lucia Richardson
b: Feb 14 1813
d: Oct. 23 1813
Buried Friends'

Henrietta Richardson
b: 1820
d: Sept 5 1862
Buried Friends'

Elizabeth Richardson
b: Oct. 9 1822
d: Sept. 25 1824
Buried Friends'

Henry Richardson
b: March 24 1820
d: Sept. 7 1843

Charlotte Richardson
b: Sept. 16 1817
d: Nov 11 1834
Buried Friends'

Mary Louisa Richardson
b: April 22 1815
Married
John Shaw Smith
b: abt. 1811
d: Jan. 29 1873
Buried Friends'
Issue

ranks and classes. In this calamitous period the contributions to the central fund of the Society of Friends, as well as to other charities, from the various firms with which he was associated, were the theme of universal remark. At home, to the numerous work-people, whose comfort he constantly studied, and amongst the poor and necessitous, whose sufferings he habitually planned to alleviate, his bounties flowed in a daily stream of considerate kindness. At a time like this, such a master and friend can be ill spared. We have the fullest confidence, however, in those who are now to take his place.-To his sorrowing and much attached and deeply-afflicted relatives it must afford a measure of consolation to know that they are the objects of a sympathy as unfeigned as it is general. Mr. Richardson died in his 67th year. *Newry Telegraph*.

BRITISH FRIEND
OCTOBER 1847

SAMUEL RICHARDSON 1817 - 1847

His loss will be severely felt by the whole neighbourhood. He was gifted with great talents for public usefulness and was actuated by a warm benevolence which induced him to exert himself actively in relieving the alarming destitution among the poor of Lisburn and in superintending the fever hospital and the county infirmary, of which he was a treasurer. He was also an exceedingly exemplary and useful member of our Religious Society, especially in his devoted attention to the Ulster Provincial School.

{*He died of Typhus and lived at the Flax Mill near Lisburn. These premises became known as "The Island Spinning Mill" under its next owners, the Clarkes.*}

(*Extract from obituary*.)

BELFAST NEWS LETTER
TUESDAY AUGUST 2 1869

DEATH OF JONATHAN RICHARDSON, Esq., J.P., GLENMORE

It is with the most sincere regret we discharge the painful duty of recording the sudden and most unexpected demise of this highly respected and deeply regretted gentleman, which melancholy event took place at an early hour yesterday morning. For some short time past, Mr. Richardson and his family had been residing at Craigdarragh, Craigavad, County Down, during the rebuilding of his mansion at Glenmore. On Sunday, as usual, he accompanied his family to Craigavad Church, apparently in the enjoyment of excellent health, which did not appear to have been interrupted throughout the evening. Having conducted family worship at eleven o'clock on Sunday night, he retired to rest, and, in an hour or two afterwards, Mrs. Richardson was awoke by his coughing. The attack continuing for some time, the servants were called; and, as it was seen he was getting weaker, medical assistance was at once sent for, but in a short time he breathed his last, and the good Jonathan Richardson was no more.

We are unwilling to intrude on domestic privacy to describe the deep grief of the widow and family; but a life like Mr. Richardson's demands fuller notice at our hands. The deceased gentleman was born on the 26th of June 1811, and was consequently in the 59th year of his age. He was the eldest son of James Nicholson Richardson, Esq., who married Miss Anna Grubb, of Anner Mills, Clonmel. The deceased commenced the linen business at his father's establishment in Lisburn, acquiring a real practical knowledge of the business. Subsequently he was taken into partnership with his father, and the firm was from that date known by the well-known name of "J.N. Richardson, Sons, & Owden." Of this firm, the gentleman we now so heartily lament was the leading member at the time of his decease. The Richardson family have been most zealous in promoting the growth, increase, and stability of the linen trade of Ireland, in conjunction with the Mulhollands, Charleys, and others. Their efforts were not confined to the brown linen trade, but were extended to the white branch as well; and the bleachgreens of the firm at Glenmore, near Lisburn, are of world-wide celebrity. In prosecuting the desires of the family, as well as the good of his country, for several years, Mr. Jonathan Richardson visited the chief towns of England, Scotland and Wales, and at a later period entered largely into various arrangements for the extension of the trade in the chief marts of the world, in all of which the name and brand of the firm have the highest repute. As an advisor or friend of the trade, Mr. Richardson was continually appealed to, and his opinion was much respected, being entirely free of bias. As a member of the various agricultural societies of Ireland he was very useful, and his loss will be long felt and deplored by the Flax Extension Society. He was also a member of the various associations for the relief of his fellow-man, and for the support of religion, of all of which he was a munificent supporter. ……….. He was a loving and faithful husband, and a fond and tender parent; and his loss is deeply mourned by a bereaved widow, daughter of Major Haughton (sic), formerly of Springfield, Lisburn, and eight children, the eldest son, 18 years of age, having only a short time ago entered upon the business of the firm. The deceased gentleman was a J.P. for the Counties of Down and Antrim, in both of which, and especially in Belfast, the news of his unexpected death has caused deep grief and the keenest sympathy with the bereaved widow and family. The funeral will take place on Thursday morning, at eight o'clock, when the remains will be removed from Craigdarragh for interment at Lisburn.

(Extract from obituary.)

BELFAST NEWS LETTER
MONDAY OCTOBER 9 1876
FUNERAL OF MR. JONATHAN J. RICHARDSON J.P.

The remains of this gentleman, whose demise was so sudden and so mush regretted, were removed from his late residence, Kircassock, near Lurgan, and interred in the quiet cemetery adjoining the Friends' Meeting-house, Lisburn. Mr. Richardson took, comparatively speaking, but little active interest in public life. He was principally known as one of the leading merchants in the staple trade of the North of Ireland, and was generally respected for his genial courtesy and strict business integrity. The son of Mr. Joseph Richardson, member of the well-known firm of J.J. & J. Richardson, which afterwards became merged in that of Richardson, Sons, & Owden, the deceased gentleman was early initiated into all the details of linen manufacture, and so far back as 1840, started flax spinning in partnership with his brother Samuel, at the Island, Lisburn. Here their joint business habits and shrewd enterprising spirit soon developed a flourishing trade; and by degrees, gradual at first, but rapidly in subsequent years, the stamp of the Island yarns became popular almost the world over. In '47 , Mr. Samuel Richardson died, and the mill became the property solely of the remaining brother. Under his aegis it continued its course of prosperity, while its proprietor grew in the good wishes and esteem of all who knew him, whether in social life or in business relationship. So much so, indeed, was this the case that in 1853, on the death of Mr. Smyth, M.P., Mr. Richardson, though advocating Liberal principles, was returned as member for Lisburn, and represented that ancient borough in Parliament for four years. In St. Stephen's his great mercantile experience and round commercial judgment were frequently elicited in aid of the government, though on party questions proper his voice was seldom, if ever, heard. After resigning his seat he took up more zealously than ever the business of the Island Mill, which he managed with enlarging success until 1866, when he sold the entire premises for a sum which might well be considered a handsome fortune. Some time after he became, by the death of another brother, the successor to an extensive provision establishment in Waterford. On this also he expended largely of his great natural energy, and the new enterprise had assumed splendid business proportions, when death stepped in and robbed it of its ruling spirit.

ROCHET

CATHEDRAL 171

This stone is for **Lewis**, or **Louis, Rochet**, or **Roché**, a Huguenot. It is believed he came to Lisburn about 1697. In 1718 Lewis Rochet was churchwarden. He had at least two daughters, **Mary** and **Alice**. Alice married **Edward Maslin** in 1725. There was an Edward Maslin who was churchwarden in 1725 and 1730/31. Mary married **Valentine Jones** (1711-22nd March 1895). There is a Cathedral record of Valentine Jones and Mary Rushett marrying on 25th February 1727. Valentine became an important merchant in Belfast, and he was engaged in commerce and a wine merchant. He is buried in Clifton Street Cemetery, Belfast. Mary and Valentine are believed to have had five children. One daughter married **John Gault Smith**, of Coleraine, and two other daughters married brothers, **William Watts** and **Edward**, sons of the **Rev. Philip Gayer** (1698-1755), vicar of Derriaghy. The Rev. Philip Gayer was nephew of **Sir John Gayer**, Lord Mayor of London 1647. William Watts Gayer's wife was called **Catherine**, and Edward's **Henrietta**. In Derriaghy Graveyard there is a grave to Edward Gayer, who died 13th September 1799, and his wife, Henrietta, who died 23rd March 1814. A daughter of the Rev. Philip Gayer, **Magdalene**, married **Capt. Poyntz Stewart,** [see Stewart No. 19 and page 269], and another daughter married a member of the **Higginson** family. Valentine and Mary Jones had a son, grandson and great grandson all called Valentine.

In the Lisburn Cathedral records there is the baptism of **Richard**, son of Mr. Valentine Jones on 2nd April 1718/19 and in 1761 a will of a Valentine Jones of Lisburn was proved.

ROMA

When Rev. Carmody wrote his book "Lisburn Cathedral and its Past rectors" in 1926 he mentioned an old gravestone near the door of the Cathedral. This gravestone cannot now be located, but in 1926 the inscription on it was legible. Carmody gives it as thus:- "**Mr. Marino Roma**, departed this life 2nd June 1689." He gives a baptism of Marino Roma, whose name was on the stone, as "Marino Roma, son of **Marino Roma, Capt.**, Baptised 1st April 1663," making Marino Roma twenty-six when he died. There is also mention of a baptism of **Olphert Marino Roma** in November 1664, and buried 29th January 1668, and **Liddia**, daughter of Mr. Marino Roma, baptised January 15th 1655, buried 20th May 1666. Another baptism was of **Frances**, daughter of **Capt. Romano Roma**, defunct on March 14th 1667, probably meaning that Romano Roma had died before his daughter was born. It is likely that Capt. Romano Roma and Capt. Marino Roma, who was buried 5th July 1667, were brothers. Capt. Marino Roma was Quartermaster in Lord Conway's troop of horse and had a large farm at Ballinderry. In his book Carmody gives an account of Capt. Roma's fatal wounding in June 1667 and that he was attended by Mr. Brook. This is probably Mr. Brooke, chirurgeon of Lisburn, buried November 14th 1694, [see Cathedral No. 134]. Marino Roma left four children.

SHANNON

CATHEDRAL 158

According to **Mary Shannon's** death notice it would appear that this family of Shannons were originally from Dublin. In October 1796 **John B. Shannon** contributed five guineas to the one thousand pound reward for the conviction of the persons responsible for the attempt on the life of Rev. Philip Johnson, vicar of Derriaghy. In 1824 John Shannon had a vitriol works in Ballymacarrett, Belfast and by 1841 the works were described as the "Belfast Vitriol Works" and he was living in 16, Chichester Street, Belfast.

BELFAST NEWS LETTER
SATURDAY MAY 24 1856

DEATH OF J.B. SHANNON, Esq.-On yesterday evening, John Baptist (sic) Shannon, Esq., one of the oldest and most respected inhabitants of Belfast, breathed his last, at his residence in Chichester Street. He settled in this town about forty years since, and with the energy which ever characterised all his actions, he early took an active part in most of the public and private charities of the town; and to every institution which had a useful tendency, he lent his zealous support. In every relation of life, he earned an unblemished reputation-a piously dutiful son; a tender and affectionate husband and father; a kind, considerate, and warm friend; an upright, active, intelligent, and successful man of business. He has left many to deplore his loss, and few who can pretend to emulate his virtues; and yet for many years he has known, and with deep humility acknowledged, the unworthiness of all his best actions as before a Holy God he deplored the corruption of his human heart, and placed all his hopes for eternity upon the free grace and mercy of God in Jesus Christ, through the Holy Spirit's blessed influence.

STANNUS

There is one grave site in the Cathedral grounds and one memorial in the Cathedral to the Stannus family. The very fine sarcophagus near the Market Square entrance is the burial site of the **Very Rev. James Stannus**, Dean of Ross and Rector of Lisburn, his wife, **Elizabeth** and one of their daughters, **Harriet Jane**. Four children who died young may also be buried here.

VERY REV. JAMES STANNUS
(1788 – 1876)

Rev. James Stannus was descended from **William Stanehouse** of Carbolzie, Scotland, who settled in Carlingford Co. Louth. His great grandson, **Trevor Stannus**, was High Sheriff of Co. Louth in 1744. Trevor's eldest son, **Thomas**, was M.P. for Portarlington, Co. Laois 1789-99 and was the father of Rev. James Stannus. He fought in the American War of Independence and was severely wounded. The Rev. James was born 10th January 1788. He was in the army first and then changed careers and entered the Church. He married **Elizabeth Borrowes** on 22nd April 1816 and came to Lisburn in 1817 as Agent to the Marquis of Hertford. He was also Rector of Ballinderry from 1820-1836 and Rector of Lisburn 1836-1870. From 1830 to his death he was Dean of Ross, Co. Cork. There were no duties attached to this deanery. He lived in Castle Street, Lisburn and had a family of at least six sons and five daughters. Of his sons, **Thomas Robert** became stamp distributor for County Antrim and lived at Magheralave, **Rev. Beauchamp Walter** was Curate of Ballinderry and then Rector of Arrow, near Alcester, Warwickshire, England. **Henry James, C.B.** was Lieutenant Colonel of the 20th Hussars and retired in 1879 with the honorary rank of General. He fought in Afghanistan in 1842, the Gwalior campaign of 1843-44, Sutlej 1845-46, Punjab 1848-49 and India 1857. The following newspaper report appeared in the Belfast News Letter 20th April 1849:-

BRAVERY OF IRISHMEN AT THE BATTLE OF GOOJERAT

It gives us no small satisfaction to state that two of the officers distinguished by the warm approbation of Lord Gough, in his official dispatches relative to the action at Goojerat, are connected with families resident in our own immediate neighbourhood. Lieutenant Stannus, of the 5th Light Cavalry, who was severely wounded during the engagement, "whilst gallantly charging a party of the enemy's horsemen," is son of the Dean of Ross. This is the third time in which honourable mention has been made by his superior officers of his gallant conduct in the field, and we believe he has served in no fewer than *eight* battles since he obtained his first commission. If we are not mistaken, Lieutenant Stannus is on the staff of the Commander-in-Chief.

The other distinguished officer to whom we allude is Captain Nicholson, who is mentioned as having accompanied Lieut.-Col. Bradford in pursuit of the enemy, twenty-four miles from Goojerat. Captain Nicholson is a native of Lisburn. His mother, who is still a resident of that town, is the sister of Sir James Weir Hogg. This officer was at Cabool during the first war in the Punjaub. His brother was killed in the disastrous retreat through the Bolan Pass, and another brother is also officer in the Indian Army. The North-East of Ireland has already given to the service of the country many a name long to live in the annals of British glory, and we rejoice to think that the list is not likely soon to be completed.

The youngest son, **Walter Trevor**, was a Deputy Lieutenant for Co. Antrim, Magistrate for Antrim, Down, Tyrone and Londonderry, and took over as Agent for the Hertford Estate from his father in 1853. He lived in the Manor House, Lisburn.

Descendants of Trevor Stannus

This is not a complete Family Tree.

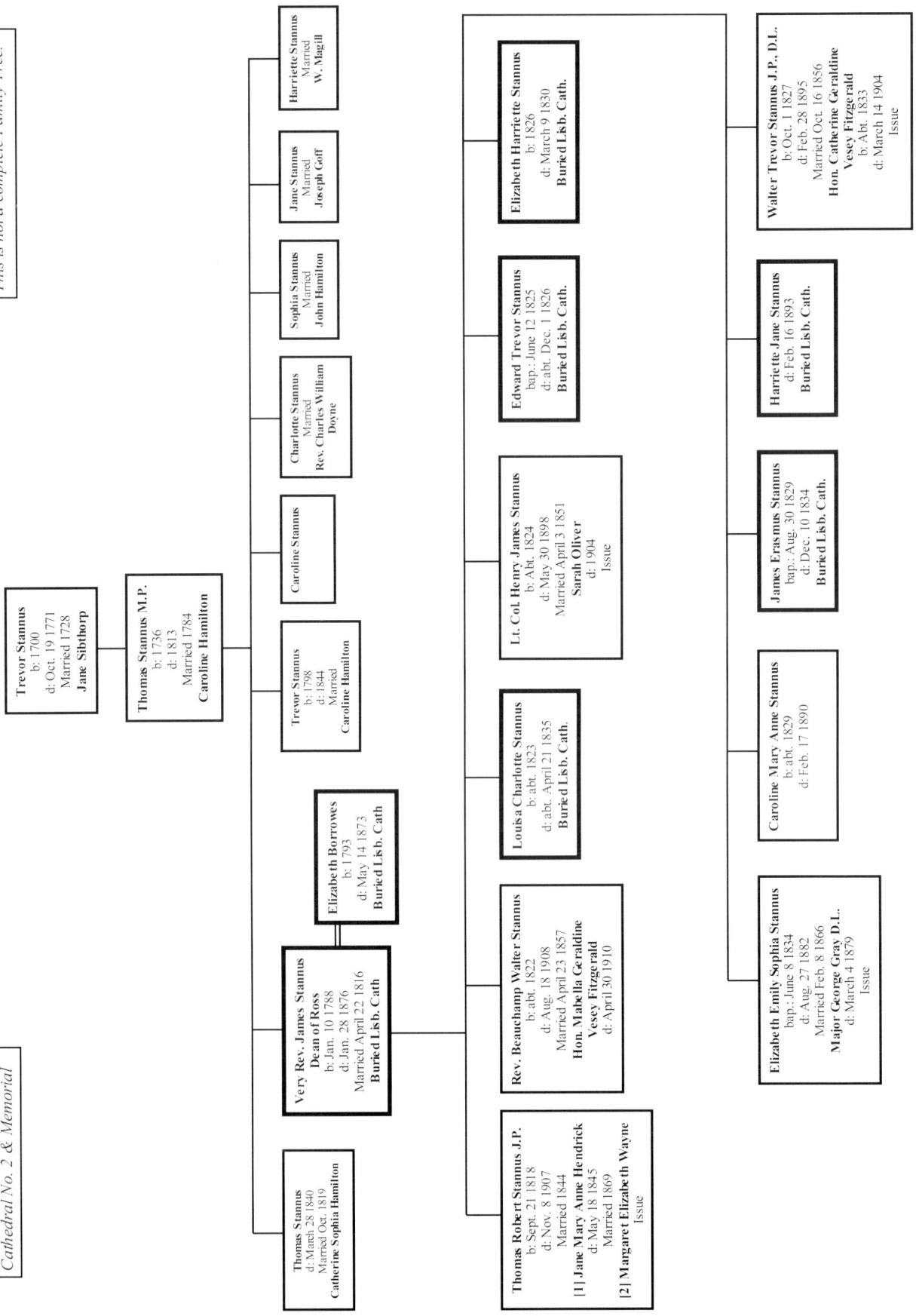

Cathedral No. 2 & Memorial

Trevor Stannus
b: 1700
d: Oct. 19 1771
Married 1728
Jane Sibthorp

Thomas Stannus M.P.
b: 1736
d: 1813
Married 1784
Caroline Hamilton

Harriette Stannus
Married
W. Magill

Jane Stannus
Married
Joseph Goff

Sophia Stannus
Married
John Hamilton

Charlotte Stannus
Married
Rev. Charles William
Doyne

Caroline Stannus

Trevor Stannus
b: 1798
d: 1844
Married
Caroline Hamilton

Thomas Stannus
d: March 28 1840
Married Oct. 1819
Catherine Sophia Hamilton

Very Rev. James Stannus
Dean of Ross
b: Jan. 10 1788
d: Jan. 28 1876
Married April 22 1816
Buried Lisb. Cath

Elizabeth Borrowes
b: 1793
d: May 14 1873
Buried Lisb. Cath

Elizabeth Harriette Stannus
b: 1826
d: March 9 1830
Buried Lisb. Cath.

Edward Trevor Stannus
bap.: June 12 1825
d: abt. Dec. 1 1826
Buried Lisb. Cath.

Lt. Col Henry James Stannus
b: Abt. 1824
d: May 30 1898
Married April 3 1851
Sarah Oliver
d: 1904
Issue

Louisa Charlotte Stannus
b: abt. 1823
d: abt. April 21 1835
Buried Lisb. Cath.

Rev. Beauchamp Walter Stannus
b: abt. 1822
d: Aug. 18 1908
Married April 23 1857
Hon. Mabella Geraldine
Vesey Fitzgerald
d: April 30 1910

Thomas Robert Stannus J.P.
b: Sept. 21 1818
d: Nov. 8 1907
Married 1844
[1] **Jane Mary Anne Hendrick**
d: May 18 1845
Married 1869
[2] **Margaret Elizabeth Wayne**
Issue

Walter Trevor Stannus J.P., D.L.
b: Oct. 1 1827
d: Feb. 28 1895
Married Oct. 16 1856
Hon. Catherine Geraldine
Vesey Fitzgerald
b: Abt. 1833
d: March 14 1904
Issue

Harriette Jane Stannus
d: Feb. 16 1893
Buried Lisb. Cath.

James Erasmus Stannus
bap.: Aug. 30 1829
d: Dec. 10 1834
Buried Lisb. Cath.

Caroline Mary Anne Stannus
b: abt. 1829
d: Feb. 17 1890

Elizabeth Emily Sophia Stannus
bap.: June 8 1834
d: Aug. 27 1882
Married Feb. 8 1866
Major George Gray D.L.
d: March 4 1879
Issue

Thomas Robert is remembered on a memorial in the Cathedral and both Thomas Robert and Walter Trevor and some of their family are buried in Lisburn Cemetery, Hillsborough Road. Some other members are buried in Lambeg, and others in England. Only the youngest daughter married. She was **Elizabeth Emily Sophia** and she married **Major George Gray** of Graymount, Co. Antrim. The Girls' School, in Lisburn, was originally founded, in 1812, by Miss Bessie Hancock and her sister, later being in the charge of two of Dr. William Stewart's daughters. In 1827 Rev. Stannus had a larger School-house erected at the end of Seymour Street. Later his daughter, **Caroline**, was an active patroness of the school and contributed to its success.

The Rev. James Stannus had a brother, **Thomas**, who was great grandfather to **Dame Ninette de Valois**, the celebrated ballerina and choreographer.

(*Extracts from obituary.*)

BELFAST NEWS LETTER
SATURDAY JANUARY 29 1876

DEATH OF THE VERY REV. THE DEAN OF ROSS

Mr. Stannus was appointed agent, and in October 1817, arrived in Lisburn, and took up his residence in the Marquis of Hertford's house in Castle Street in that town. ....The year 1816 was a most disastrous one for the agricultural interests. Prices of every product had gone down far under the lowest point anticipated, and, added to this, the harvest of that season was very unfavourable. All but continuous rains fell in August, and the few dry days in the succeeding months did not give farmers sufficient time to reap the grain, stunted and light as it was. Many fields of oats had not been reaped in November. Next year was rather more satisfactory, but fever had made sad havoc in town and village, and if crops were better than those of the previous year, prices had again fallen to a low point. Such was the state of the rural population in Ireland when the Rev. James Stannus took managerial charge of the Hertford estates. Numbers of the tenants were far behind in their rents, and had very great pressure been put on them by the new agent, wholesale desolation would have resulted. Mr. Stannus was exceedingly fond of riding on horseback, and every leisure hour he could spare from the duties connected with the rent office was spent by him in going over the estate and seeing for himself the state of the country and the position of the tenants. Those who owed three years' rent were encouraged to pay one-half the claim, and where two years were in arrears a similar proportion of the debt was received. By this mode of management the greater parts of all the rents that had accumulated was got in, and before the close of his fourth year of office the agent had the estate pretty well up as to payments; and in addition to this, there had been considerable improvements made on the lands by the farmers. In several cases too, the extreme rents at which farms had been taken in 1811, 1812 and 1813 were reduced to more moderate valuations, roads were put in better repair, many new lines of way were constructed for the benefit of the tenants who resided in backward districts, and thousands of trees were planted in different parts of the estate. These improvements were greatly to the advantage of the farmer. The good roads gave him every facility for the transport of produce, and, as the trees grew up and created increased shelter for cattle on the grazing lands, they so far aided in the successful introduction of superior breeds of stock. It will be recollected that some years ago the tenants on the Hertford estate presented Dean Stannus with a very gratifying address congratulating him on having reached the close of half a century in connection with the property. Many changes have since then taken place. Lord Hertford died in August 1870, and Sir Richard Wallace became possessor of the property. Mr. F.L. Capron was appointed agent by the new owner, but the kind-hearted baronet did not forget how well and how faithfully the aged dean had discharged his duties to the several proprietors under whom he held office, and in acknowledgement granted him a pension of £500 a year during the remainder of his life, and a free house, making a total of £600 per annum. Few men, no matter in what grade of society, ever exercised greater influence, or possessed more power over a vast population than did the Dean of Ross as land agent of the Hertford estate. In fact, for the greater portion of half a century he was all but chief of the wide domain, the different marquises under whom he held office having such implicit confidence in his management that he had supreme control of the property over which he was placed, for the proprietors left him free to pursue whatever system he thought best; and under all these circumstances and standing as he did between landlords living far away from the scene of his legislation and the people that held land in the same sections of the estate, the position of the agent was difficult in the extreme. It is true that complaints sometimes were heard respecting the administration; but, all things considered, the wonder was that, in the management of a property comprising an area of about seventy thousand acres, and the guardianship of an income the amount of which ran up to sixty thousand pounds a year, the causes of dissatisfaction on the part of the tenants were really so few. Outside the walls of the Hertford office Dean Stannus was ever found leading the way in works of charity, and when any sudden call was made for assistance in some case requiring direct aid his time was not spared, neither was the more material contribution withheld in the cause of benevolence. During the terrible visitations of cholera in Lisburn in 1849 the Dean of Ross, Thomas J. Smyth, D.L. and Captain Bolton were most munificent contributors to the fund, as well as the most active members of the sanitary committee. All the others to whom we have alluded have long since passed away, and as the last of his contemporaries, the Dean has followed them to the unseen world. We may state that immediately on the news of the demise of the venerable old man all business in Lisburn was suspended.

BELFAST NEWS LETTER
WEDNESDAY NOVEMBER 13 1907

MR. T.R. STANNUS, J.P.

Mr. Thomas Robert Stannus, J.P., who died on the 8th inst. at Gogmagog Hills, Cambridgeshire, and whose remains will be interred to-day in the old cemetery surrounding the Lisburn Cathedral, was a member of a family which figured prominently in the annals of Lisburn in days gone by. The deceased gentleman, who was in his ninetieth year, was the eldest son of the late Very Rev. James Stannus, Dean of Ross, rector of Lisburn Cathedral, and agent of the Earl of Hertford's very extensive estate, on which the town of Lisburn stands. He is survived by his brother, the Rev. B.W. Stannus, rector of Arrow, and the only representative of the family now resident in Lisburn is the daughter of the late Mr. Walter Stannus, who succeeded his father in the management of the estate. The subject of this obituary was a man distinguished by the natural attributes of a gentleman, and was most popular with all sections of the community. Until some twenty years ago he resided in a fine mansion built by himself at Magheraleave, which was burned down about sixteen years since and fully restored. After his retirement from the position of stamp distributor for County Antrim, which he held for a long period, he spent most of his time in residence in England and the Continent. He was an ardent Churchman, who deplored the Act of Disestablishment at the time of its passing, and his devotion took the practical form of a large contribution to the Sustentation Fund. During the period of his permanent residence at Magheraleave, he was master of the Killultagh Hunt, and entered with a hearty zest into the sports patronised by the gentry of the Counties of Antrim and Down. He had a great natural gift for music, which he fully cultivated, and was ever ready to help as an instrumentalist at concerts and social entertainments got up for philanthropic or religious purposes. He was also a willing contributor from his purse to every worthy object for which his aid was solicited, and although of late years generally absent from the country his name was never withdrawn from the charities he had been accustomed to support. His memory is held dear by the older members of the community among whom the early and active years of his life were spent, and who knew how to appreciate his worth. Deceased married Miss Wayne, a Welsh lady, and leaves one child—Mrs. Harold Gray-at whose residence in Cambridgeshire he breathed his last.

STEWART

We have included information on two Stewart families. One is the family of Poyntz Stewart and his son, Dr. William Stewart, and the other is for the family of Robert Stewart, who had a linen thread business in Lisburn.

CATHEDRAL 19, 20 & 18 AND ROGERS MEMORIAL

The main memorial to this Stewart family is the large slate monument attached to the north wall of the Cathedral. Unfortunately part of it is now becoming difficult to read. This memorial is for the family of **Captain Poyntz Stewart**, who was a J.P. and captain of the Derryaghy Yeomanry, and of one of his sons, **Dr. William Stewart**, who for a period of many years was a medical doctor and surgeon in the County Antrim Infirmary.

Capt. Stewart's mother is the first name mentioned on the memorial. She was **Rose Hall**, daughter of **Roger Hall**, of Narrow Water Castle, and **Christian Poyntz**, and grand-daughter of **Sir Toby Poyntz**, Acton and Brenagh, Co. Armagh. Her death date is not correct on the stone. She died February 1782. It seems likely that she may have first been married, in 1708, to **Richard Close** who was from Drumbanagher, Co. Armagh, but with Lisburn connections. Capt. Stewart's father was **Capt. Charles Stewart** of 5th (Lord Molesworth's) Dragoons. Capt. Charles Stewart, who was the son of **Alexander Stewart,** of Wester, Cluny, Perthshire, and **Isabella Stewart,** of Ballnakillie, Scotland, died in 1774. He is buried in Carrickfergus Old Graveyard (St. Nicholas') where there is a memorial to him and his wife, Rose.

Capt. Poyntz Stewart may have been married 3 times. First to **Magdalene Gayer**, then to **Ann**, and then to **Jane Casement**. He had at least four sons. Dr. William and **Poyntz** are the only sons mentioned on the stone. Another son was **Charles**, who joined the Bengal army in 1781. He was an expert on oriental languages. Two of Capt. Poyntz Stewart's sisters are also recorded on the stone. One of these, **Charlotte**, was the wife of **William Smyth** of Ballintoy, an officer in the Dragoons. They had a family of at least two sons and four daughters. One of their sons, **Rev. James Smyth**, and a daughter, **Hannah Smyth**, are recorded on the stone, and another daughter, **Ann Smyth**, married her cousin, **Major Philip Stewart**, son of Capt. Poyntz Stewart.

Dr. William Stewart married twice, first to **Margaret** and second to **Mary Angelica Crommelin**, [see De la Cherois page 213]. He had at least three sons and six daughters. One son, **Poyntz**, also became a doctor, and died in Calcutta in the service of the Hon. East India Company. Another son, **William**, was also in H.E.I.C. service. His first wife was **Ann Rogers**, grand-daughter of a Rector of Lisburn Cathedral, the **Rev. Anthony Rogers**, and her name is also recorded on the memorial in the Cathedral. William's second wife was **Arabella**.

One of Dr. Stewart's daughters, **Jane**, died in childbirth in India. Her husband was **Major Francis Crossley**, also with Lisburn connections, [see Crossley page 209]. His daughters who married were **Charlotte**, married to **Thomas Fulton Caldbeck**, [see Caldbeck page 201], and **Aemelia**, married to **Rev. Edward Johnson Smyth**, [see Johnson Smyth page 243]. Charlotte Caldbeck and Aemelia Johnson Smyth had the Longstone Infant School built in 1847. It was endowed by their sister, **Magdalene Stewart**, who was also involved with the Lisburn Religious Lending Library which was established in the Market House in 1826.

BELFAST NEWS LETTER
TUESDAY OCTOBER 29 1844

DEATH OF DR. STEWART OF LISBURN

It is to-day our painful duty to add another name to the melancholy roll of deaths which the present month has been fatally prolific - that of Dr. Stewart, of Lisburn, who expired on Tuesday afternoon, at his residence in that town, in the 76th year of his age. The language of newspaper panogyric is but too

Descendants of Alexander Stewart

This is not a complete Family Tree.

Alexander Stewart
Married
Isabella Stewart

Rose Hall
b: abt. 1690
d: Feb. 11 1782
Buried Lisb. Cath.

[1] **Richard Close**
Married 1708

[2] **Charles Stewart**
d: June 4 1774
Married

Capt. Poyntz Stewart
b: abt. 1736
d: April 9 1823
Buried Lisb. Cath.

[2] **Ann**
b: abt. 1726
d: July 21 1793
Buried Lisb. Cath.
[3] Jane Casement
d: 1828

Married Sept. 8 1763
[1] **Magdalene Gayer**

Dr. William Stewart
b: abt. 1768
d: Oct. 22 1844
Married
[1] **Margaret**
b: abt. 1777
d: May 15 1816
Buried Lisb. Cath.

Married April 16 1817
[2] **Mary Angelica**
Hutchinson (née
Crommelin)
b: 1767
d: May 26 1832
Buried Lisburn Cath.
(See Crommelin)

Ann Stewart
b: abt. 1726
d: July 26 1804
Buried Lisb. Cath.

Charlotte Stewart
b: abt. 1728
d: July 26 1822
Buried Lisb. Cath.
Married
William Smyth

Hannah Smyth
b: abt. 1768
d: Aug. 3 1792
Buried Lisb. Cath.

Katherine Smyth
d: March 19 1809
Married
Richard Stewart

Anne Smyth
Married
Major Philip Stewart
(See ✳7)

Ralph Smyth
Married
Amelia St. George
Browne
Issue

Rev. James Smyth
b: abt. 1762
d: Nov. 29 1823
Buried Lisb. Cath.
Married
Joanna Ryan
Issue

✳ **Major Philip Stewart**
d: 1837
Married Jan. 8 1796
Anne Smyth

Poyntz Stewart
b: abt. 1764
d: Nov. 5 1773
Buried Lisb. Cath.

Major Charles Stewart
b: 1764
d: 1837
Married
Amelia Gordon

Major Philip Stewart
Married
Matilda Dawson

Capt. William Stewart
d: 1857
Married
Mary Bindyshe

Charles Stewart
d: 1891
Married
Emily Parland
Issue

James Stewart
bap.: Jan. 23 1805

Dr. Poyntz Stewart
bap.: Sept. 10 1799
d: July 16 1828

Edward Stewart
bap.: Aug. 7 1802

Edward Stewart
bap.: Sept. 5 1803

Magdalene Stewart
bap.: June 4 1805
d: Dec. 5 1871
Buried Lisb. Cath.

Aemelia Stewart
d: Abt. 1808
d: April 4 1876
Married Nov. 13 1839
Buried Lisb. Cath.
Rev. Edward
Johnson Smyth
b: July 23 1815
d: July 23 1902
Issue
(See Johnson Smyth)

Mary Ann Stewart
bap.: Aug. 2 1810
d: Aug. 24 1833
Buried Lisb. Cath.

Charlotte Stewart
b: Abt. 1813
d: Feb. 2 1897
Married April 4 1851
Thomas Fulton Caldbeck
Issue
(See Caldbeck)

Margaret Stewart
b: 1816
d: May 13 1816
Buried Lisb. Cath.

Major William Stewart
Married July 30 1815
[1] **Ann Rogers**
Lisb. Cath. Memorial
d: Aug. 8 1824
[2] **Arabella**
b: abt. 1795
d: Feb. 21 1840
Buried Lisb. Cath.

[1] **Jane Stewart**
bap.: July 26 1800
d: March 1 1828
Married Aug. 20 1824
Major Francis Crossley
b: abt. 1787
d: Sept. 17 1846
Buried Lisb. Cath
(See Crossley).

270

often that of inconsiderate praise, but on this occasion we speak what we know, when we say, that a worthier citizen, a better friend, a more kindly gentleman, has seldom been summoned away from the society which he adorned. In works of charity his was an open hand - to all the benevolent institutions of Lisburn, to many of those in Belfast, his liberality was unsparing, and no object whereby the glory of God, or the good of his fellow creature could be subserved, ever appealed to him in vain. Wherever his influence could be useful, it was cheerfully bestowed — indeed he never seemed more happy than when, by disinterested exertions and anxiety, he was enabled to forward the prospects and promote the welfare of those he esteemed - and it was his privilege very often to enjoy this exalted feeling. In every relation of life his character was "void of reproach" - in disposition affectionate and cheerful - in manners polished - in mind highly educated - in profession successful and respected, his death has left a void which will be long and generally felt in the town and neighbourhood, and in the hearts of his family and friends a blank which will never be filled. Doctor Stewart was not only the descendant of one of the oldest and best families in Lisburn, but the worthy representative of a generation, now quite extinct, whose social spirit, and cordial hospitality, made the town, for many years, peculiar and remarkable. He was the last of the race, and in largeness of heart seemed to have been the general heir. Of the virtues which endear man to man in the various relations of life, he was a most amiable and unostentatious example; while, in the higher and holier, which unite man to God, we could affirm with confidence, were it not beyond our province to speak, that he was a sincere believer, and a humble follower of Christ.

CATHEDRAL 107 AND MEMORIAL

Robert Stewart, born about 1754 and died 6th May 1837, and his wife, **Ann**, born about 1741 and died 29th December 1835, the first two people mentioned on this box tomb, are the parents of **James Stewart**, born about 1781 and died 26th December 1847, and **Robert Stewart**, born about 1783 and died 4th June 1858. Robert married **Lucinda Clarke**, born about 1793 and died 11th September 1853. Robert and Lucinda had a family of at least three boys and six girls. The daughters were **Elizabeth**, born about 1821 and died 25th March 1887, **Lucinda**, baptised 3rd November 1823, **Marianne**, baptised 14th January 1827 and died 30th September 1888, **Celina,** baptised 11th July 1830, **Emily**, baptised 19th January 1834 and **Eleanor Jane**, baptised 18th June 1837.

The three sons were **Robert**, baptised 24th July 1825 and died 22nd July 1882, **James Andrew**, baptised 21st September 1828 and died 2nd November 1906, and **William**. Robert married **Maria Jackson Scott** of Rathmines, Co. Dublin, and they had a daughter, **Maria Jackson**, baptised 17th June 1868 and died 16th March 1876. She is recorded as being buried in the Cathedral grounds, although her name also appears on her parent's memorial in Lisburn Cemetery. James Andrew married **Deborah Fawcett** and then a **Miss Jardine**. Both Robert Jun. and James Andrew are buried in Lisburn Cemetery, Hillsborough Road, along with other members of their family.

Although Marianne Clarke, sister to Robert Jun. and James Andrew is mentioned on the stone in the Cathedral grounds, there is also a very fine memorial to her in the Cathedral, erected by her husband, the **Rev. Samuel Clarke**. He was a Church of Ireland rector at Gleneageary, Co. Wicklow, from 1889-96. His father was **Charles Clarke**, a surgeon, and his mother was **Emily Gertrude Hawkshaw**.

Robert Stewart (1783-1858), who, having learnt the linen trade from Barbours, set up his own flax spinning and linen thread business in 1835, in the Antrim Street area of Lisburn. At first the thread was twisted by hand.

In 1845 he brought two of his sons, Robert and James Andrew, into partnership with him and the firm then became Robert Stewart & Sons. After Robert died in 1858 his two sons continued to develop the firm. Robert Stewart jun. died in 1882. Improvements were being made to the building and while Robert was showing some visitors around he fell from some scaffolding, broke his leg and died from complications a few days later. James Andrew continued the business taking in a partner, Mr.

(Courtesy of the Irish Linen Centre & Lisburn Museum)
ROBERT STEWART & SONS' MILL SHORTLY BEFORE DEMOLITION IN 1985.

Thomas J. Porter. A new five-storey mill was built in 1889 at a cost of £30,000 and was lighted throughout with electricity. In 1888 eight hundred people were employed, but, with the new factory in 1889, this rose to about one thousand. Their speciality was shoe and tailors' threads and these products were shipped all over the world.

In 1898 the firm was declared bankrupt and in 1899 it became a limited company. James Andrew Stewart died 2nd November 1906. The firm was taken over by the Linen Thread Co. Ltd., owned by Barbours. It was eventually closed and the buildings were demolished in 1985 to make way for the Crazy Prices Supermarket complex (later Bow Street Mall). Stewart's house at 68 Bow Street, opposite the junction of Market Place and Bow Street, is still standing today.

BANNER OF ULSTER
SATURDAY JUNE 5 1858

THE LATE ROBERT STEWART ESQ. — We have this day to announce the death of this highly respected gentleman, which melancholy event took place at his house in Bow Street, Lisburn, at an early hour yesterday morning. The deceased was head of the firm of R. Stewart & Sons, of the Lisburn flax-spinning and thread works, and for upwards of half a century had been connected with the manufacturing interests of Ulster. In early life Mr. Stewart was largely engaged in the cotton trade, which business he gave up about twenty years ago, when he embarked very extensively into the thread and flax-spinning manufactures. By his fellow townsmen the deceased gentleman was very much respected, and by the religious body to which he had been more immediately attached his name is not likely soon to be forgotten. Mr. Stewart, we understand, was in his seventy fifth year of age.

SWANZY

CATHEDRAL MEMORIAL
Detective Inspector Oswald Ross Swanzy was the second son of **James** and **Elizabeth Swanzy**, formerly of Castleblaney, Co. Monaghan. Aged 39, he had been fifteen years in the Royal Irish Constabulary and had been transferred to Lisburn about three months before his death, his previous posting being Cork. He was living at 31 Railway Street, Lisburn. On Sunday 22nd August 1920 he attended morning service at Lisburn Cathedral. Just after 1 o'clock he was returning home, accompanied by Mr. Frederick William Ewart, of Derryvolgie, Lisburn (of the firm William Ewart and Sons) and his son, Major G. Valentine Ewart. As he reached the corner of the Northern Bank (now Shannon the Jewellers), he was fatally shot by the I.R.A. It is believed that four or five men were responsible and they made their escape in a taxi which was waiting for them in Castle Street, near Lisburn Technical Institute. This was a revenge killing ordered by Michael Collins. Thomas McCurtain, Lord Mayor of Cork and I.R.A. Commandant had been killed, allegedly by the R.I.C., which Swanzy had commanded.

Unfortunately the murder led to three days of civil unrest and sectarian rioting in Lisburn. This resulted in another murder and with several homes and businesses being either destroyed by burning or badly damaged by riotous mobs.

Three days later D.I. Swanzy's funeral took place to Mount Jerome Cemetery in Dublin. In February 1921 his mother and sister, **Irene**, had the memorial to his memory erected in the Cathedral. Both his father, James, and elder brother, **Henry Hubert**, had died in 1907.

The Swanzy family had connections with Lisburn as a direct ancestor, **Henry Swanzy** from Blaris, fought at the battle of the Boyne and later settled in Monaghan.

TAYLOR

CATHEDRAL MEMORIAL AND CATHEDRAL 24

The Mural tablet in the Cathedral to **Bishop Jeremy Taylor** was erected by Bishop Richard Mant in 1827. Jeremy Taylor, who was baptised 15th August 1613 in Cambridge, was the son of **Nathaniel Taylor,** a barber. Jeremy first studied at Cambridge and became a lecturer in divinity, then a Rector, before becoming Chaplain to the army of King Charles I. In 1644, after the defeat of the Royalists by the Cromwellian forces at Marston Moor, Jeremy fled to Wales and went into hiding. King Charles I was eventually beheaded in 1649. Because of his beliefs Jeremy was imprisoned at least twice, and spent some time in the Tower of London.

When Lord Conway wanted to acquire a new Churchman he appears to have consulted John Evelyn, the famous diarist, who recommended Jeremy Taylor. Perhaps, as Jeremy was a Royalist, Cromwell was only too happy to give him a permit to leave England, and so Jeremy came to Ireland in 1658 as chaplain to Lord Conway. He was given an income by Lord Conway and at various times lived in Castle Street, Lisburn, and at Portmore, Lower Ballinderry, near Lough Neagh, as well as other places.

The Rev. Carmody said in his book, "He was a great Churchman and a giant in the world of letters." Jeremy Taylor was an academic and wrote several books that are now classics of Anglican devotion, and one of these books, a treatise on moral theology, remains the most important single work by an Anglican thinker.

At the Restoration Jeremy Taylor was appointed to the bishopric of Down and Connor and Bishop or Administrator of the Diocese of Dromore. He was consecrated in St. Patrick's Cathedral, Dublin, on 27th January 1661. When he came to Lisburn the Cathedrals at Down and Connor were in ruins, as was the church of Lisburn. Again, very soon after the Restoration in 1660, Charles II raised the parish church of Lisburn to be the Cathedral of the United Diocese. Jeremy Taylor paid for the restoration of the Cathedral in Dromore and in 1664 gave money to have the Middle Church at Ballinderry built. Unfortunately he died a year before the Middle Church was consecrated.

Jeremy Taylor was ill for several days after contracting a fever from a patient he had visited, and died in Castle Street, Lisburn, on 13th August 1667. He is buried in a vault in the chancel of Dromore Cathedral. His funeral hatchment is in the Middle Church, Ballinderry. A hatchment is a tablet, usually diamond shaped, with a deceased person's armorial bearings, and was used to indicate the death of a member of a titled or landed family. [For more details see Lisburn Historical Society Journal, Vol. 7, 1989, Page 41.]

Jeremy Taylor was married twice, first, in 1639, to **Phoebe Landisdale** and secondly to **Johanna Bridges**. He had at least two daughters, **Mary** and **Joanna**. Mary married **Francis Marsh**, who became Archbishop of Dublin, and Joanna married **Edward Harrison**, of Magheralave, who became M.P. for Lisburn in 1692, in the first Parliament of William III. Edward Harrison's sister was married to **Lieutenant Thomas Conway** of Derriaghy, a kinsman of Lord Conway. Both Edward Harrison and Thomas Conway are buried in Lisburn Cathedral. Edward Harrison's sons, **Michael** and **Francis**, were also Members of Parliament, as was a descendant of his daughter, **Mary**. He was **William Todd Jones** of Ballyhomra, the son of **Dr. Conway Jones** and **Mary Wray Todd**. He was an M.P.

in the fourth Parliament of George III. His sisters, **Charlotte** and **Mary**, are buried in Cathedral No. 24, along with Charlotte's husband, **Lt. Col. Henry Wray**. Henry Wray and Charlotte Jones were married on 2nd April 1792.

Jeremy Taylor had a son, **Edward**, who was also buried in Lisburn Cathedral on 10th March 1661. His only surviving son, **Charles**, was dying of consumption in London, when Jeremy Taylor died in 1667.

THOMPSON

CATHEDRAL 42

This large burial site is for the Thompson family, who are related to the Fulton, Hogg and Bruce families. The first William (1763-1843) named on the stone was **Dr. William Thompson,** who was described as "Apothecary" of Castle Street, Lisburn, in early street directories. He and his wife, **Dora** (1749-1823), had at least three sons and a daughter. Two of the sons and a daughter died young. They were **James**, **William John** and **Jane** and they are buried in the Cathedral grave. **Francis Abbott** (1783-1865), their surviving son, married **Jane Fulton** (1782-1840) on 6th June 1805. She was the daughter of **Richard Fulton** and **Elizabeth Shanks,** [see Fulton No. 71 and page 221].

Francis and Jane had a family of at least four sons and a daughter. Both Francis and Jane Thompson are buried at Hillhall Presbyterian Church, along with one of their sons, **Richard** (1810-1856). At least one more son, **James** (1821-1854), is buried in India. The eldest son, **William**, born 7th March 1806, was a M.D. of the Edinburgh University and Fellow of the Royal College of Surgeons in Ireland. He started practicing medicine in Lisburn in 1828. He lived in Castle Street, was consulting physician and surgeon superintendent of the County Antrim Infirmary and was well known and respected through out the North of Ireland. Many patients travelled a great distance to his consulting rooms. He was also a shareholder and member of the Board of Directors of the Great Northern Railway. He married **Rosina Hogg** on 7th November 1833, [see Hogg page 239]. She had previously been married on 21st January 1826 to **Edward Maxwell** of the Bengal Civil Service, but unfortunately he died on 19th August 1826. Rosina and Edward Maxwell had a daughter, **Lilia Anna**, who married the **Rev. Edward Loftus Fitzgerald**, a curate of Lisburn Cathedral. Rosina and Dr. William Thompson had two sons and a daughter. Both the sons, **Col. William** (1834-1882) and **Stewart** (1835-1862), are buried in the Cathedral grave. Their only daughter, **Mary Hogg** (born about 1837), married firstly **George Mitchell**, of Craigavad, on 28th June 1858. She married secondly **James Bruce D.L.** (1835-1917). They lived at Thorndale, Antrim Road, Belfast, and Benburb Manor, Co. Tyrone. He was a partner in the firm of Messrs. Dunville and Co., Distillers. Mary Hogg and James Bruce had no family.

Dr. William Thompson sadly died on the 22nd September 1882, from injuries received after being hit by a train as he was crossing the railway line at Dunmurry station. At his funeral to the Cathedral his pall bearers included Dr. Samuel Musgrave, who was Dr. Thompson's first pupil, and Mr. Green, his last pupil.

As a tribute to Dr. William Thompson's memory his son-in-law, James Bruce, his daughter, Mary Hogg Bruce, and his wife, Rosina, built and endowed "The Thompson Memorial Home for Incurables" on the Magheralave Road, Lisburn. This home was erected in 1885 and in 1963 was taken over by Antrim County Health Committee and re-opened as Thompson House. The official re-opening was on Monday 9th October 1967 by His Excellency Lord Erskine of Rerrick. James Bruce also contributed generously to the Building Fund of the Royal Victoria Hospital, Belfast.

Rosina Thompson died 8th December 1884 and is buried in the Cathedral grounds. Mary Hogg Bruce, who died 4th May 1893, and James Bruce, who died 5th March 1917, are both buried in a vault at Holywood Old Church, Co. Down.

Francis and Jane Thompson had at least one other son, also called **Francis**, and a daughter, **Jane**, who are not named on the stone. Francis (1881-1904) was surgeon in the Bengal Medical Service, married twice and had two sons. Jane (born 1822) married **Rev. Adam Glasgow** in May Street Presbyterian Church, Belfast, on 30th December 1841, and they are believed to have emigrated to New Zealand.

THORNTON

In the Ordnance Survey Memoirs mention is made of **Mary Ann Thornton** who had acted as sexton of the Cathedral for fifty years. In the Cathedral burial records there is an entry on 24th July 1842 of **Margaret Thornton** of Castle Street, aged 7. There is also the comment "killed by church gate falling on her." In the Belfast News Letter of Tuesday July 26th 1842 there is the following report:-

MELANCHOLY ACCIDENT   On Friday last, a fine girl, about seven years of age, daughter of the sexton of Lisburn Cathedral, was amusing herself swinging on the large iron gate leading from the Castle-street entrance to that edifice, when it fell on the child, crushing her so dreadfully that instantaneous death was the result. It appears the gate was about to be repaired, and the stones on which it was hinged being loose, easily gave way, and caused the unfortunate accident.

VERNON

CATHEDRAL 130

James Vernon was a carpenter, and later a builder, of Bridge Street, Lisburn. Five children who died young are named on his stone. His mother, **Catherine**, and his wife, **Alis**, are also buried here. James Vernon and his firm were responsible for several notable buildings, or improvements to buildings, in the town of Lisburn, and probably in other parts of the country. They were one of the builders of Christ Church, Lisburn, which was built in 1842, and also of the various additions which were later made to it. Other work they were responsible for was the remodelling of the seats in the Cathedral, renovations to the Market House and in 1880 the building of Sir Richard Wallace's house in Castle Street, now part of Lisburn Institute. They also were involved with enlarging and remodelling Lisburn First Presbyterian Church, Market Square.

After James died his son, **John**, who was born 14th December 1841, took over the business. He had been retired about fifteen years when he died in 1924, aged 83. He is buried in Lisburn Cemetery, Hillsborough Road, along with his wife, **Hannah**, and other members of the family.

WHITLA

CATHEDRAL 48 AND MEMORIAL

For the Whitla family there is a box tomb and a memorial inside the Cathedral, on the north nave wall. Although the family have not been connected with Lisburn in recent times, they did, in the past, play a prominent part in the life of Lisburn.

It is believed the founder of the Whitla family came from Ayrshire during the plantation of Ulster and settled at Gobrana, Glenavy, Co. Antrim. **John Whitla**, son of **George** and grandson of **William**, was born in 1732 and married a **Miss Arthur**. He died 12th May 1790 and is possibly the John Whitla who was a churchwarden for Lisburn Cathedral in 1760. John had a daughter, **Rebecca**, and two sons, **William,** born 1764, and **George**, born 1765. In Lisburn Cathedral records there is the entry of a Rebecca Whitla marrying **Robert Burden** on 5th April 1780.

The box tomb in the graveyard is erected to the memory of this last named George Whitla, his wife, **Margaret Allan Carleton**, and one of their sons, **John**, and his wife, **Eleanor Haynes**. George Whitla, in 1811, is described as a muslin manufacturer and is believed to have sent Henry Monro a suit of clothes before his hanging in 1798, [see Monro page 247]. In 1790 a George Whitla had a tanyard, in 1798 a George Whitla was a sergeant in the Lisburn Cavalry, and in 1819 George Whitla is

Descendants of John Whitla

Cathedral No. 48 & Memorial

This is not a complete Family Tree.

John Whitla
b: abt. 1732
d: May 12 1790
Married
Miss Arthur

Rebecca Whitla

William Whitla
b: abt. 1764

George Whitla
b: abt. 1765
d: May 12 1831
Buried Lisb. Cath
Married Feb. 11 1792

Margaret Allan Carleton
b: abt. 1768
d: Dec. 25 1842
Buried Lisb. Cath

George Whitla
b: abt. 1803
Died young

Elinor Whitla
Died young

[1] Lieut. John Whitla
b: September 10 1795
d: March 21 1821
Buried Lisb. Cath
Married May 24 1820

Eleanor Haynes
b: abt. 1797
d: July 25 1890
Buried Lisb. Cath.

[2] Dr. John McDowall
Married June 17 1825

William Whitla
b: Feb. 1 1793
d: July 12 1861
Married Nov. 5 1830
Buried Lisb. Cath.

Elizabeth Buchanan
b: Dec. 3 1811
d: May 30 1886

George Whitla
b: July 31 1832
d: 1919
Married
[1] Susan Gooden
[2] Catherine Barbara Gould

Capt. James Buchanan Whitla
b: Sep. 2 1834
d: May 1 1911
Married
Eliza Matilda Forbes
d: Mar. 26 1899

John Whitla
b: Nov. 19 1835
d: May 8 1842
Buried Lisb. Cath

Elizabeth Clarke Whitla
b: Aug. 31 1837
d: Jan. 20 1871
Married
Thomas Peter Carr

[1] Eleanor Margaret Whitla
b: Sept. 27 1838
d: April 2 1877
Married Apr. 30 1862
Col. Lewis Mansergh Buchanan
b: Dec. 31 1836
[2] Wilhelmina Molony

Col. William Whitla
b: March 13 1840
d: 1917

Emma Hardcastle Haldane Whitla
b: July 15 1841
d: 1899
Married
Major Henry Lucas

Sydney Herbert Whitla
b: 1843
d: Feb. 27 1853

Jane Alicia Whitla
b: abt. 1845
d: 1929
Married Apr. 24 1872
Charles Cotton Bridges

Valentine Herbert Whitla
b: 1853
d: 1933

Francis Whitla
b: 1849

Ada Whitla
b: June 3 1846
d: 1919
Married Dec. 12 1871
Col. Theophilus Higginson
(See **Higginson**)

Seymour Conway Whitla
b: July 2 1845
d: Jan. 25 1853

described as a merchant of Bow Lane. George Whitla left the interest of £100 legacy to the Lisburn Male Free School and also a sum of money to the Lisburn Female School, founded in 1819 by **Miss Hawkshaw**. Mrs. George Whitla was a Governess of the Infirmary.

George's son, John Whitla, had married Eleanor Haynes in 1820, and after John's death in 1821, Eleanor then married **Dr. John McDowall**, a Dublin Physician. This was in 1825, and in 1826 she had a son called **George Whitla McDowall**.

The memorial in the Cathedral is to **William Whitla**, eldest son of George, his wife, **Elizabeth Buchanan,** and their large family. Elizabeth, is buried in Plumstead, Kent, and was a daughter of **James Buchanan** (1772-1851) HBM consul at New York, 1816 to 1843, and his wife, **Elizabeth Clarke** (1779–1851). William Whitla was on the committee of Lisburn Male Free School and was one of the founder members of the Killultagh Hunt which was started on February 28th 1832, [see THG Vol. 1 page 153]. He lived first in Bow Street and then in Seymour Street and had eight sons and five daughters.

Eleanor Margaret Whitla, daughter of William and Elizabeth Whitla, married **Col. Lewis Mansergh Buchanan**, her mother's cousin. Eleanor and her husband are buried in Cappagh Parish Graveyard, Co. Tyrone. Several of Eleanor Margaret's brothers and sisters also had military connections. Her eldest brother, **George**, was a Surgeon in the army and his brothers and brothers-in-law saw service in many parts of the world. Her father, William Whitla, and her brother, **Capt. James B. Whitla**, were churchwardens of the Cathedral in 1857 and 1872. Capt. James eventually inherited land in Manitoba from his mother, who had inherited it from her father, James Buchanan, and Capt. James and his wife went to live in Canada. There is a memorial in Christ Church, Lisburn, to **Eliza Matilda Whitla**, Capt. James B. Whitla's wife. She died in Manitoba 26th March 1899. It is thought that another brother, **Valentine Herbert**, went to Queensland, Australia. Her sister, **Ada**, was married to **Col. Theophilus Higginson**, [see Higginson memorial and page 233].

The Whitla family were mentioned in the will of **Agnes Mathewson** (née **Kennedy**), [See THG Vol. 1 Kilrush No. 79 and page 156]. This family of Whitlas are also related to the **Valentine Whitlas** of Ben Eaden, Belfast and the Whitlas of Inver Lodge, Larne.

LISBURN STANDARD
JUNE 5 1886
DEATH OF MRS. ELIZABETH WHITLA

Our readers will observe, from a notice in our obituary columns, that Mrs. Elizabeth Whitla, the widow of the late Wm. Whitla, Esq., Lisburn, died at her residence, No. 6, Chepstow, Bayswater, London, on the afternoon of Sunday, 30th ultimo, at the ripe old age of seventy-five years. The deceased lady, who was mother of Captain Whitla, and a large and distinguished Lisburn family, was connected with one of the oldest and most respected Lisburn families, and her death will be learned of with feelings of much sorrow and regret by many of the old inhabitants in our town, and, indeed by all who had the privilege of knowing her personally.

LISBURN STANDARD
SATURDAY JULY 26 1890
FUNERAL OF MRS. McDOWALL

To-day (Friday) the mortal remains of Mrs. McDowall, who died at her residence in Seymour Street on Tuesday last, were interred in the Cathedral Graveyard. Many of the townspeople showed their respect for the deceased by joining the funeral *cortege*. The beautiful burial service of the Church of Ireland was impressively said by the Rev. Canon Pounden and the Rev. G.R. Bell. Mrs. McDowall passed away at the advanced age of ninety-three years. Her first husband was John Whitla, of the 14th Light Dragoons, brother of the late William Whitla, of Seymour Street, whose family were greatly and deservedly respected in the town and neighbourhood. Mrs. Whitla, some years subsequent to her husband's death, was united in marriage to Dr. John McDowall, an eminent Dublin physician. On the demise of this gentleman, Mrs. McDowall came to live in Lisburn, where she has resided for the long period of sixty-five years. Since the death of her son, the Rev. G.H. McDowall, chaplain in her Majesty's navy, Mrs. McDowall was not able to leave her house; but, although suffering from much weakness, she maintained her cheerfulness to the last. She was attached to the congregation worshipping in the Cathedral.

JAMES BUCHANAN WHITLA
(1834 – 1911)

BELFAST NEWS LETTER
THURSDAY MAY 4 1911

CAPTAIN JAMES B. WHITLA

The death occurred at Barnes, Surrey, on the 1st inst., of Captain James Buchanan Whitla, who will be remembered by many Belfast people as a former master of the union workhouse, a position which he occupied about twenty years ago. On his resignation of that post, Captain Whitla, who had previously served in the Connaught Rangers, emigrated to Canada, where he took up farming. Subsequently he left the Dominion and settled down in England. He was 76 years of age, and was a native of the Lisburn district.

WIGHTMAN

CATHEDRAL 59

This Wightman family were Presbyterians who belonged to Market Square Presbyterian Church, Lisburn. In 1714 **James Wightman** married **Barbara**, and it is their son, **James** (2nd August 1717 – October 1767), married to **Ann Culbert** on 2nd December 1743, who is the first named on the stone. They had a family of at least six sons and a daughter. The sons were **John** (born 1747), **James** (born 1748), **Thomas**, **William** (born 1753), **Robert** (born 1757) and **George** (born 1761). The daughter was **Margaret** (born 1744). William went to the United States of America and Robert was a doctor in Southampton and died in 1843. Margaret married **Thomas Ward** in 1777 and had four sons. One of these four sons, **James**, who died 5th May 1847, married first **Eliza Fulton** (1778-1805) on 11th November 1802, [see Fulton page 221]. He then married **Margaret Craig** on 27th July 1814, [see Craig THG Vol. 1 page 151]. There was issue from both marriages.

The eldest son of James and Anne Wightman, John (c1847-15th December 1801), a damask merchant of Lisburn, also married twice. He and his two wives are mentioned on the stone. The first wife was **Margaret Kennedy**, who died 24th November 1780. John and Margaret married on 22nd April 1776. They had two sons and a daughter surviving. One son, **John**, (bap. 18th November 1780) and a daughter, **Eliza**, (bap. 1st February 1777), are named on the stone. Eliza married **Charles McAlester** on the 5th March 1807. He was a cotton manufacturer and was in partnership with Hugh Paton with calico works at Carnmoney and a calender (a roller machine for pressing the cloth) in Callender Street, Belfast. Their three children were born in Chichester Street, Belfast. Charles died on 5th March 1811 and Eliza returned to join her family in Lisburn, before going to live in Holywood, Co. Down. Eliza died on the 23rd July 1855. [For more information on Eliza's family see Craig THG Vol.1 Kilrush and page 151.] The other son, **James**, (bap. 1st February 1778), married **Margaret Fulton** on 9th August 1803. She died 30th March 1819, [see Fulton No. 71 and page 221]. They had five daughters. James is believed to have left his first family behind when he went to Pennsylvania. He may have married again. He died 7th November 1844.

John's second wife was **Mary Henderson** of Ravarnet. She died February 1819. John and Mary married on 22nd April 1783 and they had at least three sons and a daughter surviving. One son, **Robert**, (bap. 17th July 1786), died young. Of the other sons **William** (bap. 20th April 1785) married **Magdeline Patton** on 4th September 1816, and went to U.S.A. about August 1817. He died in Florence, Alabama on 22nd April 1825. **Thomas Henderson** (bap. 15th March 1791), was a surgeon in the Royal Navy and died unmarried in Glasgow on 26th October 1823. Several of his letters sent home from his time in the Royal Navy have survived. The daughter was **Nancy**. She was baptised 27th October 1792 and died on 25th May 1848 while returning from New Orleans to England.

When John Wightman (c1847-1801) died he willed £10 to the poor of Lisburn Presbyterian congregation.
[P.R.O.N.I. T/2263/1-3 and T/1475/1]

YOUNG

CATHEDRAL 28
Fred Kee in his book "Lisburn Miscellany" makes reference to this gravestone and the tragic story of how **John Young** met his death. In the Cathedral records there is the additional information that John was the son of **William Young**, a nailer.

NEWS LETTER
TUESDAY, AUGUST 27 1822

MELANCHOLY ACCIDENT

About seven o'clock on the evening of the 23rd inst., Patrick Maguire, a lad of about 16 years of age, tied John Young, a very fine boy of six years old, who had accompanied him to a field, near Lisburn, to a cow's tail. At first, the animal moved slowly forward, but soon, as it appears, became terrified, by the unusual weight appended to her tail, and ran furiously along the road, till stopped by the driver of a mail-coach. Maguire, as was proved at the inquest, called in vain to some passengers on the highway to stop the cow, which rushed violently through the turnpike on the Hillsborough Road. Before the arrival of the mail-coach, the poor child, contused and mangled by percussion on the pavement had expired. We are informed that his mother was just returning from Belfast, when she met the cow dragging the lifeless corse (sic) of her son on the highway, and was thrown into a state of distraction, in which she still continues.— Maguire has fled. He is a lad of about five feet high, stout made, with a downcast countenance, and had on when he disappeared an old artillery coat and a woollen hat.

An inquest was held on the body by Mr. Henry Allen, coroner, which found "that the said John Young came by his death in consequence of having been tied to a cow's tail, the property of John Woods, by Patrick Maguire, and that the said tying was not through malice, but youthful inadvertence of said Maguire."

APPENDIX 1
THESE HALLOWED GROUNDS VOLUME 1

Whilst researching material for Volume 2 the under noted information relating to burials in Kilrush Burying Ground was discovered.

BELFAST NEWS LETTER
DIED

Friday April 22 1825
CLOSE   In Lisburn, on the 1st inst., in the 27th year of her age, Miss Ann Close. She endured a lingering illness with Christian fortitude, and departed this life in the hope of obtaining a glorious immortality.

Saturday June 23 1860
CREE   June 19, of rapid consumption, Carleton Cree, youngest son of Mr. James Cree, of Bridge Street, Lisburn, in the 17th year of his age.

Friday April 9 1824
FULTON   On the 25th ult. near Lisburn, Mr. Wm. Fulton, aged 33 years, much lamented. His unexceptionable conduct in life, and his resignation to the divine will at death, afford his friends Christian consolation.

Tuesday May 15 1866
HICKS   February 24 at Melbourne, Australia, Robert McCall, son of Mr. Robert Hicks, aged 1 year.

Tuesday October 25 1859
MAJOR   October 21, at Lisburn, George Major Esq. His remains will be removed for interment in Kilrush Burying Ground on Wednesday (tomorrow) morning at eleven o'clock.

Tuesday May 15 1866
MAJOR   May 14, at Lisburn, George Hugh, infant son of Henry Major Esq.

LISBURN STANDARD
DIED

Saturday June 5 1886
MULHOLLAND   May 14 suddenly at Alexandria, Egypt, the Rev. James Eugene Mulholland, aged 45 (son of the late Henry Mulholland, The Quay, Lisburn) Pastor of St. Patrick's R.C. church, Philadelphia.

DAVID BEATTY (1805 – 1884)
[*SEE THG VOL.1 PAGE 149*]

APPENDIX 2

On the following pages we have included extra material giving the names of some of the people who were living in Lisburn in the late 18th century and early 19th century.

In 1782 the call was made out to Rev. Andrew Craig to come to 1st Lisburn Presbyterian Church. The following is a copy of this call, which was supported by the signatures of 132 members of the congregation.

We, the subscribers, members of the Protestant Dissenting Congregation of Lisburn, ask and invite you the Revd. Andrew Craig, to be our stated minister, and to do all the Offices thereto belonging :- And we do engage to give you for your support, on your performing those duties, Twenty pounds Sterg per year, out of the Freehold belonging to us in Lisburn, now occupied by Mr. James Read, together with whatever Stipend can be collected from the Congregation, excepting Eight Pounds per year for our Clerk : Witness our hands at our Meeting House in Lisburn, the 16th day of June 1782. Henry Bell and Robert Burden, lessees, William Martin, David Wilson, John Kenley, Elizabeth Kennedy, Richard Fulton, Magdalene Bell, Isabella Tandy, Margaret Speers, Thomas Cowdon, Alexander Alderdice, David Bredy, James Williamson, John Wightman, John Ekenhead, Henry Bell, jun., Thomas Fraiser, John Magill, Henry Mullre, Robert Bell, John Wilson, John Wilson, John Harper, William Carson, John Whitla, Ann Wightman, Eliza Stanhope, Jean Townley, Jane Douglas, Easter McCracken, John Stitt, Jane Maslin, Joseph Younger, Wm. Heron, Hu McBlain, McKneight McComb, James Crawford, Benjm. Buchanan, Nathl. Lettimore, Lillas Dixon, Edward Younge, James Read, Thomas Ward, Mathew Thompson, John McClean, John Neale, Robert Moore, Robert Fleming, Elias Clegg, junr., William Anderson, Jas. Kennedy, Alex. Crawford, John Gelston, John Patterson, Thomas Lockhart, James Kelly, Robert Parsons, Robt. Oliver, Daniel Mackay, John Clark, William Anderson, Thomas Rainey, John McKibbon, Richard Hare, Samuel Murdoch, John Maxwell, Lanty Flack, John Newill, George Rainey, James Dickey, Adam Thompson, Samuel McCleland, Patrick Sheherd, John Addams, Samuel Dawson, John Mecally, Hugh Sparks, Robert Cowdon, Mihl. Thompson, William Neill, Hugh Frazier, Thomas Rainey, George Allister, John Neapper, Robt. McAlister, David Turner, Matt. Foreman, Stephen Rowan, Thos. McGoveny, Thos. Young, John Leghorn, James Diner, Joseph Young, Edward Young, James Ledgerwood, Hugh Boyd, Thomas Cahoon, George Major, George Kairns, Hugh McDowell, Thos. Potts, Will Brown, Wm. Wilson, Thos. Rainey(?), Robt. Rainey, John McMeekin, Wm. Clark, Thos. Fulton, Lewis Cahoon, Wm. Scott, Maurice McComb, John Brown, John Todd, James Renfrey, John Oliver, James B-----, Wm. McCurry, John McCouloch, Darby Mullion, Robert Anderson, Robert Nobb, Wm. McCracken, John Magoueny, John Graham, Jas. McIlroy, J.T. Rush, Thos. Kennedy, Thos. McMurtray, David Foots, Joseph Fulton, Wm. Rea. Attested June 16, 1782. by James Caldwell.

BELFAST NEWS LETTER
FRIDAY JANUARY 2-TUESDAY JANUARY 6 1784

To the Inhabitants of the Town and Parish of Lisburn.

We whose names are hereunto subscribed, Inhabitants of Lisburn, do request your attendance at the Markethouse, on Saturday the 10th instant, at eleven o'clock, to take into consideration what further measures are necessary to effectuate a Reform of the representation of the people in Parliament.

Lisburn, 1st Jan. 1784.

Thomas Ward,	Henry Bell,
John Wightman,	William Martin,
Wm. Thompson,	Robert Bell,
James McCollom,	John Kenly,
John Biggam,	Alex. Crawford,
William Carson,	Wm. Dillon junr.,
William Whitla,	Joseph Fulton,
Robert Burden,	Arthur Johnson,
John Crossley,	William Rea,
Wm. Wheeler,	Cornelius Carleton,
James Moore Walker,	John Shepherd,
Samuel Watson,	James Kennedy,
John Shepherd, senr.,	Leonard Bullmer,
Joseph Younger,	Richard Fulton,
John Forcade,	John Hastings,
George Tandy,	Robert Douglass.

LISBURN STANDARD
MAY 1892
THE YEOMANRY OF LISBURN AND THE SURROUNDING NEIGHBOURHOOD
(FROM A CORRESPONDENT.)

The estate of the first Lord Conway, grandfather to the Marquis of Hertford, was of an oval form, about sixteen miles in length from Clogher and Ballymullan hills, in the County of Down, to Hogpark point or Shanport, in the County of Antrim, which runs into Lough Neagh, and about ten miles in breadth from Moira to Crumlin. The different yeomanry corps in this estate or territory were about one thousand men-two troops of cavalry and nine companies of infantry. The following are the names of the officers and number of men:-LISBURN Cavalry--Marquis of Hertford, William Smyth, S. Delacherois, James Fulton, 64 men. MAGHERAGALL Cavalry--Edward Wakefield, Robert Garrett, Henry Higginson, 60 men. BALLENDERRY Infantry--Marquis of Hertford, Wm. Stewart, James Campbell, William Johnston, 150 men. BALLYMACASH--P. Johnston, Francis Smith, Richard Barnsley, 150 Men. BROOKHILL--James Watson, James Patten 150 men. BROOMHEDGE--Philip Stewart, Nat. Smith, 150 men. DERRIAGHY--Poyntz Stewart, William Curtis, Richard Wolfenden, 150 men. LISBURN--N. Delacherois, Wm. Coulsin (sic), N. Delacherois, 150 men. POLLYGLASS--Robert Duncan, John McClure, John Tucker, 150 men. SOLDIERSTOWN--Stafford Gorman, Mr. Smith, Mr. Fulton, 100 men. GLENAVY--Conway McNiece, John Ridgway, Dan Allen, 150 men. The following was written about the above estate just 100 years ago:-"Leases of this whole estate for three lives or forty one years, were granted from 1740 by the late Marquis of Hertford, from two to five or six Shillings an Acre, but his Lordship got fines. Some of the lives are still in being, but they are dropping off every year; when the whole expire the estate will be between fifty and sixty thousand a year. This estate is improving in building, planting orchards, liming, &c., and will become a terrestrial paradise, or may be called the Garden of Eden in Ireland."

(*Originally written about 1803.*)

LISBURN STANDARD 1917
LISBURN VOLUNTEERS 1798

In 1798 Lisburn had a troop of cavalry Volunteers as well as infantry. In the cavalry were many well-known Lisburn names, some of which are still associated with the town.

Captain Smith	Thomas Crossey	Francis McGahey
Lieutenant Delacherois	Alex. Cudbert	George Pentland
Henry Steele, sergeant	Robert Carleton	John Oliver
George Whitla, sergeant	William Dillon	John Patten
James Fulton, sergeant	Francis Dobbs	George Paterson
James Ravenscroft, sergeant	John Drummond	John Pelan
James Willis, corporal	Robert Frazer	Arthur Richey
Thomas Beatty, corporal	Richard Greer	Henry Seede
John Boomer, corporal	John Hastings	Alex. Stewart
Henry Blainey, trumpeter	John Hill, jun.	Robert Stirling
Murray Alderdice	John Hill, sen.	William Tinsley
Francis Bennett	Isaac Hodgeon	James Townley
Charles Blackhall	John Jefferson	James Turner
Benjamin Boomer	John Johnston	Samuel Waring
John Boomer	Robert Leathem	Paul Waring
Richard Brison	Henry Mussen	William Wheeler
William Brittain	John Mercer	John Ingram
Carnl. Carleton	John Morrow	Edward Quigley
Thomas Carleton	James Mussen, jun.	Henry Sloane
Richard Cahoon	James Mussen, sen.	Thomas Townley
Wm. Coulson	William Mussen	
John Crossley	John McDowell	

In the county of Antrim, situated on the river Lagan <Lougan>, which serves by means of a canal to connect the Lough of Belfast with Lough Neagh <Neugh>. It is 7 miles S.W. of Belfast, and 73 N. from Dublin. Here are extensive manufactures of brown and white linens, lawns, cambrics, damask and diaper cloths, muslin, calicos, &c. Lisburn sends one member to parliament. Market on Tuesday: and fairs on July 21st, and October 5th.

Agnew <Aynew>, George, Moss Vale
Alderdice Alexander, grocer
Andrews Edward, grocer
Armstrong George, tailor
Ballantine James, tanner
Barbour and Duncan, thread and muslin manufacturers
Barcroft John, linen-draper
Barnsley Richard, merchant
Beatty Thomas, tanner
Bell Samuel, woollen-draper
Benson Francis, publican
Boomer George, muslin-manufacturer, Heelcaw
Boomer George, farrier
Boomer John, farmer
Boucher and McCuchen
Boyd Hugh, tailor
Brady Henry, hosier
Brittain <Briltain> Terrence, publican
Bryson Richard, agent to John Hunter, Esq.
Caird John, timber-merchant
Carleton Cornelius, Esq.
Carleton Cornelius, spirit-merchant, Blaris <Blures>
Chambers Thomas, baker
Clarke Charles, muslin-manufacturer
Clarke John, dealer in muslin
Clarke Ellen, grocer
Clegg Joseph, tanner
Clegg Thomas, glazier
Collins William, publican
Coulson John and William, damask and diaper manufacturers
Coulson Walter, grocer
Coulson Rev. Hill, curate
Conran Joshua, linen-draper, Maze
Craig Rev. A. <S.> Prebyterian Minister
Crawford Alexander, M.D.
Crossley John, spirit-merchant
Cupples Rev. Dr., rector
Curtis <Curteis> Edward, linen-draper, Glenburn
Davis Thomas, muslin-manufacturer
Davis Jeremiah, publican
Davis Arthur, grocer and publican
Dawson John, innkeeper and grocer
Dawson James, Sun Inn
Delacherois Nicholas, Esq.
Dillon William, conveyancer
Dixon George, watchmaker
Dixon Thomas, grocer

Dornan James, whitesmith
Dowdall John, publican
Dubourdieu Rev. S.
Dunn George, muslin-manufacturer
Ferguson John, grocer
Fitzsimmons John, grocer
Fletcher Rev. Philip
Foots Richard, nailer
Fulton, **Thompson, and Cursa**, woollen-drapers and thread-merchants
Fulton Joseph, Master of Chancery, Commissioner for taking affidavits for the King's Bench, Exchequer, and Common Pleas
Fulton Andrew, woollen-draper
Fulton James, attorney
Fulton Richard, Esq.
Garrett Robert, brewer
Gelson John, cabinet-maker
Gill William, yarn-merchant, Maragall
Graham William, grocer
Gray William, schoolmaster
Greer Richard, chandler and soap-boiler
Gregg Dominick, linen-draper
Griffith George, surveyor of excise
Hames Abraham, publican
Hancock John, linen-draper
Hancock Jacob, linen-draper
Hawkshaw William, J.P.
Helsey John, jun. linen draper
Higginson Rev. Thomas, academy
Hill John, linen-draper, Dunuey ht.
Hodgen James, wool-hatter
Hogg James, linen-draper
Hughes Elias, yarn merchant, Maze
Hull Eliza, grocer and haberdasher
Hunter Joseph, veterinary-surgeon
Hunter William, Dunmurry, Seymour
Johnson Robert, linen-bleacher
James John F.P., baker and grocer
Johnson William, publican
Johnson Ann, haberdasher and milliner
Johnson Rev. Philip J.P. Ballymacash <Ballymucath>
Jordan Matthew, publican
Kelly Mary, circulating-library
Kelsey John, linen inspector, Drumbridge
Kennedy Samuel, muslin-manufacturer
Kennedy William and Co., muslin manufacturers
Kennedy John, woollen-draper

Kennedy Henry, attorney
Machlin Robert, linen-draper
Major William, muslin-manufacturer
Major George, grocer
Marmion Henry, gent
Marshall John, publican
Martin Thomas, publican
McArdle John, rope-maker
McBlain James, architect
McCull Robert, publican
McClure John, grocer
McClure John, grocer
McClure Joseph, sadler
McCollom James, prawnbroker
McCombs John, Hertford Arms <kin>
McCoull Walter, muslin-manufacturer
McCoull John, muslin-manufacturer, Ballylesson
McDowell John, tobacconist
McFerran George and Co. thread-manufacturers
McFerrow George and Co. thread-manufacturers
McGaghey <**McGuyley**> Francis, dealer in linen-yarn
McGee Lance, publican
McHewen Robert, publican
McIlroy M., publican
McNamara <**McNumurad**> John, currier
Meade Christopher, Gent
Mercer A.H., linen-draper
Miller David and Co., muslin-bleachers
Moore George, seedsman &c.
Moorwood George Esq.
Mulhollan Hugh, spirit and timber-merchant
Mulhollan Bernard, muslin-manufacturer
Muhollan John, mason &c.
Mulhollan Henry, grocer
Mulhollan Hugh, publican
Munro -------, grocer
Murray John, linen-draper, Stoneyford
Murray John, sadler
Musgrave Samuel, surgeon and apothecary
Mussen James, soap-boiler and chandler
Mussen George, grocer
Mussen Matthew, soap-boiler
Neely Benjamin, schoolmaster
Newburn Thomas, hosier
Osburn Roger, publican
Palmer Thomas, shoemaker
Patten R., yarn-merchant
Patten James, linen-draper, Strumeren
Patten William, wheelwright
Pelan Richard B., grocer
Pelan James, soap-boiler and chandler
Pelan Mary, grocer
Pentland George, farrier
Phillips Edward, grocer

INN.—King's-Arms, Thomas **Shaw**

Ravenscroft James, attorney at law
Richardson James, muslin-manufacturer
Richardson James, John and Joseph, linen-drapers
Richardson Jonathan, Esq.
Rogers John, grocer, dealer in earthenware, &c.
Rogers Pat, shoemaker and publican
Rogers William, Esq.
Seed Henry and Co., millers
Shaw Thomas, King's-Arms Inn
Shepherd John, attorney at law
Smith William, master in chancery
Smith Alexander, gauger of excise
Smith Roger Johnson, Esq. J.P.
Sorrell ___, milliner and haberdasher
Spence James, shoemaker
Spence William, publican
Stephens Thomas, muslin manufacturer
Stewart William, M.D. and surgeon of the County of Antrim Infirmary
Stewart Pointz, Esq. J.P.
Stewart John, Esq. Wilmount
Thompson Thomas, Maze, Hug yarn-merchant
Thompson William, apothecary
Thompson Thomas, shoemaker
Thornton Philip, publican
Townley James, publican
Trail Rev. archdeacon
Walker Mary, apothecary
Ward James, bookseller, &c.
Watson James, Esq. Brookhill
Weir Matthew, shoemaker
Wheeler William, dealer in timber, spirits, &c.
Wheeler John, grocer
White John, publican and muslin-manufacturer
Whitla George, muslin-manufacturer
Wightman Jas. flour-miller and cotton-spinner
Wightman William, spirit-dealer
Wiley Alexander, watchmaker
Williams James, spirit-dealer
Williams Thomas, grocer and spirit-dealer
Williams William, pawnbroker
Williamson Robert, and Co. cotton-yarn-merchant and linen-drapers
Williamson Alex. cotton-yarn-merchant
Wilson Thomas, muslin-manufacturer, Blaris <Bluris>
Wolfenden Richard and Co. cotton-spinner
Wolfenden Richard, felt-manufacturer
Wolfenden Thomas, blanket-manufacturer
Wolfenden John, thread-manufacturer
Wolfenden Robert, cabinet-maker
Woods John, baker
Wrigley William, bookseller and auctioneer
Younghusband John, Ballydrain <Bullydrain>, linen-draper

SOURCES

BOOKS

BASSETT, GEORGE HENRY, *The Book of Antrim.* 1888

BEST, E. JOYCE, *The Huguenots of Lisburn.* 1997

CALDICOTT, C.E.J. & GOUGH, H. (eds) *The Huguenots and Ireland.* 1987

CARMODY, THE VERY REV. J.P., *Lisburn Cathedral and its Past Rectors.* 1926

CHRIST CHURCH CATHEDRAL, LISBURN, *Visitor's Guide.* 1993

DAY, A., & McWILLIAMS, P. (eds), *Ordnance Survey Memoirs of Ireland. 1832 – 8, Lisburn and South Antrim. (Volume 8)* 1991

GREENE, W.A., *Concise History of Lisburn.* 1906

HARRISON, RICHARD S., *A Biographical Dictionary of Irish Quakers.* 1997

HOPE, SIR THEODORE, *The Memoirs of the Fultons of Lisburn.* 1903

KEE, FREDERICK, *Lisburn Miscellany.* 1976

LEWIS, SAMUEL, *County Antrim – A Topographical Dictionary.* Reprint 2002

LISBURN MUSEUM, *The Huguenots and Ulster 1685-1985.* 1985

MACKEY, BRIAN, *Lisburn, The Town and its People 1873 – 1973* 2000

NEWMAN, KATE, *Dictionary of Ulster Biography.* 1993

PIKE, W.T., *Contemporary Biographies.* 1910

POTTERTON, HOMAN, *Irish Church Monuments 1570 – 1880.* 1975

RANKIN, KATHLEEN, *The Linen Houses of the Lagan Valley.* 2002

REFAUSSÉ, RAYMOND (ed), *Register of the Church of St. Thomas, Lisnagarvey, Co. Antrim 1637-1646.* 1996

RICHARDSON, JAMES N., *Reminiscences of "Friends" in Ulster.* 1911

TROTTER, CAPT. LIONEL J., *The Life of John Nicholson.* 1897

YOUNG, ROBERT M., *Belfast and the Province of Ulster in the 20th Cent.* 1909

JOURNALS

Lisburn Historical Society Journals

Ulster Journal of Archaeology Third Series Vol. 1, 1938

Ulster Star Borough Supplement, Saturday 27th June 1964

NEWSPAPERS

Banner of Ulster 1842 – 1869

Belfast Commercial Chronicle 1805 – 1855

Belfast News Letter 1737 –

Belfast Telegraph 1894 –

Irish Times 1859 -

Lisburn Standard 1878 – 1959

Northern Whig 1824 – June 1991

Tyrone Constitution 1844 -

OTHER SOURCES FOR INFORMATION

Public Record Office of Northern Ireland

Street Directories

Personal Names Index cards

Annual Will Calendars

Church Records

Maps

Death Indexes from 1864

Irish Linen Centre & Lisburn Museum

Belfast Central Library and Newspaper Library

Linen Hall Library, Belfast - Blackwood Pedigrees, Burke's Irish Family Records and Landed Gentry of Ireland, Church of Ireland Clergy books, 3 volumes of "Abstract of Wills, Registry of Deeds, Ireland", U.H.F. series of Gravestone Inscription books.

S.E.E.L.B. Library Headquarters, Ballynahinch – Irish and Local Studies Section

Lisburn Branch Library

INDEX

290

295